HARDPRESS.NET

ISBN: 9781314238549

Published by:
HardPress Publishing
8345 NW 66TH ST #2561
MIAMI FL 33166-2626

Email: info@hardpress.net
Web: http://www.hardpress.net

OPTOMETRIST'S MANUAL

A Treatise on the Science and Practice of Optometry

By C. H. BROWN, M. D.

Graduate University of Pennsylvania; Professor of Principles and Practice of Optometry; formerly Physician to the Philadelphia Hospital; author of "Clinics in Optometry," Etc.

VOLUME II

Hypermetropia, Myopia, Astigmatism and Muscular Anomalies

WITH ILLUSTRATIONS

PUBLISHED BY
THE KEYSTONE PUBLISHING CO.
Bourse Building
Philadelphia, U. S. A.
1921

OPTOMETRIST'S MANUAL

VOL. II

CONTENTS

PREFACE TO VOLUME II

THE subject-matter of the second volume of OPTOMETRIST'S MANUAL is a direct continuation of Volume I, and together they cover thoroughly the modern science of refractive optics. Both volumes originally appeared under the title "THE OPTICIAN'S MANUAL," but the new title more correctly indicates the nature of their contents.

The popularity of these two volumes as text and reference books is explained by their remarkable lucidity of statement and the omission of confusing technicalities, which makes them especially valuable to students.

The author's quarter of a century experience as a teacher of practical optometry in conjunction with his profound knowledge of the subject, qualify him in a special manner to compile a work of this character, the value of which is best shown in its universal popularity.

THE PUBLISHERS.

HERMANN VON HELMHOLTZ

HERMANN VON HELMHOLTZ shares with Donders the glory of laying the foundation on which the modern science of ophthalmology is built. This eminent investigator is the bright, particular luminary in the field of physiologic optics. He was born in 1821, and took his degree of doctor of medicine at Berlin in 1842. He served as a military surgeon until 1847, during which time he published his important article on the conservation of energy. In 1850 he went to the University of Koenigsberg as professor of physiology and general pathology, and here it was where, in 1851, he announced his invention of the ophthalmoscope, which revolutionized ophthalmology. He was called to Heidelberg in 1858, and he here devoted a great deal of study to physiological optics, as a result of which his celebrated "Handbook of Physiological Optics" appeared during the ten years from 1856 to 1866, a book noted for its depth of original investigation, historical research and profound erudition. A second edition of it appeared during the decade of 1885 to 1896. This work, which is too mathematical and profound for the average student, is published in German and French only, but the portions of it of practical interest to the refractionist will be found incorporated in simplified form in Tscherning's "Physiologic Optics," translated into English by Carl Weiland M. D., and published by THE KEYSTONE PUBLISHING CO. Helmholtz was called to Berlin in 1871 as professor of physics and director of the physical laboratory at the University of Berlin, and remained there until 1887, when he became director of the great Physico-technical Institute at Charlottenburg. He died in 1894.

CHAPTER XI.

HYPERMETROPIA

Having given a careful representation of the anatomy of the eye and the physiology of vision, as well as of the simpler laws of optics and the properties and uses of lenses, and having enumerated the outfit required and given minute directions as to the method of examination of a case of supposed optical defect, together with a detailed description of the loss of accommodation and the diagnosis and treatment of presbyopia and its complications, we pass on to the consideration of the various optical defects. The first one to be studied will be *hypermetropia,* as being perhaps the error of refraction with which the optometrist meets most frequently.

The word hypermetropia is made up of three Greek words, signifying *in excess of the measure of the eye.* It may be defined as that condition of the eyeball in which the antero-posterior (from in front backward) axis of the ball is too short; in other words, the globe of the eye is too flat, which is equivalent to its refracting power being insufficient, so that parallel rays of light entering the eye cannot be brought to a focus upon the retina when the accommodation is at rest, as it should be when we are looking at distant objects.

HISTORY OF HYPERMETROPIA

Although hypermetropia had been mentioned and described by previous writers somewhat indefinitely, it was reserved for Donders to reduce the knowledge concerning it to scientific accuracy; but it was not until 1848 (little over half a century ago) that he published his first description of this defect, and cleared the optical atmosphere surrounding it, which had previously been cloudy and misty with speculation and error.

The elucidation of this hitherto mysterious defect was the magnificent result of many years of patient toil and systematic investigation of the subject, in the light of the knowledge concerning it which was at that time the property of the scientific men of the day, together with the added fruit of Donders' own research and discovery, just as many other great truths have been evolved by a similarly slow process but by a persistent application, such as has characterized the labors of many of the great minds of the age.

Previous to this time many affections of the eye were misunderstood, because of the imperfect knowledge of these matters available at that day, and were supposed to have their origin in the nervous system of the eye. In the light of our present knowledge, however, many of these cases were hypermetropic, and the distressing symptoms were caused by the strain imposed upon the accommodation in its unaided efforts to overcome the defect.

DONDERS' OWN WORDS

"He who knows by experience how commonly hypermetropia occurs, how necessary a knowledge of it is to the correct diagnosis of the various defects of the eye, and how deeply it affects the whole treatment of the oculist, will come to the sad conviction that an incredible number of patients have been tormented with all sorts of remedies, and have been given over to painful anxiety, who would have found immediate relief and deliverance in suitable spectacles.

"It is a great satisfaction to be able to say that asthenopia need now no longer be an inconvenience to any one. In this we have an example, by what trifling means science sometimes obtains a triumph, blessing thousands in its results. The discovery of the simple fact that asthenopia is dependent on the hypermetropic structure of the eye, pointed out the way in which it was to be obviated."

PROF. DONDERS

is one of the best-known men connected with the ophthalmology of the preceding generation, and his name is a familiar one to every optical student of the present day. His death was an irreparable loss to ophthalmology and to optics, which is shared and felt by every individual practitioner and worker in this field. But it has been truthfully said by one of his biographers that "we do not lose the master, since his works remain and will always remain, forming the life, the soul of ophthalmology."

PROF. DONDERS

Donders pursued a medical course, and at the early age of twenty-two years occupied a teacher's chair, followed two years later by his elevation to the professorship of anatomy and physiology in the University of Utrecht, from which he had so recently graduated, and in which he continued during all of his active professional life, building up an international reputation that was limited only by the size of the world, and making of this little city of Utrecht a scientific center that emitted its radiance in every direction, and attracted the attention of learned men of every clime. Donders was indeed a foremost representative of Holland in the noble galaxy of savants that were cultivating the fertile fields of science.

Donders did not confine his researches to any one portion of the field, but his labors extended over the whole domain of science, in which are found everywhere the evidences and results of his indefatigable investigations. To us, as optometrists, he is best known and most revered for having enriched our science as no man before or since has done, and particularly through the medium of his great work on the accommodation and refraction of the eye, the fountain of knowledge from which every writer and teacher on the subject draws his inspiration.

Donders' preference in his work was always for teaching, and he is said to have possessed in an eminent degree all those essential qualities which go to make up the perfect professor. "An erudition as profound as extensive; an excellent memory; an intelligence capable of adapting itself to his audience; a wit which colors abstract matters; a rich flow of language; a voice sonorous and flexible; gesture noble and significant; something sublime emanated from the man; physically grand and beautiful, something at once imposing, captivating and sympathetic; great knowledge and great desire to impart it."

DONDERS' MODESTY

It seems as if Donders' learning was equalled only by his modesty, and the latter quality is scarcely less an element of greatness than the former; it certainly increases one's admiration for the man. Several instances exemplifying this trait of his character are related, and they are so distinctive of the man as to bear repetition.

On one occasion an admirer was felicitating him on the discovery of astigmatism, when he made the following magnificent reply: "Pardon me, my friend, astigmatism was known a long time before my day; I only discovered astigmatic people."

When the time came for Donders, on account of the limitations which age imposed upon him, to retire from the professor's chair, which he had honored for so many years, it was made an occasion of paying special homage to his merits by his countrymen, pupils and admirers. His modest response to all the glory which was sought to be showered upon him was, "Talk not to me of my merits, but congratulate me on my lucky star."

CHARACTERISTICS OF A HYPERMETROPIC EYE

Hypermetropia may be looked upon as a congenital defect, in fact the statement has been made that all babies are born hypermetropic. It is supposed to be due to an arrested development in the formation of the eyeball, which may vary from the slightest degree to an extreme condition of smallness.

The hypermetropic eye differs somewhat from an emmetropic eye, and the following have been enumerated as some of the characteristic points of an eye suffering from this defect. The eye is said to look smaller, but this is a change that is not always noticeable, although as a matter of fact the ball is smaller than the normal eye in all of its dimensions, but particularly antero-posteriorly. The lens and iris advance forward, which makes the anterior chamber shallower. The pupil is small and contracted.

The ciliary muscle, by reason of its action on the accommodation, upon which the eye depends for whatever clear vision it may enjoy, is much larger and more fully developed than in emmetropia, this development being particularly noticeable in the anterior portion, which is composed chiefly of circular fibers, and is due to the constant strain imposed on the accommodation by the hypermetropia.

On account of the constant relation existing between the accommodation and the convergence (as has been fully explained in the previous chapters) this excessive accommodation is apt to cause an excessive convergence, the result being a case of convergent strabismus.

In hypermetropia of high degree, the optic nerve is diminished in size and contains a less number of fibers, which accounts for the lessened acuteness of vision so often found in these cases.

In this defect the face is said to have a characteristic flat appearance, the nose depressed, orbits shallow, and the distance between the eyes to be increased. It should be remarked, however, to the optometrist that these points are often absent, and that there may be no distinctive features apparent in the face

It is not unusual to find a hypermetropic eye disposed to astigmatism.

HYPERMETROPIA HEREDITARY

It is not an infrequent occurrence to find many members of the same family affected with hypermetropia. This is so commonly the case that when the diagnosis of hypermetropia is reached in the examination of a patient, the question naturally presents itself in the examiner's mind as to whether some other members of the family are not similarly affected; and when this question is put to the patient, the answer generally corroborates the assumption, at least to the extent of admitting that one or both parents commenced to wear convex glasses for reading at a very early age. (Hypermetropia in some cases first shows itself as an early presbyopia, as remarked in the preceding chapter.)

Cases will sometimes be met with in which one eye is emmetropic and the other eye hypermetropic; and in such cases there may be a very marked difference in the form of the bones on the two sides of the face, thus illustrating the shallowness of the orbits and the flatness of the face with the diminished prominence of the nose, which so often accompanies and indicates hypermetropia. A writer relates a case of this kind, the patient being a young lady who presented herself for treatment of stricture of the nasal duct. The lack of symmetry between the two sides of the face and in the size of the eyeballs was strikingly noticeable, and on examination showed the presence of hypermetropia in one eye.

It will be remembered that the normal or emmetropic eye, when the accommodation is at rest, is accurately adapted for parallel rays, which come to a focus on the retina, forming on this membrane sharply defined images of distant objects, from which these rays emanate. This is accomplished without any action of the accommodation, which is left unrestricted for its normal purpose of adjusting the dioptric apparatus of the eye for the divergent rays issuing from objects close at hand.

In hypermetropia, on the contrary, we find the dioptric system of the eye, when the accommodation is suspended (this is a supposed condition, however, and one that seldom occurs, because in this defect the accommodation is in active and continuous use), on account of the shallowness of the ball, arranged for the refraction of convergent rays, as no other form of rays can be united on the retina in the production of a clearly defined image. Now it is a well-known fact that in nature all rays of light are either parallel or divergent, and hence the hypermetropic eye, being conformed for convergent rays, is adapted for a condition which does not naturally exist.

THE FAR POINT IN HYPERMETROPIA

In emmetropia the far point of distinct vision is situated at infinity, or at any distance far enough removed from the eye that the rays proceeding from it shall be parallel. While in hypermetropia, on account of the adaptation of the eye for the unnatural convergent rays, the far point is negative, or may be said to be situated beyond infinity, if such a condition can be imagined.

In emmetropia the parallel rays are united on the retina, and distinct vision is the result; in hypermetropia these same parallel rays strike the retina before they have converged to a focal point, which renders distinct vision an impossibility, because each point of the image is surrounded by diffusion circles, and these circles from points of the image close together overlap each other.

DEFINITION OF HYPERMETROPIA

Hypermetropia may then be defined as that condition of the eye in which there is a shortening of the antero-posterior diameter of the ball, or the positive refracting power of the eye is deficient, and the result in either case is that the focus is behind the retina. Or, in other words, the diameter or length of the eye-ball is less than the focal length of its dioptric apparatus.

THE DIFFICULTIES OF HYPERMETROPIA PRACTICALLY DEMONSTRATED

A concave lens is a negative lens and diminishes refraction; a hypermetropic eye is one in which there is naturally a deficiency of refraction. Now if we consider these two facts together, it follows that a concave lens placed before an emmetropic eye will lessen its refraction, and to that extent will make it equivalent to, and place it in the same optical condition as a hypermetropic eye. Therefore if any one enjoying emmetropic eyes desires to experience a practical demonstration of the difficulties and hindrances which are ever present to annoy and harass the hypermetrope, he can very easily place his own eyes in the same condition by making them artificially hypermetropic by the use of concave lenses.

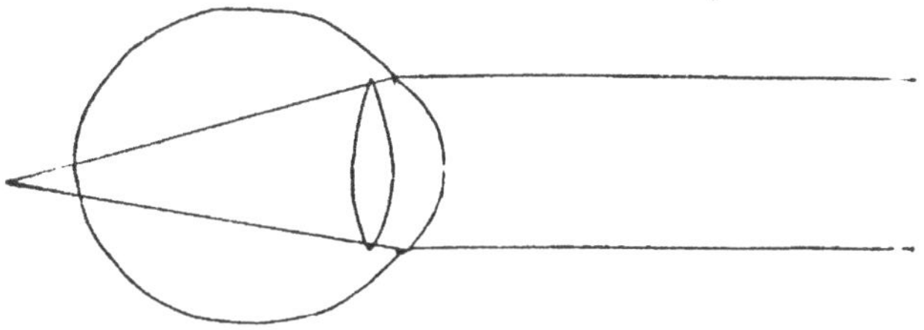

Outline of a Hypermetropic Eye, Showing the Focus of Parallel Rays to be Back of Retina

If he tries first weak lenses and by changing them gradually increases their strength, he will in the beginning find that by the exercise of his accommodation he is able to neutralize and overcome the diminishing effect of the concave lenses. As, however, he gets into the higher numbers, it becomes a more and more difficult task for the accommodation to counterbalance these increasing negative lenses.

If, in spite of these warnings that the accommodation has reached the extreme limit of its powers, and its greatest effort is required to preserve vision clear through the concave lenses, a step farther be taken with stronger glasses, it would entirely drain all the resources of the ciliary muscles, and they would be no longer equal to the task of supplying the necessary refractive power, and vision would become blurred, and the eyes would be in a condition of absolute hypermetropia.

Convex lenses sufficiently strong placed before the concave ones, would supplement the exhausted accommodation, and would partly or wholly nullify the diminishing effect of the concave lenses, and distant vision would again be restored clear and distinct.

FORMS OF HYPERMETROPIA

Hypermetropia may be classified as *original* and *acquired.*

In the acquired form the eye was primarily emmetropic, but on account of the lessening of its refraction, toward which all its senile changes tend, the focus for parallel rays falls behind the retina, and the refraction of the eye passes over from a condition of emmetropia to that of hypermetropia.

The changes that take place in the eye with the advance of years, more especially as to the loss of accommodation, and the rationale of the appearance of hypermetropia in old age, have been fully described in the chapter on presbyopia.

Original hypermetropia may be either congenital or developed at a very early age by an interruption in the growth

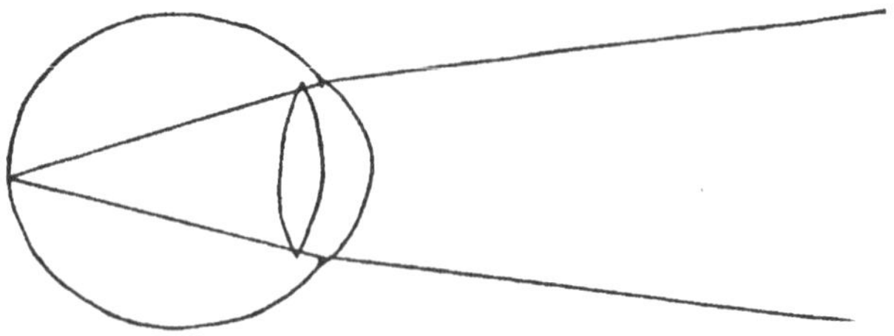

Outline of a Hypermetropic Eye, Showing its Adaptation for Convergent Rays

of the eye, especially in its antero-posterior diameter. The weight of authority seems to favor the opinion that the eyes of new-born babes are hypermetropic, which condition may soon develop into emmetropia, and then pass over into myopia; and when once these changes have occurred by a lengthening of the axis of the eye-ball, they become permanent, and the eye cannot again return to its original hypermetropic condition. This would indicate a tendency for the eye-ball to elongate, and the natural inference would be that myopia is apt to increase, while hypermetropia seldom grows greater, but frequently diminishes.

DIVISIONS OF HYPERMETROPIA

Original hypermetropia may be divided into *manifest* and *latent,* and in order to ascertain the *total* hypermetropia it is necessary to add the manifest to the latent.

In hypermetropia of not too high a degree it is usually found that the distant vision is quite up to the standard, and the sight is apparently that of an emmetropic eye. This is accomplished by means of the accommodation, which increases the convexity of the crystalline lens and adds to the refractive power of the eye, and thus bends parallel rays so as to advance their focus from behind the retina on to this structure. It is the same effect that is produced by a convex lens placed in front of the eye; and the amount of accommodation required, which can be expressed by a certain number of convex lens, will represent the degree of hypermetropia present.

The division of hypermetropia into manifest and latent depends on the action of the accommodation; manifest hypermetropia is possible only with a suspended accommodation, while the latent form is that which is concealed by the contraction of the ciliary muscle. Hence it follows that the more passive the accommodation, the greater the manifest hypermetropia; and the more active the accommodation, the greater the latent hypermetropia.

The *manifest* hypermetropia is usually apparent without a mydriatic, and is measured by the strongest convex glass that will be accepted for distant vision. The *latent* defect can be made manifest, or can be detected only by the use of a mydriatic. As the person advances in life and the power of accommodation weakens, in the same proportion the latent defect decreases and passes over into manifest, until finally there remains no more latent trouble, but it has all become manifest.

The manifest hypermetropia is, for the purposes of convenience, written Hm, the latent hypermetropia Hl, and the total hypermetropia Ht.

ILLUSTRATIONS OF THE DIVISIONS OF HYPERMETROPIA

Perhaps this subject can be made more clear by the exemplification of a case of hypermetropia tested at a distance of twenty feet with Snellen's test types. Possibly the eye can distinguish only the larger letters, and the vision would be recorded as follows: V = 20/100. If now there is placed before the eye a convex lens of 2 D., the vision is raised to normal, and V = 20/20. In this case the accommodation is supposed to be at rest, and the total hypermetropia (Ht) is 2 D.

If, however, the eye would call into action a portion of its accommodative power, the hypermetropia would be corrected thereby and the vision raised to 20/20 without the employment of a convex lens, and this is usually the state of affairs as it is found in young hypermetropes. If now the eyes are tested with convex lenses, the vision remains the same, so that we find V = 20/20 either with or without convex lenses. This illustrates manifest hypermetropia, and the strongest convex lens through which vision still remains 20/20 would represent the degree of manifest hypermetropia (Hm).

The record of this case would read V = 20/20, Hm. = + 1 D. That is to say, vision is normal or 20/20, and remains as good when a convex lens of 1 D. is placed before the eye. Now in this case we presume that a certain amount of the defect is latent or concealed by the action of the accommodation, because the patient is unable to completely relax it.

In this imaginary case we have a total hypermetropia of 2 D., and a manifest hypermetropia of 1 D., and therefore the difference between the two would indicate a latent hypermetropia of 1 D.

The latent hypermetropia can seldom be revealed except by the use of atropine, and we would remark in passing that this is not always necessary for the following reasons: we can scarcely ever give a glass to do more than correct the manifest hypermetropia, which can be measured without the use of the drug; why then should it be considered essential to determine the latent defect, which after all will not bear correction.

THEORY OF THE CORRECTION OF HYPERMETROPIA

It would be theoretically correct to place before hyper metropic eyes, convex glasses of such strength as to completely neutralize the error of refraction and correct the total hypermetropia, thus giving to parallel rays the degree of convergence for which the refractive media are adapted, and in this manner obviating the necessity for calling into action any part of the accommodation for vision of distant objects, so as to leave the entire accommodative power unimpaired for the necessary adjustment of the eye for the divergent rays proceeding from small objects close at hand. This would be the ideal method of correction of this oftentimes distressing defect.

Although it would seem to be the proper thing in hypermetropia to prescribe such glasses as would completely correct the defect, yet practically such a method of procedure has been found not to answer, except in but few cases, and even then not until after repeated trials with glasses, and not until the eyes have adapted themselves to their use.

THE OBSTACLE IN THE WAY OF THE COMPLETE CORRECTION OF HYPERMETROPIA

The hypermetropic eye, ever since it commenced to fulfill its function in looking at the lettered blocks and picture books of childhood has been accustomed to associate with the act of vision a certain amount of muscular action, or, in other words, a definite contraction of the ciliary muscle to overcome the defect, for only by this means is the hypermetropic eye able to enjoy clear and distinct vision; and as the natural instinct of the eye impels it to produce well-defined vision if within the range of its possibility, this effort of the muscle of accommodation is purely an automatic and involuntary one, and is ever present, from the time the dawn of morning opens the eyelids and allows the rays of light to enter through the refractive media, until they are closed in sleep.

It has been said that man is a creature of habit, which becomes to him a second nature, and from which it is difficult, and oftentimes impossible, for him to break away. The habit thus acquired, of contraction of the ciliary muscle coincident with the act of vision, is hard to abandon entirely, even after the error of refraction is fully corrected by convex glasses placed before the eyes and all necessity for the use of the accommodation thus removed.

Hence it follows if there is a correction (either partial or entire) of the hypermetropia by means of the accommodation, and in addition there is a correction of the same defect by means of convex glasses, there is evidently a surplus of correction, and the glasses appear to be too strong and cannot be worn.

In other words, we are able to correct, by the employment of glasses, only that portion of the hypermetropia which the accommodation by its relaxation will permit us to do, or which we can coax the accommodation not to correct, and this brings us back to the point from which we started and which we emphasized in the last issue, that we can scarcely ever give a glass to do more than correct the manifest hypermetropia.

BLURRING OF IMAGES DUE TO THE SCREEN BEING TOO CLOSE TO THE REFRACTIVE MEDIUM

In hypermetropia the focus of parallel rays is behind the retina, and hence the rays strike the retina before they have been united in a focal point, the reason being that the retina (or the screen on which the images are formed) is closer to the crystalline lens than the focal distance of the dioptric media of the eye.

Any student of optics who is sufficiently interested in these matters can take a strong convex lens from his trial case and see for himself how the images of objects will be blurred when the screen on which they are formed is closer than the focal distance of the lens.

The student will stand in front of a window and hold the lens in such a position that the light coming from the outside will fall upon it and pass through it. A sheet of white paper is to be used for a screen and placed at the focal distance of the lens. If the strength of the latter is 5 D., the sheet of paper will be placed eight inches from it, and small and distinct images of external objects, such as trees and houses, will be formed upon it; every detail of the objects; every leaf and branch of the tree, all the doors and windows of the house, will be clearly defined, and form a beautiful (though diminished and inverted) picture. This illustrates the formation of distinct images on the yellow spot of the emmetropic eye, the retina being at the exact focal distance of the dioptric system of the eyes, which may then be said to be IN MEASURE.

If now the screen of white paper be moved slightly so as

to bring it closer to the lens, the sharpness of the images is at once destroyed; the trees may still be seen in blurred outlines and the shape of the house be discerned, but none of the fine details can be perceived. If the screen be moved still nearer the trees will gradually fade out of sight and even the outlines of the house will be lost. This illustrates the forma-

The Image as Formed on the Retina of the Emmetropic Eye

tion of the indistinct images on the yellow spot of the hypermetropic eye, the eye-ball being flat and the retina too close to the crystalline lens, which may then be described as an eye *out of measure*. The flatter the eye, the closer the retina to the crystalline lens and the higher the degree of hypermetropia, the more blurred will be the images formed in the eye, and the less satisfactory the vision.

RESTORATION OF THE CLEARNESS OF THE IMPERFECT IMAGES

When the screen of paper is moved up to seven inches, the images are noticeably blurred, and when it is moved to six inches there is no distinct definition of objects. If at this distance a second convex lens of 1.50 D. be placed before the first lens of 5 D., an instantaneous and marvelous effect is

The Image as Formed on the Retina of the Hypermetropic Eye

produced in the restoration of the images to perfect clearness and distinct definition, a stepping, as it were, from twilight to mid-day.

The student who performs this experiment for himself will be the better able to understand and appreciate the effect of convex glasses in the correction of hypermetropia, and how they produce distinct images on the retina without any accommodative effort.

PRACTICAL ILLUSTRATIONS OF THE DISTINCT IMAGES OF EMMETROPIA AND THE INDISTINCT IMAGES OF HYPERMETROPIA

In order to emphasize these points, and to afford a practical illustration of the marked difference in the clearness of the images formed in the emmetropic and hypermetropic eyes, as well as to show the difficulties under which the hypermetrope labors, we present on page 24 a cut of the title page of a holiday number of THE KEYSTONE as its image would appear when formed on the yellow spot of the emmetropic eye, which the reader can compare with the image of the same object formed in the hypermetropic eye on page 25.

The first cut was made with the dioptric apparatus of the photographic camera in perfect adjustment, so that the rays proceeding from the title page were accurately focused on the screen. In making the second cut, the screen was moved closer to the condensing lens of the camera, thus simulating the relative positions of the retina and crystalline lens in the hypermetropic eye, and in this case the rays struck the screen before they were united in a focus, and, as a consequence, the image there formed is imperfect and indistinct.

These illustrations have reference to the refractive condition of the emmetropic and hypermetropic eyes, that is, with the eyes in a state of rest and the function of accommodation in a passive condition. The student knows that if the accommodation is brought actively into play, the results obtained will be entirely different.

The hypermetrope, if the degree of defect be not too high, by the exercise of his accommodative power is able to supplement and increase the refractive strength of his eye, and in this way bring the focus of parallel rays forward so as to coincide with the retina, and thus counteract the disturbing influence caused by the nearness of the retina to the lens.

This would clear up the retinal image and give the hypermetrope perfect vision, but it would be accomplished only at the expense of a constant strain on the accommodation, which Nature will not sanction, as she expects distant vision to be entirely devoid of accommodative effort.

SUB-DIVISIONS OF HYPERMETROPIA

Manifest hypermetropia has been further divided into *facultative, relative* and *absolute.* We do not attach very much practical value to these sub-divisions, but we feel that our readers should not be entirely ignorant of them.

Facultative hypermetropia is the term applied to those cases of hypermetropia in which distant objects can be clearly seen, either without or with convex glasses. In these cases the accommodation is sufficiently strong to overcome the defect and afford perfect vision; and at the same time it is obliging enough, when convex glasses are placed before the eyes, to subside and retire from the field, and allow the convex lenses to do its work.

Relative hypermetropia is the term applied to those cases of hypermetropia in which, by the addition of the entire accommodative force to the natural refractive condition, the eye still does not possess sufficient power to bring the parallel rays of distant vision, much less the divergent rays of near vision, to a focus on the retina, except by an over-convergence of the visual axes, or, in other words, by squinting.

Absolute hypermetropia is the term applied to those cases where distinct vision is impossible without artificial assistance. The entire refractive and accommodative power of the eye, reinforced by the strongest effort of convergence, is insufficient to bring parallel rays of light to a focus on the retina, much less the divergent rays proceeding from near objects. Such an eye is entirely dependent upon convex glasses for any vision at all.

The facultative form of hypermetropia is most common in youth, when the accommodation is vigorous and able to overcome the defect. The relative form occurs a little later in life, when the accommodation weakens and no longer suffices to correct the defect without the added assistance of the convergence. In old age the accommodation has become entirely exhausted, and then the hypermetropia becomes absolute.

From the very nature of it, acquired hypermetropia can never occur in the latent form, but it is always manifest. Neither can it come under the head of facultative, but it may possibly be relative, although it is more apt to be absolute. All this becomes clear and easily explained when it is remembered that acquired hypermetropia is due to a natural diminution of refraction, and occurs only after the accommodation has been shorn of its strength by age, and when all that remains of it is memory.

Facultative hypermetropia is almost the same as manifest hypermetropia; although we consider the latter term preferable because it is more expressive, the word itself indicating that it is not concealed, but that it is easy of detection, by the ready acceptance of a convex lens.

CAUSES OF HYPERMETROPIA

As has already been shown, the essential condition in hypermetropia is that the retina is too close to the dioptric apparatus, so that the rays of light strike this membrane in diffusion circles before they have had the opportunity to unite in a focus. This condition may be dependent upon several different causes, which we will enumerate as follows:

1. Axial hypermetropia, in which the dioptric system may measure up to the same standard as an emmetropic eye, but the eye is flat and there is a lessening of the antero-posterior diameter of the globe of the eye, and a consequent shortening of its axis. This is by far the most common cause, and it has been illustrated in the earlier part of the chapter.

The *axial* form of hypermetropia is congenital, and is due to an arrest of development of the eye in its growth, particularly noticeable in the antero-posterior diameter. Such eyes are distinguished by their smallness and mobility, the diminution in size being oftentimes a noticeable feature.

2. The length or depth of the eye-ball may be the same as an emmetropic eye, but the refractive power of the dioptric apparatus may be too feeble to bring the rays of light to a focus on the retina, which they strike in un-united circles, producing the same effect as the axial form.

This *deficiency of refractive power* may be due to several different causes: there may be a depression of the cornea or a lessening of its convexity, as the result of inflammation or disease; or it may normally be lacking in convexity; there may also be a diminution in the natural convexity of the crystalline lens; and there may also be a reduction in the index of refraction of the refracting media, the aqueous humor, the crystalline lens and the vitreous humor.

3. Aphakia, or the absence of the crystalline lens either naturally or artificially, is a cause of the most pronounced hypermetropia. In such cases there is an absence of all refractive power and the eye becomes intensely hypermetropic.

AMOUNT OF SHORTENING IN AXIAL HYPERMETROPIA

The following table (after Donders) shows the amount of shortening of the axis of the eye-ball for the various degrees of hypermetropia:

Degree of Hypermetropia	Diminution of Axial Line
.50 D.	.16 mm.
1 D.	.31 mm.
1.50 D.	.47 mm.
2 D.	.62 mm.
2.50 D.	.77 mm.
3 D.	.92 mm.
3.50 D.	1.06 mm.
4 D.	1.22 mm.
4.50 D.	1.4 mm.
5 D.	1.6 mm.
6 D.	1.9 mm.
7 D.	2.2 mm.
8 D.	2.6 mm.
9 D.	2.9 mm.
10 D.	3.2 mm.
11 D.	3.3 mm.
12 D.	3.4 mm.
13 D.	3.5 mm.
14 D.	3.7 mm.
15 D.	4. mm.
16 D.	4.2 mm.
17 D.	4.4 mm.
18 D.	4.6 mm.
19 D.	4.7 mm.
20 D.	4.9 mm.

The axial line of the emmetropic eye is nearly 23/25 of an inch; in 3.50 D. of hypermetropia this would be reduced to 22/25 of an inch; in 7 D. of hypermetropia to 21/25, and in 10 D. of hypermetropia to 20/25 of an inch. This shows in the latter grade of the defect a shortening of 1/8 inch, which is quite a considerable amount.

PREVALENCE OF HYPERMETROPIA

Hypermetropia is the predominant error of refraction. Babies in the majority of cases are born hypermetropic (perhaps in all cases), although this condition may afterward develop into emmetropia, and finaly pass over into myopia. The reason why infants are almost invariably hypermetropic is undoubtedly due to the fact that at birth the eye has scarce reached its full development.

Various animals, such as frogs, rabbits, cats and dogs, have been examined with the ophthalmoscope to determine their refraction, and all have been found to be hypermetropic, sometimes as much as 3 D. or 4 D. The ciliary muscle in these animals is but poorly developed, the hypermetropia therefore existing in a manifest form; in view of which their near vision must be very indistinct. This, however, is a matter of no inconvenience to them, as they are not called upon to use their eyes in near vision for those employments which so much tax the human eye, reading, writing and sewing.

DEGREE OF HYPERMETROPIA

Ordinarily the degree of hypermetropia may be expressed by the convex lens that is required to correct it. In *axial* hypermetropia it depends upon the flatness of the eye, or the distance of the retina from the focus of the refracting media.

In *refractive* hypermetropia it depends upon the deficiency of refractive power, or the amount to which this falls below the normal standard.

In emmetropia the distance of the retina and the location of the principal focus exactly coincide, and the extent of their departure from each other in hypermetropia would indicate its degree, and the greater this departure the higher the degree of defect. In one case we reckon the distance from the nodal point to the focus of the hypermetropic eye, and the distance from the nodal point to the retina of the same eye, and then compare the two, and the difference between them will denote the hypermetropic deficiency.

In the table given we can see the amount of diminution of the axial line for every diopter of hypermetropia, and conversely a certain diminution in the axial line implies a certain degree of hypermetropia, and each increases in equal proportion. A convex lens corresponding to the grade of the defect will bring forward the focus to the position of the retina, and thus tend to counterbalance the diminution in the axial line. While in refractive hypermetropia, the convex lens directly supplies the deficiency in refractive power, and at the same time reveals its extent and expresses it in definite terms of refraction.

A good idea of the difference in shape between the emmetropic eye and the hypermetropic eye may be obtained by comparing a round apple with a flat turnip. The round apple represents the normal or emmetropic eye, and the turnip the flat or hypermetropic eye, and a comparison of them will convey to the mind a well-defined conception of the difference in shape between emmetropia and hypermetropia.

SYMPTOMS OF HYPERMETROPIA

When a child complains of headache and pain in the eyes, and is taken from school and charged with stupidity, or punished for idleness, and the family physician advises abstinence from study or change of occupation, and puts the patient through a course of powerful medicines or (puts a course of medicines through him) for an imaginary nervous trouble, the intelligent optometrist will recognize these as symptoms of hypermetropia; and he knows (and why shouldn't the family physician know?) that medicines are worse than useless in such a case, but that a pair of properly adjusted convex glasses will remove the headache and pain in the eyes (when nothing else can), and will, perhaps, make the child as bright and studious as any of his companions. Otherwise if the cause of the trouble is not recognized and rectified, the child's prospects are blighted for life.

The hypermetrope (if the defect is not of too high degree) usually sees well at a distance, but the presence of the defect is made known even in early life, by the pain and symptoms of fatigue that follow any close use of the eyes. By a tension of the accommodation the hypermetrope may be able to read well for awhile, but sooner or later the constant effort to contract the muscle of accommodation sufficiently for near work causes fatigue and exhaustion of the muscle, and the accommodative effort can be maintained only by the greatest difficulty, and the patient is reminded that he has eyes and that they are weak and painful ones.

The eyes feel strained and painful, the letters run together and become blurred, and there is an instinctive desire to rest the eyes by closing them for a moment or two and compressing them. After this a fresh start can be made, only to break down in a little while as before. In short, the symptoms of hypermetropia may be said to consist of pain and discomfort on using the eyes, and an indistinctness of the letters on a printed page.

SELF-CORRECTION OF HYPERMETROPIA

The condition of every hypermetrope would be a sorry one indeed, if he could not alter and increase the refraction of his eye, and make vision clear and distinct by bringing the focus of rays forward to the retina. While a hypermetrope with no inherent power over the defect would see nothing clearly at any distance, fortunately he possesses in his accommodation a means by which he can increase his refraction and overcome his trouble. While it is possible for distinct vision to be thus purchased by the hypermetrope, it is accomplished only at the expense of a constant strain upon the accommodation, the amount of strain depending on the degree of hypermetropia.

Since hypermetropia can be thus corrected by the individual himself by the use of his accommodation, no ill effects may be noticed for some time, and indeed the presence of the defect may not even be suspected. At length there comes a time when the accommodation breaks down, and it is no longer equal to long-sustained efforts required by reading and near work.

Anything that weakens the accommodation will precipitate this breakdown, hence it is especially liable to show itself after a protracted illness, or if the patient's system has been run down from overwork or anxiety. It also becomes apparent as the patient approaches the presbyopic period of life, when the accommodation fails from the natural changes in the eye.

The illustration previously given, showing the outline of a hypermetropic eye, represents it as refracting parallel rays of light, or those proceeding from a distance of twenty feet or more, in which case the focus is behind the retina and vision is more or less indistinct. As has just been described, this focus is advanced to the retina and vision made clear by the action of the accommodation, which is thus kept on a constant strain.

But when the rays proceed from close objects or from those nearer than twenty feet, they become divergent, and the nearer the object is brought to the eye, the more divergent the rays that proceed from it to enter the eye. Now it does not require much reasoning to show that when divergent rays are refracted by a lens, the resulting focus cannot be at the same place as that of parallel rays, but it will be farther removed; or if it is desired to keep the focus at the same place, it is equally evident that more power is necessary in a lens to focus divergent rays at that point than is required to bring parallel rays to a focus at the same distance.

THE ACCOMMODATION IN HYPERMETROPIA

Hence when we apply these principles to the hypermetropic eye we find that the focus of divergent rays is back of that of parallel rays, or still further removed from the retina, when the accommodation that is in force for distance remains unchanged. Therefore the accommodation of the hypermetrope, which must be constantly exerted even for distance, is put to a still greater strain for near vision.

As a consequence, it follows in reading, writing or sewing, to which the emmetrope comes with fresh and strong eyes, that in the case of the hypermetrope, who is compelled to use some of his accommodation for distant vision, and whose ciliary muscle is in the harness (as it were) from the time the eyes are opened in the morning until they are closed in sleep at night, the start is made with that much of a deficit from the normal strength of the eyes, and near vision is maintained and continued only by calling into action the reserve of accommodative power, and in some cases the totality of accommodation of which the eye is capable.

THE RESERVE MUST NOT BE IMPAIRED

Just as the use of its reserve will impoverish a bank or an insurance company, so the use of its reserve accommodative power will exhaust an eye and cause it to break down; for it must be remembered that a tension of only a portion of the accommodation can be sustained for any length of time. Therefore in the case of the hypermetrope, who is compelled to use a part of his accommodation for distance and the balance of it for reading, there soon appear pain and fatigue of the eyes and general symptoms of asthenopia, which gradually increase and become so pronounced as to compel a frequent interruption of the strain on the accommodation by closing the eyes and resting them for a moment or two.

The laws of State prohibit the officers of a bank or an insurance company from touching the reserve fund, which must be kept intact, under heavy penalties; but not more so than do physical laws forbid any encroachment on the reserve of accommodative power, else equally severe punishment may follow. As a rule, banks and insurance companies are so conservatively managed that not only is the reserve not infringed upon, but, on the other hand, it is from time to time increased, and to that extent is the institution inherently strengthened and raised in public estimation. Rectitude of character, as well as fear of the law, averts any violation of the reserve in banks and insurance companies, except in rare instances, when the offender is forced to pay the penalty for his crimes. But no high sense of duty to one's self, nor even the fear of the suffering that is sure to follow, prevents violation of the laws of health, as is noticeably evidenced on every hand by the abuse of the eyes and of the stomach. The hypermetropic eye is urged to the full extent of its accommodative power, until it breaks down from sheer exhaustion, while the stomach is overloaded at all hours of the day and night with rich and indigestible food, until it finally rebels and is unable to perform its functions.

FAR-SIGHTEDNESS

The popular term for hypermetropia is far-sightedness or long-sightedness, and the use of these words has led the laity to believe that such eyes can see better at a distance than emmetropic eyes; but these terms are misnomers and are misleading, because a hypermetropic eye cannot see any better at a distance than an emmetropic eye, and besides, what it does see is only at the expense of an unnatural use of the accommodation. The student who understands the shape of the hypermetropic eye, and the difficulties under which it labors, will realize that it is far from being as good an eye as the normal. Then, too, it frequently happens that hypermetropia, if of high degree, very much diminishes the acuteness of vision.

HYPERMETROPIA CONFOUNDED WITH MYOPIA

On account of this impairment of vision, hypermetropia is sometimes mistaken, even by the patient himself, for myopia. These are cases of hypermetropia of high degree, in which the person finds that he is able to materially improve his reading vision by holding his book close, which increases the size of the retinal image, intensifies the illumination, and by contracting the pupil cuts off some of the circles of diffusion. Is it any wonder under these circumstances that the case is looked upon as one of myopia? These matters can perhaps be best emphasized by a few illustrative cases taken from the writer's record book.

A CASE OF HYPERMETROPIA SIMULATING MYOPIA

William F. Aged ten years. School-boy. Comes to me with the statement that he has always been near-sighted, and that of late his eyes are getting worse. They hurt when he reads and vision is quite indistinct, so much so that he is compelled to almost close his lids in order to see. There is also a convergent squint, which alternates between the two eyes. R. V. = 10/200, L. V. = 5/200. Reads Jaeger No. 9, 2 in. to 5 in.

A history such as this, with so imperfect near and distant vision, is very apt to mislead the average optician into supposing that he had a case of myopia to deal with; and really, to any but a skilled refractionist, this would be a most natural error, for is not the boy compelled to hold his book very close to his eyes, and is not his distant vision imperfect and indistinct, and does he not half close his eyelids, as all myopes are apt to do?

In testing his eyes with convex lenses, I soon found it was a case of high hypermetropia, but vision was scarcely satisfactory even with the best glasses I could give him. As this was an unusual case and as he desired the removal of the strabismus, I instilled atropine in his eyes for a week, during which time I operated on his eye for correction of the strabismus. I kept him under observation for two weeks, and then ordered the following glasses:

$$\left.\begin{matrix} R. \\ L. \end{matrix}\right\} + 13 \text{ D. for constant wear.}$$

Some three weeks later he reports eyes as comfortable, able to read and study with satisfaction, and does not have to hold book so near, nor half close lids, in reading, as formerly.

ANOTHER CASE OF HYPERMETROPIA, IN WHICH CONCAVE GLASSES WERE PRESCRIBED

ANNIE F. Aged seventeen years. A sister of the boy in case above narrated. She comes with nearly the same history as her brother. She says she has always been near-sighted, but does not have much pain in her eyes unless she uses them for too long a time. Some months ago she purchased a pair of glasses from an optician (which she showed me, and which I found on examination to be — 3.50 D.), but they have been of no benefit to her and she has used them but little. R. V. = 15/100, L. V. 15/200. Refraction = manifest hypermetropia of 3.50 L. Reads Jaeger No. 9, 2 in. to 7 in. With + 3.50 D. can read the same print out to 11 in. Prescribed for her

$$\left.\begin{matrix} R. \\ L. \end{matrix}\right\} + 3.50 \text{ D. for constant wear.}$$

Two months later she reported that her sight had improved very much, and that she can see better than she ever could, and is now able to use her eyes a great deal, without pain or discomfort.

THE MORAL OF THESE CASES

One lesson to be learned from the above cases is that too much reliance should not be placed on the patient's statements. Both the boy and the girl called themselves near-sighted, and they both accepted concave glasses when placed before their eyes. Under these circumstances nothing is more natural to the unskilled optician than to regard these as cases of myopia, and hence every man should be constantly on his guard to avoid falling into such a grievous error.

The reader of these pages, even though he possesses only a moderate amount of knowledge and experience, is aware that to give concave glasses to either of the above cases would not only fail to relieve them, but would make their eyes infinitely worse than to wear no glasses at all; it would, in fact, only be adding fuel to the fire.

In the boy's case he came to me at first hand and I was able to correctly diagnose the trouble and prescribe the proper glasses, and hence he suffered no injury to his eyes from improper lenses. But the girl ran a great risk of ruining her eyes with the concave glasses that were prescribed for her, and she escaped only because the glasses were of no benefit and she did not wear them.

Another interesting point that impresses us in the study of these cases is the occurrence of two such marked cases of hypermetropia in the same family.

ANOTHER CASE OF HYPERMETROPIA SIMULATING MYOPIA

Mary H. Aged fifteen years. About a year ago her eyes commenced to trouble her. She consulted an oculist, who told her it was necessary to drop atropine into her eyes, to which she and her parents objected. She was then taken to another oculist, who said she didn't need any glasses.

She comes to me with the statement that she has always held her book close to her eyes, but recently is compelled to hold it closer than ever. Complains of a great deal of headache, and of a dull, heavy pain over eyes, which is much worse after reading.

V. = 15/20. Hm. = 1.25 D., with which V. = 15/12. Reads Jaeger 3, 2½ in. to 9 in. With the + 1.25 glasses the range of accommodation is from 3 in. to 33 in. Ordered

R. } + 1.25 D. for constant wear.
L. }

Three years later she reports that glasses have given the greatest satisfaction in every particular, and she wants them put into a gold frame.

One interesting point about this case is the limited range of accommodation for so small a degree of hypermetropia, and the wonderful effect of the glasses in increasing her reading limit from nine inches to thirty-three inches. Cases like this are afforded untold benefit from the proper glasses, while at the same time they are a source of great satisfaction to the optometrist.

The distance of the far point in this case (nine inches) would point toward myopia, although with an acuteness of vision of 15/20 but a slight degree would be possible.

ANOTHER SIMILAR CASE

Mrs. Sarah K. Aged thirty-eight years. Says she has been near-sighted all her life, but has never been able to get glasses to suit her eyes.

V. = 15/200. Hm. + 5.50 D., with which V. = 15/70. Can read only large size print, and can read no farther off than seven inches. With the + 5.50 D. lenses can read out to twelve inches. As these glasses correct only her manifest hypermetropia, and as she is approaching the presbyopic period, she will consequently need a stronger pair for reading. After testing her eyes for reading I ordered R. and L. + 8 D., which afforded her the greatest satisfaction.

The point of interest in this case is that this woman should have reached thirty-eight years of age without having been able to obtain suitable glasses, which can be explained on one of two grounds: Either the optician gave her concave glasses because she said she was near-sighted, which would only hinder her eyes instead of helping them; or he did not know how to properly test her eyes for hypermetropia, and hence gave her only a weak convex glass of not sufficient strength to afford her relief, because he was afraid he might injure her eyes by giving her too strong a glass.

ANOTHER CASE OF HYPERMETROPIA, CLASSED AS ONE OF MYOPIA

LIZZIE H Aged twenty-eight years. Says she has always been near-sighted, and when attending school the teacher allowed her to go close to the windows in order to be able to see to read. On examination I found her vision 15/75, and with the unassisted eye was unable to read even the largest size print on the reading test card. A pair of + 8 D. enabled her to read ordinary print with ease and comfort, and gave her good distant vision.

A CASE OF HYPERMETROPIA TREATED WITH CONCAVE GLASSES

SUSAN G. Aged ten years. Complains of a great deal of pain in eyes, and headache. She showed me a pair of — 4 D. glasses which an optometrist had given her, but which she had not been able to wear. She cannot see at a distance with them, nor can she read with them; neither can she read without them, as her eyes have gotten into such a weak and irritable condition. An examination showed her vision equals 15/30, and a manifest hypermetropia of + 1.25 D. Is able to read newspaper print no farther away than nine inches.

As the girl was young it semed best to commence with weak lenses, and hence she was ordered + .75 D. for constant wear. A week later she returned to have the glasses set in a gold frame, and her report was that they had given the greatest satisfaction; she can see well with them both far and near, with entire relief from the pain in her head and eyes.

The error of the optometrist in giving this young girl a concave lens of 4 D. is a most inexcusable one. It is difficult to understand how such a mistake could have been made by an optometrist of any intelligence, except on the supposition that it was looked upon as a case of myopia, and the concave glasses were prescribed according to the rule in myopia that the distance of the far point expresses the degree of defect and at the same time the correcting glass.

If the optometrist had examined her distant vision, he could hardly have made such an error, because a vision of 15/30 is not compatible with a myopia of 4 D.; and besides, if he had measured her refraction according to the methods laid down in The Manual, he would certainly have found some evidence of the existence of hypermetropia; at least nothing to lead him to prescribe a — 4 D. glass. A grievous error of this kind would permanently injure the eyes if the patient continued to wear the glasses, and when discovered it brings reproach on optometrists as a class.

A FINAL CASE OF HYPERMETROPIA IN WHICH CONCAVE GLASSES WERE PRESCRIBED

Mrs. K. G. Aged twenty-three years. Had been having trouble with her eyes for some time previously, and about three months ago consulted an optometrist, who gave her a pair of — 1 D. glasses. She has tried to wear these glasses, but they cause her eyes to ache, and she is unable to thread a needle with them.

A careful examination was made with the following result: R. E., vision 12/20; with + 1 D. = 12/15. L. E., vision = 12/15, with a manifest hypermetropia of .75 D. Is able to read Jaeger No. 4 only, 6 in. to 11 in. The above lenses increase the reading far point to sixteen inches. Ordered R. E. + 1, L. E. + .75, for constant wear, and these afforded the greatest comfort and satisfaction.

MORAL OF THESE CASES

The writer could give the history of a great many more similar cases from his own case-books, but sufficient have probably been narrated to call attention to, and to emphasize, this most important point; that is, the great danger to the eye when concave glasses are prescribed in cases of hypermetropia. Of course it is a natural error, into which the examiner may easily be misled by the patient's statements that he is near-sighted, and by his answers when test lenses are placed before his eyes, but it is to be hoped that no reader of The Manual will ever allow himself to fall into such an error, and he certainly will not if he carefully follows the directions given in this chapter and in the chapter on Method of Examination.

Too much stress cannot be laid on the importance of the proper differential diagnosis between hypermetropia and myopia, and at the risk of repetition (which, after all, serves as the best means of fixing a fact in the student's mind) we will repeat the rule as follows: In testing the refraction of an eye *always commence with convex lenses*, and if these make vision clearer, or if they are accepted at all, it is *prima facie* evidence of the existence of hypermetropia; for the diagnosis of hypermetropia, in testing with the trial case, depends upon the acceptance of a convex lens for distance, and in such a case concave lenses should not be used, else they too will be accepted, and then the optometrist becomes mixed and the diagnosis is in doubt. For it should be remembered that weak concave glasses are accepted for distance by almost every eye, and rarely fail to cause some slight improvement in vision; and hence if they are tried first and at once accepted, the examiner may too hastily jump to the conclusion that the case is one of myopia, and may be led to commit the unpardonable error of prescribing concave glasses in a case of hypermetropia.

LATENT HYPERMETROPIA

The optometrist will sometimes meet with cases of suspected hypermetropia that will not accept convex lenses; their vision is 20/20, and all convex lenses blur it. In spite of this all the symptoms may point to hypermetropia, and the optometrist may be able to detect its presence by the retinoscope and by other means which will be described later on. Such patients are unable to relax their long-contracted ciliary muscles in the slightest degree; and in these cases the total hypermetropia is all latent. This condition of non-relaxation of the muscle of accommodation is most frequently found in young persons, in whom it is strong and vigorous. In some cases where convex lenses are thus rejected when each eye is tested separately, it may be possible to secure their acceptance by trying the eyes together in binocular vision, when the accommodation relaxes more readily.

THE OPHTHALMOSCOPE IN HYPERMETROPIA

It has been stated that the hypermetropic eye, when at rest, is adapted for convergent rays, and hence when the eye is strongly illuminated, the emergent rays will follow the same course in returning, and as a consequence will diverge from the surface of the cornea. During the ophthalmoscopic examination of the hypermetropic eye by the direct method, the instrument is held very close to the eye under observation, and the optometrist rotates behind the mirror, and into its aperture, a convex lens of sufficient refractive power to render parallel the divergent rays issuing from the patient's eye, when an erect, virtual, magnified image of the retina of this eye will become visible to the observer. The focal power of the convex lens necessary to make the divergent rays parallel will represent the degree of the hypermetropia.

This method of determining the refraction does not always yield accurate results, and should not be relied upon to the exclusion of the test by trial lenses; but in cases where the answers are unsatisfactory with the trial case, and particularly in children, it suffices to give a very satisfactory clue to the condition of the refraction and the degree of defect. With the improved ophthalmoscopes of the present day, the proper correcting lens can be found by simply rotating the disk until the strongest convex lens is reached that does not blur the retinal picture.

FAR-SIGHTEDNESS

The common term in use among the laity for hypermetropia is "far-sightedness," in contradistinction to near-sightedness, the common name for myopia. As this term would indicate, the idea generally prevails that the hypermetropic eye can see at a greater distance and can see better far off than an emmetropic eye. This is a great mistake; nothing can be better for vision than a normal or emmetropic eye. Instead of being more advantageous, the hypermetropic eye is an undeveloped eye, and because of this incompleteness there is apt to be an insufficiency in the layer of rods and cones of the retina, as well as of the optic nerve fibers, and therefore the vision can scarcely measure up to the normal standard of distinctness for distant objects, much less for near ones.

COURSE OF HYPERMETROPIA

While myopia inclines to increase in proportion to the close use of the eyes and in consequence thereof, hypermetropia, on the other hand, rarely increases, but rather tends to decrease. It has been shown that the hypermetropic eye possesses a larger ciliary muscle than the myopic or the emmetropic eye, and that its circular fibers particularly are more highly developed, few or none of which are found in the myopic eye. The statement is also made that the yellow spot is situated farther toward the temporal side than is the case in the emmetropic eye, thus increasing the distance between the disk and the macula.

VISION IN HYPERMETROPIA

In the lower grades of hypermetropia during adolescence, vision usually equals 20/20, and the defect is almost or altogether latent, and is therefore difficult of detection; but in the higher grades of the defect vision is more or less impaired, even when the hypermetropia is completely neutralized by the proper convex lenses.

This deficiency of sight depends partly on the insufficiency of the rods and cones of the retina as mentioned above, but more perhaps on the nearness of the retina to the nodal point, which causes the size of the retinal images to be smaller than in emmetropic eyes, and being smaller they are able to impress fewer of the perceptive nervous elements. Even when the size of the images is increased by the magnifying effect of convex lenses, the vision is not always raised to normal, which tends to prove the scarcity of the rods and cones.

For these reasons persons with a marked degree of hypermetropia cannot see well at night or in dimly-lighted rooms. Such persons fall into the habit of partially closing their lids and bringing small objects well illuminated quite close to the eyes, where for a short time they can be seen distinctly. The holding of objects close to the eyes is so contrary to the popular ideas about far-sightedness, that an explanation of this phenomenon would not be out of order. As the object approaches the eye the size of the retinal image increases to a much greater extent than the circles of diffusion. The strong illumination which is necessary to enable the objects to be seen causes a contraction of the pupil, which shuts out the circumferential rays and diminishes the diffusion circles, in which it is aided by the half-closed lids. At the same time the hypermetrope learns to suppress the impressions of any un-united rays that fall upon the retina. In this way these hypermetropes are sometimes able to do fine work and read small print even without the aid of glasses, a fact that is almost incredible. Is it any wonder then that these cases are sometimes confounded with myopia? They can, however, see distant objects with convex glasses, which would be quite impossible in myopia.

The ability to read so close to the eyes requires a very strong supply of light, not only to illuminate the letters, but also to contract the pupil to its smallest size, which, assisted by the partially closed lids, acts as a stenopaic apparatus, very much on the same principle as the improvement in vision caused by the pin-hole disk; we consider a single ray as emanating from each point of an object, and passing through the dioptric media and forming an image on the retina.

ESTIMATION OF THE TOTAL HYPERMETROPIA

The total hypermetropia can be determined upon by paralyzing the accommodation by a strong solution of atropine (or one of the other mydriatics) and then selecting the glass that affords the best distant vision. The total hypermetropia as thus ascertained is oftentimes very much greater than the manifest error. The writer has seen many cases where the manifest hypermetropia was less than 1 D., and some in which there was no evidence even of any manifest defect, where he found the total hypermetropia, as revealed by the mydriatic, to be 3 D. or 4 D. and even more.

THE USE OF ATROPINE DISCOUNTENANCED

But the employment of atropine belongs wholly to the province of the physician or oculist, and we advise against its use by the optometrist. It produces a most alarming disturbance of vision in hypermetropic eyes, which in some cases has so frightened the individual, even where he was advised in advance of its probable effect, that he has refused to submit to a second instillation of the drug, and either tried to get along without glasses or sought them elsewhere.

Many persons have consulted the writer, who have attributed (whether justly or unjustly) much of their trouble to the atropine that had been dropped in their eyes, and have declared with the greatest positiveness that their sight has never been as good since the drug was used as it had been before. In view of the possibility of such an experience, it would scarcely be policy for the optometrist to run the risk of injuring his reputation in this way.

Nor indeed is it really necessary in a majority of cases; for even though the total hypermetropia is ascertained by the use of the mydriatic, the patient would be unable to wear glasses strong enough to correct it all. In fact, the custom of the writer is to advise his students to correct only the manifest error, and in almost all cases it will be found that such glasses are about as strong as the patient can wear. This is particularly true of young persons, in whom the accommodation is strong and active. As the person grows older, and the accommodation lessens and weakens, more and more of the latent defect becomes manifest, and stronger and stronger glasses can be borne and are called for.

We repeat the statement that almost any case of hypermetropia can be corrected without the use of atropine, at least temporarily. The writer does not employ the drug nearly so much as he did in the earlier years of his practice. He has frequently found that the glasses that were indicated by the preliminary examination, were the same glasses that were prescribed after repeated examinations under atropine, because his experience had taught him that the total error could not all be neutralized; and this experience has occurred so often that he was led to look upon atropine as almost superfluous in the detection and correction of the majority of cases of optical defect, because the result of a careful examination without atropine indicates glasses about as strong as they can be borne even after the use of the drug.

While atropine is used and the glasses are prescribed while the eyes are still under its influence, such glasses usually prove to be too strong, so much so as to prohibit their use, because the attempt is made to correct too much of the latent defect. We will cite a case in illustration, in which there is only a slight manifest error, but probably a marked degree of latent defect. Atropine had previously been used by another physician, which developed the latent hypermetropia and the glasses had been prescribed accordingly, with the result, as so often happens, that they could not be worn.

CASE OF HYPERMETROPIA CORRECTED UNDER ATROPINE IN WHICH THE GLASSES WERE NOT SATISFACTORY

J. L. B. Aged eighteen years. Always had weak eyes and has suffered a great deal with neuralgia in eyes. About two years ago was given a pair of glasses, which were fitted after repeated examinations under atropine, but they have never been of any benefit to her, and in fact she had not been able to wear them. Vision of both eyes is 10/12, and she accepts + .25 C. axis 90°. Reads Jaeger No. 4, 4½ inches to 36 inches. These cylinders were ordered for constant wear; they afforded her the greatest satisfaction and relieved all the unpleasant symptoms of which she complained.

There is possibly some latent hypermetropia in this case in connection with the slight hypermetropic astigmatism, but which would not bear correction, as evidenced by the trouble with the glasses first prescribed.

LATENT HYPERMETROPIA VS. MANIFEST

In some cases the hypermetropia may be almost entirely latent, and a casual examination would show very little, if any, manifest error. In other cases the hypermetropia may be almost entirely manifest, and an examination under atropine would reveal very little, if any, latent defect. Another point with which the optometrist should be familiar, is the fact that the amount of discomfort is not always proportionate to the degree of hypermetropia.

These points are well illustrated in the two following cases, both of whom happened to be under my care at the same time:

A CASE IN WHICH THE HYPERMETROPIA IS ALMOST ENTIRELY MANIFEST

Mrs. J. M. H. Aged forty-two years. About eight years ago eyes first commenced to trouble her, but they have been getting worse during the past two or three years. Has had her glasses changed frequently, but to no advantage. Her present glasses, which were given her for reading only, are + 1.50 D., besides which she also has a pair of + 2 D. Complains of frequent attacks of neuralgia. Unable to read or sew more than five minutes at a time, when she begins to feel sick and dizzy. V. = 15/40; Hm. = + 2.50 D., with which V. = 15/15. Can't see to read without glasses; with + 3.50 D. reads Jaeger No. 4, 8 to 32 inches.

Under atropine, V. = 15/200. Ht. = + 3.50 D. with which V. = 15/15.

Ordered + 2.50 D. for distance, and + 4 D. for reading. These glasses relieved the neuralgia and enabled her to use her eyes with comfort.

The optician who fitted this case with + 2 D. for reading evidently did not or could not test her refraction to determine if she was hypermetropic or if any other error existed. He mistook it for a case of early presbyopia, and as she was not very far advanced in years, he was afraid of giving her glasses too strong; they were not sufficient to correct the manifest hypermetropia, much less to enable her to read or sew with any degree of comfort.

A CASE IN WHICH THE HYPERMETROPIA IS ALMOST ENTIRELY LATENT

Mrs. Dr. G. A. K. Aged thirty-one years. Has been wearing glasses more or less for reading and sewing for the past eleven years. Her reading glasses are + 1.50 D., which she uses without much discomfort. Her eyes trouble her most when from any cause her system is run down, while they annoy her but little when she enjoys her usual health. She has no particular difficulty with her eyes at present, but her husband, being a physician, advises her to have her eyes examined.

V. = 15/15. Hm. = + .75 D. Reads Jaeger No. 3, 11 in. to 30 in. Under atropine V. = 15/200. Ht. = + 4 D., with which V. = 15/15. Ordered + 2.50 D. for reading, but she complained that these were too strong, and not entirely comfortable in spite of the degree of hypermetropia present, and I was compelled to reduce them to + 1.50 D. for reading, the same number she had been using. As her distant vision was unimpaired and she had no trouble with her eyes, glasses for constant wear seemed unnecessary.

THESE CASES COMPARED

A careful study and comparison of these two cases will amply repay the practical optometrist, and to assist him we will make mention of a few of the important points. In the first place Mrs. H., with a total hypermetropia of 3.50, suffers greatly with neuralgia and inability to use her eyes, while Mrs. K., with a total error of 4 D., has no pain and uses her eyes with comparative comfort.

In the next place, Mrs. H. shows a manifest defect of 2.50 D., while Mrs. K., whose total defect is .50 D. greater than Mrs. H., reveals a manifest error of only .75 D. This accounts for the difference in the glasses prescribed for each lady, and explains why Mrs. K. needs no glasses for distance, and why such weak glasses suffice for her for reading. Of course, the difference in the age of these patients is the reason for the variance in the symptoms referred to. In the first case the accommodation is weakened by age and is unable to overcome the defect, and in the second case it still retains the vigor of youth and suffices to keep the refractive power of the eye up to the necessary degree.

HISTORY OF HYPERMETROPIA

The slighter degrees of hypermetropia occasion but little inconvenience until the individual reaches the thirties, when it manifests itself chiefly as an early presbyopia. In cases where the defect is a little more marked (from 1 D. to 3 D.), it usually causes the condition of convergent strabismus. In still higher degrees of hypermetropia, strabismus may be absent, but a group of symptoms known as "asthenopia" may be produced. This is a pen picture of the effects of the several degrees of hypermetropia, varying in different cases according to the peculiarities of each individual (his muscular power and nervous susceptibility). Sometimes a very slight degree of hypermetropia may be the cause of much distress; in other cases a much higher amount of refractive error produces but little discomfort.

The asthenopic symptoms of hypermetropia are especially liable to manifest themselves after an illness, or if the health of the patient is impaired from overwork, anxiety or other causes.

Distant objects are seen by the emmetropic eye without any effort of accommodation, consequently its whole power is free for use in near-vision. But in hypermetropia, on the contrary, there is no distinct vision of any object even at a distance, without more or less effort of accommodation. Hence there is a deficiency of accommodation to start with, or in other words an extra weight to carry, and as a matter of course under such circumstances the accommodation gives out much sooner than it otherwise would. The less the degree of hypermetropia, all other things being equal, the longer the eyes can be used before the annoying symptoms supervene. Therefore it becomes evident that the length of time the tension of the accommodation can be kept up is to a great extent dependent upon the degree of defect, or the amount of extra weight the ciliary muscle has to carry.

In the earlier years the soft and yielding crystalline lens and the strong and well-developed ciliary muscle enable the eyes to do their work without much complaint even in the face of a high degree of hypermetropia. But as years pass on and the lens becomes firmer and the muscles weaker, then the troublesome symptoms manifest themselves and become very annoying.

HYPERMETROPIA IN CHILDREN

The eye-strain that is caused by hypermetropia cannot fail to have an effect upon the character and natural disposition of children, and frequently tends to render them peevish and fretful, as well as desponding and lacking in self-reliance. The constant effort required for vision retards the quickness of perception and comprehension, and the exhaustion that is sure to follow this continued straining of the eyes interferes with the concentration of the attention; for these reasons the child unconsciously and without knowing the reason why, acquires a distaste for books.

A hypermetropic boy sits down to study his lessons full of the enthusiasm of youth and with a determination to perform his task. Sooner or later a feeling of uneasiness creeps over him and makes him restless. He thinks he needs more light and he moves near to the window or close to the lamp. Then the glare of the increased light irritates the eyes and they begin to feel heavy, and the face becomes flushed. He makes effort after effort to continue his work, but he finds it is of no use; his head droops over the table and he finally falls asleep.

This struggle is repeated day after day, and the naturally bright boy becomes backward and stupid. He gradually loses his desire for study, and he continues through life without the habit of application and the power of concentration, which are so essential to success, and all on account of a neglected optical defect, which should have been corrected at the commencement of his education.

DETERMINATION OF HYPERMETROPIA

The optometrist will be able to determine the existence of hypermetropia when any one of the following conditions is found to be present:

1. When distant vision is improved by a convex lens, or when the acuteness of vision equals 20/20 and is just as good with a convex lens as without.

2. When a patient is able to read fine print through a convex glass at a greater distance than the focal length of the lens.

3. When the near point lies at a greater distance from the eye than is proper for the age, or when the amplitude of accommodation falls below the normal standard. A reference to the tables in the Chapter on Presbyopia will show the distance of the near point and the amount of amplitude of accommodation at the various ages, a departure from which can be readily detected.

4. When with the ophthalmoscope the fundus of the eye can be distinctly seen with a convex lens in the aperture of the instrument.

The presence of any or all of these conditions indicates the existence of hypermetropia, which is then to be measured and corrected by the means to be described.

AMOUNT OF HYPERMETROPIA

The amount of hypermetropia may vary from a fraction of a dioptric to fifteen dioptrics; when it exceeds 6 D. it is looked upon as a case of high hypermetropia. When the defect is under 4 D. in young persons with a good accommodation, the acuteness of vision as a rule is normal and equals 20/20. Such patients may accept weak convex lenses, but without any improvement in vision, which has not fallen below the normal standard, the defect existing in the latent form. When the degree of hypermetropia is greater than 4 D., the vision is apt to be more or less impaired, which in moderate degrees is raised to normal by the proper convex lenses. In extreme cases of high hypermetropia it is impossible to secure normal vision by the most carefully adjusted glasses.

SIGNS OF HYPERMETROPIA

The presence of hypermetropia makes it a matter of more or less difficulty to maintain distinct vision of small objects for any great length of time. The vision begins to blur and the patient is compelled to stop reading and rub his eyes. This for the moment seems to clear up the vision, and the book is again taken up and a fresh start is made; but the blurring occurs again and again until finally the accommodation becomes entirely exhausted and the reading must be discontinued.

The book is often held in a very strong light, which serves to contract the pupil and thus render vision clearer. At the same time many hypermetropic persons fall into the habit of holding the book quite close to their eyes, thus increasing the size of the visual angle, when vision is also assisted by the half-closed lids acting as a stenopaic apparatus.

PAIN IN HYPERMETROPIA

One of the principal subjective symptoms of which the hypermetropic patient complains is pain, which varies very much as to its character and location. Sometimes it is in the eye-ball, sometimes over the brow and through the temple, sometimes on the top of the head, sometimes in the back of the head and nape of the neck, and in extreme cases the pain may be accompanied by nausea and vomiting. Headache is a very common symptom, and is often described under the French term *migraine*.

TESTING HYPERMETROPIA

If the symptoms have indicated the existence of hypermetropia, and the preliminary examination has confirmed this, the eyes must then be carefully tested to determine the degree of defect. Each eye should be tested separately, noting first its visual acuteness, and then commencing the test with weak convex lenses.

If a mild convex glass is accepted the diagnosis of hypermetropia is assured, and then stronger and stronger glasses are placed before the eye in rapid succession, until the strongest convex lens is reached with which the patient is able to read 20/20; or if it is impossible to raise the acuteness of vision to normal, then the strongest convex lens that affords the best sight in looking at the card hanging twenty feet away. This is the measure of the *manifest hypermetropia*.

If the acuity of vision is not raised to normal by a convex spherical lens, there is a possibility of the existence of an astigmatic element in the case, for which a careful examination should be made. If, however, vision equals 20/20 with the spherical lens, it is hardly likely that any astigmatism is present, but still every case should be tested with a view of its detection if it exists. If none is present, the convex lens is all that is necessary to correct the ametropia. In order to insure accuracy, this examination should be repeated two or three times on as many different days.

In cases where vision is found to be exactly alike in the two eyes, and if spasm of the accommodation is suspected, the two eves may be tested together, when more suitable glasses car oftentimes be obtained in this way by the acceptance of stionger glasses, than when one eye is excluded from the act of vision, because with parallel axes the accommodation is more apt to relax.

THE METHOD BY OVER-CORRECTION

In cases where the hypermetropia exists largely in a latent form, and where there is consequently difficulty in having the patient accept convex lenses, the following "method by over-correction" will often yield satisfactory results.

Place in the trial frame a stronger convex lens than is required; that is, one strong enough to greatly over-correct the defect. This, of course, blurs the vision, but at the same time it encourages the accommodation to relax, as the more the relaxation of the accommodation the greater the improvement in vision.

Then place in the trial frame, in front of this convex lens, a weak concave lens, which at once causes an improvement in vision. Then try successively stronger and stronger concave lenses until the *weakest* one is found that affords a vision of 20/20, and then the difference between the two lenses will be the measure of the manifest hypermetropia.

For instance, a + 6 D. lens is placed in the trial frame, with which perhaps vision is only equal to 20/200. Concave lenses improve this vision, and it is found a — 4 D. enables the patient to read 20/20, in which case + 2 D. is the measure of the manifest hypermetropia.

LATENT HYPERMETROPIA BECOMES MANIFEST

As age advances and the vigor of accommodation lessens, if there is any latent hypermetropia it gradually becomes manifest. A person may have 6 D. of latent hypermetropia at ten years of age, when the defect is difficult of detection, or perhaps its existence may not even be suspected. At thirty-five years of age half of it (3 D.) may have become manifest and is easily discovered by the usual tests, and after middle age the whole of it becomes manifest and complicates and augments the natural condition of presbyopia, and then the total hypermetropia and the manifest hypermetropia are synonymous terms.

A HYPERMETROPIC EYE CHANGING ITS REFRACTION

The normal condition of refraction in childhood is one of hypermetropia, as has been stated; some persons retain this condition all through life, a considerable number become emmetropic as they grow older, while a certain percentage pass over into a condition of myopia. In all these changes, from hypermetropia to emmetropia and from emmetropia to myopia, there is a gradual lengthening in the antero-posterior diameter of the eye-ball, and the rapidity of the changes and the degree of myopia finally attained will depend on the amount of lengthening and the recession of the retina from the focus of the parallel rays.

When these changes occur they usually take place before adult age is reached. In childhood and youth the membranes and tissues of the eye are soft and yielding, and can offer but little resistance to the causes that tend to elongate the ball. After twenty years of age the tunics of the eye, and especially the sclerotic, become tough and firm, after which there is little danger of these morbid changes taking place, or if they have already commenced, their progress is now checked.

SPASM OF ACCOMMODATION

On account of the persistent contraction of the ciliary muscle which is necessary to overcome the error of refraction and render vision distinct, hypermetropia often gives rise to a condition which has been termed *spasm of the accommodation.* This simulates myopia in all of its symptoms, the resemblance being particularly noticeable in the impairment of distant vision and the confirmed habit of holding the book close to the eyes. In these cases concave lenses are often accepted and may cause a great improvement in distant vision; but it need hardly be said that no well-informed optometrist would order them, as they would only aggravate the trouble and impose a greater strain on the accommodation.

This state of spasm is apt to occur in persons whose nervous system is in a low state of vitality, and, strange to say, it seems to bear no relation to the vigor of the accommodation. It is almost incredible that persons with a weak accommodation should suffer with constant contraction of the ciliary muscle; but such is really the case. It might be well to remark in passing that spasm of accommodation may occur in conditions of refraction other than hypermetropia.

TREATMENT OF HYPERMETROPIA

In absolute hypermetropia vision is indistinct at all distances. The accommodation is not equal to the task of uniting even parallel rays (those from a distance) in a focus on the retina, much less divergent rays (those from near objects). In such cases the rays must be rendered convergent before they enter the eye; and this changing of parallel diverging rays into a convergent form is accomplished by means of convex lenses.

The treatment, then, of hypermetropia consists in the application of a convex lens of such strength as will impart to parallel rays sufficient convergence to make them focus upon the retina without any effort of the accommodation.

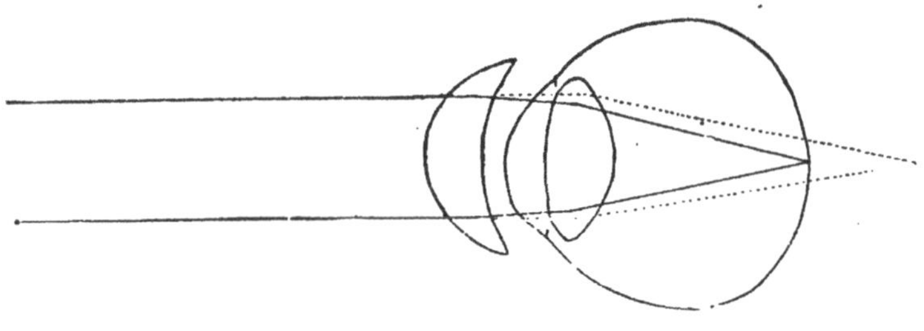

Diagram of a passive hypermetropic eye, the focus of parallel rays lying behind the retina, as shown by the dotted lines. A convex lens placed in front of the eye converges the rays to a focus on the retina, as shown by the plain lines, the accommodation all the while being quiescent.

TWO PAIRS OF GLASSES MAY BE REQUIRED

In many cases two pairs of glasses may be required; one pair to enable distant objects to be distinctly seen, and another pair to permit of fine print being easily read at the ordinary reading distance. Two pairs of glasses become a necessity under one of two conditions—in high degrees of hypermetropia and in hypermetropia complicated with presbyopia.

When the range of accommodation is much diminished, this deficiency may be compensated for by a change in the position of the glasses. If very strong convex glasses are worn, a slight alteration in their distance from the eyes is equivalent to a change for those of a greater or lesser power, as may be needed to make objects distinctly seen at different distances, thus supplementing the use of the accommodation and obviating the necessity for glasses of an intermediate focus. Therefore great care should be taken to see that such glasses are properly adjusted and centered. As these glasses are usually required for near vision, where a marked convergence of the visual axes is called for, the centers of the lenses should be slightly approximated, so that the visual lines may pass through them. If this precaution be overlooked and the rays of light pass through the peripheral portions of the lenses, their prismatic effect is called into play, which may cause a disturbance of the close relation which should exist between the functions of accommodation and convergence, and this may be followed by a train of symptoms making up the condition of asthenopia.

In facultative hypermetropia where both near and distant vision is good, and the use of the accommodation can be continued without fatigue almost as long as may be desired, no glasses are necessary until the near point has receded beyond eight or nine inches. This occurs much earlier than in the normal eye, and such persons are required to wear glasses for close work in many cases when only twenty-five or thirty years old.

AN UNNATURAL USE OF THE ACCOMMODATION

In hypermetropia, as has already been shown, either on account of the faulty formation of the eye-ball or of a deficiency of refractive and accommodative power, an excessive amount of muscular power is required to adjust the dioptric apparatus of the eye for near vision. Now, the placing of a convex lens before such an eye does away with the necessity for a certain amount of muscular effort, and, therefore, the lens represents, or is equivalent to, the expenditure of a certain amount of muscular force. In other words, the convex lens lifts a load from the shoulders of the overburdened muscle, which is then called upon to perform only its legitimate work.

In hypermetropia the brain abhors the circles of diffusion that would naturally be formed on the retina and the blurred vision that would result therefrom, and instinctively turns to the function of accommodation and appeals to it to bring the focus of rays forward to the retina and thus restore clearness of vision.

In giving the hint to the nerve centers that control the accommodation as to what is expected of it, and while notifying it when the time arrives for action, the brain despatches sufficient nerve force (no more and no less) to the ciliary muscle to accomplish the purpose of clear vision. The most wonderful thing about this whole matter is the accuracy with which the brain measures the work that is to be accomplished and the nicety with which it sends forth just the amount of force required.

This is an unjust use to which the accommodation is put but it must be continued until the necessary glasses are supplied. Transgression on any of Nature's laws is sure to be followed by punishment sooner or later, and the breaking of this law proves no exception to the rule, as is shown by the torture which some of these hypermetropic and asthenopic patients are compelled to suffer.

WHAT GLASSES TO PRESCRIBE

In the correction of hypermetropia by convex lenses in the light of the above statements, the important question naturally arises as to what shall be the power of the glass required in each individual case? This brings up the subject of the total amount of error, and what proportion of the latent portion it is advisable to attempt to correct. The total hypermetropia is made up of the sum of the manifest and the latent, the divisions between which are plainly marked.

The former can be easily measured, but the latter can be detected only by the employment of atropine, the use of which by the optometrist has been discountenanced on these pages on every occasion. But, for the sake of argument, suppose the drug had been used and the total error determined in this way. Theoretically it would seem to be the proper thing to at once and completely neutralize it, but practically such glasses are found to be much too strong.

Previously there had been an excessive and unnatural contraction of the ciliary muscle, by means of which a portion of the defect had been rendered latent. When the total neutralizing glasses are placed before the eyes, the muscle should completely relax and allow the defect, which it had rendered latent, to now become manifest and correctible by glasses; but instead of this, the contraction of the muscle still continues, which, with the action of the convex lens, supplies an excess of refractive power, which may result in an aggravation of the very symptoms it was intended to relieve. Hence the rule has been formulated not to attempt to correct the total amount of hypermetropia at the first fitting of glasses.

CORRECTION OF TOTAL HYPERMETROPIA

When a hypermetropic eye is under the influence of atropine, vision at all distances is blurred and indistinct. The full correction of the defect is necessary to clear up distant vision, and a lens 4 D. or 5 D. stronger will enable the patient to see at reading distance. As soon as the effects of the drug have worn off (which may not be for a week) and the accommodation is again allowed to exercise its function, then distant vision is dimmed when the same glasses are placed before the eyes, and his haziness, which envelopes all distant objects, continues until the glasses are taken off. The tension of the accommodation, which is the disturbing feature in this problem, is a variable quantity in different individuals, some few persons bearing almost or quite the full correction with little discomfort, while a great many others will tolerate but a small part of the correction.

Oculists who are accustomed to employ atropine in the correction of hypermetropia, use different methods in dealing with this difficulty. Sometimes the full correction is ordered and placed before the eyes while still under the influence of the mydriatic, and the patient is instructed to wear them constantly all the while that the influence of the drug is wearing off and the accommodation is returning to its normal state. In this way it is hoped to coax the eyes to accept the glasses.

It might be well at this point to remind the optometrist that when the glasses are fitted at fifteen feet (and even at twenty feet), there is really an over-correction of about .12 D. to .25 D., because the rays proceeding from these distances are not strictly parallel, and hence the lens that is required to focus them perfectly on the retina is a little too strong to exactly focus parallel rays. Therefore, even when it is desired to order a full correction, the glass which affords the best vision under atropine at fifteen or twenty feet should be weakened by .25 D. This is a slight step in the direction of enabling patients to wear a full correction.

THE FULL CORRECTION MAY NEED TO BE REDUCED

In other cases the oculist may employ a different method, as follows: The effect of the atropine is allowed to wear off and the eyes regain their full power of accommodation, after which an interval of one or two weeks is permitted to pass before the eyes are given their final trial for the glasses which are to be prescribed.

The full correction as found by the atropine is then placed before the eyes, and the effect on the distant letters is noted. If they afford a normal acuteness of vision (which unfortunately is rarely the case) the oculist would be justified in ordering them. If, however, as is usually the case, the acuteness of vision is impaired by these full strength glasses, they are gradually reduced little by little until the lens is arrived at that permits a vision of 20/20. This may require a reduction of one-fourth, one-third, or even one-half of the full amount, and these weakened glasses are the ones that are then ordered.

WHY THEN USE ATROPINE?

This practically amounts to a correction of the manifest hypermetropia only, and now the question naturally arises, "Of what benefit is the use of atropine to determine the total error (which will not bear neutralization), when only the manifest defect is after all corrected, the amount of which can be just as well determined without the use of the mydriatic?" This question carries its own answer.

Exophoria may act as a frequent cause of the inability to wear the full correction of convex glasses in hypermetropia, on account of its accompanying insufficiency of the internal recti muscles. In this condition an extra supply of nervous force is required by these muscles in order to maintain parallelism of the visual axes, which implies a corresponding stimulation of the muscle of accommodation. It therefore follows that in the face of this constant incentive to action on the part of the accommodation, it can hardly be expected to relax to any appreciable extent to admit of the acceptance of a convex lens. A displacement of the optical centers of these glasses inward may be of some benefit, as this will assist the overtaxed convergence, and in like manner will tend to diminish the accommodation.

A PRACTICAL ILLUSTRATION

The writer of these lines has seen many cases of hypermetropia coming from the hospitals and dispensaries of this city who were unable to wear the glasses given them. The rule in these institutions is to use atropine and correct the total error, the refracting being done by assistants and beginners. If the patient returns with any complaint he is assured the glasses are made according to the prescription, and that the latter is correct, and he is advised to persevere in their use. If the luckless patient ventures to return again to find further fault with the glasses, he is given the scant courtesy that is so common in charitable institutions, and is dismissed with the statement that nothing more can be done for him.

He finally drifts into the office of some oculist or falls into the hands of some optometrist, who hears his story and quickly perceives the cause of his trouble, and by reducing the strength of his glasses, gives him immediate comfort. This is a very common occurrence and hence we feel safe in making the statement that the optometrist, in the great majority of cases, if he exercises the proper care, will be able to fit his cases of hypermetropia as satisfactorily as the oculist who uses atropine. Therefore, the practical optometrist will have to do only with the *manifest* hypermetropia, which he is able to measure and correct by the methods set forth in this chapter.

After the glasses have been worn for awhile, some additional portion of the latent hypermetropia becomes manifest, when the glasses may be advantageously changed for those a little stronger. After a time another change may be made in the same way, and finally in some cases the latent error becomes almost or entirely manifest, when glasses corresponding to the degree of the total hypermetropia are the proper ones to prescribe, and no further changes are likely to be necessary until the presbyopic period of life arrives.

SHOULD THE GLASSES BE WORN CONSTANTLY?

This is a question that frequently arises, and it is one which the optometrist will be called upon to answer, which can only be done by taking into account all the peculiarities of each individual case, with special reference to these three points—the age of the patient, the degree of the hypermetropia and the symptoms of which he complains.

If the degree of the defect is not high, and the patient is young and in vigorous health, and the eyes are strong with distant vision perfect, there would scarcely seem to be any real necessity for their constant use. When such a person is engaged in long-continued sight-seeing, as at a theater or at an exposition, symptoms of fatigue of the eyes may appear, when recourse should be had to the glasses. Even when glasses are not worn for customary distant wear, there is every reason why they should be brought into use on such special occasions, in order to assist the ciliary muscle and lessen the strain on the eye.

WHY GLASSES SHOULD BE WORN

In many cases where the optometrist may find it necessary to advise his patient to wear the glasses constantly, the latter will sometimes protest and say that he can see perfectly well at a distance without them, and that therefore he does not need them. Under such circumstances the optometrist must take the trouble to explain the reason why the glasses are to be worn for distance, and that they are intended not so much to improve vision as to enable the patient to see with less strain and to assist the ciliary muscle, which is overtaxed.

If the patient is no longer young, if the degree of hypermetropia is marked, or if there is much pain in the eyes, and headache and symptoms of asthenopia, then in any or all of these cases the use of glasses for constant wear is no longer a question or a matter of fancy, but becomes an actual necessity. In any case where the distant vision is impaired and where it is raised to the normal standard by the glasses, there is sufficient reason why the glasses should be used for constant wear.

The fact is that when hypermetropia exists in any marked degree, no amount of resting the eyes nor the observance of any fixed rules can possibly prevent such eyes from becoming weak and painful in the absence of convex glasses, which will, when regularly made use of, do much to render them more useful and comfortable.

In the prescribing of glasses two objects must be kept in view—to select that glass which will afford the greatest acuteness of vision, which results only when the rays of light are sharply focused on the retina, thus producing a distinct image. This sharp focus may be effected by the accommodation alone, by a convex lens alone (as in an eye under atropine), or by a combination of action of a convex lens and the accommodation; and hence the optometrist must make the effort to so associate the glasses and the accommodation that this clearly defined focus may be maintained. In the second place, that glass should be chosen which will enable the eyes to perform their functions with the greatest ease and comfort.

A COMMON COMPLAINT

It frequently happens that when convex glasses are first given to a hypermetropic person for constant wear, they will make objects appear magnified, and, therefore, closer than they really are. Such a person may return to the optometrist with the complaint that the pavement seems to approach him, and therefore he feels as if he was walking up-hill or taking a step upward. It may be well for the optometrist to make a re-examination, so as to be sure that the glasses that have been prescribed are not at fault, and then the patient should be assured that if he will persist in their use these annoying appearances will speedily pass away and the sight will become so natural that he will scarcely be conscious of having glasses before his eyes.

RULES FOR DETERMINING THE GLASSES

Some authorities, instead of prescribing the strongest convex lenses, with which the patient retains his full acuteness of vision, think it best to order a lens somewhat weaker, perhaps .50 D. to .75 D. less, and in this way they feel confident the eyes will at once take kindly to the glasses, and will begin to reap the benefit to be derived from their use at the start, whereas the stronger ones would probably annoy the eyes at first and might require some time before they became habituated to them.

In cases where atropine has been applied, Donders advised the prescribing of a glass that would correct all the manifest hypermetropia and one-fourth of the latent. Another author recommends a convex lens equal in strength to one-half the sum of the manifest and the total error. For example, if the manifest error was 2 D. and the total error 4 D., the sum of the two would equal 6 D., and the glasses ordered would be + 3 D. This last rule can scarcely be considered a scientific one, and, in fact, neither of these rules appeals to the optometrist, as they are both based on measurements made under atropine. We repeat, then, and would emphasize the advice, that the optometrist should not attempt to do more than correct the manifest error.

DONDERS' WORDS

"He who knows by experience how commonly hypermetropia occurs, how necessary a knowedge of it is to the correct diagnosis of the various defects of the eye, and how deeply it affects the whole treatment of the oculist, will come to the sad conviction that an incredible number of patients have been tormented with all sorts of remedies, and have been given over to painful anxiety, who would have found immediate relief and deliverance in suitable spectacles."

These words are as true now as when first uttered by our distinguished teacher, and they have been verified by the experience of many persons who have had this defect from childhood and who have suffered greatly while attending school, but who did not understand the cause of their distress until they grew up and learned the nature of hypermetropia.

BEFORE HYPERMETROPIA WAS UNDERSTOOD

Such persons were unable to use their eyes for any length of time, and therefore failed to complete their studies, and in this way fell behind their classmates and appeared to be stupid. If they complained of pain in the eyes or headache, it was regarded as an excuse to get away from their books. Occasionally such a child would chance upon a pair of grandfather's discarded spectacles, and, with childlike curiosity, would try them on, when it found to its amazement that it could read with comfort, and the print seemed large and plain. Of course, as soon as it was discovered in this presumptuous use of the old spectacles, the latter were taken away and the child warned never to touch them again under penalty of losing its sight and becoming blind. While the parents acted entirely for the best interests of the child according to their own limited knowledge, yet to us of this day, who are so familiar with the symptoms of hypermetropia and its method of correction by convex glasses, this deprivation of the child of the only means of relief seems little short of barbarous.

In former years many ambitious young men, with a fondness for study and high hopes for professional distinction, have had their anticipations nipped in the bud by increasing difficulties experienced in continued near vision, and have been advised not to wear glasses, but to abandon all their chosen plans and go to the country and seek some occupation that does not call for any close use of the eyes. Could any disappointment be greater?

There are many pupils attending school at the present time who cannot use their eyes in study without pain and headache and irritation of the eyes, especially noticeable when they are used by artificial light, due to a hypermetropia, the correction of which by properly adjusted convex glasses would cause these annoying symptoms to vanish as rapidly as the morning dew before the rising sun. The frequency with which these cases are met with by parents and educators emphasizes the importance of an early recognition of the cause, in order that it may be removed before permanent injury is done to the sight, and that the complaints of children and their apparent stupidity may receive due allowance, and not be met with undeserved punishment.

Formerly there existed a great prejudice against the wearing of convex glasses by children, which doomed them to a continuance of suffering and handicapped them in the acquirement of an education. The prevailing idea was that convex lenses were suitable only for aged persons and that children were debarred from their use.

A TYPICAL CASE OF HYPERMETROPIA

In order to point the moral for the preceding remarks, we will relate the history of a typical case, which was originally reported by Dr. Fenner.

A young man of sixteen years comes for advice, with the statement that his eyes are weak; they are small, prominent and set widely apart, and present no external appearance of disease. The pupils act quickly and freely to the stimulus of light. On inquiring into the family history it is learned that he has a brother who suffers like himself, but to a less degree, a sister who has convergent strabismus, and his father was compelled to wear glasses at the age of thirty.

The patient's health is good; he attends school and is inclined to be studious, but after reading or writing for a short time his eyes grow tired and the letters become indistinct. He moves the book further from his eyes, which enables him to see better for a little while, but soon the letters begin to blur again; another change in the position of the book affords a temporary improvement, which, however, is soon lost, and any further changes are futile. The eyes become more and more fatigued, there is a slight watering accompanied by a sensation of smarting and supra-orbital pain, the print pales and the borders and angles of the letters widen out so that they appear as confused, irregular spots on the paper, and he is compelled to discontinue his reading. He closes his eyes, rubs and presses the lids with his fingers for a few moments, when he is able to look around and see distant objects distinctly. After a few minutes of rest in this way he is again able to take up the book and see the letters with their original clearness, but the eyes give out sooner than before and he goes through the same process of closing his eyes and compressing the lids. The pain over his eyes increases and develops into a severe headache, the conjunctiva becomes bloodshot, and if he persists in reading he becomes nauseated.

Thus he worries along through the day, and if he attempts to study at night all the symptoms are intensified, because his eyes are sensitive to strong artificial light, which produces a painful dazzling and causes a sensation of scratching and roughness as if sand was under the lids. When he awakes in the morning he finds his eye-lids somewhat adherent, but after washing his face and bathing his eyes he feels all right again and starts in with his studies with all the vim and enthusiasm of an ambitious youth; soon the well-known symptoms return and he goes through the experience of the previous day. A Sunday's rest invigorates his eyes and on Monday he has less trouble than on any other day, and during a vacation he experiences no difficulty whatever. He says he has been under the treatment of a physician, who told him he had an "affection of the optic nerve," gave him medicines, blistered his temples and dropped "eye-water" into his eyes.

On examination his vision is found to equal 20/20. Convex lenses were tried, commencing with + .50 D., and increasing to + 1.75 D., which were the strongest accepted; + 2 D.

blurred the letters. Hence his manifest hypermetropia is + 1.75 D. His reading vision is now tried and his amplitude of accommodation measured. He is able to bring the print as close as six inches, but says it requires an appreciable effort: he gradually moves the book farther away as he reads, and by the time he has finished the paragraph it is out as far as fourteen inches. His near point of six inches represents an amplitude of accommodation of 6.50 D., and, as the normal amplitude at this age is 11 D., there is presumptive evidence of the existence of 4.50 D. of hypermetropia, and, as the manifest error was 1.75 D., the balance exists as latent hypermetropia.

Glasses of + 2 D. are ordered for him and he remarks, "Why, doctor, you don't want me to wear spectacles, do you?" "Certainly," the oculist answers, "or at least I wish you to try them." He then said, "I used to wear my grandmother's spectacles at night to get my lessons and I could see as well as ever, but when I told our doctor he said I must not use any more, for they would ruin my eyes and make me blind." Notwithstanding his doctor's advice he takes the glasses, returns to school, and has no further trouble with his eyes.

While ignorance of these matters might be excused in the laity, it is reprehensible in a physician; but now, since the nature of the defect and the proper means of correcting it are well understood, it is hoped, by the diffusion of knowledge, to overcome the prejudice which has so widely existed in the public mind against the wearing of convex glasses by children.

TWO PAIRS OF GLASSES

In the higher degrees of hypermetropia, and in hypermetropia of persons approaching the presbyopic period of life. two pairs of glasses are required—one pair for distant vision, and the other pair to enable fine print to be easily read at the customary distance.

PROPER FITTING OF GLASSES

It should be remembered that when strong convex glasses are worn, the removal of the lenses a little farther from the eyes increases their power and makes them equivalent to glasses of a higher number; and, as this is sometimes not desirable, it would not be out of place for the optometrist to instruct his patient just how they should be worn.

Another point that should not be overlooked in the fitting of such glasses is to see that they are close enough together that the patient looks through the centers of the lenses when converging his eyes for near work, as otherwise, if the line of vision was through the edges of the lenses, the rays of light would be refracted as by prisms with curved surfaces; and, while this might not be undesirable in selected cases, unless it is specially indicated, and particularly if the decentering is outward, it might destroy the harmony between the functions of accommodation and convergence and be productive of asthenopic symptoms.

THE PROPER GLASSES

It has been stated on a previous page that the hypermetropic eye is unable to see any object distinctly, not even the most remote, without an effort of accommodation, and the closer the object the more the strain. Consequently, in hypermetropic eyes the accommodation is in a state of constant tension.

When convex glasses are placed before the hypermetropic eye it is found that the ciliary muscle, which has been in a state of contraction for so long a time, cannot wholly relax; there still remains a certain amount of involuntary contraction of the muscle, but this is an element that cannot be measured (except by atropine, which is out of the question), and varies in different individuals.

Hence, in fitting such eyes with convex lenses, the strongest they will bear without blurring distant vision is just equal to the amount of relaxation of the muscle of accommodation, and this is known as the manifest hypermetropia. The degree of involuntary contraction of the muscle that remains is the measure of the latent hypermetropia, with which the optician need not concern himself, as he will have done his whole duty in correcting the manifest error.

Sometimes there is no manifest hypermetropia, it is all latent, which is particularly the case in young persons. At about twenty years of age some of it becomes manifest, the proportion of which increases with advancing years, the latent decreasing in the same ratio, until, finally, in middle life it has entirely disappeared, and all of the hypermetropia is then manifest.

A CASE OF MANIFEST HYPERMETROPIA IN WHICH THE LATENT PORTION IS REVEALED BY THE DIMINISHED AMPLITUDE OF ACCOMMODATION

JOSEPH F. Aged twenty-one years.

Has no trouble in using his eyes in daytime, but complains of inability to read at night. He went to an optician, who gave him a pair of + .50 D. glasses, but they have not been of much benefit to him. On examination his vision is found to equal 12/10 and a manifest hypermetropia of .50 D. A test of his reading vision showed a range of accommodation of eight inches to thirty-three inches.

A near point of eight inches indicates an amplitude of accommodation of only 5 D., whereas the normal amplitude of a person at this age is at least 9.50 D., and hence we are justified in assuming the existence of 4.50 D. of total hypermetropia; and as the test showed only .50 D. of manifest error, there remains 4 D. of latent defect. It was not deemed advisable to correct the total error, and hence his reading vision was tested with the following results:

With + 1 D., range of accommodation 7 in. to 33 in.
With + 1.50 D., range of accommodation 5½ in. to 33 in.
With + 2 D., range of accommodation 5 in. to 32 in.

+ 2 D. glasses were ordered for reading, and gave the most perfect satisfaction.

A CASE OF SLIGHT MANIFEST AND MARKED LATENT HYPERMETROPIA

MRS. S. M. R. Aged thirty-eight years.

Eyes have been failing for the past year. Has constant headache and a great deal of pain and smarting in eyes. Complains that she can't see to thread a needle. Vision = 15/15. Manifest Hy. = .50 D. The near point has receded to sixteen inches, which implies an amplitude of accommodation of 2.50

D., and as the normal amplitude at this age is about 5 D., we have evidence of 2.50 D. of hypermetropia.

It is a curious coincidence that if we calculate the reading glasses according to the rules given under Presbyopia the same result is obtained. Subtract the glass representing the receded near point (16 in. = 2.50 D.) from the glass representing the point which we wish to make the near point (8 in. = 5 D.), which leaves + 2.50 D. as the glass required.

One would expect at this age that more of the latent portion would become manifest, and that it has not indicates an exceptionally vigorous condition of the accommodation. Glasses of + 2.50 D. were ordered for reading, and for distance + .75 D. will answer at present, although stronger ones will soon be needed, as the latent trouble becomes manifest.

A CASE OF HYPERMETROPIA IN WHICH READING GLASSES FAILED TO GIVE SATISFACTION UNTIL DISTANCE GLASSES WERE WORN

Mrs. J. H. S. Aged fifty-nine years.

Her eyes have been troubling her for past fifteen years, and she has great difficulty in getting glasses to suit. Has been compelled to change glasses frequently, those for reading at present being + 4 D., with which she can see fairly well, but in spite of this they do not give her satisfaction. Vision = 15/70. With + 1.50 D. — 15/15. Ordered + 1.50 D. for distance and constant wear, and advised her to continue the + 4 D. glasses for reading.

In this case the uncorrected hypermetropia kept the eyes on a constant strain, and consequently when the patient desired to read she commenced the task with eyes already fatigued, and, therefore, her reading glasses did not seem suitable, even though they were accurately adjusted for their purpose. But, now that her reading glasses are supplemented by distance ones, the constant strain will be relieved, and when she begins to read her eyes will be fresh and the reading glasses prove all that can be desired.

There has been a marked change of late years in the attitude of the public in regard to the wearing of convex glasses, and when their use is imperatively demanded for the rectification of some optical defect, there is at least no stubborn protest; but there is still room for improvement, and instead of this placid acquiescence in their employment we would like to see such a sentiment prevail as would recognize their worth and demand their use wherever and whenever indicated.

CARE IN THE WEARING OF GLASSES

When glasses are prescribed for the correction of hypermetropia, whether for constant wear or only for reading, the optometrist should give his patient definite instructions that he wear them always for the purpose for which they are given. If they are laid aside at intervals, a return of the old symptoms is apt to follow, and in this way little progress can be made in relieving the eyes and freeing them from irritation. Whereas, if the glasses are worn persistently, comfort is at once experienced and the eyes become better and stronger, so much so, in some cases, that the glasses may be dispensed with for general wear and used only for reading.

In young persons, whose eyes are strong enough to easily overcome the hypermetropia, whose distant vision is good, and who experience no trouble except in reading, the glasses may be given with the distinct understanding that they need be worn only for close use. As the patient grows toward the presbyopic period of life, these glasses will need to be exchanged for those of a higher power, and then the old pair will suffice for distant vision and should be used for that purpose.

In the case of intelligent persons who are desirous to be properly fitted the use of the trial case is the decisive method, and the test that is sufficiently trustworthy is the patient's own statement that such or such a lens does not blur the sight, or makes vision clearest, or feels the most comfortable to his eyes.

But in the case of stupid persons, or of children, where definite answers can only be obtained with the greatest difficulty, or where it is desired to verify the statements made, the optometrist should have recourse to his ophthalmoscope and retinoscope, the latter especially affording an inexpensive and satisfactory method of determining the state of the refraction.

Even with the assistance afforded by these additional methods, some cases will still be obscure, and the optometrist must fall back on his own experience and be guided by general principles, always endeavoring to press the patient to the most satisfactory answers obtainable.

There is no limit of age as regards the wearing of convex glasses for hypermetropia (or in using the proper glasses for the correction of any other optical defect). They may be placed before the eyes of a child as soon as he is old enough to understand that they are not playthings, that being about the age when the child commences to go to school. In those cases of hypermetropia which tend to produce squint, the persistent wearing of convex glasses will usually prevent this tendency from being developed. For the same reasons, they should be worn after an operation for strabismus, as a preventive of a return of the defect.

THE PUNCTUM REMOTUM IN HYPERMETROPIA

The emmetropic eye, when at rest, has been shown to be adapted for parallel rays, or those proceeding from infinite distance, consequently its punctum remotum is said to lie at infinity. The hypermetropic eye, on the other hand, is adapted only for convergent rays; but there are no convergent rays in nature, and consequently such an eye is adjusted for a condition that does not exist. The focus of parallel rays lies behind the retina, and the punctum remotum becomes a *negative* quantity in hypermetropia.

The position of this negative point can be found by (or, in other words, the distance of the punctum remotum behind the eye will be equal to) the focus of the convex lens which is required to correct the hypermetropia. The writer finds that this subject is not clearly comprehended by the optical student, and a glance at the various standard text-books shows such conflicting and ambiguous statements that there is no wonder the reader is puzzled and confused and unable to gather a proper understanding of it. And as it is a matter of considerable theoretical importance, we will endeavor to describe it so clearly that the beginner of the study cannot fail to understand.

This illustration shows the punctum remotum of the hypermetropic eye and the lenses that give to parallel rays sufficient convergence to meet upon its retina.

The location of the far point behind the eye is the spot to which rays must converge before entering the eye, in order that they may be focused upon the retina. From this statement we are enabled to formulate the following corollary: The hypermetropic eye, when its accommodation is at rest and its refractive power at a minimum, is adjusted for rays converging to its far point, and such converging rays exactly meet upon its retina.

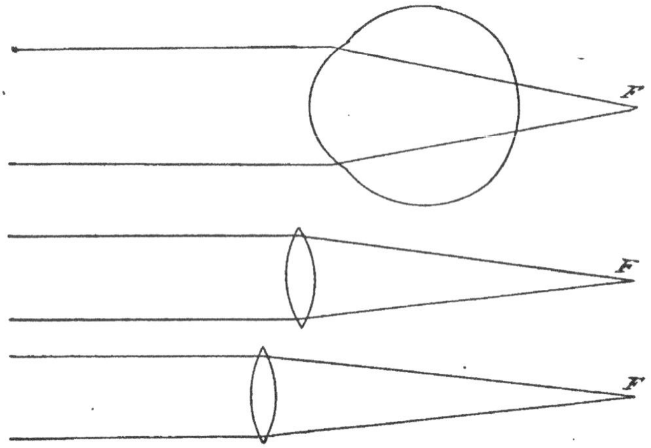

The focus of a convex lens is at a certain definite distance depending upon the refractive power of the lens, and therefore the convex lens that is needed to give to the rays the proper convergence, so that if continued they would meet at the punctum proximum, which holds a conjugate relation to the retina, must be a lens whose focal distance exactly corresponds to this point.

In the diagram of the hypermetropic eye, given above, the position of the focus of parallel rays is at *F*, which is a certain distance behind the retina, and the convex lens immediately below it brings parallel rays also to a focus at *F*, which is a corresponding point. If now this convex lens be raised to a position just in front of the diagrammatic eye, and almost touching the cornea, it is evident that the rays that pass through it and enter the eye will possess just the proper convergence to be focused on the retina of the eye, and hence this lens will be the proper one to correct the hypermetropia.

If the lens was placed farther from the eye a weaker one would suffice, because, the punctum remotum remaining at the same point, the farther the lens is removed from it the less refractive power it needs to focus parallel rays at this point. This fact is well illustrated in the diagram, where the second lens is removed from the eye, and although of weaker power has its focus at the corresponding point *F*. Therefore, when the convex correcting lens is to be worn a definite distance in front of the eye, it must be of a certain strength; if it is approached closer to the eye its strength must be increased; if it is removed farther from the eye a weaker lens will answer.

FAULTY CONCEPTIONS OF HYPERMETROPIA

So much has been written of late years as to the growing prevalence of myopia and its direct causation by the increased use of the eyes for reading and writing that is required by our habits of civilization, that we are almost unconsciously led to regard it as the most common error of refraction. This impression is heightened by the fact that myopia can with difficulty be concealed, and we readily recognize it by the stooping position, by the nearness with which the book is held, and by the well-known nipping of the eyelids together. But the fact is that hypermetropia is the most frequent defect, although it is not patent to others, and even the individual himself for a long time may not be aware of it until an impaired condition of health, or a severe attack of illness, or the approach of the presbyopic period of life makes it manifest by an unmistakable train of symptoms.

When these evidences of the defect become noticeable, as they are especially apt to do after a prolonged use of the eyes, it seems natural to place them in the relation of cause and effect; the one follows the other, and would seem to be directly produced by it. While this may be said of myopia, it is not true of hypermetropia; no amount of abuse or overtaxing the eyes can result in the production of hypermetropia, or can increase it when already present. Of course, any immoderate use of the eyes will aggravate the symptoms and render the eye apparently weaker, but it cannot originate the essential condition of hypermetropia, an undeveloped or flat eye-ball, which is a congenital condition.

Another error that has crept in and gained credence, is the supposition that hypermetropia is better for distant vision than emmetropia. The fact that its far point is negative and that the hypermetropic eye is adapted for a point beyond infinity, shows that its accommodation is under a constant strain, and therefore its distant vision suffers from the disadvantage of being accomplished only at this expense. Whereas the emmetropic eye by nature is adjusted for the parallel rays of distant vision, and no other form of eye can be better than this.

No well-read optometrist should fall into the error of supposing that a person must be myopic simply because he holds his book close. Attention has already been called in the earlier part of this chapter to the fact that in high degree of hypermetropia the book is sometimes approached quite near to the eyes, and the caution was given not to mistake hypermetropia for myopia, and a number of cases illustrative of this point were narrated. This matter is of such great importance as to call for a repetition at this place, while mentioning some false conceptions about hypermetropia.

SEQUELAE OF HYPERMETROPIA OR ITS DELETERIOUS CONSEQUENCES

All the defects of the optical construction of the eye, and especially those that impose an unnatural tax upon the accommodation, are not only accompanied by a certain train of symptoms, but are liable to lead to the production of other troubles. The evil effects flowing from hypermetropia may be enumerated as follows:

1. Headache and neuralgia.
2. Spasm of accommodation.
3. Blepharitis, styes, etc.
4. Glaucoma.

5. Cataract.
6. Myopia.
7. Asthenopia.
8. Convergent strabismus.
9. Retinitis and neuritis.
10. Nervous derangements.

1. HEADACHE AND NEURALGIA

These forms of paroxysmal pain are very common, and there is scarcely a family but can disclose one or more sufferers. There is usually no direct evidence of actual disease of the affected nerves or brain, or even of any of the vital organs of the body, and yet there must be some underlying cause in every case of intractable headache or neuralgia. These ailments may be classified under several different headings, but by far the most common form, and the one in which the optometrist is particularly interested, is the *reflex*.

Under this head (of reflex troubles) may be mentioned the headaches and neuralgias that result from a decayed tooth, hardened wax in the ear, disease or obstruction of the nasal cavities, some obscure rectal or pelvic irritation, and lastly, and most important from our standpoint, those that are caused by some error of refraction or some anomaly of the ocular muscles. None can deny that remarkable cures of headache and neuralgia have been accomplished solely by the removal of one of the causes mentioned above, and without the use of drugs.

Therefore, in any case of intractable headache and neuralgia, the condition of the refraction of the eye and of its muscular equilibrium should be carefully inquired into; and when the family physician has such a case under his care and does not himself possess the skill or the instruments required to make the necessary examination, he should refer his patient to a skilled optometrist in whom he has confidence, in order that this source of suffering may be removed.

Many cases of headache have been treated by the physician on the presumption of cerebral congestion or cerebral anæmia, by the remedies that are ordinarily useful in such conditions, without benefit; and, finally, after every other hope of relief had failed, the thought has occurred that perhaps the eyes were at fault, and recovery immediately followed the proper correction of any existing anomaly.

The literature on this subject of headaches and neuralgia due to eye-strain is very extensive, and within the last few years there has been a large amount of additional testimony to prove the importance of a thorough examination of the eyes in all cases of headache. It is proper to state that correction of the ocular anomaly does not always cure the pain in the head immediately; sometimes the relief comes gradually, and again a course of constitutional treatment may be necessary in addition.

2. SPASM OF ACCOMMODATION

The constant contraction of the ciliary muscle in hypermetropia that is necessary to overcome the refractive error and afford clear vision, often gives rise to the condition known as "spasm of the accommodation," which is simply a high tension and persistent contraction of the affected muscle. Such spasm is apt to occur in persons of a nervous temperament, and, strange to say, it bears no direct relation to the vigor of the accommodation; that is, persons with a strong and vigorous accommodation may never be troubled in this way, whereas patients with a relatively feeble accommodation may suffer with a marked cramp of the ciliary muscle.

The symptoms of spasm of the accommodation are photophobia (dread of light), lachrymation (excessive watering of the eyes), pain, contracted pupils and congestion of the eye. In addition to these symptoms, distant vision is impaired and there is a condition of false or simulated myopia, so marked that concave glasses have been ordered on account of the improvement they afford in distant vision; this, however, is a grievous error that should not be committed by any well-informed optometrist. The cause of spasm of the accommodation is not limited to hypermetropia.

3. BLEPHARITIS, STYES, ETC.

The constant strain under which the hypermetropic eye labors causes an increased flow of blood to the organ, which results in a congestion of some of the structures of the eye and a subsequent inflammation. In this way the edges of the lids become red and swollen, with the formation of scales and crusts, and the dropping out of the lashes, which are sometimes not reproduced. The statement has been made by competent authorities that "chronically inflamed eye-lids are almost always dependent upon hypermetropia or hypermetropic astigmatism."

This congestion may result in a localized inflammation, and there are few diseases of the lids more common or more annoying than styes, oftentimes one following another in quick succession, seeming to come without any apparent cause. The inflammation is seated in and around the bulb of an eyelash, and rapidly results in the formation of pus, which breaks naturally or is discharged by a small incision made in the apex of the tumor. The cause is usually to be found in some ocular anomaly, principally hypermetropia, and the treatment consists in the correction of the error by properly adjusted glasses.

4. GLAUCOMA

This is a disease characterized by abnormally increased intra-ocular tension, which gradually advances to blindness. The majority of the cases of this dreaded disease occur in hypermetropic eyes, and hence the value of correcting glasses becomes evident as a means of prevention. In one of the latest text-books on diseases of the eye the statement is made that "overuse of the eyes, especially with improperly corrected refractive error, has a distinct tendency, by causing ocular congestion, to bring on glaucoma in an eye predisposed to the disorders by changes in the ciliary region."

5. CATARACT

Investigations by competent authorities show that the majority of cataractous eyes are hypermetropic, and it follows that the use of the proper correcting glasses must be looked upon as an important preventive measure.

6. MYOPIA

Hypermetropia is the prevalent condition of refraction in childhood, and the strain caused by this defect in the use of the eyes during these tender years, for reading and studying for long periods of time and under unfavorable conditions, results in an elongation of the eye-ball and the development of myopia. This has been proven by abundant statistics.

7. ASTHENOPIA

This term means weak sight, and may be defined as a lack of sufficient muscular strength to maintain for any length of time the adjustment of the dioptric apparatus required for near vision. It may be divided into *muscular* and *accommodative,* the latter being the form which occurs as the result of hypermetropia, for the reason that a portion of the accommodation is diverted from its legitimate purposes of focusing the eye for near vision and used for uniting the parallel rays from distant sources, thus leaving a corresponding deficiency in the power of adjustment for close use, and requiring an unnatural tension of the muscle of accommodation for the latter purpose. The result is that the muscles become exhausted and symptoms of asthenopia make their appearance.

Asthenopia does not usually manifest itself in young persons, because their accommodation is sufficiently vigorous to overcome the hypermetropia without feeling the strain, and because they are seldom required to use their eyes for any considerable length of time in looking at small objects. But after the age of ten years, when the accommodation naturally begins to gradually fail, and when more and longer use of the eyes is required for reading, writing and studying, then the symptoms of asthenopia begin to be apparent, cause much annoyance and suffering, and even give rise to painful forebodings of future blindness.

In asthenopia there may be comfortable vision for a short time, but the necessary effort of accommodation required for close vision cannot be long maintained, and, notwithstanding an increased nervous impulse is transmitted to the eye to compensate for the unnatural tension that is called for, there are soon a feeling of fatigue within the eyes, pain in and around them, excessive irritability, and a blood-shot appearance of the conjunctiva. Vision becomes blurred and the constant straining of the accommodation to form clear images aggravates all the symptoms, renders the eye sensitive to light, particularly if it be artificial, causes a painful dazzling and a sensation of smarting and roughness as if there was sand beneath the lids; there is often a resulting conjunctivitis with swelling of the lids and sometimes a mucous discharge, which dries during sleep and causes the edges of the lids to adhere.

The patient is inclined to close his lids and rub his eyes or press them with his fingers, and, after a short period of rest, all the symptoms disappear; but they return with increased violence after another attempt to use the eyes in close vision, until, finally, the pain and irritation become so great that reading, writing, sewing and all fine work have to be abandoned, and some occupation sought that does not call for use of the eyes in sharp vision of small objects.

The treatment of asthenopia is the removal of the cause by the correction of the hypermetropia.

8. CONVERGENT STRABISMUS

In this form of strabismus the visual line of one eye is directed to the object looked at, while the visual line of the other eye is deviated inward, and in four-fifths of all cases it is caused by (or at least it is associated with) hypermetropia; and therefore it is fair to presume that this condition of squint might have been corrected by the timely use of glasses.

When convergent strabismus is due to hypermetropia, it usually makes its appearance about five or six years of age, at the time when pictures, letters of the alphabet and small objects are first noticed. Sometimes it does not show itself until after the child has been attending school for a time, when the close use of the eyes is more pronounced and more persistent. There is scarcely any ailment that may befall a child that will cause more alarm to the anxious mother than the appearance of strabismus; and a cross-eyed child in a family is something to be greatly dreaded, not only on account of the impairment of vision in the squinting eye, but also because of the unpleasant disfigurement.

The explanation of the production of convergent strabismus by hypermetropia is as follows: The presence of this error of refraction in an eye imposes upon its accommodation a constant strain to maintain distinct vision. It has been found that by convergence of the visual axes an increase in the power of accommodation will be gained, and the greater the degree of convergence the more the resulting power of accommodation. In this way the visual lines are made to cross each other at a point nearer than that of binocular fixation, and while an increase in the force of accommodation is thus gained, it is at the expense of binocular vision, which gives way to diplopia or, perhaps, to monocular vision because the image cannot be formed on the yellow spot of each eye.

The visual line of one eye fixes the object looked at, and its image is formed on the yellow spot, while the visual line of the other eye is directed to another point, the eye itself being placed in such a position with reference to the object fixed by the straight eye, that its image is formed on the retina at a distance from the yellow spot. These two images therefore being formed on parts of the retina, which are not identical, cannot be fused into one, and double vision is the result.

This diplopia, while very annoying at first, does not last very long, for the following reason: The image of the object which is desired to be seen is received in the fixing eye and formed on the most sensitive portion of its retina, and hence the impression carried to the brain is clear and distinct, whereas the corresponding image in the deviating eye is formed on a portion of the retina which is much less sensitive, and hence the impression carried to the brain is not of a perfect image.

Under such circumstances (in cases of diplopia where one image is much clearer than the other) the sharp image of the straight eye commands of the brain a more distinct recognition, which is only disturbed and confused by the feeble impression received from the squinting eye, and hence the effort is made by the percipient elements to suppress the recognition of the latter in order that monocular vision may be secured and prove satisfactory.

The hypermetropic child, when he begins to use his eyes for close vision, finds that he cannot see distinctly except by a considerable effort, of which he is conscious, and he soon finds, as if by instinct, that if he allows one eye to turn inward he receives a clearer image in the other eye, and with less apparent effort of accommodation. Hence, when he desires to see distinctly at a close range, he unconsciously fixes the object with one eye, while the visual axis of the other eye converges and crosses the first visual line at a point nearer than the object.

As soon as the gaze is removed from close objects and fixed on those more remote, the squint disappears and the eyes assume their normal parallel condition, and continue so until again called upon to adjust the vision to a near point, when the strabismus returns. The natural instinct of the child (if it may be termed such), or some guiding impulse, leads the child to prefer clear monocular vision to blurred or strained binocular vision.

At this stage the squint is periodical, manifesting itself whenever the eyes are under the strain of close vision and vanishing with every relaxation of the accommodation. With the growth of the child and his advance in school, the eyes are used more and more in close vision, and consequently the condition of the squint is present for a greater length of time, and there is less tendency for the eyes to resume their normal position, the turning inward of one eye lasting even after the accommodation is passive, until finally the strabismus becomes fixed and permanent and binocular vision is forever lost.

IMPAIRMENT OF VISION IN THE SQUINTING EYE

In some cases the squint appears first in one eye and then in the other, and under such conditions, when each eye shares alternately in the act of vision, the sharpness of sight is equally retained in both of them. But it usually happens that one eye is preferred for vision and is always used, and then the squinting eye, constantly receiving its image on a non-sensitive portion of the retina gradually loses its powers of perception and its acuteness of vision is very much impaired. There may be no organic change in the retina that can be detected by the ophthalmoscope, but from non-participation in the act of vision the nervous sensibility becomes blunted, and the eye is said to be amblyopic.

If an operation be performed early and the muscular equilibrium be restored, resulting in a return of binocular vision and the action of the two eyes in harmony, the sensibility of the retina may again be raised to normal, in which case it may become necessary, in order to hasten the improvement, to exclude the good eye and exercise the other for a few minutes each day in reading with a convex lens. In those cases where the strabismus has lasted for many years, the impairment of vision becomes permanent, and no operation or any amount of exercise of vision will avail in restoring the sight.

WHY DOES NOT STRABISMUS OCCUR IN EVERY CASE OF HYPERMETROPIA?

We have classed convergent strabismus as one of the evil effects that may result from hypermetropia, but in reading the rationale of its production the query may logically arise in the student's mind, why does not strabismus occur in every case of hypermetropia? While this question is perhaps easier asked than answered, still we have some very good reasons for its non-occurrence in every case.

In the normal eye there is a constant natural desire for single vision, which holds equally good in hypermetropia, and it becomes the duty of the ocular muscles to maintain binocular vision if at all possible. This results in a struggle between two contending impulses; in the first case binocular vision is preserved at the expense of clearness of sight; in the second case a more distinct perception is enjoyed, but with a sacrifice of single vision. In the former condition the brain, in its abhorrence of double vision, strives to obtain the clearest possible image and still retain single vision; in the latter predicament the endeavor to secure perfect vision, which can be accomplished only by the use of one eye, induces the brain to suppress the image formed on the retina (but not on the yellow spot) of the squinting eye.

In this contest between these struggling influences, the abhorrence of double images and the desire for single vision are in many cases the most powerful, resulting in the maintenance of binocular vision and the prevention of squint.

In addition to this, the theory has been advanced that some hypermetropes may pass through childhood without discovering that they are able to secure clear and distinct images by an over-convergence; but this proposition we are not altogether prepared to accept, because this is a natural instinct, and on account of the close relation existing between accommodation and convergence the youthful hypermetrope will as naturally learn to increase his power of accommodation by an excessive convergence, as he will to use his legs in walking.

In absolute hypermetropia, where the entire refractive and accommodative power of the eye, even when assisted by the strongest effort of convergence, is insufficient to form a clear image on the retina, there is no motive for excessive convergence because there is nothing to be gained by it, and hence, in such cases, strabismus is not likely to occur.

PREVENTION OF STRABISMUS BY CONVEX LENSES.

Inasmuch as convergent strabismus is one of the results of hypermetropia, on account of the strain imposed upon the accommodation, it naturally follows that the correction of the defect and the removal of the strain would be an important measure of preventive treatment, in the shape of properly adjusted convex lenses. When a suggestion of this kind is made to the mother she is horrified at the thought of her child wearing glasses; and if perchance her scruples are overcome and her consent given, there is constant difficulty in coaxing and persuading a child of five or six years of age to wear them.

The child is too young to appreciate the useful purpose for which they are given, nor is he inclined to accept them as playthings given for his amusement; and hence they do not appeal to him in any language that he can understand. Consequently there is a constant strife between parent and child in the endeavor to control the inclination of the latter to remove the glasses and to prevent their being broken. After this struggle continues for a while the parents become annoyed and disgusted, and their duty in this respect becomes so irksome that they neglect it, until finally the child has his own way, the glasses are laid aside and lost, and the periodic squint becomes permanent.

OCCURRENCE OF PERMANENT STRABISMUS

Even after the squint has become permanent, the duty of the parent does not cease, because by compelling the use of the eyes in alternation, the sight of both may be kept up to the normal standard. The usual tendency is for the child to use one and the same eye constantly for all purposes of vision, and then of course the sight of the other eye soon deteriorates. In order to obviate such a condition the good eye should be covered with a handkerchief or a light bandage for an hour or two each day, thus compelling a use of the squinting eye and maintaining its visual powers unimpaired.

The advantages to be gained from such a practice are obvious; in fact, the patient retains two good eyes instead of one, and in such a case, if the sight of one is impaired or lost by injury or disease, the other at once becomes available for immediate and satisfactory use. Also if an operation be performed for the cure of the strabismus and the restoration of the natural position and movements of the eyes, there would be much more hope for a return of binocular vision if both eyes were of the same acuteness of vision.

PREVENTION BETTER THAN CURE

However, the prevention of the periodic squint from becoming permanent is of much more importance to the child than is an operation for its cure, for it is very doubtful if a strabismus operation, even though apparently successful, ever restores the ideal singleness of vision with two eyes—a perfect binocular vision. In many cases this is most likely due to the fact that the two eyes vary in their acuteness of vision, and this fact only serves to emphasize the advice given above, that the attempt should always be made to keep both eyes up to the normal standard by alternating their use.

The occurrence of convergent strabismus in a child just commencing to go to school almost certainly indicates the existence of hypermetropia, and should at once lead to a careful and skillful examination of the refraction, in order that the defect may be quickly discovered and the remedy applied before the squint becomes fixed; because strabismus is never due, as is popularly supposed, to fright, imitation or naughtiness.

The statement has been made by some authorities that "the greater the degree of hypermetropia the greater, obviously, is its tendency to produce strabismus"; and while on first thought this seems like a reasonable assumption, yet it is a proposition from which we are compelled to dissent. In the higher degrees of hypermetropia, where the accommodation, with all the added assistance of convergence, is still not strong enough to overcome the refractive error, convergent strabismus can be of no advantage and does not occur. But it is in the moderate degrees of the defect (from 2 D. to 4 D.) that the accommodation is made equal to the task of neutralizing the defect by the assistance of the convergence, and here the strabismus is most commonly found.

The theory has been advanced by some authors that the amblyopia that is usually found in a squinting eye is not the result of the strabismus, but is the cause of it. They argue that the defective sensibility of the retina is congenital and thus leads to the production of strabismus; but they are able to present no convincing evidence in support of this theory, and the opinion of the writer is that the amblyopia is the direct result of the strabismus as explained in the foregoing.

9. RETINITIS AND NEURITIS

Inflammations of the retina and of the optic nerve are oftentimes symptoms of grave constitutional diseases, as syphilis and Bright's disease, and yet there is abundant evidence to prove that these conditions may develop in patients who are entirely free from such maladies, and as the result of overuse of the eyes or the strain caused by hypermetropia; and an examination of a large number of cases of retinitis and neuritis has shown the existence of hypermetropia (perhaps in a latent form) in a great majority of the cases.

Of course, it is quite possible that there may exist in these cases some underlying constitutional cause, some predisposition to these inflammatory conditions, and when the eyes are thus rendered susceptible, it requires but a little strain or a trifling irritation to start up the disease.

10. NERVOUS DERANGEMENTS

The strain imposed upon the eyes by an uncorrected hypermetropia has a decided effect upon the nervous system by a leakage of nerve force, and may lead to a train of evils far more extended that we are accustomed to suppose. When the various organs of the body perform their functions harmoniously, each receives its normal supply of nerve force, and there is no cause for irritation. But hypermetropia, by overtaxing the ciliary muscle and destroying the normal relation that should exist between accommodation and convergence, calls for an excessive supply of nervous energy and acts as an irritant to the central nervous system, with the final result of a breakdown and prostration of this important system, which not only causes misery and suffering, but statistics are not wanting to prove that the duration of life is materially shortened thereby.

Chorea. The clinical experience of hospital physicians has demonstrated most positively that there is a direct relationship between hypermetropia and chorea or St. Vitus's dance; the percentage of this defect in choreic cases being placed as high as seventy per cent. Therefore it follows that such cases are rapidly cured by eye treatment alone, the correcting glasses stopping a leakage of nervous force that may have been going on for years.

Epilepsy is one of the most terrible diseases that can befall any human being, and its treatment by drugs alone is very unsatisfactory. Of late years specialists on nervous diseases have found that errors of refraction, and especially hypermetropia, bear a direct causal relation to the attacks, and that properly adjusted glasses are an indispensable adjunct to the treatment, if they do not even supersede all other methods of treatment.

Nervous Prostration and Insanity are very closely related, the former leading to the latter, and it does not require any stretch of the imagination to see how an uncorrected hypermetropia, by causing a leakage and excessive expenditure of nerve force, may develop a nervous debility that leads to mental disturbance and ends in insanity.

TESTS FOR HYPERMETROPIA

The outfit required by optometrists for use in refraction tests has been described in the chapter devoted to that subject, and a repetition of the paraphernalia seems scarcely necessary at this place; but their use and the methods of making the practical tests will receive a detailed description.

The various tests for the detection and determination of hypermetropia may be enumerated as follows:

1. Trial Case.
2. Skiascopy.
3. Ophthalmoscopy.
4. Chromatic Test.
5. Scheiner's Test.
6. Amplitude of Accommodation.

THE TRIAL CASE

The most reliable test for hypermetropia, and the most satisfactory on which to rely for the determination of the proper glasses, is by means of the test lenses from the trial case. The improvement of distant vision by convex lenses, or in cases of normal acuteness of vision where such a lens is accepted for distance, is regarded as proof positive of the existence of hypermetropia. From this fact it does not follow that the acceptance of a concave lens disproves it, as frequently a spasm of accommodation is an accompaniment of hypermetropia, and in such a case a concave lens improves distant vision and makes the case apparently myopic, when in fact it is hypermetropic.

ACUTENESS OF VISION

The first step in the examination is the determination of the acuteness of vision, which is ascertained by means of the test card hanging twenty feet away. This may equal the normal standard of 20/20, or it may fall below it. The degree of acuteness of vision present does not throw much light on the existence or absence of hypermetropia.

If the visual acuteness is 20/20, the only certain deduction that can be drawn is that the case is not one of myopia, but it does not afford any information as to the presence of hypermetropia, because a normal vision may mean either emmetropia or hypermetropia.

On the other hand, if the vision is 20/30, or 20/40, or 20/70, the only undisputed inference that can be drawn is that the case is not one of emmetropia, but there is no knowledge afforded as to the existence of hypermetropia, because a lower visual acuteness may mean either hypermetropia, myopia or astigmatism.

CONVEX LENSES THE TEST

How then is the presence of hypermetropia to be determined? By the acceptance or rejection of convex lenses for distant vision. A weak convex lens (usually + .50 D.) is placed before the eye, the effect of which at once becomes apparent, one way or the other.

If the acuteness of vision is 20/20, and this convex lens blurs it, it is fair to presume that the eye is emmetropic; but if the convex lens is accepted, that is, if the vision remains just as good with the lens as without it, and if the No. 20 line can be just as clearly read, the case is proven to be one of hypermetropia. But the test does not end here, as the refraction has only been shown to be hypermetropic, the degree of which may be much greater than that represented by the + .50 D. lens. A + .75 D. lens is next placed in the trial frame, with which the No. 20 line is still clearly seen. But still the optometrist must not be satisfied, and he proceeds to use the next stronger and another stronger, continuing as long as the patient's vision remains 20/20, and the letters on this line are distinctly visible.

Finally a lens is reached that causes the patient to shake his head and say the letters are not quite as plain as they were before. He may be able to name them, because he has probably learned them by heart by this time, but he is conscious of the fact that their sharpness of outline is less marked, and some of the letters he is doubtful of. What has been determined now? The amount of the manifest hypermetropia has been measured, by placing stronger and stronger convex lenses in front of the eye until the vision was made worse. In other words, the refraction of the eye was increased more and more by the addition of the convex lenses, until at last the focus of rays of light was formed in the vitreous humor in front of the retina, which simulated a condition of myopia, and distant vision was correspondingly impaired.

In that class of cases where the vision falls below 20/20 the test is commenced with convex lenses, which are not only accepted, but cause a marked improvement in vision. A + .50 D. lens is tried first, and at once the patient notices that the letters are clearer and blacker, and perhaps he is enabled to read a few letters on the next line below. Then a + .75 lens is tried, and a + 1 D., with a noticeable improvement each time, and still stronger lenses until the acuteness of vision is raised to 20/20. But even when this point is reached the test does not stop, but is continued by the addition of still stronger lenses until the No. 20 line begins to be dimmed. Perhaps a + .50 D. or a + .75 D. lens stronger will be accepted than that which raises vision to normal; but as the amount of defect is not measured by the lens that first makes the No. 20 line readable, but by the strongest lens with which this line remains so, the test is not ended until this latter lens is reached.

NEVER TRY CONCAVE LENSES IN HYPERMETROPIA

The optometrist should be cautioned always in cases of suspected hypermetropia to commence the test with convex lenses, and if they improve vision, or at least if they do not make it worse, the refraction is proven to be hypermetropic. Whereas if weak concave lenses are tried first, they will most likely be accepted on account of the spasm of accommodation which is generally present; and when once accepted they serve to stimulate the accommodation to still further contraction, and then if convex lenses are tried afterward, they will be promptly rejected; for the detection of hypermetropia by means of convex lenses depends upon a relaxation of the accommodation to the extent of the strength of the convex lenses used. In either case (with or without convex spherical lenses) the rays of light are brought to a focus at the same place, and vision remains the same.

In the first case this was accomplished by the refractive power supplied by the crystalline lens of the eye, and in the second case by the convex lens in front of the eye. But when concave lenses are used first they excite the accommodation and cause convex lenses to be rejected, and in this way the diagnosis of the case becomes doubtful, and the optometrist may be led into serious error.

CAUTION IN CHANGING THE LENSES

As the optometrist changes the test-lenses in front of the eye for stronger ones, he should not make too much of a jump or increase their strength too rapidly, else the ciliary muscle contract spasmodically and he fail to discover the hypermetropia. But he should increase only .25 D. at a time, leaving each lens in front of the eye for a short space of time, thus giving the ciliary muscle an opportunity to relax and encouraging it to do so, and by thus changing the lenses slowly and increasing their strength gradually, the test lenses will be used to the greatest possible advantage in developing and detecting hypermetropia.

THE METHOD BY OVER-CORRECTION, OR THE FOGGING SYSTEM

After ascertaining the acuteness of vision, a strong convex lens is at once placed before the eye, about + 6 D. in ordinary cases, or even stronger if there is reason to suspect a marked degree of hypermetropia. This blurs the letters on the distance test card, and the patient involuntarily exclaims that he is unable to see with it. The optometrist encourages him to look quietly at the card for a moment or two without straining his eye, and after the eye recovers from the shock of suddenly placing such a strong lens before it, the vision may slightly improve.

The action of the convex lens is to induce a relaxation of the accommodation, as only in this way can the vision be made even slightly better. The natural tendency for the ciliary muscle is to contract, but a contraction of this muscle when a convex lens is before the eye instantly makes vision very much worse. The eye is not slow to appreciate this fact, and then, as the natural instinct of the eye is for clear vision, the effort is made in the other direction; that is, in a relaxation of this muscle, which at once tends to slightly clear the vision, and thus a further relaxation is encouraged.

Now a weak concave lens (— .50 D.) is placed over this convex one, and by diminishing its strength improves vision quite noticeably and encourages a still further lessening of accommodation. After this lens remains a brief moment, it is replaced by a — 1 D. lens, which affords another improvement in vision and enables the patient to see more of the letters. Then — 1.50 D. is tried, followed by — 2 D., — 2.50 D. and — 3 D., with amelioration of vision each time until the normal standard is reached, and then the difference between the convex and the concave lens will be the measure of the hypermetropia.

AN ILLUSTRATION OF FOGGING

A patient presents himself with all the symptoms of hypermetropia as they have been described in this chapter. On examination his acuteness of vision is found to be 20/20. Each eye is tested separately with convex lenses, but only + .50 D. is accepted and a stronger lens blurs the vision. Then the eyes are tried together, and it is found in binocular vision that they will bear + 1 D., but nothing stronger.

If the optometrist desires to make his examination thorough, he will not stop here, but will make use of the fogging method. He places a + 6 D. lens in the trial frame, with which the patient is unable to read even the largest letter on the card at first, although after a moment he may be able to discern the form of the No. 200 letter. A — .50 D. lens is then placed in the front groove of the trial frame, which renders this letter clear and easily discerned. Then it is replaced by a — 1 D. lens, which brings out the No. 100 line. Next, a — 1.50 D. lens is tried with the effect of making clear the No. 70 line of letters; a — 2 D. clears up the No. 50 line, a — 2.50 D. the No. 40, and a — 3 D. brings into view the No. 30 line, and, finally, a — 3.50 D. brings the vision up to 20/20 clearly and distinctly.

Now what has been done and what has been accomplished? The + 6 D. lens first placed before the eye has been partially neutralized by the — 3.50 D. lens and reduced to + 2.50 D., with which vision is 20/20. In other words, the eye has been led to accept a + 2.50 D. lens, with which the acuteness of vision is unimpaired, and hence this is the measure of the defect.

TEST FOR HYPERMETROPIA BY SKIASCOPY

The essentials for the test by skiascopy are a darkened room, a bright light (either electric, gas or oil will answer), and a retinoscope, to which may be added the trial case.

The distance of the optometrist from the patient is a matter of considerable interest, for which, however, there is no fixed rule, each observer within certain limits selecting his own distance. The beginner may try the method at different distances, and then decide for himself at what distance he obtains the best results. When the plane mirror is used this is a comparatively simple matter, but with a concave mirror any great variation in the distance requires a corresponding variation in the focus of the mirror; the nearer the optometrist approaches his patient the shorter should be the focus of the mirror, and the greater the distance the longer the focus.

The preference of the writer is for a plane mirror and a distance of one meter, the advantages of this distance being that it is close enough to get a good view of the reflex and shadow, that a lens can be placed before the patient's eye and changed at will without requiring the optometrist to leave his seat, and that a uniform allowance of 1 D. is thus called for in the estimate.

The light should be steady, clear and white, and as bright as possible; the Welsbach light, the incandescent electric light or an Argand burner of either gas or oil will answer the purpose; and in order to obtain the brightest part of the flame, it is customary to use an asbestos chimney or screen with an aperture opposite the most brilliant part of the flame.

The room should be darkened by removing all sources of light except the one in use. It is not essential that the ceiling and walls of the room should be black, but the covering of all windows by black shades, that fit closely, will suffice.

The position of the light is varied by different authorities. Formerly, the advice was given to place the light in such a position above the head, and slightly behind, that the patient's eyes will be in the shadow, and that no light can fall on the trial lenses that may be placed in the frame. Or the light may be close to the observer, and thence reflected on the patient's eyes, the optometrist's eye, the light and the patient's eye all being on the same plane. The closer the light is to the mirror, the brighter will be the reflected rays.

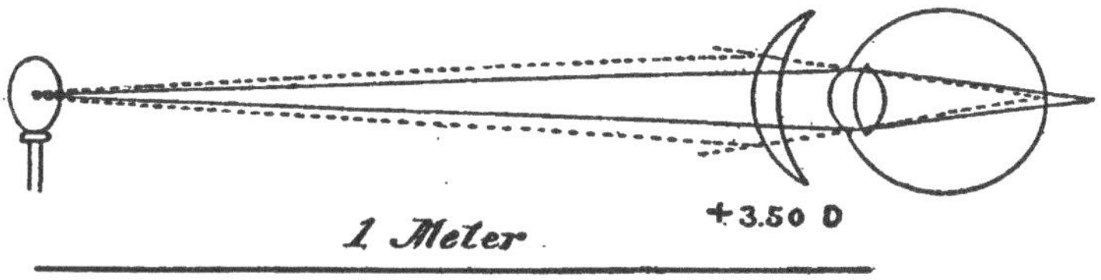

This drawing shows the mirror at a distance of one meter from the eye under examination, and the dark lines represent the reflected rays from the mirror, which illuminate the retina, and as in all hypermetropic eyes, focus behind the retina. The dotted lines indicate the diverging rays proceeding from the retina, and the convex lens of 3.50 D., which is placed in front of the eye, and which possesses just sufficient refractive power to bend these dotted diverging rays and bring them to a focus at the position of the mirror one meter away.

METHOD OF CONDUCTING THE TEST

The patient and optometrist being seated at the proper distance, the latter takes his retinoscopic mirror, holds it in front of his own eye, looks through the sight hole, and reflects the light on the patient's pupil, which at once appears more or less brilliantly illuminated, according to the condition of the refraction of the eye, and the portion of the fundus which is being observed.

If the optic disk is in the direct line of view, the examination is more easily conducted; but as the refraction at the disk may possibly vary 1 D. or even 2 D. from that at the macula, the latter is really the proper part of the fundus to be corrected, to obtain which the patient must look at the sight-hole of the mirror during the whole examination.

The reflection from the eye of a blonde is much brighter than from a brunette, on account of the greater amount of pigment in the eye-ground of the latter. The reflection is much brighter in cases of low refractive error than in high degrees of defect, where it is dull.

The *shadow* is the dark portion of the retina that immediately surrounds the illumination; they adjoin each other, and the contrast between them is most marked and more easily recognized when the illumination is the brightest. It is this combination of light and shadow that gives the "shadow test" its name. In a darkened room the retina is in darkness, except that portion which is illuminated by the light from the mirror. As the mirror is rotated, the retinal illumination moves and shadow takes its place. It is this change of place of the illumination followed by the shadow that causes it to be spoken of as the movement of the shadow.

As the mirror is slowly and slightly rotated first one way and then the other, around an imaginary vertical axis, the light reflection moves with it across the face from right to left, and from left to right. Just here the beginner should know that the illumination of the patient's face *always* moves in the same direction as the mirror is rotated, but in the pupillary area it *may* move in the same or in the opposite direction, as it is affected by the condition of the refraction. Hence when the movement of the illumination is spoken of it is that which is seen in the pupil and not on the face.

When the movement of the retinal illumination is *the same* as the movement of the light on the patient's face, the case is presumably one of emmetropia or hypermetropia, in the determination of which convex glasses must be used and placed before the eye. The trial frame is used on the patient's face with a + 1 D. lens over the eye under examination, and the light is again reflected on the pupil, and the direction of the movement is again observed. If this lens causes the light to travel in a direction the reverse of that on the face, the refraction is proven to be emmetropic. Whereas if the shadow still moves in the same direction as the light, the eye is hypermetropic, and the lens must be changed successively for stronger ones until finally a glass is reached which reverses the movement.

HOW TO MAKE THE NECESSARY CALCULATIONS

When this glass is found it is compared with the previous lens, and the refraction of the eye is between the two. In other words, the number of the lens is found between the weakest glass which reverses the movement of the reflection and the strongest glass which does not reverse it. If when a + 3.25 D. lens is placed in the trial frame, the illumination is diminished in size and very faint, appears to move rapidly and *with* the light on the face, the hypermetropia is still slightly uncorrected, and a stronger lens must be found. If a + 3.75 lens is substituted for it, and the retinal illumination is then found to move *opposite* to the movement of the light on the face, the measure of the defect will be between the + 3.25 D. and the + 3.75 D., which is + 3.50 D.

This lens has converged the emergent rays issuing from the patient's eye and brought them to a focus in the examiner's eye, which is at a distance of one meter; and in so doing and fixing the far point at one meter, it has practically made the eye myopic to that extent, just one diopter. Therefore when the patient's vision is tested with the letters at twenty feet, this 1 D. of artificial myopia partly neutralizes the 3.50 D. of hypermetropia, and the result of adding — 1 D. to + 3.50 D. gives 2.50 D. as the amount of the hypermetropia.

This + 2.50 D. lens, when placed before a hypermetropic eye, suffices to render parallel the divergent rays proceeding from it, and conversely would so refract parallel rays of light entering the eye, as to exactly focus them upon the retina. But the additional + 1 D. is necessary to refract the emergent rays still more in order to bring them to a focus at one meter.

The reader who follows these explanations carefully will readily understand why the correcting glass should be 1 D. less than that shown by the retinoscope, and the writer desires to draw especial attention to this point, as it is one that is more or less confused in the mind of the beginner in retinoscopy.

TEST FOR HYPERMETROPIA BY THE OPHTHALMOSCOPE

The room should be darkened and the same light can be used that was found available in the shadow test. It should be placed (by an adjustable bracket) on the same level as the eye that is to be examined, and on the same side of the head. Patient and optometrist sit facing each other and side by side. The pupil is then illuminated by reflecting the light from the concave mirror, and the red reflex is obtained. If there are any opacities in any of the refracting media, they at once become apparent by marring the clearness of the reflex.

Presuming there are none, the optometrist at once passes on to the *direct method* of the use of the ophthalmoscope, which is the one preferred for estimating the refraction. This gives an upright, enlarged picture, but only a very small portion of the fundus is visible at one time. The optometrist uses his right eye to examine the patient's right, and approaches as close as possible, all the while keeping the pupil well illuminated. The beginner finds some difficulty in keeping the light on the pupil as he approaches, and as soon as it loses its bright red reflex he may know he is at fault with the position of his mirror.

In an emmetropic eye, parallel rays are brought to a focus exactly on the retina without any effort of accommodation. Conversely, the rays proceeding from the retina of such an eye are bent by its refracting media in such a way as to issue from the eye parallel.

THE OPTICAL PRINCIPLES INVOLVED IN THE OPHTHALMOSCOPIC TEST

In hypermetropia the focus of parallel rays is behind the retina, and only convergent rays can be focused on the retina. As no such rays are present in nature, the hypermetropic eye is adapted for a condition that does not naturally exist. The rays proceeding from the retina of such an eye are bent by its refracting media, but as their power is less than normal, the rays emerge from the eye divergent, just as if they came from a point behind the eye. These diverging rays can be rendered parallel only by the interposition of a convex lens of the proper strength.

If the eye is viewed through the ophthalmoscope at a distance of twelve or fourteen inches, the condition of the refraction may be determined by the appearance and behavior of the blood-vessels as they are seen at the fundus of the eye, that is, the direction in which they will travel upon the moving of the head of the observer.

In hypermetropia a more or less clear view of the fundus can be obtained at this distance with the mirror alone. The image is enlarged, erect and virtual, and as the optometrist moves his head from side to side, the disk and blood-vessels will seem to move in the *same* direction.

In emmetropia the optometrist must approach much closer to the observed eye in order to get a distinct view of the disk and vessels, and then as he moves his head their behavior will be the same as in hypermetropia.

The power of accommodation in the eyes of both patient and optometrist is supposed to be at rest. In order to favor the relaxation of the accommodation in the patient's eye, the room is darkened and he is requested to turn his eyes in a distant direction, without, however, endeavoring to fix any one particular object in distinct vision. For the optometrist it is sometimes a difficult matter to place the accommodation at rest, because, in looking at the fundus of the patient's eye, he is inclined to adjust his accommodation as for a near object, whereas he should endeavor to relax his eye and place it in the condition for viewing distant objects. If the fundus be viewed as at a near point, the amount of accommodation brought into play will render the optometrist's eye practically myopic, and this is the reason why so many beginners can get a clearer view of the eye-ground by rotating a weak concave lens in the sight-hole of the ophthalmoscope. Therefore, it should be borne in mind that the improvement caused by a concave lens must not be considered as proof positive of the existence of myopia.

RELAXATION OF THE ACCOMMODATION

The power to completely relax his ciliary muscle is a faculty that should be cultivated by the ophthalmoscopist; and as it is so essential in the determination of hypermetropia, the following procedures will be found of benefit in assisting to that end.

The optometrist looks upward and at the same time holds above his eyes a white card on which there is a black spot. He then endeavors to relax his accommodation, and as soon as he succeeds the spot will appear double; then the card is to be lowered, the eyes following it, and as long as the spot continues to appear double he will know that his accommodation is at rest.

Another exercise which is adapted for the same purpose is to hold a pen or pencil about ten inches in front of the face, and if the ciliary muscle can be relaxed and the vision adjusted for distance, the pencil will appear double, and will continue so as long as the ciliary muscle can be kept quiescent.

Still another method of practicing the same thing is to hold a book as close to the eyes as possible; then the observer is to commence to read, and while thus engaged he endeavors to look through the book or beyond it, when the letters will run together and become obscured, because when the accommodation relaxes the letters are no longer focused upon the retina; at the same time the optometrist will probably feel that the act of convergence lessens and the eyes gradually turn outward until their visual axes assume a parallel position.

By a frequent repetition of one or all of the above exercises, the beginner can learn to approximate an object close to his eyes, and at the same time keep his accommodation and convergence in abeyance. Having thus secured control of his accommodation, the optometrist will be in a position to estimate by the use of the ophthalmoscope the amount of hypermetropia in any particular case.

WHAT TO LOOK FOR

The optometrist should familiarize himself with the appearance of the normal fundus; first by a careful study of the colored plate given in a previous chapter, and then by actual use of the ophthalmoscope with healthy eyes. The optic disk, that is, the entrance of the optic nerve, is the object to be looked for, it being circular in shape and much lighter than the retina, which presents a bright, rose-red, granular appearance. In brunettes there is more pigment matter in the retina, which brings out in strong contrast the difference in color of the disk and the retina.

The optometrist now endeavors to get a clear view of the details of the fundus, and if he and his patient are both emmetropic this is a comparatively simple matter. If the observer is not emmetropic he must wear his correcting glasses. If he looks into a hypermetropic eye (of moderate degree) he will again see the features of the eye-ground clearly and distinctly, but by the involuntary use of his accommodation. A distinct picture being thus obtained in both emmetropia and hypermetropia, how can it be determined which condition is present? By the revolving of a convex lens into the sight-hole of the ophthalmoscope, and if the picture still continues as clear (or is made more distinct) the case is known to be one of hypermetropia. And the strongest convex lens with which the optometrist can get a clear view of the optic disk and the blood-vessels will be the measure of the defect, presuming that both persons have been able to relax their ciliary muscles.

In order to insure an exact measurement of the patient's refraction by means of the ophthalmoscope, the advice is given by some authorities to use the region of the yellow spot for the examination. But unless the eye is under the influence of a mydriatic, this is a difficult matter, because the pupil sharply contracts as soon as the yellow spot turns toward the mirror; and besides there is no marked feature here, such as a blood-vessel, which can be used for accurate focusing.

For all practical purposes the optic disk will be entirely satisfactory for this examination, and preferably the side of the disk toward the temple, because its margin here is generally well defined. The small blood-vessels as they pass over the edge of the disk are to be observed; this makes a delicate test, as the variation of but a fraction of a diopter is sufficient to throw them in or out of focus.

The optic disk is seen if the patient turns his eye slightly inward toward the nose, while the yellow spot comes into view when he looks directly at the hole in the mirror, while the course of the main retinal vessels can be traced by the optometrist moving his head, and directing the patient to turn his eye in an appropriate direction as the course of each vessel is being followed.

CHROMATIC TEST FOR HYPERMETROPIA

This test has been fully described and illustrated with colored plates in the chapter on "Method of Examination." It is a ready and convenient test for detecting hypermetropia, in which defect the retina, being farther front than normal, approaches the focus of the blue rays, causing the flame to appear with a blue center and a red border. The convex lens that neutralizes the flame and fuses it into a single color will be the measure of the defect.

SCHEINER'S TEST

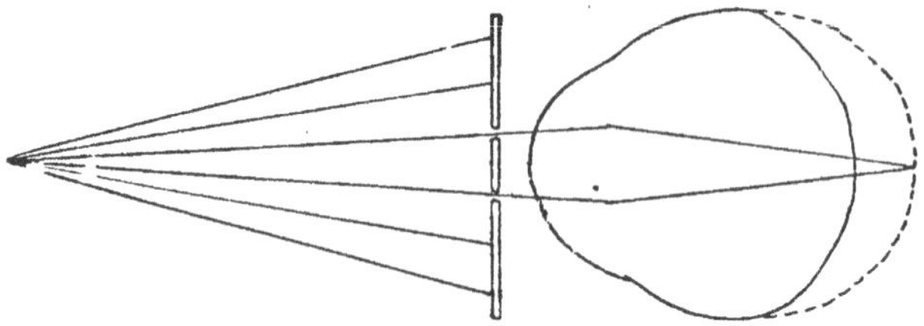

In this illustration the rays are shown which emanate from the candle flame and pass through the perforations in the card, and, being bent by the refracting media of the eye, are focused on the retina of the emmetropic eye. which is shown by the dotted lines. The hypermetropic eye being flatter, its retina is farther forward, as shown by the black line, and the rays striking it before their union produce there two images of the flame, and therefore to such a person the flame is seen double.

This test for hypermetropia is one that is not in common use, and yet it illustrates so beautifully certain optical principles that it is desirable the optometrist should be familiar with it. A card with two small holes, so close together that rays passing through them will enter the pupil, is placed in front of the eye to be examined. The patient looks through these holes at a candle flame twenty feet away, and if the eye is hypermetropic two flames are seen, instead of one as in emmetropia.

The explanation of this phenomenon is as follows: The rays of light proceeding from the candle flame travel in all directions and fall upon the card, a few of them passing through the perforations; and if the eye is adapted to the flame; that is, if it be emmetropic, these two sets of rays will exactly meet on the retina, and form there a single image of the flame.

If, however, the eye be hypermetropic and the defect be not corrected by the accommodation, the two sets of rays will strike the retina before they have had the opportunity to meet, and each set will form an image of the flame. The greater the degree of the hypermetropia, the farther apart the two images will be. Convex lenses are then taken from the trial case and placed between the card and the eye, and that convex lens which causes the flame to be seen singly will be the measure of the defect.

DETECTION OF HYPERMETROPIA BY MEASURING THE AMPLITUDE OF ACCOMMODATION

The amplitude of accommodation is the power exerted by the eye to change its adjustment from a far point to the near point, and is measured by the closest point at which the patient is able to read the fine print. The lens whose refractive power corresponds to this focal distance will represent the amplitude of accommodation.

For instance, if twenty inches is found to be the distance of the near point, the amplitude of accommodation would be 2 D. If the near point is thirteen inches the accommodation is equal to a lens of 3 D.; and if the near point is ten inches the accommodation is 4 D.

In emmetropia the amount of amplitude of accommodation is a constant one for the different ages all through life, as shown by the following table:

Years	Amplitude of Accommodation	Years	Amplitude of Accommodation
10	14 D.	40	4.50 D.
15	12 D.	45	3.50 D.
20	10 D.	50	2.50 D.
25	9 D.	55	1.50 D.
30	7 D.	60	.50 D.
35	6 D.		

This is the standard by which every case must be gauged, and any departure from which, at any certain age, can be readily detected.

A hypermetropic eye requires some of its accommodation for distant vision, and hence for close use there is a deficiency of that amount; therefore the amplitude of accommodation present in a hypermetropic eye at a given age would be less than is indicated in the table for the same age; and the amount by which it is less would indicate the degree of defect.

For instance, if on examination a patient thirty years of age has a near point of eight inches, representing an amplitude of accommodation of 5 D., it is at once evident there is a deficiency of 2 D., and a presumption of the existence of a hypermetropia of that amount.

With the same amplitude of accommodation it is evident that the near point is farther away in hypermetropia than in emmetropia, as is shown in the above instance, where the near point is at eight inches instead of five and a half inches, the normal distance. In this way the existence of a latent hypermetropia can often be determined, that could not, perhaps, be detected by the usual test with trial lenses.

THE TESTS FOR HYPERMETROPIA COMPARED

In considering the value of the tests that have been described for the determination of hypermetropia, the examiner soon discovers that the two objective tests (ophthalmoscopy and retinoscopy) are somewhat difficult to learn. Of course he knows that the theories involved and phenomena observed are simple and easily understood, but it requires much time and practice to become an expert in the use of these methods. Therefore they may be considered subordinate to the test by the trial lenses, which is really the decisive one. And then, finally, even this test yields to that which is given by the patient himself when he commences to wear the glasses which have been ordered.

REMARKABLE ACUTENESS OF VISION IN HYPERMETROPIA

In a description of this defect of hypermetropia it should be noted that hypermetropic eyes sometimes enjoy an unusual degree of acuteness of sight, and, in fact, when young, they are very apt to boast of their power of vision. They cannot only read all the No. 20 line without an error when seated at twenty feet, but will also call off the letters on the next line quite as readily. The parents of such a boy will tell how the child can see things with an ease and distinctness which they themselves do not possess. They may laugh at the suggestion of any defect in the eyes of their child, and ridicule the thought of glasses as long as the child can get along without them.

PREJUDICE AGAINST GLASSES

There is no use denying the universal prejudice that has existed in the public mind, but which, fortunately, is not so pronounced now as formerly, that glasses are an injury when they can be avoided for fear the patient may become so dependent upon them as never to be able to remove them. This is certainly not good grounds for an argument, but the proper light in which the matter should be viewed is that if Nature is dependent upon a glass which affords relief and removes strain, such means of assistance should not be withheld.

If the pain in hip disease is arrested by a properly-adapted support, should the splint be denied the patient because he feels his dependence upon it? Is there any more reason why a patient with defective eyes should go through life without the relief that glasses only can afford, simply because of unfounded prejudice against their use?

A case is related of a physician who refused to allow an oculist to examine his children's eyes, with the statement that no child of his should ever wear glasses with his consent. The children suffered from weekly attacks of sick headaches, and finally one was fitted with a + 3.25 D. lens, another with the same sphere combined with 5° prisms, and the third was also highly hypermetropic and astigmatic. Immediate relief was afforded in each one of these cases by the correction of an optical defect which had rendered their early life one of suffering. This is not an uncommon experience with oculists and optometrists.

SICK HEADACHES

There is every reason to believe that there are thousands of sufferers from sick headache who are struggling through life with an uncorrected hypermetropia, who have made unsuccessful efforts for relief at the hands of doctors and drugs, and who have in despair abandoned all hope of cure. This is an interesting study for the ambitious optometrist, and forms a wide and promising field for the exercise of his skill and judgment.

The statement is made by eminent authorities that the gastric symptoms which accompany typical attacks of sick headache are not due to "biliousness," or "disordered liver," or "dyspeptic conditions," or "the use of tobacco to excess," or "living too high," but they are reflex in character, and, in the majority of cases, due to hypermetropia. These attacks often occur without any explainable cause, and they are sometimes even cured by eating, drinking or smoking, while at other times they are aggravated by similar indulgences. Every known remedy in the pharmacopœia has been tried, at first with success, acting almost as specifics, and later proving entirely valueless, until finally life is rendered really unendurable.

The brain and central nervous system preside over all the functions of life. If now this ruling spirit is disturbed by the irritation caused by a constant strain to use the eyes in the face of an uncorrected hypermetropia, may not this disturbance manifest itself by an interference with the normal functions, as shown by nausea, vomiting, dizziness and other evidences of impaired animal life? This reasoning is plausible, and although they are the views of an extremist, they contain much of truth, and suggest a train of thought and experiment that can be successfully carried out by every intelligent optometrist.

RECAPITULATORY REMARKS

Before concluding this chapter on hypermetropia, at the risk of possible repetition it seems desirable to mention again a few of the important points that should be borne in mind in adjusting glasses for the correction of this defect.

In obtaining the history of the case the optometrist should ascertain whether or not the patient has been wearing glasses, and if so, what kind, what number, and how long. Even though they are entirely unsuitable, they may serve as a guide in making the test and prevent the prescription of similiar glasses, which the optometrist might be led to give if he was not thus warned.

In testing the vision at twenty feet, every letter in the No. 20 line may seem black and the outlines of the letters clearly defined, and the presumption would be that the patient was emmetropic, *but he might be hypermetropic*; the determination of which depends on the acceptance or rejection of a convex lens. A weak lens is used (generally + .50 D.), and if the patient rejects this it is reasonable to infer there is no hypermetropia present (barring those cases of latent defect, which do not enter into our consideration now).

If, on the other hand, this convex lens is accepted, it is fair to assume the case is one of hypermetropia. Then a stronger one is tried, and still a stronger, the patient all the while looking at the No. 20 line, until he says the letters are slightly dimmed or less distinctly seen. This lens is then to be compared with the previous one and with several weaker and stronger, until finally the one chosen is the strongest that affords the best vision. If the degree of defect is found to be considerable, the lenses may be increased .50 D. at a time, but ordinarily the better plan is to change only .25 D., and thus allow the accommodation to gradually adapt itself to the convex lenses.

It is customary to fit one eye at a time, but this monocular vision is never as satisfactory with either eye as is binocular vision, and, in fact, if there is not much difference in the acuteness of vision of the two eyes they may be tried together, when a stronger lens will usually be accepted. When the refractive power of the eyes varies so much as to produce discomfort, then they must be measured separately and the best eye accurately fitted, and an approximate correction given to the other eye, not allowing a great enough difference between the lenses to cause discomfort. In these latter cases the eyes will gradually accustom themselves to the glasses, so that in time a much greater difference will be borne than at first seemed possible.

When presbyopia begins to steal over the hypermetropic eye, as it does earlier in life than normal, and the accommodation becomes unequal for reading and fine work, two pairs of glasses are required, the new and stronger glasses for close use, while the old and weaker glasses which the patient has been wearing for his hypermetropia, and to which his eyes have become accustomed, remain good for distance. A person with a hypermetropia of 2 D. and wearing glasses of that strength to correct it, would, in the ordinary course of events, at the age of forty-five years, have a presbyopia of about 1 D.; such a person would therefore need + 3 D. for reading, and continue to wear his + 2 D. for distance.

ARTIFICIAL HYPERMETROPIA, OR APHAKIA

Aphakia is the term used to represent that condition of the eye in which the crystalline lens is absent from its position in the center of the pupil. This may result from luxation of the lens and its removal from the plane of vision, or if the capsule of the lens be punctured or ruptured its substance may be dissolved in the aqueous humor and removed by absorption.

By far the most frequent cause, however, for the absence of the lens is its extraction from the eye by one of the various operations for cataract. Inasmuch as the crystalline lens is the principal refracting medium of the eye, its removal leaves the eye intensely hypermetropic and destitute of all accommodative power; it is in a state of absolute hypermetropia. It has been conclusively proven that in the absence of the crystalline lens there remains not the slightest trace of accommodation. This fact establishes the correctness of the universally adopted theory (if, indeed, it needs any corroboration) that the power of adjusting the dioptric apparatus of the eye for close vision depends entirely upon changes in the convexity of the crystalline lens.

In chapter VI. of this work on "The Physiology of Vision" will be found an illustration of candle-flame images in the eye, three in number, the first being erect and reflected from the cornea, the second, also upright, is formed on the anterior convex surface of the crystalline lens, and the third is inverted and reflected from the posterior concave surface of the lens. When the flame is moved up and down, the two erect images move with it and the inverted one in an opposite direction. In aphakia there remains only the single image on the cornea, the two reflected from the surface of the lens being absent.

The eye being left in a condition of absolute hypermetropia, it becomes necessary to measure its degree, which can be readily accomplished by means of the test by trial lenses. Strong convex lenses will be required to take the place of the absent lens, the strength of which will, of course, be influenced by the previous condition of the refraction of the eye; if formerly hypermetropic, stronger glasses will be called for, and if myopic, weaker convexes will suffice.

If the degree of myopia was as high as 10 D. or more, its aphakial condition might readily be one of emmetropia.

When the crystalline lens is removed from an emmetropic eye, the glass that is needed to take its place and bring parallel rays to a focus on the retina is usually about +10 D., sometimes a little stronger. On account of the absence of all accommodation, stronger glasses will, of course, be required to focus on the retina the divergent rays proceeding from near objects. In order to determine the proper glass for reading, we add to the first glass one whose focus represents the distance at which the patient wishes to read. For instance, if 10 D. was found to be the proper lens for distance, and ten inches was decided on as the desired point for reading; then the latter, which equals 4 D., is added to the former, and the result is a lens of + 14 D. for reading.

An artificial accommodation may be produced by a change in the distance of the spectacles from the eyes, thus adapting them for intermediate points, on the principle that as the spectacles are moved farther away down the nose, their refractive power is increased and the reading point is brought nearer, while as they are pushed up close to the eyes their power is lessened and the reading point is moved away.

APHAKIAL VISION

In addition to the hypermetropic refraction caused by the removal of the crystalline lens, a certain degree of astigmatism is also the result of the operation, most likely due to failure of the wound to heal properly. This astigmatism is generally "against the rule," and is apt to be more noticeable during the first month or two after the operation, or until the cicatrization has become complete, and then it gradually diminishes for several months. It usually does not amount to more than 3 D., but even a slight astigmatism should be sought out and corrected.

Even after the most successful operations for cataract vision very rarely equals 20/20, for the reason that there is not perfect transparency in the line of vision, on account of slight opacities on the posterior capsule of the lens, which can often be detected by the ophthalmoscope. The amount of vision varies very considerably; an acuteness of 20/200 (that is, one-tenth of the normal standard) is considered sufficient to class the case among the successful operations, while a vision which will enable the patient to find his way around is not to be despised.

In adjusting glasses for patients after a cataract operation, it is customary to wait until all redness has disappeared from the eyes, which may be a month or two, and even then they should not be worn constantly at first. In the meantime smoked glasses of various degrees of tint are worn as protectives. The "cataract" glasses should be set in strong spectacle frames, because their great convexity makes them thick and heavy.

TWO PAIRS OF GLASSES

When two pairs of glasses are required, for both distance and reading, either on account of the high degree of hypermetropia or on account of the approach of presbyopia, there are several ways of arranging the glasses to meet the requirements of the person's occupation.

In one case two separate and distinct pairs of glasses may be given, one pair for distance, and the other pair for reading, and the patient changes from one pair to the other, as occasion requires. This is the best way to place the glasses for the welfare of the eyes and is to be recommended to patients, although it involves so much more trouble and the possibility of not having the second pair of glasses when needed, that many persons object to it and prefer to arrange their glasses in some other way.

In such cases the person may wear his distance glasses constantly, put them on in the morning when he arises and take them off at night when he retires, and then when he wants to read or write or look at small objects close at hand, he

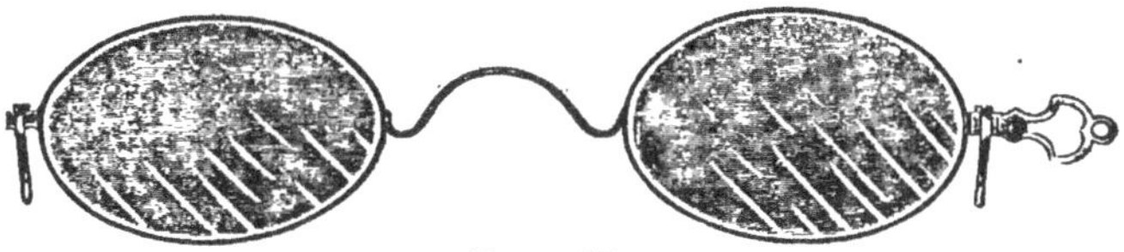

Extra Front

places an additional pair of glasses over his distance glasses, the sum of the two pairs being equal in strength to the lens required for reading. This extra pair of glasses may be either in the form of eye-glasses, or a spectacle front that should correspond in dimensions with the frame that is worn for distance, and in place of the usual temples is provided with small hooks at each end that are readily fastened to the constant spectacles, with but little danger of dropping or displacement. This is a very convenient arrangement, as many hypermetropes can testify.

BI-FOCAL GLASSES

In other cases bi-focal glasses are preferred, the upper and larger portion being for distance, the lower and smaller portion for reading. The split bi-focals, in which the distance and reading portions were of the same size, are no longer used, they having given way largely to the cemented form, the reading strength being obtained by cementing a small convex shell on the lower portion of the distance glass.

The *advantages* of bi-focal glasses to those persons who need assistance for both distance and reading, are the convenience and satisfaction of having both pairs of lenses constantly before the eyes, and only a slight turn of the head and eyes required to bring either pair into use as desired. Many persons wear this form of bi-focals with the greatest comfort, and declare they could not get along without them.

The *disadvantages* of double-focus glasses are the annoyance caused by the line of separation between the two glasses and the difficulty in walking. This latter trouble is due to the fact that the patient must look through the reading glasses, and as these are adapted for vision at twelve to fifteen inches, the floor or pavement which is so much farther away is seen indistinctly, and hence there is danger of stumbling and especially in going up and down stairs. This difficulty can be overcome by tilting the head downward so as to look through the upper lenses, and the eyes in time learn to adapt themselves to the new form of glasses, but in spite of this, many persons find themselves positively unable to wear bi-focal glasses. The ability to wear them with satisfaction is a matter that can be determined only by actual trial.

In fitting reading glasses for the correction of hypermetropic presbyopia it would be well for the optometrist to keep in mind or refer to the table given in the chapter on presbyopia, showing the approximate reading glasses required by emmetropic eyes, in order to use it as a check against giving too strong a glass, or as a verification of the glasses about to be prescribed.

For instance, if a patient fifty-five years of age, with a hypermetropia of 2 D. (as has been ascertained by measuring the refraction with the usual tests for this defect) chooses a + 5 D. for reading, a reference to the table will show that he is not out of the way, as the strength of this glass for reading is just equal to the sum of his hypermetropia and the average presbyopia at his age: Hypermetropia 2 D. and presbyopia 3 D., equals 5 D.

THE VALUE OF WEAK CONVEX GLASSES

Many optometrists never give glasses weaker than .50 D., thinking that if the defect is any less than this it is too slight to require correction. But the writer, in his practice, has met with a large number of cases in which great benefit has been derived from .25 D. lenses, spherical and cylindrical convex. and even sometimes concave, and he often finds occasion to order these weak numbers, to the great relief of the patient.

and hence we would advise the optometrist not to disregard these apparently valueless glasses.

Mrs. M. E. F. Aged thirty-nine years. About three years before one of our leading oculists ordered + .50 D. glasses for reading, but she has never been able to use them because they made her eyes ache. Vision = 12/10. All convex lenses rejected, which we regard as evidence that the eyes are emmetropic. Reads small print 9 inches to 22 inches.

According to the rule given in the chapter on presbyopia for determining the reading glasses, we subtract 4.50 D. (as shown by the near point of 9 in.) from 5 D. (representing the normal near point of 8 in.), which leaves + .50 D. as the proper lens; but as she had tried these with so much discomfort, + .25 D. were ordered for reading, which gave her the greatest comfort and relief.

HYPERMETROPIA VS. PRESBYOPIA

It is to be hoped that no reader of these pages will ever in any way, confound hypermetropia and presbyopia. Of course, the symptoms are similar and both require convex lenses for their correction, but in every other respect they are essentially diverse; one is an error of refraction, the other an error of accommodation. Hypermetropia is due to a change in the shape of the eye-ball, which impairs the refraction of the eye; while in presbyopia the ball is perfect in shape and the refraction normal, the accommodation alone being impaired. The diagnosis and treatment of hypermetropia and presbyopia have been fully described in this and the preceding chapters.

A CASE OF HYPERMETROPIA, SHOWING THE USELESSNESS OF A MYDRIATIC

Adam B. Aged twenty-two years. Student. Complains that after reading a minute or two the letters run together. After looking up and resting eyes, he is able to read again for a short time. Has a great deal of pain in eyes, but during vacation in summer they do not trouble him at all. But as soon as he returns to his studies in September, eyes again commence to annoy him. At the present time is unable to read more than a minute or two at a time, and eyes are constantly aching. V = 15/15. Accepts + 3 D., with which vision equals 15/12, showing a manifest hypermetropia of that amount.

Under homatropine V = 15/200, which was raised to normal by + 3.50 D. lenses, evidencing a total hypermetropia of that amount, the difference between the manifest and total leaving but .50 D. of latent defect.

As this patient was young and had never worn glasses, it seemed advisable not to give too strong a glass to commence with, and hence a pair of + 2 D. were prescribed for constant wear. In a week he returned with the report that his eyes were free from ache or pain, and that he could read comfortably for two hours, which is in marked contrast with the moment or two's reading which was his limit before.

It is interesting to note that although a mydriatic was employed, it was of no real value in determining the glasses required; and the writer is free to say that he could have corrected the defect just as well without the use of the drug. And what is true in this case applies equally to other cases, in the great majority of which satisfactory glasses can be prescribed without the thought of a mydriatic.

CHAPTER XII

MYOPIA

Myopia is an optical defect, the condition of its refraction being such that the focus of parallel rays lies in front of the retina. It is the direct antithesis of hypermetropia, from which it differs in every respect.

In myopia parallel rays of light are converged to a focus in the vitreous humor before they have reached the retina. After meeting in focus the rays cross and continue until they strike the retina in circles of diffusion; consequently, the image formed is blurred and indistinct.

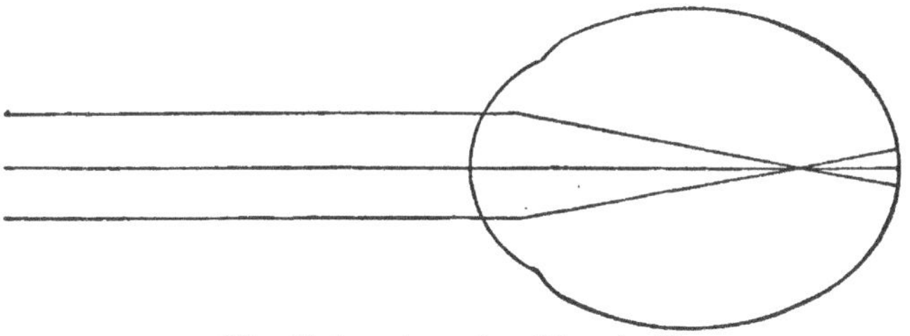

The Refraction of a Myopic Eye

In hypermetropia (as was demonstrated in the last chapter) the rays of light strike the retina before they have had an opportunity to unite in a focal point. In myopia, on the other hand, the rays have met in focus and over-crossed before they reached the retina. In both cases the retina receives only circles of diffusion, and in neither case is the formation of a distinct image possible, this latter being found only at the principal focus of the eye, where the rays at this point of union produce a sharp and well-defined image.

FORMS OF MYOPIA

1. Refractive Myopia.
2. Axial Myopia.

In the first case there is an excess in the static refraction of the eye, due to an increase in the curvature of one or more of the dioptric surfaces, or to an augmentation of the index of refraction of the nucleus of the lens, thus causing the rays to meet in focus too soon in front of the retina, which may be at its proper position.

In the second case, the eye-ball is too long antero-posteriorly in the direction of its visual axis, oftentimes on account of pathological changes in the coats of the eye. This removes the retina from the principal focus of the eye, and is the form in which myopia usually occurs.

This elongation of the ball of the eye depends, in the great majority of cases, upon the formation of a *posterior staphyloma,* which means a protrusion backward. The coats of the eye first become softened and thus are rendered liable to give way under pressure; this bulging occurring at the outer side of the optic disk, toward the yellow spot, and causing a thinning of the tissues and oftentimes an atrophy of the choroid. This elongation of the visual axis is so constant that every certain degree of myopia corresponds to a definite increase in the length of the eye-ball.

AMOUNT OF LENGTHENING OF VISUAL LINE IN AXIAL MYOPIA

The following table (after Donders) shows the increase in length and the total measurement that corresponds to the degree of myopia:

Amount of Myopia	Increase in Length	Length of Axis
.50 D.	.16 mm.	22.98 mm.
1 D.	.32 mm.	23.14 mm.
1.50 D.	.49 mm.	23.31 mm.
2 D.	.66 mm.	23.48 mm.
2.50 D.	.83 mm.	23.65 mm.
3 D.	1.01 mm.	23.83 mm.
3.50 D.	1.19 mm.	24.01 mm.
4 D.	1.37 mm.	24.19 mm.
4.50 D.	1.55 mm.	24.37 mm.
5 D.	1.74 mm.	24.56 mm.
5.50 D.	1.93 mm.	24.75 mm.
6 D.	2.13 mm.	24.95 mm.
6.50 D.	2.32 mm.	25.14 mm.
7 D.	2.52 mm.	25.34 mm.
7.50 D.	2.73 mm.	25.55 mm.
8 D.	2.93 mm.	25.75 mm.
8.50 D.	3.14 mm.	25.96 mm.
9 D.	3.35 mm.	26.17 mm.
9.50 D.	3.58 mm.	26.40 mm.
10 D.	3.80 mm.	26.62 mm.
10.50 D.	4.03 mm.	26.85 mm.
11 D.	4.26 mm.	27.08 mm.

Amount of Myopia	Increase in Length	Length of Axis
12 D.	4.73 mm.	27.55 mm.
13 D.	5.23 mm.	28.05 mm.
14 D.	5.74 mm.	28.56 mm.
15 D.	6.28 mm.	29.10 mm.
16 D.	6.83 mm.	29.65 mm.
17 D.	7.41 mm.	30.23 mm.
18 D.	8.03 mm.	30.85 mm.
19 D.	8.65 mm.	31.47 mm.
20 D	9.31 mm.	32.13 mm.

The antero-posterior diameter of the normal eye is 22.82 mm., which is about 91/100 of an inch. In the higher grades of myopia an increase of 1 D. represents a much greater addition in length of the ball than in the lower grades. For instance, a myopia of 1 D. causes an increase of 32/100 of a millimeter, as compared with 66/100 the enlargement in an eye of 20 D. myopia over one of 19 D., the increase in the higher degree being more than twice as great as in the commencement of the defect. The average increase for every dioptric of defect is about 47/100 of a millimeter, which equals nearly 1/50 of an inch.

In an organ so small as the eye, which measures less than an inch in diameter, the addition of even 1/50 of an inch cannot be disregarded. And when we consider the eye as an optical instrument, comparable to a photographer's camera or a microscope, and when we call to mind how the slightest movement of the screw will throw both of these instruments out of focus, it can be readily understood that the addition of 1/50 of an inch to the length of the eye-ball is sufficient to disturb the dioptric adjustment of the eye and to impair the clearness of the image formed upon its retina.

In a myopia of 5 D. the amount of lengthening is 1¾ millimeters, or 1/41 of an inch; in a myopia of 10 D. the amount is 3 4/5 millimeters, or nearly 1/6 of an inch; in 15 D. of myopia, 6¼ millimeters, or ¼ of an inch; while in an extreme case of myopia of 20 D., 9 3/10 millimeters is added to the length of the ball, which means the addition of more than 1/3 of an inch, making such an eye measure 1 7/25 inches as compared with 23/25 of an inch, which is the normal standard.

A careful study of this table is interesting and important,

and serves to impress upon the optometrist the actual organic changes in the coats and shape of the eye-ball, upon which the production of myopia depends.

CAUSES OF MYOPIA

The one great cause of myopia is long-continued use of the eyes for small objects close at hand; and, therefore, myopia may be considered as a product of civilization—as a penalty of progressiveness. The use of the eye for close vision calls for an effort of accommodation, and when long continued, may cause a spasm of the ciliary muscle. The adjustment of the dioptric apparatus of the eye for the divergent rays of near vision, transforms it temporarily into a condition similar to myopia; and if the accommodation continues its spasm and fails to relax, a condition of *accommodative myopia* is produced. In this case the eye-ball is not elongated and there is no real myopia, but all the symptoms are present and the defect is simulated by the spasm of accommodation.

The permanent production of real myopia depends upon the congestion, inflammation and giving way of the coats of the eye-ball. The ciliary muscle is connected with the choroid, and, therefore, in the exercise of the function of accommodation there is a strain upon the latter, and when the eye is overtaxed, as is frequently the case with school children and those compelled to use their eyes continuously for near work, an inflammation of the choroid is apt to follow.

In addition to this, the close position at which the object is held necessitates a marked convergence of the optic axis, which causes a strain of the muscles and a pressure upon the tunics of the ball. Then, too, the stooping position that is generally indulged in during such employment also tends to increase the congestion and inflammation by favoring an accumulation of blood in the eye. In this way a continuation of the congestion and pressure gradually leads to a bulging at the posterior pole of the eye.

THE EFFECT OF SCHOOL LIFE UPON THE SIGHT

There is no doubt that the origin of many distressing diseases can be traced to the school life of the sufferer. The pathological conditions are not in all cases the direct result of unsuitable school existence, but it may be that the improperly constructed school buildings and badly managed school life simply fan into a flame the spark of heredity which many unfortunate children receive from diseased parents.

The deleterious influence of education and intellectual advancement upon the bodily health is everywhere apparent. The mind is cultivated at the expense of the body, and it almost seems as if mental advancement goes hand in hand with physical retrogression. Certain it is, that uneducated and untutored races present types of bodily development superior to those nations that are renowned for civilization and knowledge.

The eye furnishes a striking example of the truth of these statements. The vision of those persons who are engaged in farming and kindred occupations is but seldom impaired, while in savage and barbarous races the statement is made that myopia and astigmatism are positively unknown. We are compelled to regard school life as disastrously prolific of refractive errors, by far the most frequent of which is myopia.

SCHOOL STATISTICS

As early as the beginning of the last century the fact was recognized that the oftentimes unnatural requirements of school life resulted in injury to the eyes of many of the children, and several writers in those early days called attention to these important matters and to the relation that seemed to exist between the demands of civilized life and the production of myopia.

The statistics that have been compiled bearing on this subject are enormous. The examination of the eyes of more than ten thousand school children in Breslau and vicinity by Cohn, and the published results of his extensive investigations, in 1865 and 1866, called public attention to school hygiene and gave a great impetus to the discussion of this important subject. Similar examinations have been repeated from time to time by other observers in different cities, until at the present time the children who have been subjected to a study of ocular conditions by competent examiners for statistical purposes.

compose an army of more than two hundred thousand. These investigations have occurred in all civilized countries, and have been made under all circumstances of age, sex, race, health, heredity and school architecture and management. Many of these investigations have been so arranged as to follow a certain number of pupils from class to class and from school to school, and they all point to one inevitable conclusion, viz., that mental culture is obtained at the sacrifice of ocular perfection, and that such imperfections are usually myopic in their nature.

Certain facts have been established by the investigations, which may be briefly mentioned as follows:

1. The eye at birth is hypermetropic, and during early childhood the hypermetropic eyes greatly outnumbered the emmetropic and myopic ones. An examination by one observer of children three months old showed them to be all hypermetropic.

2. Emmetropia was comparatively rare, but the percentage of those eyes which most nearly approached this condition remained almost uniform throughout school life.

3. Myopia was entirely absent, or very rare before the commencement of school life, and was found to increase steadily in percentage with the progress of the pupils in the schools, while the percentage of hypermetropia diminished in approximately the same degree. Not only does the number of myopic scholars increase from the lowest to the highest schools, but the increase is in direct proportion to the length of time devoted to the strain of school life.

We cannot burden this chapter with the statistics compiled by the various European and American observers, but as Prof. Cohn's work was the most extensive and most notable, and stands as the representative of all the others, we give his figures as follows:

Primary schools..............	1.4	per cent.	of myopia.
Elementary schools...........	6.7	"	"
Intermediate schools..........	10.3	"	"
High schools..................	19.7	"	"
Gymnasia......................	26.2	"	"
Universities..................	59.5	"	"

The fact that in the universities fifty-nine students out of every hundred are myopic is an appalling one, and when contrasted with the small percentage in the primary schools (only one out of every hundred), there is certainly abundant food for the most serious thought, which appeals, however, more to those engaged in the education of children than to us as optometrists.

GENESIS OF MYOPIA

The manner in which abnormal circumstances act in causing an elongation of the axis of the eye, which is the physical condition present in myopia, has been well described by Fenner in the following graphic words:

"As a nation or community becomes wealthy, refined and elevated in social position, the inhabitants are more inclined to cultivate the intellectual faculties; hence they spend much time in close study, requiring a great and prolonged tension of accommodation in reading, writing, etc. They usually sit bending over a desk in stooping position, the abdominal organs are compressed, preventing the free return of the blood from the head.

"The insufficient illumination at many schools and colleges necessitates the bringing of the eyes very near the book, so as to obtain a larger visual angle, and as the book usually rests on a desk or table, the head has to be bent over; this posture produces an increased flow of blood to the eyes, whilst the higher degree of convergence necessary causes an increased pressure of the lateral recti muscles on the equator of the globe, thus increasing the intraocular pressure.

"The congestion of the fundus oculi causes softening of the scleral tissue, which gives way under the increased pressure, and the organ is elongated backward (a condition of posterior staphyloma); the other portions of the sclerotic coat are supported by the broad muscles. The retina is then pushed backward behind the focus of the dioptric apparatus.

"When this condition once commences, all the causes which first gave rise to it, act with increased force. There is a greater stooping posture necessary, because the eyes have to be brought still nearer the object; an increased convergence is demanded, and the congestion of the fundus oculi increases; consequently, the softening processes progressively augment, causing the posterior portion of the sclerotic to yield more and more. Hence myopia is usually progressive, particularly in its higher grades.

"There is greater tendency to the development of this condition of the eye in youth from the causes above mentioned, because then the scleral tissues are softer and consequently more yielding than in later life. With the increase of age this coat hardens, becomes firmer and better able to withstand intraocular pressure; hence it is rare that the posterior staphyloma giving rise to near-sightedness commences after the twentieth year."

WHY CHILDREN ARE MORE PRONE TO MYOPIA

From the foregoing statements that the development of myopia depends upon a daily and continuous use of the eyes upon small objects close at hand, accompanied by strong convergence and with the patient in a stooping posture, it might naturally be expected to find this error of refraction of frequent occurrence among tailors, seamstresses, embroidery and lace makers, and all artisans whose trades require accurate near-vision.

But the fact is myopia is much more rare among these people than in the wealthier and more intellectual classes. This apparent paradox can be explained as follows: These working people do not engage in their occupations until they are of adult size, when the tissues of the sclerotic and the other coats of the eye have become sufficiently firm to resist the disturbing influences which their work engenders. While in the case of the higher classes, the eyes are exposed to the dangers of myopia at the tender age at which these children are usually placed at school.

In addition to the difference in the ages of these two sets of people, there is probably another factor that is brought into action, and that is the well-known fact that when the mind is actively engaged in study, an increased quantity of blood flows through the brain causing a temporary congestion, which is shared by the eye on account of its proximity, thus adding to the previous plethora of the fundus of this organ.

ANATOMICAL CHANGES IN THE FUNDUS OF THE MYOPIC EYE

In view of what has been said, that myopia means staphyloma and that the degree of myopia corresponds to the amount of extension of the fundus, it follows that myopia and posterior staphyloma are almost synonymous terms, and it is evident that the *myopic eye is essentially a diseased eye,* more so than any other error of refraction. The invention of the ophthalmoscope places in our hands the means of observing the changes taking place in the fundus of the eye upon which the production of myopia depends, and of noting the progress of the morbid processes.

The extension of the globe of the eye is at the expense of the sclerotic coat, which grows thinner and thinner, until in high degrees of myopia it becomes transparent, and sometimes when the eye is turned inward, the dark pigment of the choroid becomes visible through it. As the property of the dense and firm sclerotic coat is to give the eye its form and to support its interior structure, it naturally follows if this protecting coat be stretched at any part, the contents of the eye-ball lying adjacent to this will suffer a corresponding change in position.

Thus it happens that the choroid coat also becomes extended and atrophied, particularly on the outside of the optic disk, as well as in the region of the yellow spot.

THE MYOPIC CRESCENT

The choroid attains its greatest thinness around the outer edge of the optic disk, where it forms a white, shining concentric disk, resembling a meniscus in shape. The dark pigment cells are obliterated, the small capillary blood-vessels no longer carry the red blood, and there remains the marble-white, crescent-shaped patch of atrophy. If the distention extends entirely around the disk, the atrophic portion becomes annular in shape.

The ophthalmoscope admits of careful observation of these changes. Some remains of pigment are often seen about the convex border of the crescent. Although the atrophy usually assumes the crescentic form, yet it may vary, sometimes forming a complete ring around the disk as already stated, or extending outward in an irregular patch. This increase in atrophic surface around the optic nerve enlarges the size of the normal blind spot.

The presence of the crescent just described depends largely upon the degree of myopia; in slight cases in young persons it may be entirely absent, but in cases of 6 D. and over in adult persons it is almost invariably present.

The position of the yellow spot may also be changed; it approaches the posterior pole of the eye-ball until the visual line almost corresponds with the optic axis. In very high degrees of the defect, it may even pass to the inside of the axis of the ball.

HEREDITY

Myopia is regarded as a hereditary disease, and there is a universal popular impression that the defect is handed down from parent to child. When a myopic patient is questioned, he can usually name some other member of his family as being similarly affected, perhaps a parent or grandparent, an uncle or aunt, a brother or sister.

But there are many difficulties that stand in the way of a thorough investigation of hereditary influence, and perhaps all that can be claimed is that a *predisposition to myopia* is often transmitted to posterity, and not the disease itself. So that it may be regarded as an established fact that myopia rarely develops in an emmetropic eye, and never in a hypermetropic eye, without a predisposition to it derived from ancestors.

PREVENTIVE MEASURES

Whatever an ounce of prevention may be to other members of the body, it certainly is worth many pounds of cure to the eye. This delicate organ will stand a great deal of use, and not a little abuse, but when once thrown off its balance, it very rarely can be brought back to its original perfection of action, and it becomes liable ever after to a return of disability of function.

On this account and from the fact that modern civilization has imposed upon the eye an ever-increasing amount of strain, one might suppose that the greatest precaution would be observed to maintain the organ in a condition of health. And yet it is safe to say that there is no organ in the body, the welfare of which is so persistently neglected, as the eye.

It is not uncommon, and certainly not improper, to have the first teeth of children four and five years of age filled instead of extracted; while the eye, the most intellectual, the most apprehensive, and the most discriminating of all our organs, receives scarcely a passing thought, much less an examination.

HOW THE CHILD SUFFERS

It seems never to occur to parents that the principal agent in acquiring an education is the eye. The child is placed in school without the slightest inquiry on the part of either parent or teacher as to whether it has the normal amount of sight, whether it be near-sighted or far-sighted, whether vision is clear or blurred, whether it sees with one eye or two eyes, or whether the act of vision is accomplished at the expense of an unnatural strain upon the nervous system.

It has been truthfully said, and cannot be repeated too often, that "a near-sighted eye is a sick eye," and it not infrequently happens that a near-sighted child is a sick child, the reason for which is as follows: A myopic boy is unable to successfully compete with his schoolmates in their usual games, for the reason that most of them lie beyond the range of his vision. Subjected to ridicule on the part of his companions for clumsiness and inaptitude, due to a defect of which neither he nor they are aware, he relinquishes in disgust one by one of the health-giving sports in which he can never hope to excel, and takes to books until reading becomes a passion.

Not only the abstraction from fresh air and exercise, but the very conditions under which the eyes are used, are detrimental to the general health. The book is brought nearer the eye, the head is bent upon the chest or over the table, till the shoulders become curved and the chest contracted, and normal respiration is interfered with.

Such a child cannot see clearly the features of his companions, his parents or his teachers, nor catch the ever-varying expression of the eye, or the subtle change in the muscles of the face, by which an idea is emphasized or a principle enforced. His sense of the beautiful in nature is hampered and curtailed. Earth, sea and sky make up for him a world different from that of his companions, and it is no wonder that his views of men and things are different also.

He judges of men and their intentions rather by the sound of the voice than the expression of the face, and is apt for that reason to be suspicious of strangers. In unfamiliar neighborhoods and with insufficient light, he is timid and cautious. With all this studiousness and devotion to books, the statement is made that near-sighted people, as a whole, are not any more intellectual than those who have normal eyes, because studiousness and intellectuality are not always convertible terms, as most people think they are.

Of course these remarks do not apply to those cases of myopia which have been corrected at the commencement of school life with the proper concave lenses, but to those other cases of the defect which exist among young and growing children and which, being neglected, gradually become worse as adult age is reached.

ORIGIN OF THE TERM MYOPIA

In hypermetropia, as was demonstrated in the last chapter, the patient is able, by the use of the accommodation, to overcome the defect and maintain clear vision. But in myopia, on the contrary, the exercise of the accommodation would only make the eye more near-sighted; nor does the eye possess any other power of its own to correct this error of refraction, except that such a patient falls into the habit of half-closing the lids, or nipping them together. In this way the more circumferential rays are cut off and the central rays only are allowed to enter the eye, the lids thus forming a stenopaic apparatus to the improvement of the clearness of the image formed on the retina. This gives rise to the word myopia, which is derived from two Greek words, meaning to "contract or close the eye."

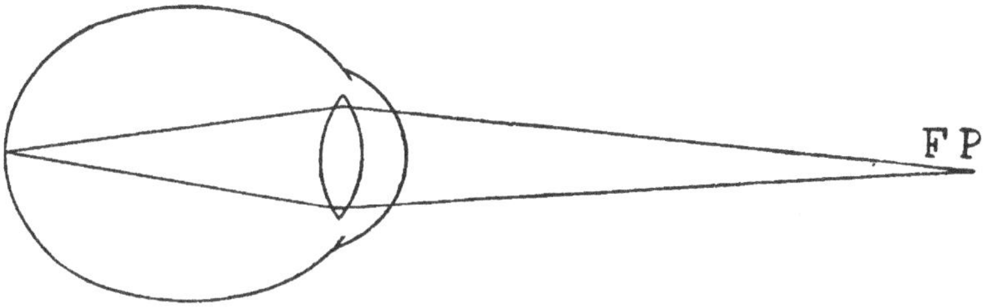

Diagram of a Myopic Eye, showing that the divergent rays which proceed from F. P. (the far point) are exactly focused upon the retina

HOW DIVERGENT RAYS ARE FOCUSED IN MYOPIA

When parallel rays pass through a convex lens, they are brought to a focus at a certain point on the other side of the lens, which is known as the principal focus of the lens. If divergent rays are made to pass through the same lens, the focus would be farther away; while in the case of convergent rays the focus would be nearer than the principal focus.

The statement has been made in this chapter that in myopia the rays meet in front of the retina, but it should be remembered that this refers only to parallel rays, or to convergent rays which focus still farther in front. The focus of divergent rays is farther back than parallel, thus approaching the retina, and if of the proper degree of divergence will meet on this membrane.

Now in nature there are no convergent rays of light; such rays exist only when made so artificially. Hence we are interested at the present time only in parallel and divergent rays, the two forms in which we find light to exist, the former proceeding from distant objects and meeting in front of the retina of the myopic eye; the latter issuing from objects near at hand and focusing on the retina as shown by the diagram.

There is in front of the myopic eye a certain space within which vision is clear and beyond which it becomes indistinct, the dividing line of which is marked by the far point, which varies with the degree of defect. The higher the grade of myopia the closer the far point, the lower the degree the more distant the far point. It follows from this that if any object can be brought close enough to be within the far point of any myopic eye, it will be clearly seen. While if it is moved farther away so as to get beyond the far point, the rays begin to lose their divergence and focus in front of the retina and vision is no longer distinct. Thus it is seen that the myope is shut up in a little world of his own, the limits of which are determined by the distance of the far point.

In the correction of myopia, the concave lens that is prescribed causes the rays that pass through it to enter the eye divergently, thus throwing the focus back upon the retina, and restoring distant vision to normal clearness.

PREVALENCE OF MYOPIA AND ITS COMPARATIVE FREQUENCY IN DIFFERENT CLASSES OF SOCIETY

Myopia is more common in the cities, and in those nations and among those classes of people, whose advanced civilization, and whose occupations require extended use of the eyes for close objects. It is not equally prevalent in all civilized countries, nor in all parts of the same country.

It is much less frequently found among persons brought up in rural districts, or among those who devote themselves to occupations requiring but little use of sharp vision for small objects. On the contrary it is among this class that hypermetropia prevails to a much greater extent.

VISION OF MYOPES

It is not unusual to find in the slighter degrees of myopia, where the error of refraction is less than 2 D., that the patient himself is not conscious of its existence, until perhaps it is accidentally discovered when comparing distant vision with some emmetropic friend; or by trying on the concave glasses of some myopic friend, when it is found that everything is more clearly seen and objects are visible at greater distances.

With such a myopia the patient will be able to read fine print without convex glasses until he is probably fifty or fifty-five years of age. Thus the late appearance of presbyopia will tend to compensate for the diminished range of vision for distant objects. It is for these reasons that Donders gives his preference to the slightly myopic eye, because he argued that the slight indistinctness with which distant objects are seen in early life, is more than counterbalanced by the ability to read and write at a later period of life without the use of convex glasses.

In higher degrees of myopia if there is a fair amplitude of accommodation present, the patient naturally falls into the habit of bringing small objects close to the eyes, oftentimes much nearer than there is any necessity for, and as it is inconvenient to bring his book or work close to his eyes, he bends the body so as to assume a stooping position, the more so the higher the degree of defect.

The half-closed lids and the wrinkling of the skin of the forehead, gives the features a peculiar expression, by which the myope can often be recognized; and this habit, like many others when once formed, is hard to abandon and is often kept up even after the myopia has been entirely corrected by concave glasses, and the necessity for using the lids as a stenopaic apparatus no longer exists.

As has already been stated, objects situated beyond the far point are seen in diffusion circles; while within this point vision is just as good as in an emmetropic eye, or perhaps even a little better. Inasmuch as small objects in order to be sharply defined, must necessarily be held much closer in this defect than normal, the visual angle under which they are seen is proportionally larger; consequently the image formed on the retina is of greater size, thus impressing more of the percipient elements of the layer of rods and cones.

In addition to this the pupil is more dilated in myopia, thus allowing additional light to enter the eye and enabling the patient to see with less illumination. But while near vision is possible with a feeble light, distant vision on the contrary is improved by a brilliant illumination, because the strong light contracts the pupil and thus diminishes the size of the diffusion circles. For this reason the myope can see very much better by looking through the pin-hole disk from the trial case.

When the degree of myopia is greater than 6 D., there is generally more or less disturbance of near vision in addition to the impairment of distant vision, and this is not to be wondered at when the morbid changes that have taken place at the fundus of the eye are considered. Excessive use of the eyes in near vision produces a feeling of strain and they become painful, following which there appears redness of the conjunctiva and an increased flow of tears.

MUSCAE VOLITANTES

In all forms of ametropia, but especially in myopia, complaints are often made of dark spots or floating bodies, which make their appearance in the field of vision and dance before the eyes, and which have received the name of *muscae volitantes.* The constant appearance of these floating specks is a source of considerable annoyance and alarm to myopes, not only from the way in which they engage the attention, but also from the fears which they excite.

They are variously described by different persons, and are most noticeable when the eyes are turned toward a white surface, such as a whitewashed wall or ceiling, or a white cloud. They follow the movements of the eye, and are especially annoying during the act of reading, as they float across the page. They do not, however, interfere with vision, as it is characteristic of them that they never cross the axis of vision, nor obscure or conceal the object looked at, but rather move about the lateral portions of the field.

There is no real opacity of the vitreous humor, and an examination by the ophthalmoscope fails to detect in these cases any floating opaque particles. They are caused by shadows thrown upon the retina by very minute particles in the vitreous body, perhaps the remains of embryonic tissues. They are more visible to myopic persons than to others, because of the greater length of the eye-ball, thus allowing a shadow of larger size to be cast upon the retina. The number of these spots may be increased by any condition which disturbs the balance of the circulation and thus alters the density of the fluids within the eye.

If not excessive in size or number,. these spots may be regarded as more or less physiological and the effort must be made by the individual to ignore them. Patients often complain of the exaggerated and fantastic shapes they assume, ascribing them to disorders of digestion and torpidity of the liver. But when they are abundant and increasing, they may indicate serious structural change, and should lead to a careful examination by a competent oculist.

Donders says: "I have seen instances in which anxiety about muscæ volitantes amounted to true monomania, against which all reasoning and the most direct demonstrations were in vain."

Any marked increase in the size and number of these spots may be regarded as evidence of morbid changes taking place in the vitreous humor, and if they become so bad as to seriously disturb vision, an examination by the ophthalmoscope will generally reveal turbidity in this humor. Sometimes there are such subjective symptoms as sparks, luminous chains, flashes of light, brightly illuminated white or colored rings, which often appear in the field of vision; they are more noticeable in darkness than in daylight and are, of course, very alarming to the sufferer. Their appearance is an indication that some serious condition is impending in the fundus of the eye, and which may result in amblyopia. Even after the onset of these unpleasant symptoms, if great care is exercised in the use of the eyes and all excesses and irregularities of habits are avoided, vision may be preserved in a fairly good condition for a long time.

The myopic eye is more liable to be attacked by disease of its internal structures than is the emmetropic eye, as choroiditis, which often leads on to hyalitis and inflammation of the vitreous, conditions which are serious and very much to be dreaded; hence the great importance of care in the use of such eyes, which require careful watching in order that complications may be early detected and receive skillful treatment.

DETERMINATION OF THE EXISTENCE OF MYOPIA

The presence of myopia and its degree can be readily determined by the test letters of Snellen, which are hanging on the wall twenty feet away.

If the patient is able to read the No. 20 line there can be no myopia; if, however, he cannot see the letters on this line, but can perhaps barely distinguish some of the larger lines, a weak convex lens is placed before the eyes; this at once blurs the vision and excludes hypermetropia. A convex lens is used as a matter of proper routine, even though the symptoms all indicate myopia, in order to escape the grievous error of mistaking hypermetropia for myopia, as has been frequently done, to the discredit of the optometrist and the suffering of the patient.

After this procedure the way is clear for the use of concave lenses: a weak one is first tried which instantly clears vision and enables more letters to be seen. A stronger one is used with the result of a still greater improvement; thus by a gradual increase in the power of the lenses the acuteness of vision is brought up to 20/20 clearly and sharply. This proves the existence of myopia, and the number of glasses will indicate the degree of the defect.

As soon as the vision is raised to 20/20 the optometrist must stop, because then he has measured the grade of the myopia. In this defect it is a not uncommon thing for glasses to be prescribed very much stronger than are really necessary. If the patient is not old, and the power of accommodation unimpaired, an increase in the strength of the glasses will allow the distant type to be seen equally well, or, perhaps, even a little better.

When a concave lens is placed before a myopic eye of greater strength than is necessary to neutralize the defect, the eye is rendered hypermetropic and the ciliary muscle is called into action to overcome the diminishing effect of the minus lens, just as is the case in hypermetropia. This tension of the accommodation carries with it a contraction of the pupil (which in myopia is apt to be large), thus cutting off the peripheral rays and acting on the principle of the pin-hole disk, improves the distant vision. Hence there is a constant tendency for the glasses chosen in myopia to be stronger than are necessary, and such glasses at once begin to strain and irritate the eye.

This logically leads to the rule that is laid down in myopia, *that the very weakest glasses* with which the No. 20 line can be seen at twenty feet, are the proper ones to prescribe. In hypermetropia, it will be remembered, the strongest convex glasses which were accepted at twenty feet were recommended; in myopia, the weakest concave glasses. The reason is the same in both cases—to assist the accommodation or at least to avoid overtaxing it. The stronger the convex glasses the more support given to the ciliary muscle; the weaker the concave glasses the less tax upon this muscle.

DIAGNOSIS OF MYOPIA

The diagnosis of myopia is not usually a difficult matter. Distant vision is below the standard, and is at once raised to normal by the proper concave lenses. The impairment of distant vision by itself is not an evidence of myopia, because this may be present in a great many other conditions. But when this diminished acuteness of vision instantly yields to the proper concave lenses, the proof is positive that the case is one of myopia and nothing else. In cases of impaired vision from other causes, the application of concave lenses will produce little, if any, improvement.

In the chapter on hypermetropia great stress was laid on the importance of distinguishing that defect from myopia, and the reader was warned that impaired distant vision and holding objects close to the eyes, did not necessarily indicate myopia, but might occur in hypermetropia. The skilled and wide-awake optometrist will hardly fall into this error, and yet it has happened quite often among mere spectacle sellers, and thus tends to bring discredit upon optometrists as a class.

In any case of impaired vision where it is desired to measure the refraction by trial lenses, *the invariable rule is to commence the test with convex lenses*, and if they are accepted at all, the case is regarded as one of hypermetropia and concave lenses must not be tried. Perchance the latter were placed before the eye, they would most likely be accepted also; then the case would be obscured and the optometrist in a quandary—convex and concave lenses both accepted, which is correct?

But if the rule just mentioned be adhered to, the case is kept free from any such doubt. Then, if convex lenses are absolutely rejected, it is proper to try concaves, and if the latter raise the vision to normal, myopia must be the defect that is present.

MYOPIA AND AMBLYOPIA

The term amblyopia usually signifies *dimness of vision,* and as this is the one prominent symptom of myopia, there is some danger that the two conditions may be confounded. In both cases the acuteness of vision is impaired, and there is the tendency to bring small objects very close to the eyes in order to get the benefit of the magnified retinal images.

Strictly speaking, amblyopia is only a symptom; it is a term used to express the defective vision from which the patient suffers, which is not dependent upon an error of refraction, but is due to functional disturbance or disease of some part of the visual apparatus, either the retina, the optic nerve or the brain. It is possible that this condition may exist without any evidences of it visible to the ophthalmoscope, although we usually expect to find some atrophy of the optic nerve.

This is not the place to give a detailed description of amblyopia, but we will simply mention some of the forms in which it occurs—congenital or acquired, temporary or permanent, and symmetrical or non-symmetrical. *Amblyopia ex anopsia* is due to lack of use of eyes; *reflex amblyopia* to irritations in some other part of the body; *traumatic amblyopia* to injury; *uraemic amblyopia* to kidney disease; *tobacco and alcohol amblyopia* to abuse of these agents; *hysterical amblyopia, night-blindness, day-blindness,* etc.

The one diagnositc feature of amblyopia by which the optometrist will be able to recognize it, is its inability to respond to any glass that may be placed before it, and the failure of the pin-hole disk to afford the slightest improvement in the acuteness of vision. By attention to these points myopia can always be readily distinguished from amblyopia.

NEAR VISION IS GOOD

While in myopia the distant vision is very much impaired, at the same time the near vision is quite good, and the recognition of myopia is made possible by the existence of these two factors. If either one of them is missing it cannot be myopia; while if both are present there is little room for doubt.

There are very good reasons why close vision should be good in myopia. Such an eye by its refractive condition is adapted for near vision, the divergent rays of which are focused without any accommodative effort, and hence reading, writing and sewing may be done without any tax on the ciliary muscle. Then, too, on account of the excess of refractive power which such an eye possesses, there is a slight magnification of the image formed on the retina, and hence small print and fine stitches in sewing which might be intolerable to other eyes, are quite possible to the myope.

On account of this sharpness of proximate vision, near-sighted persons consider themselves fitted for occupations requiring good vision for small objects close at hand, as engraving, watch-making, etc., but if the occasion presents itself they should be warned that myopic eyes are usually sick eyes, and if their defect is of high degree they should be advised against the choice of these trying occupations, and recommended to others that do not require such contiguous use of the eyes.

How often do we see persons bending over their desks when writing, with their eyes very close to the paper or sometimes looking obliquely at it. This, in many cases, is only a habit, and may occur with emmetropes or with those only slightly myopic; but habits once formed are hard to break, and gradually such changes take place in the eye that develop or increase the myopia, and the near-sight that was once a habit becomes a necessity.

If, at the commencement of these symptoms, the patient is advised of their serious tendency, and is instructed how to avoid the danger, by keeping the book at the proper distance, by holding the head erect and by frequently resting the eyes in looking for a few minutes at distant objects, the trouble can probably be nipped in the bud and the eye prevented from becoming myopic.

SO MANY PERSONS WEARING GLASSES

The middle-aged individual of to-day is astonished as he walks along the streets at the great number of persons wearing glasses, and he is particularly struck by the large proportion of spectacled children. He hears so many young people complaining of their eyes that he involuntarily remarks that things must be different from the time when he was young, and that children didn't wear glasses then. There is no doubt that defects of the eye are on the increase, and our present school system, with its increased demands upon the eyes and brains of children far beyond the capacity of their years, can be justly charged with a large part of the growing trouble.

The eye, like any other organ, or like any delicate instrument, may be abused, and the bad effects of such abuse are more noticeable during its growing period. The coats of the eye-ball do not reach their full firmness and power of resistance until about twenty years of age, the time when the rest of the body approaches maturity Consequently, before this age, and particularly between the ages of six and sixteen, during what may be called the school years, the eye is liable to injury from overwork. Thus is the causation of myopia in youth accounted for, and if ever "an ounce of prevention is worth a pound of cure." it is in the attention that should be given to the eyes of growing children.

After twenty years of age a good eye can be abused in many ways by overwork without much danger of the production of myopia, although a train of other evils may result. One-fourth of the same application of the eye at the age of ten, with its walls and structures soft and yielding, would cause its posterior wall to give way and bring about myopia; whereas when the eye is well hardened by full growth a much greater amount of eye application can be borne continuously without the fear of causing the walls of the eye-ball to bulge and injuriously changing the shape of the organ. Hence the well-known fact that the danger of the production of myopia by abuse of the eyes is peculiar to youth and to its growing state.

CAN MYOPIA BE CURED?

The question naturally arises, and it is one that is often asked the optometrist, "Is there any cure for myopia?" The answer to this is unfortunately always in the negative. It would scarcely be reasonable to expect that the dense and firm fibrous tissues forming the sclerotic coat of the eye, after having been softened and extended and thinned out, could ever be returned to their normal condition and position, so that the weakened and yielding fibers would contract and regain their original tonicity, and thus restore the posterior part of the sclerotic to its primary form and thickness, and replace the retina again in the position where parallel rays of light would focus upon it when the eye is at rest. A little reflection will show that such a change is impossible.

But while myopia cannot be cured, much can be done to lessen its progress and alleviate its dangers. That by improved school hygiene, education of the laity and careful and uniform correction of refractive errors, it is susceptible of material mitigation in a community, has been fully proven by the careful and painstaking investigations of many oculists in different cities.

DOES AGE IMPROVE THE MYOPIC EYE?

The popular notion that the degree of myopia grows less or is entirely neutralized with age, is far from correct. It is true that in slight degrees of myopia (as 2 D. or less), the inevitable senile changes which tend to diminish the refractive powers of the dioptric media, are sufficient for a time to neutralize the effect of the changed position of the retina, and enable such eyes to dispense with convex glasses for near vision until a very late period of life.

In addition to this the myope begins to notice that he does not hold his book so close as formerly, not because his myopia is growing less, as might naturally be supposed, but because the presbyopic changes are stealing on and his eye is no exception to the rule.

In myopia the focus of rays is in front of the retina, partly because of excessive refraction and partly on account of the length of the eye-ball. Now as the person gets into middle age the over-refraction is reduced and, as a consequence, the rays do not come to a focus so soon, which thus approaches the retina, the source of the rays of course remaining at the same distance. For similar reasons the object may be moved farther away and the rays will meet in focus at the original location. Therefore, as age creeps on, the myope increases his reading distance, using his eyes with the same ease as before. Not because the myopia has undergone improvement, but on account of the recession of the near point due to the presence and progress of presbyopic changes. The actual myopia has not been diminished, as shown by the far point of distinct vision remaining at the same place, all the changes and apparent improvement having taken place in the position of the near point.

There is one change in the eye that accompanies age, that does seem to improve the vision of the myopic eye, and that depends on the size of the pupil. As years creep on the pupil contracts, sometimes almost to a pin point, thus cutting off some of the circles of diffusion, which are so annoying to a myope when looking at a distance, and in this way clearing the vision by allowing only the central rays to pass, but without in any way influencing the degree of myopia.

EFFECT OF HOLDING THE BOOK FARTHER AWAY

The attempt has been made to lessen the amount of myopia by requiring the patient to hold his book or keep his work at a greater distance, and thus after a few weeks' practice the myope is often able to read considerably farther off, and he thinks that his defect has diminished; but the experienced optometrist knows that he has been holding his book closer than is really necessary (as all myopes are apt to do), and that, furthermore, the degree of defect is measured by the far point instead of the near point, and that for any distance less than the former the accommodation is brought into action.

Suppose an emmetrope is accustomed to hold his book twelve inches from his eyes and by the advice of some friend he tries to habituate himself to read at a distance of sixteen inches instead; he simply reads with less effort of accommodation.

So it is with a myope; if he increases the distance at which his book is ordinarily held he simply sees with less exercise of accommodative power. No matter where the reading is held the normal eye still remains emmetropic and the near-sighted eye is no less myopic, as evidenced by its far point being unchanged in position.

While this plan of treatment of holding the book at the greatest possible distance does not diminish the degree of the myopia, yet it is most timely advice for the myope to act upon, and it yields most excellent results in checking the progress of the organic changes taking place in the fundus of the eye. It lessens the amount of convergence needed, and thus removes a great part of the pressure of the lateral muscles on the ball, while the erect position of the head retards the flow of blood to the already congested tissues, and thus restrains the softening processes upon which the giving way of the scleral tissues mainly depend. Therefore, the myope should be instructed to cultivate the habit of keeping his book and work as far from his eye as possible.

MYOPIA NOT DEPENDENT UPON CONVEXITY OF THE CORNEA

Formerly myopia was thought to be due to an excessive convexity of the cornea, and systematic efforts were made to lessen this by compression; but now since the defect is known to be dependent upon an extension of the posterior walls of the eye, it becomes apparent that such treatment is not only useless, but injurious, because the pressure might have a tendency to still further increase the elongation. Myopia then is incurable, and only the lower grades are neutralized (and that but partially) by the compensation of senile changes during the later years of life. As the eye then cannot be restored to a normal condition, the management must consist in endeavoring to arrest the progress of the abnormal changes, and at the same time to render vision easy and comfortable by neutralizing the error of refraction, as far as it can be done without injury to the eyes, and to increase the distance of the near point in order to diminish the excessive convergence and thus lessen the tension of the recti muscles, so as to remove their pressure from the ball.

DISTANT VISION IMPAIRED

To all near-sighted persons distant objects appear as in a fog, which increases with the degree of defect until even close objects present blurred outlines. Where the myopia is but slight, there is so little inconvenience that the patient himself may not be aware of his defect until contrasted with the sharper sight of some friend. On the other hand, a highly myopic person will be unable to distinguish the features of a person who is no farther away than three or four feet.

The first intimation that a child's eyes are growing defective comes in the form of a complaint that the blackboard in the school-room, which could be clearly seen last year, is now very much blurred when viewed from the same desk, and the teacher is requested to allow a change of seats, nearer to the board, in order that the letters and figures upon it may be visible to the pupil. A little questioning will develop the fact that the child cannot see faces across the street and cannot even recognize his own parents at a distance.

Now that attention has been called to the matter, it is noticed that in reading and studying at home the book is held much closer than formerly. If the parents themselves are myopic (as is not unlikely) they recognize the symptoms in their child as corresponding with their own myopic condition. Probably then the parent tests the child with his concave lenses, and if distant objects are brought out clearly a similar pair are purchased for the child.

But this is a very improper and injudicious thing for the parent to do, and it is a well-established rule that concave glasses should never be supplied to a child except after a most careful and thorough examination by some one especially skilled in this line. It is possible there may be no myopia at all, but only a condition simulating it, dependent upon a spasm of accommodation, and if concave glasses were given under such circumstances the eyes would suffer irreparable injury.

Such a case of spasm of the accommodation may present all the symptoms of myopia, so much so that even an expert refractionist may almost be misled. But if the symptoms are rightly interpreted and the condition early recognized, the danger of a confirmed defect may be averted. Whereas, if improperly managed, the defect which at first was only apparent becomes real and the vision gradually grows worse and worse.

SECOND SIGHT

This term is applied to those cases occurring in persons of advanced years who have been using the regular convex lenses for the correction of their presbyopia, and who begin to find that their glasses are too strong; that they can read better with weaker ones, or perhaps with none at all. In other words, it is a return of reading vision late in life, and persons of advanced years are able to dispense with their customary convex lenses. But it should be remembered that this improvement in near vision is accompanied by a corresponding impairment of distant vision.

The explanation of this (seemingly mysterious) occurrence is as follows: Ordinarily in old age the crystalline lens has become harder and denser and flatter, thus crippling the act of accommodation and necessitating the use of convex glasses to supplement it. This is a physiological change which occurs in every eye without exception.

Now in certain cases the lens commences to imbibe fluid and to lose its dryness and hardness. This is accompanied by swelling of this humor, which is made possible by the elasticity of its capsule. Then, instead of being hard and flat, it is soft and swollen, and having become more convex it has increased its refracting and magnifying power. This is the first step in the formation of cataract, although for many months and even years the lens may retain its transparency, even though altered in shape and consistency. But sooner or later opaque streaks or spots begin to make their appearance in it, and gradually the whole lens loses its clearness, and when it has become entirely opaque the condition is known as cataract.

The statement has been made that when second sight makes its appearance before seventy, it foreshadows blindness from cataract in a comparatively short time—perhaps in six months, certainly within a few years.

When the privilege of second sight makes its appearance in extreme old age—that is, in persons of eighty years and upward—the pathological changes in the lens are not likely to progress very rapidly, and the eyes will probably last as long as the patient does, because the debility of old age is apt to prove fatal before the opacity in the lens has made sufficient advance to restrict the sight.

Concave lenses, for a longer or shorter time, will improve the distant vision in these cases, just as in regular myopia, while reading may be possible without any glasses. But after a time, as the degeneration in the lens substance progresses, the passage of light to the retina is impeded and obstructed, and then vision becomes impaired both near and far, and glasses are no longer of any assistance.

THE FAR POINT THE MEASURE OF THE MYOPIA

The distance of the far point represents very closely the grade of the myopia, and therefore in order to save time and to quickly determine the approximate glass required in any case of myopia under examination, without going through the process of trying a great many different numbers of glasses, a procedure both tedious to the patient and tiresome to the optometrist, the far point can be soon located and the extent of the defect at once becomes apparent.

The patient is requested to read small-sized print, not necessarily the finest on the reading card, but somewhat smaller than the letters on this page, while the card is slowly moved away to the farthest distance from the eyes at which the letters still remain legible. If the myopia be of high degree and the near point very close to the eyes, the very smallest print can be used. If ten inches is found by this means to be the far point, then 4 D. is the approximate measure of the myopia and a concave lens of that number is the proper correction, or nearly so.

In order to determine if such glass is the one that ought to be prescribed, it is placed before the eye of the patient, who is requested to look at the test-card, hanging twenty feet away, and read the lowest line he can make out; and then by trying alternately weak convex and weak concave lenses, placed before the original glass, the proper number is soon determined.

If the — 4 D. lens affords a vision of 20/20, a + .25 D. is placed before it, and if the No. 20 line still remains legible then a + .50 D. is tried. If this dulls the vision quite notice ably, then the — 4 D. lens reduced by the + .25 D. would be the proper correction, and the prescription would be — 3.75 D., because the rule in myopia is to order the very weakest glass with which satisfactory vision is possible.

If, however, the — 4 D. lens does not raise the acuteness of vision to 20/20, then a — .25 D. is placed before it; this improves vision slightly, but still it is not up to the normal standard. Then a — .50 D. is tried, and this brings out the

FIG. 112.

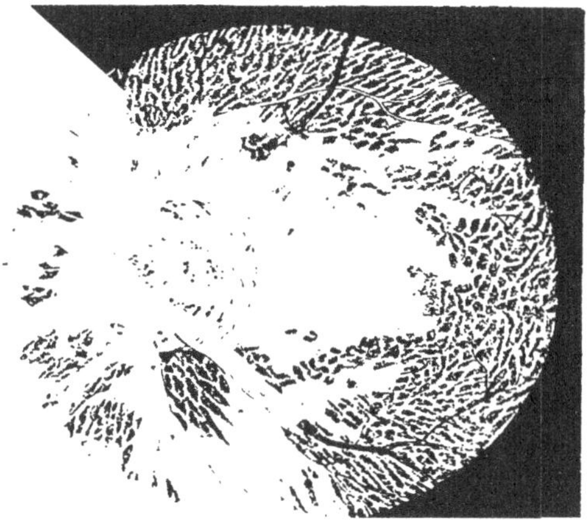

(*De Wecker and Fuchs*)

The Posterior Staphyloma of Myopia, showing not only the white crescent around the optic disc, but also white patches of atrophic choroiditis in the region of the yellow spot, and general exposure of the choroidal vessels by absorption of the retinal pigment epithelium.

No. 20 line clearly, every letter being sharp and distinct. This proves that the first lens is not quite sufficient to entirely correct the refractive error, and a higher number must be substituted, which we have found to be — 4.50 D.

EXPLANATION OF THE FAR POINT

The myopic eye is at rest when adjusted for its far point, just as an emmetropic eye is at rest when adjusted for infinite distance; the divergent rays from the far point in the first case, and the parallel rays from infinity in the second case, being each focused on the retinæ of their respective eyes without any effort of accommodation.

Now, when a concave lens of the proper focal distance is placed before the eye, the rays that pass through it from a distance will assume the same divergence as if they proceeded from the far point, and hence will be exactly focused upon the retina in the same way. Therefore, the parallel rays from a distance, after having been made artificially divergent, will afford distinct vision of the remote objects from which they proceed; just as in the case of the naturally divergent rays from a close point, which enable near objects to be clearly seen.

This will explain why a far point of ten inches indicates a myopia of 4 D., and why a concave lens of the latter strength will correct the defect, and is a beautiful illustration of the adaptation of the refractive properties of lenses to the correction of the errors of refraction of the human eye.

WHY MYOPIC EYES ARE REGARDED AS STRONG EYES

There is a widely prevalent, popular notion that the eye of the myope is superior in strength to any other form of eyeball. Notwithstanding the statement that has already been made that such an eye is a diseased eye, there is some foundation for this idea to become fixed in the public mind, in that the myope, more readily than the emmetrope, can distinguish minute objects, in the examination of which he is able to bring them much closer to his eyes, just as an emmetrope would be compelled to place a magnifying glass before his eye for the same purpose.

This proximity increases the size of the image formed on the retina as well as the quantity of light reflected upon it, and as a consequence vision is made much more distinct. The dilated pupil, which is common in myopia, allows of a still further increase in the illumination.

If an optical student (who is emmetropic) desires to test for himself the supposed superiority of the myopic eye, he can make himself artificially near-sighted by placing before his eyes a convex lens; in this way an addition is made to the refractive power of the eye, parallel rays are brought to a focus in front of the retina, distant vision is very much blurred, and even near vision is not entirely satisfactory. Such an experiment will tend to demonstrate the fact that the apparent superiority of the myopic eye is more fancied than real, except in slight degrees (2 D. or 3 D. or less).

In these latter cases it is not uncommon to find many persons who are utterly unconscious of any defect in their sight. Not having any special need for sharp distant vision, they walk along the streets without a suspicion that others can see better than themselves. Only a few moments ago the writer had an illustration of this fact in his own office; a lady had compound myopic astigmatism and a visual acuteness of only 20/100. Very naturally and properly we suggested glasses for constant wear and to improve distant vision. The lady indignantly repelled the suggestion, and going to the window she pulled aside the lace curtain and triumphantly exclaimed: "I don't need glasses for distant vision; I can see those numbers on the doors (they were very large), and if I was acquainted with those people I could recognize every one of them. My sight is all right; all I need is glasses for reading." Such a remark seemed ridiculous from a patient whose acuteness of vision was only 20/100, but she was so determined that it seemed useless to argue with her.

PROGRESSIVE MYOPIA

Myopia is a defect which does not decrease in degree; in fact, it even does not usually remain stationary, but its natural tendency is to increase. Such a condition is more than a simple error of refraction; it is really a disease, and one that is fraught with many dangers to the eye.

The *optical* characteristic of a myopic eye is that the position of the retina is behind the focus of parallel rays; its *anatomical and pathological* characteristic is that this departure of the retina from its normal condition is due to a distention of the eyeball, caused by a giving way of the coats of the ball at the fundus. As the membranes thus become attenuated, their power of resistance is at the same time diminished; in the face of this fact it is hardly to be expected that the trouble would remain stationary, when all the conditions are favorable for its increase. As the distention grows the myopia progresses, dependent upon a real disease of the eye.

On account of the elongation of the myopic eye-ball in its antero-posterior diameter, resembling somewhat the shape of an egg, its very form causes it to suffer its greatest pressure backward. This fact, together with that mentioned above (thinning of the coats of the eye and diminished power of resistance), will account for the progressive tendency of myopia.

Of course, it can be easily understood that the higher the degree of myopia the more likely it is to assume the progressive form, even in more advanced years; while in youth almost every case of myopia shows a tendency to be progressive, and this is really the critical period for the myopic eye.

The term progressive myopia is reserved for those cases where the defect increases rapidly and is accompanied by symptoms of congestion and irritation, and does not apply to those cases where the progress of the defect is very slow and where the eye is free from all unpleasant symptoms.

POSTERIOR STAPHYLOMA

The general acceptance of posterior staphyloma as the anatomical basis of myopia rests upon two factors:

1. Descriptions of myopic eyes after death.
2. Ophthalmoscopic examinations during life.

Myopic eyes of low or medium degrees (such as are usually acquired during school life) do not present this condition of posterior staphyloma, but it is always found in eyes having a myopia exceeding 10 D.

The axial diameter of a normal eye is about 23 mm., which is considerably increased by the presence of posterior staphyloma; of the recorded cases the shortest measured 27 mm. and the longest 32 mm. corresponding respectively to a myopia of 11 D. and of 20 D.

As the thinning of the walls of the eye in these cases usually extends forward, the transverse diameter is also, as a rule, greater than normal, ranging from 24½ mm. to 28 mm., as compared with 22 mm. to 23 mm., the normal measure.

The ophthalmoscopic appearances of posterior staphyloma are marked and unmistakable. The characteristic symptom is a white crescent at the edge of the optic disk, generally at the outer side. This crescent varies greatly in size, from a small arc to a large zone, and may extend all around the disk, and even encroach on the region of the yellow spot, its greatest extent being always in this direction. Its edges may be sharply and distinctly defined, or may be irregular and gradually merge in the surrounding healthy structure.

There may be patches of pigment about the margin of the white crescent, or scattered over its surface. The crescent itself is of a brilliant white color, which makes the disk by contrast appear abnormally pink. On account of this whiteness of the background, the small blood-vessels that pass over it are rendered more visible and are more easily discerned than elsewhere on the retina. The whiteness is due to a thinning and an atrophy of the substance of the choroid, which, indeed, may be found entirely lacking at this spot, thus allowing the glistening sclerotic to come into view. Hence the white crescent is simply a portion of the sclerotic, which, for the reasons mentioned above, becomes abnormally visible.

On account of the wasting of the choroid there is an absence of the pigment cells, and this removal of the natural protection against excessive light gives rise to the sense of glare which such patients frequently complain of. As might be expected from this, the sight of these myopes is often much improved by a tinted glass, which, under the circumstances, is not only allowable, but advisable.

DEGREE OF MYOPIA

The writer has frequently asked the following question of his optical students: "Upon what does the degree of myopia depend?" and the almost invariable answer has been, "The distance of the far point." This shows an incorrect conception of the point involved. The location of the far point simply *indicates* or *represents* the amount of the myopia, which *depends* upon the distance of the focus of parallel rays in front of the retina. The nearer the focus is to this membrane the lower the degree of defect; the farther the focus is removed from it, the higher the grade of myopia.

This distance of the focus cannot be directly estimated, but can be determined indirectly by measuring the excess of refractive power. When the refraction of the eye exactly corresponds with the length of the optic axis, the condition is one of emmetropia; when the former exceeds the latter, the eye is known as a myopic one, and the concave lens that neutralizes the surplus will indicate the grade of myopia. Suppose a — 4 D. lens is required; this proves that there is a myopia of 4 D., and that there is an excess of refractive power of 4 D., which causes parallel rays to focus in front of the retina. The concave lens diminishes the refraction of the eye and gives to parallel rays sufficient divergence to throw their focus back upon the retina and thus afford clear vision.

APPARENT OR ACCOMMODATIVE MYOPIA

The attention of the optometrist should be called to a condition of apparent or false myopia, which is not myopia at all, but is made to simulate it on account of a spasm of the accommodation, by means of which the refraction of the eye is increased and parallel rays are brought to a focus in front of the retina.

Ordinarily the ciliary muscle acts just sufficiently to focus divergent rays on the yellow spot and to adjust the eye for the every-day purposes of close vision. But this little muscle may fall into a condition of abnormal activity, known as spasm of the accommodation, where the muscle refuses to relax and continues indefinitely to keep the eye in a condition of over-refraction. This is the optical condition present in myopia, and gives rise to all the symptoms of this defect. This ciliary spasm may occur in emmetropia or more often in hypermetropia, as explained in the last chapter, where we gave warning of the danger of mistaking hypermetropia for myopia.

Spasm of the accommodation is of more frequent occurrence than is generally supposed, and in addition to the apparent myopia which it causes, also gives rise to marked symptoms of asthenopia during reading or close work. The pupil is contracted and the ophthalmoscope will show congestion of the optic disk and retina.

When the vision of such a patient is tested with the

trial lenses there will be noticeable variations in the apparent refraction; sometimes he will prefer one glass, sometimes another. When the amplitude of accommodation is measured there will be quite a discrepancy between the position of the far point and the degree of apparent myopia. For instance, the location of the far point may be ten inches from the eye, which would lead to a suspicion of a myopia of 4 D. But when the acuteness of vision is taken, such an error would be at once discovered. The patient can read all the letters on the test card, and only a weak concave lens is required (perhaps — 1 D.) to raise the vision to the normal of 20/20. In this way the diagnosis between real myopia and apparent myopia due to spasm can often be made.

The fact should not be overlooked that spasm of the ciliary muscle may be dependent upon an insufficiency of the internal recti muscles. The excessive muscular effort required to maintain the necessary degree of convergence carries with it an extreme contraction of the ciliary. Just as in hypermetropia the extra accommodation causes an extra convergence which may result in convergent strabismus; in both instances produced by the close relation which naturally exists between the functions of accommodation and convergence. In these cases a pair of prisms, bases in, may assist in relaxing the ciliary spasm.

Spasm of accommodation is most apt to occur in nervous individuals, when the system is enfeebled or the nervous force exhausted; and, strange to say, the degree of spasm bears no relation to the vigor of the ciliary muscle. In fact, it is usually found in connection with a weakened accommodation, and instead of being an evidence of extra strength, must be regarded as an indication of nervous debility. This is proven by the fact that eyes exhausted by overwork are the ones that are subject to spasm, and the accompanying asthenopia tends to increase the spasmodic action.

The *treatment* of cases of spasm of accommodation will oftentimes tax the skill and ingenuity of the examiner. One method of management consists in the use of convex lenses, a moderately strong pair for reading and a weak pair for distance. As is well known, the use of the convex lenses constantly and persistently encourages a relaxation of the spasm, and the patient who was apparently near-sighted, is soon able to read the No. 20 line without the concave glasses that were formerly necessary.

Of course, the wearing of convex lenses in this way makes vision indistinct, and the patient is apt to rebel. Sometimes, with intelligent persons, if the rationale of the treatment is explained, their co-operation may be secured. But if not, the distance glasses may be dispensed with and reliance placed on the reading glasses, to which very few persons will object.

In some stubborn cases it may become necessary to invoke the services of a physician, and place the eyes under the influence of atropine, which may need to be continued for several weeks before the spasm is overcome and the ciliary muscle completely paralyzed. Then the exact condition of the refraction can be determined, and if hypermetropic, as it often is, the correcting convex glasses should be prescribed at once and the patient directed to wear them and become accustomed to them while the muscle is recovering from the effects of the drug.

SYMPTOMS OF MYOPIA

The two principal symptoms are the impairment of distant vision and the improvement of close vision. The eyes are usually large, full and prominent, and the pupils dilated, although as age creeps on they gradually contract, thus diminishing the circles of diffusion and slightly improving vision. The young myope makes use of the same principle to assist vision by half-closing his lids, which habit indeed is so characteristic of this defect as to give occasion for its name, the word myopia originating from two Greek words meaning, "to close the eyes."

On account of the impairment of distant vision, myopes are inclined to avoid outdoor sports, and rather prefer indoor amusements, as reading, drawing, etc., which do not require good vision at a distance. But, unfortunately, such habits cause congestion of the eyes, and thus favor the increase of myopia. Of course, where the correcting glasses are worn early in life, the boy has his range of vision widened, and in this respect is placed on an equality with his companions, and then he has the same desire as they to join in all their games.

In progressive forms of myopia the field of vision may be limited and besides show numerous blank spots, on account of patches of retinal atrophy.

In some cases of myopia there may be evidences of considerable irritation of the eyes, especially after using them by artificial light for any great length of time. The conjunctiva may be blood-shot and the lids red, while the patient complains of pain, sensitiveness to light, a feeling of eye-strain, eye-balls sore to the touch, and the annoying "muscæ volitantes," which have already been described.

The symptoms of myopia that have been enumerated are both subjective and objective, the former depending on the visual sensations of the patient, and the latter on what the optometrist himself observes.

PREVENTION OF MYOPIA

The importance of the prevention of myopia cannot be too forcibly impressed upon parents, teachers and school directors, in order that the conditions which cause it may be understood and removed. This is an age of prevention rather than cure. Everywhere efforts are made to prevent disease and all questions pertaining to hygiene and sanitary reform receive the closest study and attention. The prevention of small-pox, diphtheria, yellow fever, cholera and tuberculosis is enforced by law, and is facilitated by laboratory work with the microscope and test tube. This certainly shows the unselfish interest physicians manifest in the welfare of mankind, because it is evident that the existence of disease is more profitable to the medical profession than its absence; but the discovery of a prophylactic measure affords more satisfaction to a physician than a new method of cure.

The optical profession should measure up to the same standard, and should exhibit the same commendable spirit in developing measures of hygienic reform as it pertains to the eye, and in educating the public along the same lines. The scope of this book will not permit an extended reference to this subject or a complete description of the work that has been and should be done in this field, but a brief mention of some of the practical points bearing on the prevention of myopia is at least necessary.

Consideration must be given to those conditions of school life which tend to develop this defect; and the first thought that arises is that children should not be sent to school unless their general health is robust enough to endure the strain. In addition, the refraction of the eye should be examined, as well to detect any possible defect as to determine their capacity for the work on which the child is just entering. The importance of this latter procedure as a prophylactic measure will commend itself at once to those interested in the welfare of children's eyes.

LIGHTING OF SCHOOL ROOMS

The school building should be lighted sufficiently and properly, and should also be so constructed as to afford the pupils all the advantages possible in the way of location, ventilation, sanitary plumbing, pure and abundant water, etc. The light in the school room should be direct, and not reflected from the walls of adjoining buildings.

Light that is insufficient or ill-arranged is the most potential factor in the causation of myopia in the school room, because such light compels a lessening of the distance between the eye and the book when reading or writing, and therefore the question of proper light becomes an all-important one.

The light should be sufficient in quantity, should come from above the level of the eyes and, as far as possible, should fall upon the desk from the left-hand side. This arrangement of light could be best secured if the school rooms were of an oblong shape, all the windows located in one of the long sides, the desks placed in rows at right angles to this wall, and the scholars facing that end of the room which allows the light to fall from the left. The windows should extend upward to the ceiling, starting about four feet from the floor. The total window surface should be one-fifth of the floor area, with the panes as large as possible.

It would be better if the education of children could be carried on entirely by daylight, but in cloudy weather, in the afternoons of the short days in mid-winter, and in night schools, artificial illumination becomes a necessity. The usual naked gas jets are mentioned only to be condemned. The improved Welsbach burners afford an excellent light, and if properly placed over the children's heads and in sufficient numbers, would constitute a satisfactory method of artificial illumination. If electricity is available for introduction into the building, the incandescent light is perhaps the best substitute for daylight. It is capable of uniform distribution and concentration, and does not heat or vitiate the atmosphere. The lights should be ample in number, properly shaded and brought close enough to the desk to afford an abundant illumination.

SCHOOL DESKS AND SEATS

In addition to the proper lighting of the school-room, the question of the construction of desks and seats is one of no little importance, as it doubtless is partly responsible for the increasing percentage of myopia found in school children, and certainly improper seats and desks produce injurious results upon the health of the children, particularly affecting their lungs, abdominal organs, spine and figure.

A crooked and stooping posture cannot always be blamed upon the pupil, because for anatomical and physiological reasons it is impossible for a child to assume and maintain a good posture with unsuitable seats and desks. The faults may be enumerated as follows:

1. Improper backs or no backs.
2. Too great distance between seat and desk.
3. Disproportion between height of seat and of desk.
4. Unsuitable form and slope of desk.

This naturally leads to a brief mention of the essentials in proper school furniture. The seat must be of such height as to allow the feet to rest upon the floor, which is accomplished by adjustable seats and measuring the distance from the sole of the foot to the inner bend of the knee. The seat should be generously wide, slightly concave, but without any inclination and its front edge about two inches under the edge of desk. Some authorities consider this overlapping of the desk as unnecessary, claiming that the edge of desk and of seat should be on same plane.

The seats should have comfortable backs, corresponding in size to the height of pupil. They must not be too high,

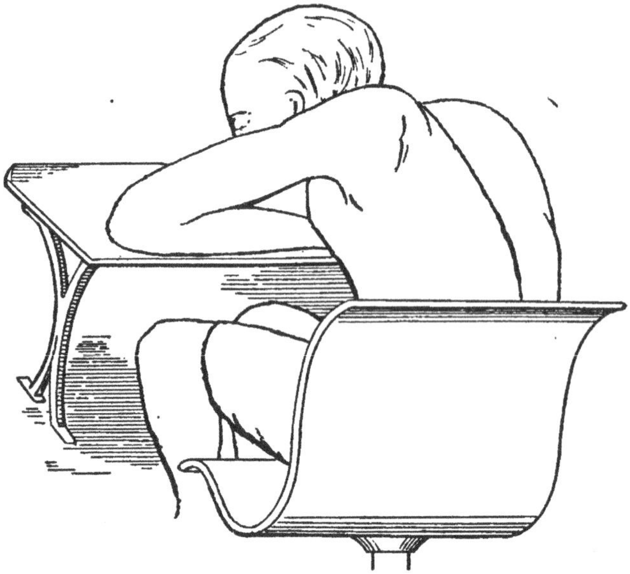

Showing the improper position assumed by the pupil because the seat and desk is too low, and the edge of the desk is too far in front of the seat. The child is compelled to sit on the front of the seat, the body falls forward and finds support upon the elbows, which rest upon the desk. In writing, the left arm is used for support while the right hand is employed, which causes the vertebral column to be partially turned upon its long axis and the body to be placed in a distorted position. The head falls forward toward the work and turns to the right; this brings the face too near to the page, the left eye closer than the right. The normal relation between the plane of the face and the work is thus disturbed, while the abnormal near point adds greatly to the strain upon the accommodation and convergence.

coming only far enough to support the shoulders and leave the head free to assume the proper position. The top of the desk must be just high enough to allow the elbow to rest upon it without displacing the natural position of the shoulder.

In order to meet all the requirements, it is evident that

the size of the desk and seat should correspond to the size of the pupil. But it is equally obvious that a desk rigidly constructed for all the pupils of a certain grade or a certain age,

Showing the correct position which the student should assume, the lower part of back and pelvis being supported by the forward curve in the back of the seat. The forearm of the pupil rests lightly upon the desk, which is not so high as to raise the shoulders, but sufficiently high to avoid the necessity of stooping in order to reach it. Both the desk and seat are adjustable in height by means of the nuts on the pedestal of each. The front edge of the seat projects an inch or two under the desk, which allows the correct upright sitting posture to be assumed and maintained, and in fact the child finds it easier to sit in this position than in any other he can assume.

would fall short of answering the purpose on account of extremes in size which may exist. Therefore it is not only necessary to have desks and seats of different sizes for the various grades, but they should also be easily adjustable to meet the requirements of each pupil in that particular grade. After the seat and desk has been adapted to the length of the leg and height of body the adjustment must be fixed by a key, which should be in the hands of the teacher, so as not to allow of any alteration by the pupil himself.

INCLINATION OF TOP OF DESK

The reasons given why the top of the desk should slope are so interesting and important from a physiological and hygienic standpoint for the benefit of adults as well as children, that the optometrist should not be lacking in the knowledge which is therein implied.[2]

The eyes are moved in different directions by six muscles. The movements of the two eyes are associated, and only certain sets of muscles of both eyes can be brought into simultaneous action. For instance, we cannot turn one eye up and the other down, but we can only move both eyes at the same time in the same direction, either up or down. We can use both internal recti muscles in the act of convergence, but we cannot use the two external recti muscles and turn the eyes from parallelism to divergence. We can use the internal rectus muscle of one eye with the external rectus of the other, as when the eyes are turned to the right or left.

Of the various combinations of muscles, some can be comfortably kept in action for a length of time, others only for a few seconds. Thus it requires considerable effort to converge the eyes and look upward at the same time; while, on the other hand, we can converge and look downward with ease. If we want to see distinctly a line or a plane, instead of a point, a particular turning of both retinæ is necessary for each position of the object. When this turning can be produced by a combination of muscles which can be effected with ease for a length of time, then we can look at the object steadily and comfortably.

Therefore the proper position of the book in reading does not depend on chance, but is a physiological necessity. If it is constantly disregarded the eyes become fatigued and a condition of asthenopia may intervene. This is the reason why it is so tiring to look at those pictures in a gallery which are hung high on the wall, while the same number of pictures can be examined without fatigue if placed on easels below the level of the eyes. Likewise it is hurtful to the eyes to read while lying down, and if this pernicious habit is persisted in will sooner or later produce a painful and weak condition of the eyes.

Consequently, if we want to look for any length of time at any plane surface, as for instance, the page of a book, it is necessary to place it and hold it in such a position as to form an angle of about 45° with the horizon, and then direct the axis of vision of our eyes downward at an equal angle of 45°, so that a right angle will be formed by their intersection, or in other words, that the visual axis may be perpendicular to the surface of the book. This is the ideal position for the book and eyes in reading, and if the reader will look around him he will see how many persons disregard these plainly proven propositions. For writing, the same inclination for the paper would be equally advantageous, but for obvious reasons this would scarcely be practicable, and for this purpose a less angle is recommended, usually about 20°. It is possible to have a desk so constructed that the inclination of its top might be changed by a simple mechanism.

It is obvious that a flat-top desk not only prevents the direction of the visual axis at that angle most favorable to the natural and easy movement of the eye-ball, but also encourages a stooping position with its attendant evils of close sight and gravitation of blood to the eyes.

The influence of school life upon the figure of the child and in the causation of curvature of the spine, as well as the disastrous effects that crooked and stooping positions at school may have upon the heart and lungs and abdominal organs, are important matters for serious consideration, but it is not in place to discuss them here, as they are beyond the scope of this work.

BLACKBOARDS AND MAPS

Attention should also be given to the distance and location of blackboards, as an important factor in the hygiene of school vision. They should not be placed so far away from any scholar as to necessitate a strain in order to see the marks upon their surfaces, but those pupils who have defective vision should be given front seats near the board. No blackboard should ever be placed between two windows, as the scholar could not see the writing upon it without subjecting his eyes to the irritating glare of light which enters the eye from an improper direction, while the board remains in shadow; but the light should be so arranged as to illuminate the board without causing its rays to be reflected in such a manner as to obscure the characters that are inscribed thereon.

Some authorities have recommended, as a desirable substitute, white surfaces with black crayons, on the presumption that black marks on a white background can be seen at a greater distance. But on the other hand the reflection from a large extent of white surface is more apt to be annoying and irritating to the eye than is the same amount of black surface, and therefore we think the old form of blackboard and white crayon cannot be improved upon. For similar reasons, the writer has been using in his office for determining the acuteness of vision and measuring the refraction, a black card with white block letters upon it, and finds it very satisfactory.

THE TYPE OF TEXT-BOOKS

The size and form of the type used in school books are of great importance from a hygienic standpoint. All authorities agree that the Latin letters are the best for all kinds of reading. The crooked zig-zag lines of the German letters are by common consent considered very trying to the eyes, and hence that form of letters should never be employed in text-books. It is altogether likely that this type, in connection with the studious habits of the German nation, are responsible for the larger percentage of myopia in that country, in speaking of which an author says, "it is certain that if Germany would absolve itself from nationalism sufficiently to declare an emancipation from its miserable type, there would be less myopia among its people."

The normal acuity of vision is based upon the ability to distinguish letters which subtend an angle of five minutes, but it would be very unreasonable to expect the eyes to keep at a task for any great length of time which called forth their utmost endeavor. This will become evident to anyone who compares the strain and effort to read small (diamond) type, with the ease and comfort with which a larger type (long primer) is read, and the latter (the size in which this book is set) is the smallest which should be allowed in school books, or for that matter in any book intended for general reading.

The distance between the lines has much to do with the legibility of the page and with the ease with which it is read. When the lines are crowded as closely together as the type will permit, the page has a dark and unattractive appearance, and the labor of reading is relatively increased, as is evident to any one who will compare a closely set page of reading matter with one that is liberally leaded. The fact is, a proper spacing between the lines is really of more importance than the size and height of the letters, and the weight of opinion is that this space should not be less than two and a half millimeters, or one-tenth of an inch. The printing should be well done, so that the letters show up clear and distinct. If a large edition of a book is issued, those first run off are clearest, and later on the print begins to appear somewhat blurred and defective. As soon as this is noticeable the type (or electrotype which is generally used) should be rejected and new metal demanded.

The paper should be of good quality, as otherwise the beneficial effect of large type properly spaced would be neutralized. It should be reasonably thick and opaque, so that the impression of the type on the opposite side should not show through. The surface of the paper should be dulled, so that there may be no unpleasant reflection from it, and of a cream tint.

PROPER PENMANSHIP

We do not propose to go very deeply into the consideration of the question of vertical or slanting handwriting, but some mention of it is due on account of the agitation of the subject at the present day. There was for a time some sentiment in favor of the erect system, because the slanting form seems to favor an unnatural position of the body and of the paper, and thus tend to the development of myopia. But if the desk and seat are of the proper proportions, and the pupil rightly seated with the paper in a central position in front of him, the question of the selection of the kind of script is immaterial from the standpoint of the hygiene of vision, which is the only point in which we, as optometrists, are interested.

HOURS OF STUDY

Young children should not be expected to use their eyes more than a few hours each day; all their work should be done in the school room, and when they leave it their minds and bodies should be free from any set tasks. As the child increases in years and advances into the higher grades, some amount of study is necessary out of school, and it seems possible that more harm may be done to the eyes by indiscretion in the home work than in school hours. Children are usually under less discipline at home than at school; they are often allowed to read what, when and how they please; no provision is made for proper desks, seats or light; the child assumes various positions and often reads while reclining, with light that is perhaps insufficient or coming from a wrong direction.

As a rule, children are sent to school too early in life; in many instances because the mother wishes to be rid of the annoyance of the child for a few hours each day, and because the law allows it. Seven years of age is young enough for a child to enter school, although six years is the legal age; but really such an important matter cannot be regulated by statute, but should depend on the physical condition of each individual child.

PREVENTIVE MEASURES

In the prevention of the development of myopia in children, the importance of giving to the child for his playthings objects of considerable size becomes evident. Small ones, books with fine print and games with minute figures, all impose a tax upon the accommodation and should be avoided. On the other hand, out-door plays should be encouraged, because they do not require any close vision, or at least all play objects should be sufficiently large not to require any effort of accommodation. After the child enters school he should not be required to keep his eyes uninterruptedly upon the book, as some teachers with mistaken zeal insist upon, under penalty of receiving a bad mark for misconduct, but he should rather be encouraged to rest his eyes and relieve their fatigue by looking up from his books and glancing around at more distant objects.

Frequent interruption of any kind of confining work is essential to symmetrical development and the maintenance of a healthy condition of the body, and this is especially true of the young. If one attempts to hold up an object at arm's length, and thus imposes a continued effort upon these muscles, a feeling of strain and exhaustion soon becomes apparent, and the act must be quickly discontinued; and yet the muscles of the eyes are often forced to do similar work; is it any wonder then that myopia results?

Myopia is seldom congenital, although it may be hereditary and appear soon after birth. It rarely develops, however, before the eighth year of life, more often the tenth, and reaches its maximum about the age of twenty. Where an inherited predisposition to myopia exists, the child should be kept out of the school room as long as possible; perhaps until he is ten or eleven years old. In the meantime, and in fact all through life, open-air sports should be encouraged, with gymnastic exercises for the development of the body and perhaps an intermixture of properly assigned manual labor.

The fact should be impressed upon the minds of parents and educators that it is better to devote the years of youth to laying the foundation of a healthy constitution and strong eyes than to encourage forced intellectual advancement at the expense of feeble health and impaired vision. The moral of this advice is emphasized by the country boy, raised upon the farm and receiving but few educational advantages, who so often outstrips his city cousin, whose life from four years of age has been spent in kindergartens and graded schools.

For those predisposed to myopia, mental education should be always subject to the physical condition, and earnest, systematic study should not be commenced until the sixteenth year, when the body is stronger and the coats of the eye firmer and better able to resist the encroachments of myopia. Even then it would be better if the child could be taught privately instead of being placed in the general class and expected to keep pace with his normal-sighted companions.

In order to prevent the onset of myopia, or its increase, the stooping position and a close approximation of the book, which taxes both accommodation and convergence, must be avoided; the patient should be instructed never to read in a moving car or carriage, where the continual jarring requires a constant change in the accommodation; not to continue close vision too long at a time without suitable periods of inter mission; to maintain a reading, writing or working distance of at least twelve inches, and more if possible; to select books and newspapers printed in clear, large type; to avoid fine sewing and tedious fancy work; to write a large hand (as myópes are especially prone to small writing); to see that daylight is sufficient in quantity and coming from the proper direction; not to use the eyes by artificial light, or as little as possible; and if symptoms of irritation become manifest, or there is a marked increase in the myopia, to give the eyes complete rest.

TESTS FOR MYOPIA

In myopia the distant vision is impaired, while the close vision remains fairly good, and therefore if a person is unable to make out the large letters on the test card, hanging twenty feet distant, but can easily read the small print six or seven inches away, it is fair to presume he is myopic. This is a rough test, but it is one of value, and can be made at any time and under any circumstances and without any outfit. An ordinary newspaper can be made to suffice, the letters of the title line forming the distance test and the small type the near test. Of course, if with the impairment of distant sight near vision is also defective or impossible, there is something more than myopia; perhaps amblyopia, or some diseased condition.

The differential diagnosis between myopia (which is correctible with glasses) and an organic disease (which is beyond the reach of optical help) can be quickly made by means of the pin-hole test, which is described and illustrated in the chapter on Method of Examination. The trial case contains one or two of these pin-hole disks, made of hard rubber and mounted in a metal ring with handle; but in the absence of a test case, a card or a stiff piece of paper can be punctured with a pin, an equally efficacious pin-hole test is at hand, and one that can be made and used in any lonely cabin in the backwoods.

The principal tests for myopia are:

1. Trial case and test types.
2. Ophthalmoscope.
3. Retinoscope.
4. Refractometer, optometer, prisoptometer.
5. Scheiner's method.
6. Chromatic test.

TEST WITH TRIAL LENSES

The patient is seated facing the test card of Snellen, which is well illuminated and hanging twenty feet away. The trial frame is placed on his face and carefully adjusted for height of nose and pupillary distance. Both eyes should be kept open, but only one eye should be tested at a time, the other being excluded from vision by a solid rubber disk being placed in the trial frame over it.

The left eye being thus covered, the patient is asked to name the letters on the lowest line which is legible to him. If he reads the No. 20 line, that is if his visual acuteness is 20/20, the eye is presumably emmetropic, although latent hypermetropia may be present. If he reads the line hesitatingly and makes some mistakes in naming the letters, there is probably some astigmatic element in the case. But either of the above conditions precludes the existence of myopia, which cannot be present if the vision is wholly or even partly 20/20, because this defect markedly impairs the acuteness of vision

If, however, the patient cannot distinguish any letters on the No. 20 line, and perhaps cannot even read the 30 or 40 lines, we may infer the possibility of myopia; but first in order to prevent error, convex glasses must be tried in order to detect any hypermetropia. If they are immediately and positively rejected, it is then proper to begin to suspect myopia, and we ask the patient to take the fine near type (which a myope is easily able to read) and move it away from him to the greatest possible distance from the eye at which it can still be seen distinctly. The distance from the eye to the type is then carefully measured, which, when converted into dioptrics, will represent (at least approximately) the degree of myopia, and the corresponding concave lens will be the proper correction. This glass is placed in the trial frame in front of the eye and the distant vision is again tested. The strength of the lens is diminished or increased, if necessary, until the maximum acuity of vision is obtained, always remembering to give the preference to the weakest glass.

The other eye is then similarly tested, and when both eyes are corrected an effort should be made to reduce the strength of the glasses by placing weak convex lenses in front of them. If any glass above + .50 D. is thus accepted, the examiner's suspicions should be aroused as to the possible existence of spasm of accommodation. Otherwise the lenses may be considered as correct.

A recent books says: "Take in your hand a + .50 D. S. and a — .50 D. S., trying first one and then the other before the eye you are testing. Whichever lens gives the best vision, after a careful trial, will be an indication of what kind of lenses (convex or concave) the patient is going to need."

Now we are compelled to take issue with the author of this work, as we cannot consider such a method of testing as proper. It is a well-known fact that a weak concave lens will be accepted for distance by almost any eye, even by emmetropic and hypermetropic eyes, and in slight degrees of the latter defect will be preferred to weak convex. Therefore when weak plus and minus lenses are tried alternately, the patient will most likely select the concave, or else he will be confused and will be unable to decide between them. The writer feels that he can make the positive statement that in such a method of testing the convex lens would never be chosen; this makes the test entirely one-sided and robs it of its value.

The advice given on these pages has always been to commence the test with convex lenses, and if they are accepted at all, not to confuse the patient or run the risk of error by trying concaves, and this advice is especially applicable in cases where the vision is 20/20 or nearly so. Where the vision is markedly below normal, the rule still holds good to begin the examination with convex lenses, and only in case of their positive rejection is it proper to try concaves.

After these preliminaries, suppose — .50 D. lens quickly and unmistakably improves vision on the test card, it is probable the case is one of myopia and needs concave lenses. Then the — .50 D. is removed and a — .75 D. is substituted for it, with a still greater improvement in vision, which possibly may now reach the normal standard of 20/20, in which case this lens would be the measure of the defect. If not, a — 1 D. is next tried, and as long as a further improvement in vision is obtained, the lenses are gradually increased in strength a .25 D. at a time until the best vision is secured that it is possible

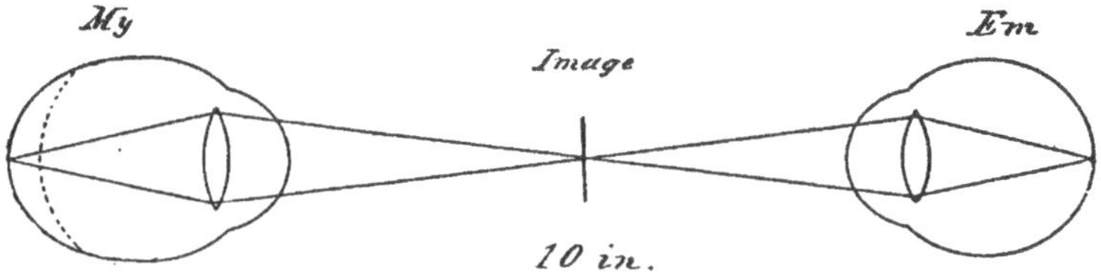

This diagram shows the path of the rays and the position of the image. The rays issue from the myopic eye convergently and focus ten inches in front of it; they then cross and enter the emmetropic eye and are united upon its retina.

to get with concave spherical glasses, always remembering that the weakest glass is the one to be preferred.

This lens is then placed in the back groove of the trial frame and the rubber disk slipped in front of it, and a similar test made of the other eye. After the second eye has been carefully measured, the rubber disk is removed from before the first eye and the patient can see with his both eyes together, each properly corrected as far as can be with spherical lenses.

The frequent change of lenses in the trial frame is more or less confusing to the patient, and should be avoided as much as possible. Hence in high degrees of defect, instead of increasing .25 D. at a time, it is better to jump .50 D., or even 1 D., until something near the normal acuteness of vision is reached, and then proceed more cautiously and with shorter steps. When lenses are found that afford pretty fair vision, instead of removing the lens and replacing it with another, its strength may be increased or decreased by holding before it alternately a — .25 D. and a + .25 D. If with the convex lens vision remains as good, then the concave lens in the frame is stronger than is necessary, and should be reduced a quarter of a dioptric. If on the other hand the — .25 D. produces a marked improvement in vision, then the lens in the frame is not quite strong enough, and should be replaced by one a quarter of a dioptric stronger.

NORMAL VISION NOT ALWAYS POSSIBLE IN HIGH MYOPIA

If with the lenses found according to the above methods the patient, at twenty feet, can read the No. 20 line clearly and distinctly, it is right to assume that the full defect has been measured and the proper correcting lenses found. Even if the vision is less than 20/20, with these glasses it does not prove they are incorrect; it simply shows this is the best vision attainable with concave spherical lenses.

In high degrees of myopia it is an unfortunate fact that vision cannot be raised to normal by any glass, and this may perhaps be comforting knowledge to some conscientious persons who have vainly endeavored to find some glass that would afford a vision of 20/20. There are two reasons for this—the impaired sensibility of the retina and the diminishing effect of concave lenses. Either one of these would be sufficient to account for the lessened vision, while the two together only serve to make it more pronounced.

In extreme cases of myopia there is great bulging of the fundus and stretching of all the coats of the eye,' in which process the retina is the membrane that suffers the most, its layer of rods and cones being separated and fewer of them being impressed by the image formed, and therefore the degree of vision would be lessened. The function of a concave lens is to minify, and the diminution of an image by strong minus lenses is very marked, and hence such a glass, by reducing the image formed, would tend to impair the acuteness of vision very perceptibly. When these two causes act together and an image smaller than normal is received by a less number of rods and cones than natural, the wonder really is that the vision is as susceptible of as much improvement as it is.

TEST WITH OPHTHALMOSCOPE

In emmetropia parallel rays are brought to a focus exactly on the retina and, therefore, inasmuch as the retina is located precisely at the principal focus, the divergent rays proceeding from it (after being acted on by the refracting media of the eye) would emerge from the cornea parallel.

In myopia, on the other hand, the retina is placed beyond the principal focus and parallel rays unite and cross over before reaching it. Under such conditions the rays proceeding from the retina would emerge from the eye convergent and would meet at this far point.

When looking into an emmetropic eye with an ophthalmoscope, the observer must approach within two or three inches in order to see the details of the fundus clearly. In myopia, on the contrary, nothing can be clearly seen at such a close distance with the naked eye, but on withdrawing the instrument from fifteen to twenty inches, the optic disk and blood-vessels will gradually come more or less clearly into view.

In a case of myopia of 4 D. the rays reflected from the retina would converge and meet at a distance of ten inches from the eye and form there an inverted image, which can be clearly seen by the examiner, at his ordinary distance for small objects (say from ten to twelve inches), by calling into action his accommodation and adjusting his eye for that particular spot at which the aerial image is formed. In this case, where the image is at ten inches and the observer's eye ten inches from that, it will be found that a distance of twenty inches will be the proper one to assume. The precaution must be taken not to approach the image too close—that is, the optometrist must always keep beyond his own near point, else his accommodation will not suffice to afford him a distinct view.

That this image is inverted is proven by the fact that when the observer moves his head slightly from side to side the image moves in the *opposite* direction, hence a contrary movement of the image, when the ophthalmoscope is held some little distance away, is one of the diagnostic tests for myopia.

Direct Method.—Inasmuch as the emergent rays from a myopic eye are convergent, it is evident that such converging rays cannot be focused upon the retina of an emmetropic observer, and hence an erect image of the myopic fundus is impossible without the aid of a concave lens to lessen their convergence.

The rule then in simple myopia is to ascertain the weakest concave lens that will render the fundus clear and distinct as being the approximate measure of the defect. After a few trials it is easy to decide which concave lens, rotated into the sight hole of the instrument, will afford the clearest image.

The accuracy of this method (the direct method of the ophthalmoscope) presumes the corneæ of observer and patient to be in actual contact, but as that is impossible, the distance between them should be added to the focal length of the lens found as above.

For instance, by referring to the illustration (page 164) the rays are seen to cross ten inches from the myopic eye. Suppose the observer placed his eye one inch in front of it, then the position of the focus is nine inches back of his cornea, and therefore a — 4.50 D. lens in the aperture of the ophthalmoscope would render the rays parallel and allow them to be focused on his retina without any effort of accommodation. But as is evident from the illustration, this — 4.50 D. lens is more than the full measure of the defect; but by adding the distance between the eyes of patient and observer to the focal distance of the lens found as above, the result will be the exact measure of the myopia present in patient's eye (1 inch added to 9 inches = 10 inches focal distance, or a refractive power of — 4 D., it being understood that an increase of distance represents less optical defect).

The rule then is that the weakest concave lens that renders the details of the fundus clear and distinct will be the extent of the myopia. Suppose when the optometrist looks into an eye through the aperture of his ophthalmoscope everything about the fundus appears blurred and indistinct; a convex lens is then rotated into the sight hole, with the effect of making it worse; now the weakest concave lens is tried, and at once the fundus begins to look clearer; then another and another is used, until finally all the details of the eye-ground are brought out distinctly, and this lens will approximately represent the degree of the myopia. It should always be remembered that preference is to be given to weakest concave lens that renders the fundus distinct.

SELF-RELAXATION OF THE ACCOMMODATION

In attempting to determine the amount of myopia by the direct method of the ophthalmoscope, the accommodation of both observer and patient is supposed to be at rest, and upon this fact rests the accuracy of this method. Otherwise a condition of false myopia is temporarily produced by the involuntary use of the ciliary muscle in either examiner or patient, which would require a concave lens to enable the details of the fundus to be clearly seen. This is an error into which many beginners fall, thinking they have a case of myopia to deal with, because a concave lens brings out the blood-vessels and optic disk more sharply, whereas it may be emmetropic or even hypermetropia metamorphosed by the accommodation.

The patient's accommodation is encouraged to relax by the dark room, and bv requesting him to direct his eyes to a distance, without however attempting to fix the vision on any particular object. But it is not so easy for the optometrist to relax his power of accommodation, because he is inclined, naturally, to look at the fundus of the patient's eye as at a near point; whereas it should be viewed as if at infinite distance with a relaxed ciliary muscle.

The faculty of placing the ciliary muscle at rest is one that can be acquired by the optometrist, in the practice of which the following exercises have been recommended as facilitating that end.

1. The optometrist directs his eyes toward the ceiling, and while in that position holds above them a sheet of white paper upon which there is a black ink spot. When he notices that the spot appears double, the paper and the eyes are to be slowly lowered and the endeavor made to keep the gaze directed into distance and the accommodation at rest, in which

case the dot will continue to appear double, even when it is below the level of the eyes. It is comparatively easy to get the double vision when the spot is high up over the eyes, but the difficulty increases as the object is lowered to the level of or below the eyes.

2. The finger or a pencil should be held ten or twelve inches in front of the face, and as long as the gaze is kept at a distance and the accommodation remains quiescent, the object will appear double.

3. While reading a book or card of fine print, held quite close to the eyes, the optometrist attempts to look through and beyond the book or card, as it were, when the lack of accommodation will cause the letters to run together and become blurred. At the same time the convergence can be felt to lessen and the eyes to assume a parallel condition.

By a frequent repetition of these exercises, the optometrist can learn to bring an object close to the eyes without bringing into play his accommodation or convergence, and with the accommodation thus under his control, he is in a position to obtain the most accurate results in the estimation of the amount of myopia by the direct method of the ophthalmoscope, which, however, should always be verified by the subjective examination.

INDIRECT METHOD OF OPHTHALMOSCOPE

By the indirect method the eye is viewed at a distance of twelve to fifteen inches (usual reading distance) through a strong convex lens held at its focal distance from the patient's eye. An inverted image of the optic disk and blood-vessels is seen, which is sharper but smaller than by the direct method. In myopia this inverted image of the disk is smaller than in emmetropia, but increases in size as the strong convex lens is withdrawn from the patient's eye. While the indirect method gives a larger field and thus favors a more rapid examination of the whole fundus, yet for determining the refraction of an eye the direct method is much to be preferred, and besides it is not so difficult for the beginner to learn.

TEST WITH RETINOSCOPE

The essentials for the retinoscope test, with full instructions as to how it should be conducted, were described in the chapter on "Hypermetropia." When the shadow in the pupil moves in an opposite direction to the light on the face, the eye is known to be myopic (the plane mirror being used), and concave spherical lenses are placed in the trial frame until the weakest glass is found which reverses the movement of shadow and makes it travel in the same direction as the light on the face. This is the correcting lens at the distance at which the examination is conducted, to which must be added the lens representing that distance (— 1 D.).

Suppose, for example, the far point of the myopic eye is at ten inches, and if the eye was examined at a distance of twenty feet a concave lens of 4 D. would render the rays of light parallel and stop all retinal reflex. But as the examination is conducted at a distance of only one meter, or forty inches, a lens of — 3 D. will be sufficient to halt the reflex; and, therefore, in estimating the total amount of myopia, 1 D. must be added.

TESTS WITH INSTRUMENTS

Refractometer.—As the patient looks through this instrument at the test card, hanging fifteen or twenty feet away, any desired number of convex or concave lens can be placed before his eye by simply rotating a wheel on the side of the tube, which is marked in diopters and fractions thereof, and numbered in red and white to distinguish between convex and concave. The revolving dial is first placed at the zero mark, so that no focus whatever, either spherical or cylindrical, may be before the eye at the time the test is begun. The patient is asked to name the lowest letters which are visible on the card. In myopia he will be able to see only the largest letters, or in high degrees none at all. As a matter of precaution, the wheel is turned toward convex lenses, which at once throws a deeper blur over the card and letters. Then the rotation is made toward concaves, with the effect of brightening and clearing the card, and the degree of myopia is estimated by reading the graduation on the indicator after the focusing adjustment had been turned as far to the right as necessary to make the small letters clear and distinct, and then back a little, if possible, without casting a blur upon them. The most important point, and one to be kept constantly in mind when dealing with myopia, is to obtain the best vision with the instrument so adjusted that it registers the very smallest amount of defect, and to prescribe accordingly the weakest glass.

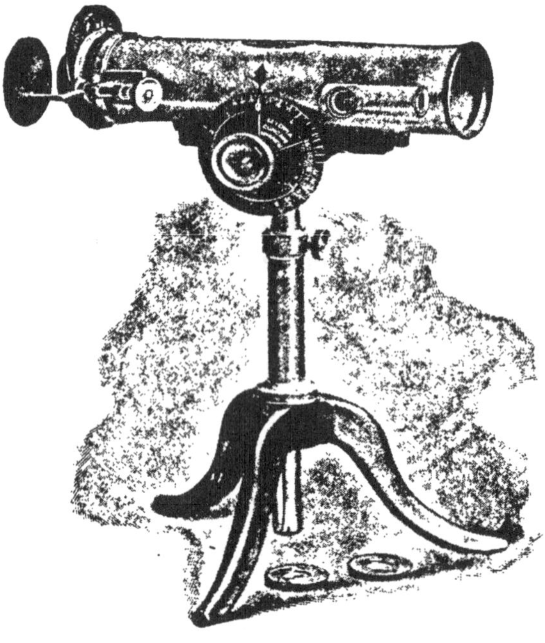

The Refractometer

Optometer.—This instrument consists of an adjustable stand supporting a horizontal rod, which has two movable slides for holding lenses, with a test card at the far end and an eye shield at the near end. To measure the amount of myopia, a concave lens of 8 D. is placed in the clip of the eye shield and a convex lens of the same strength placed in the slide and moved away from the eye. The patient looks at the small test card, and the point where the type appears brightest will indicate the proper correcting lens, as shown by the scale marked on the rod.

Prisoptometer.—This instrument contains a double prism, set in a large disk, which can be revolved from 0 to 180°, and which has the effect of doubling all objects which the patient looks at. The test object is a white circular disk hanging sixteen feet away, and if the person is emmetropic the two disks seen are just touching each other. If, however, there is an excess of refraction, as in myopia, the disks will overlap and then minus lenses must be placed in the holder of the instrument to separate them, and that lens which makes them merely in contact will be the measure of the myopia.

These three instruments are the ones in most common use for measuring the refraction of the eye. They are all based

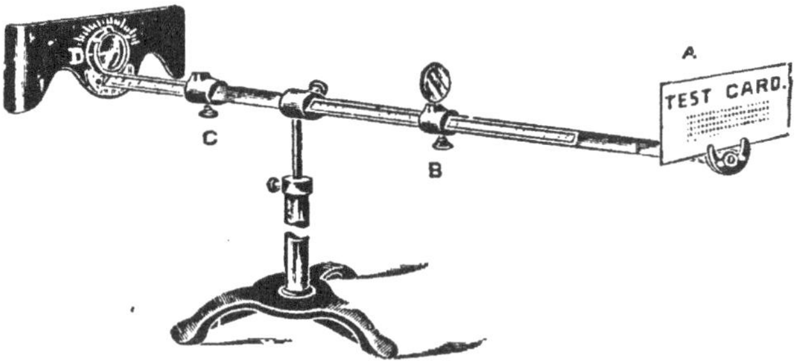

The Optometer

on scientific principles, but all act in a different way. Any one or all of them would prove valuable adjuncts to an optometrist's outfit, but they must always be considered as subordinate to the test case.

SCHEINER'S TEST

Two small perforations are made in a card close enough together so that rays passing through them will enter the pupil. The patient looks at a candle flame twenty feet away, which in emmetropia will appear single, because the two sets of rays passing through the two holes exactly meet upon the retina. In the elongated eye-ball of myopia the two sets of rays will have united and crossed before reaching the retina, and as these diverging sets of rays strike this membrane two images of the flame are formed. That concave lens placed behind the card which fuses the two images into one, will be the measure of the amount of myopia. In this defect the two images are homonymous in contrast with hypermetropia, where the images are crossed. In order to determine which form is present, a red glass should be placed in front of one perforation, and if the flame on the same side is red the diplopia is homonymous and the case one of myopia.

CHROMATIC TEST

This test depends upon chromatic aberration, or the unequal refraction of the different colored rays of which white light is composed. The red rays being the strongest, are turned least from their course, and the violet being the weakest, are deviated most. A cobalt lens is used for this test, because it suppresses all the intermediate colors and allows only the red and blue to pass. The blue rays being more strongly refracted, are brought to a sooner focus, and the red rays being least refracted to a later focus. In the myopic eye, where the retina is too far back, it approaches the position of the focus of red rays, whereas the blue rays have already met in focus and strike it in divergent rays. Hence when such an eye looks through such a lens at a lighted candle twenty feet away the flame will appear of a distinct red center with a blue border. This subject has been illustrated and explained in detail on pages 78, 79, 285, 286 and 287, of Volume I.

TREATMENT OF MYOPIA

As the one thing of which the myopic patient will chiefly complain is poor vision, so his single desire is to get glasses that will enable him to see well; consequently the treatment of myopia by the optometrist, and, indeed, the principal remedial measure, even in the hands of the physician, consists in the careful adaptation of the proper concave glasses for the correction of the anomaly. To afford good vision both for distance and reading, as well as to prevent unnecessary convergence, requires no little skill on the part of the optometrist. A myopic person should never be allowed to choose his own glasses, because he is apt to pick out those that are too strong and thus impose an extra tax upon his accommodation (which in this defect is weaker than normal), and this would tend to aggravate and increase the very defect which he is endeavoring to correct.

TREATMENT BY CONCAVE LENSES

The first step in the adjustment of glasses for the correction of myopia is to ascertain the acuteness of vision, as shown by the lowest line the patient can read on a Snellen's test card, hanging twenty feet away. One eye is to be tested at a time, and preferably the one that has the best vision, the other being covered with an opaque disk. If he can distinguish only the largest letter, the one that is marked 200, his visual acuteness equals 20/200. In high myopia even this large letter will not be legible, and then it becomes necessary to place the card at a closer distance or allow the patient to approach the card until the No. 200 letter becomes readable, and the distance at which it is first seen will represent the numerator of the fraction that is used to express the visual acuity. For instance, if he has to come as close as eight feet his vision would equal 8/200.

The patient is then asked to resume his seat at twenty feet from the card, and the test with concave lenses commences. The optometrist having satisfied himself that the case is one of myopia, places a weak concave lens before the eye and notices how much improvement in vision is afforded. Then a stronger and a stronger is tried, until that one is found that produces the greatest amount of vision, the preference invariably being given to the very weakest glass that accomplishes this result. It is always better in myopia to err on the side of giving a glass that is too weak than one too strong.

GLASSES IN LOW MYOPIA

In the low grades of myopia as 2 D. or 2.50 D. or less, the glasses are necessary only to enable the patient to get a distinct view of distant objects. At school, to discern the blackboard; at church, to see the preacher; at the theater, to view the actors; when outdoors, to behold the scenery, or any occasion when it is desirable to see distinctly farther away than arm's length; in a word, to comprehend the world and the beauties of nature and art as other people do; these are the purposes fulfilled by glasses in the slighter degrees of this defect. Of course, there are many persons, after having once experienced the satisfaction of perfect distant vision afforded by the concave glasses, who are unwilling to do without them and get into the habit of wearing them more or less constantly even indoors and for close work.

But in these slighter degrees of the defect the use of glasses is entirely unnecessary for close vision, and not only so, but they even impose a strain upon the accommodation, and hence should be removed when engaged in reading or writing. The reason for this is obvious: In these cases vision is perfectly good out to the far point, which is situated at eighteen or twenty inches from the eyes, sufficiently removed to allow of good vision in the customary close use of the eyes; such being the case, there is no need for glasses, and especially as instead of improving vision they tend to impair by diminishing the size of the retinal image and calling into action the ciliary muscle. Their persistent use under these circumstances would favor an increase in the error of refraction, or might even give rise to the progressive form of myopia, which is always a source of anxiety to both optometrist and patient.

GLASSES IN HIGH MYOPIA

While in the lower grades of myopia glasses may be regarded somewhat as a luxury, and their use a matter of indifference, in the higher degrees of the defect they become an actual necessity and cannot be safely dispensed with. In these cases they are needed not only to improve the distant vision, but also to increase the reading distance, and in addition they play an important part in harmonizing the accommodation and convergence and preventing an increase of the defect.

In the medium degrees of myopia (5 D. or less), where the patient is not old and the range of accommodation good, the full correction, as a general rule, may be allowed. But in the higher grades two pairs of glasses must be prescribed, because the glasses needed for the full correction are entirely too strong for close work and impose an unnecessary and unbearable tax upon the accommodation, and then the question naturally arises as to what is the proper strength of glass to adopt in each particular case?

Without glasses the myope is compelled to hold his book unnaturally close, which is not only very uncomfortable, but in addition proves a source of strain to the function of convergence. If he wears his full correction glasses, the lessening in the size of the retinal image by the strong concave lenses, and the impairments in the function of the retina due to the stretching which it has undergone, originate and encourage a desire to bring the object nearer to the eye in order to obtain a larger visual angle. In the first case, there is tension of accommodation and convergence, the greatest strain being on the latter; in the second case there is a similar tension of both functions, but now the greater strain is upon the former. Between two evils, the proper plan is to choose the least, but a still better method is to avoid both of them if possible. In this case it might be difficult to decide which was the greater evil of the two—the strain upon the accommodation or upon the convergence, but the way is open by which both in a measure can be avoided.

RULE FOR DETERMINING THE READING GLASSES IN MYOPIA

Instead of allowing the patient to read with his full correction glasses we select a pair which only partly neutralizes the error of refraction, or in other words those glasses which remove the far point to a convenient reading distance of twelve to fifteen inches. The rule may be expressed somewhat as follows: *Subtract from the glasses which are the full measure of the myopia those glasses the focus of which represents the distance at which the patient desires to read or work.*

As thirteen inches is regarded as a proper reading distance, and as a glass of + 3 D. represents a distance of thirteen inches, therefore it is customary to subtract about 3 D. from the full measure of the defect in order to arrive at the correct glasses for close use. In some cases it may be desirable to subtract a little more and in some cases a little less, depending on the age, the amount of available accommodation and the distance at which the patient desires to use the glasses. This point can readily be determined by the trial of several numbers slightly weaker and slightly stronger than those indicated by the above rule, and the choice being given to that one that affords the most satisfactory vision at the distance desired.

Finally, the glasses must be submitted to the test of actual experience, and the patient, after a few weeks' trial, will be able to say whether they are pleasant or unsatisfactory, whether the eyes are comfortable or whether symptoms of asthenopia have been provoked, and thus will be decided the question as to the suitableness of the glasses for continued wear or whether they should be changed for others of a different power. Sometimes no glasses can be found which render near vision entirely comfortable, and then it becomes necessary for the person to abandon all work or occupation requiring close use of the eyes.

In high myopia, if the person had not previously worn glasses it is inadvisable to prescribe the full correction at first, because such strong glasses are unpleasant and they are apt to disturb the relative association of accommodation and convergence. In these cases the better plan is to commence with weaker numbers and gradually increase their strength from time to time, as the eyes become accustomed to them, until finally the full correction can be worn for distance without producing unpleasant symptoms or injurious disturbances.

It is important that the patient, and still more so the optometrist, should have a clear idea of the purposes for which the reading glasses are prescribed in myopia. They are not intended so much to magnify the print or enable the person to see better (in fact, concave lenses necessarily minify objects seen through them) as to increase the distance at which reading can be accomplished to enable the person to read at the customary distance and thus relieve the strain upon the convergence. If the old habit of holding objects close to the eyes is still continued, then reading glasses are not only useless, but positively harmful. Hence the importance of impressing upon the patient the necessity of keeping the book as far away as the glasses will allow.

There can be no fixed rules by which glasses should be adjusted in every case, but each must be treated upon its own merits. Many myopes wear their full correction constantly, both for near and distance, without suffering any inconvenience and apparently without any injury to their eyes, while others can scarcely bear their correction for distance much less for reading.

While the writer was penning these lines a patient consulted him; thirty-five years of age and wearing — 6.50 D. glasses. Has worn these same glasses for twenty-three years, using them for all purposes, near and far, and without any difficulty. Recently has suffered from headache, which he attributes to an attack of la grippe, but his physician advised him to consult an oculist. On examination I was surprised to find a myopia of only 5 D. in R. E. and 4 D. in L. E. The remarkable point about this case is that his glasses should have been so comfortable for close work all these years, in spite of the fact that this defect was over-corrected (thus rendering his eyes really hypermetropic) and that he was approaching the time of life when a lessened accommodation would call for a weaker concave lens.

DONDERS' ADVICE

In discussing the importance of the proper selection of glasses in individual cases of myopia, Donders' remarks are so apropos that they are worthy of reproduction on these pages, and especially as everything issuing from the mouth or pen of this gifted man is universally accepted as gospel truth by all seekers after optical knowledge, alike by oculists and optometrists. He says: "The prescribing of spectacles for myopes is a matter of great importance. While emmetropic and hypermetropic eyes do not readily experience any injury from the use of unsuitable glasses, this may in myopes, particularly on account of the morbidly distended condition of the eye-ball and of the tendency to get worse, be very dangerous. There exists in general a dread of the use of too strong glasses. It is laid down as a rule: Rather too weak, or no glasses, than too strong. In this rule the necessary distinction is lost sight of. Too strong glasses make hypermetropic eyes myopic, and myopic eyes hypermetropic. The rule therefore cannot be equally true for both. In fact, it is in general much less injurious to produce a certain degree of myopia than of hypermetropia, in which last particularly much is required of the accommodative power. The rule would therefore be more correctly stated thus: In hypermetropia we must beware of giving too weak; in myopia of giving too strong glasses; a rule the second part of which we should especially insist upon But even by this little is gained. Not using glasses, or using too weak glasses, may also be injurious to myopes. All the circumstances must therefore be studied, which can exercise an influence on the choice of glasses. It is difficult to reduce these to definite rules."

A PERSONAL EXPERIENCE WITH CONCAVE GLASSES

M. Sarcy, a well-known French critic, had congenital myopia, and in later life became temporarily blind. In one eye he suffered a retinal detachment, and in the other a cataract. By means of an operation vision in the latter eye was restored and became better than ever. He relates an interesting bit of personal experience in the following words:

"I was born near-sighted; many physicians assert that persons are never born near-sighted, and only become so. Science may say what it pleases; I was born myopic. One day, prompted by a spirit of mischief, I got hold of the big silver spectacles which my father wore and clapped them on. Fifty years have passed since then, but the sensation I experienced is keen and thrilling to this day. I gave a cry of astonishment and joy. Up to that moment I had seen the leafy dome above me only as a thick green cloth, through which no ray of sunshine ever fell; now, oh wonder and delight! I saw that in this dome were many little brilliant chinks; that it was made of myriad separate and distinct leaves, through whose interstices the sunlight sifted, imparting to the greenery a thousand forms of light and shade. But what amazed me most, what enchanted me so that I cannot speak of it to this day without emotion, was that I saw suddenly, between the leaves and far, far away beyond them little glimpses of the bright, blue sky. I clapped my hands in ecstacy and was mad with astonishment and delight."

HOW MYOPIA DISTURBS THE NORMAL RELATION EXISTING BETWEEN ACCOMMODATION AND CONVERGENCE

The far point of a myope is always situated at a finite distance, and is determined by the degree of the defect. A myope of 4 D. has a far point of ten inches, and can see at that distance without any effort of accommodation, but he must converge four meter angles in order to maintain binocular vision. Now, in the case of an emmetropic eye the accommodation and convergence are used in equal proportion, and hence a distance of ten inches would call for 4 D. of accommodation and four meter angles of convergence.

Therefore in myopia the convergence is necessarily used in excess of the accommodation, a condition just the reverse of hypermetropia where the accommodation is used in excess of the convergence. Nature will allow to a certain extent the use of one function in excess of the other as a result of nerve education, but she inflicts a penalty for this as shown by the frequency of "eye-strain" under these conditions.

In myopia the fusion effort must be greater than in emmetropia, and the greater this effort the more the fatigue of the internal recti muscles; this fatigue leads to "insufficiency" of the muscles and thus matters are made worse. A myope requires more convergence of the visual lines because vision takes place so close to the eyes, and this is particularly difficult in this defect on account of the elongated shape of the eye-ball which impedes its movements. There may be no actual weakness of the internal recti muscles, but only apparently so on account of the excess of work they are called upon to perform.

DIVERGENT STRABISMUS

In the previous chapter it was shown that hypermetropia was the direct cause of a majority of the cases of convergent squint. And as myopia is a condition of the eye exactly the reverse of hypermetropia, it will be found that many of the cases of divergent squint occur in connection with near-sightedness. The accommodation is used but little, while the convergence must be excessive, which latter continues until the eyes have reached the maximum state of convergence, and then the energy and tone of the internal recti muscles soon become exhausted, and as it tires and gives way the eye turns outward. The power of accommodation still remains unimpaired, but the power of convergence is worn out, because the limit within which the two functions may vary has been overstepped.

As soon as the object is brought nearer than the extreme limit of convergence in binocular vision will permit, divergent strabismus necessarily takes place, and this may occur even if there be no actual insufficiency of the internal recti muscles, just as in hypermetropia there may be no actual weakness of the ciliary muscle; but simply that in each case the muscles have laid upon them work which is beyond their power to perform. While the convergent strabismus of hypermetropia usually makes its appearance in childhood, the divergent squint of myopia is rarely developed until a more advanced age, and is usually connected with the progressive form of the defect.

If the myopia develops slowly, the internal recti muscles may gradually increase in size and strength sufficiently to perform the excessive labor demanded of them, but usually there is a deficiency of power of one or both of these muscles to maintain the required convergence for any length of time, and especially if the progress of the myopia has been rapid. In such cases the internal recti muscles are too weak to resist the action of the external, and the eye rolls outward and double vision results. When once an insufficiency of the internal recti has manifested itself, the muscles do not readily regain their strength even after considerable periods of rest; they become less and less able to sustain prolonged action, until finally the insufficiency becomes so annoying that artificial assistance must be sought or binocular vision abandoned.

TREATMENT OF THE MUSCULAR INSUFFICIENCY ACCOMPANYING MYOPIA

Insufficiency of the internal recti muscles is usually found in cases of myopia ranging from 4 D. to 7 D., and when it occurs the advice is at once gratuitously offered by all the friends to rest the eyes, which the patient is inclined to adopt because it affords temporary relief. If these muscles are not strained, naturally they will cease to ache. But, as in the case of all other muscles, if they are not used they undergo loss of tone, and hence the more they are rested the less they will be able to work. Therefore the common prescription of rest is bad, unsound in principle and disastrous in practice. The writer has seen cases of this kind who could not use their eyes at all, where reading for only a minute brought on pain and lachrymation. Such persons being debarred from reading and almost every use of the eyes, have nothing to do but to dwell upon their own troubles, and they are constantly worried by the fear they will some day become blind.

The proper principle to adopt in the management of these cases is to train and strengthen the muscles by discreet use and by gymnastic exercises. The right lenses for reading are carefully chosen according to the directions already given, and then they must be accorded a patient trial to see how far or how long their use is practicable. By increasing the reading distance these glasses lessen the effort of convergence, which is thus made more nearly equal with the accommodation. If, however, this method fails to afford the desired relief it may become necessary to combine prisms.

In the slighter degrees of myopia, some authorities recommend that the glasses should be worn constantly, for the following reasons: In this way the eyes are practically made emmetropic; the accommodation is brought into action instead of allowing it to remain idle; there is no occasion to hold the book close, a habit which has much to do in the causation and aggravation of myopia. Priestley Smith says: "My present custom is to encourage rather than discourage, with proper limits, the use of the accommodation; in other words, to advise those who can to use the same glasses for reading and distance, and where this is impossible, by reason of weak accommodation, still to give reading glasses as strong as can be worn with comfort."

The full correction of the myopia restores the harmony between the functions of accommodation and convergence, a procedure which may be quite practical in young persons, but for this very reason in older patients it is not well borne. The habit of converging in excess of accommodation has become so fixed for so many years, that it cannot even by practice be easily relaxed, and under such circumstances if the wearing of the glasses be insisted upon, they may become a cause of eye strain instead of a means for its removal.

For such persons, if the myopia be less than 5 D., the wearing of glasses for distance will be all that is necessary. As a matter of fact there are many persons with a myopia of 3 D. or less, who never use glasses at all; they are not inconvenienced by the partial indistinctness of distant vision, which is scarcely marked enough to prevent the recognition of ordinary-sized objects, while their near work can be accomplished at the usual distance without any strain upon the eye.

THE OTHER SIDE OF THE QUESTION

Landolt's views are somewhat different from those given above. He hays: "A myope must be prohibited from wearing a concave glass for any distance at which he can see clearly without accommodation. Correcting glasses have a very serious disadvantage for the myope, because they force him to make an effort of accommodation from which his ametropia grants him dispensation, and they deprive him of another advantage, *i. e.*, of the larger size of the retinal images obtained by the naked eye, and which the glasses make smaller."

After all, each case must be managed on its own merits; on the one hand we must avoid an overtaxing of the accommodation by a too strong concave lens, and on the other hand we must prevent the strain of excessive convergence, because the stooping position of the head which accompanies it favors congestion and leads to increased intraocular pressure, and thus tends to the increase of the defect. With this in view, the concave glasses that lengthen the reading distance to twelve or fifteen inches, play an important part in relieving eye-strain and preventing increase of the myopia.

MUSCLE TESTS

In order to determine the relative or absolute weakness of the internal recti muscles, a trial should be made to see what strength of prism they are able to overcome. For this purpose the patient looks at a lighted candle placed at a distance of twentv feet. Then a weak prism is placed before one eye, base out, causing a momentary diplopia, which soon disappears. Now a similar prism is placed before the other eye, with a like result. This is repeated with increasing prisms until the double images of the candle flame can no longer be united into one by any muscular effort.

If it is found the muscles can thus overcome a pair of prisms of 12° each (making a total of 24°), they cannot be considered as deficient in strength, and the prismatic element will scarcely need to be added to the necessary concave lenses, the use of which alone may be all that is necessary to restore the normal relation between accommodation and convergence, and thus relieve all the eye symptoms. Such use of the eyes may be regarded as gymnastic exercise, to be stopped before it produces undue fatigue, and to be resumed at regular intervals. Sometimes there will be a good deal of pain at first, especially with nervous persons and those who have been trying the "rest" cure, but they must be encouraged to persevere notwithstanding.

If, however, the internal recti muscles cannot overcome the diplopia caused by a pair of prisms of 12°, bases out, they must then be regarded as absolutely weak, in which case it may become necessary to combine prisms in order to assist and strengthen them.

In cases of high myopia (that is, from 6 D. to 20 D.) the eyes are often saved the convergence effort at the expense of binocular vision; that is to say, the person uses only one eye for vision and the other squints outwardly. If such a condition has continued long enough to become a confirmed habit, it is scarcely worth while to attempt to correct it; in fact, it is an almost impossible task to restore binocular vision and cause the two eyes to work in harmony. In many of these cases it will be found on examination that one eye is used chiefly for reading and the other principally for distance, and to make the effort to disturb such an arrangement oftentimes does more harm than good, and here the optometrist must be content to give the proper glass to each eye for its own particular use.

In contrast with the 24° prism, which the eyes can overcome when placed base out, we find that not more than 6° or 8° can be borne when placed base in. This marked difference is owing to the fact that in the first case the internal recti muscles are brought into action, and in the second case the external, and that the former are so much stronger than the latter because they need to be used so much more.

When it comes to prisms being placed vertically, but very few persons can overcome more than 1° or 2°, because the superior and inferior recti muscles are relatively so much

weaker than either the internal or external recti. The nomenclature of, and the tests for, the various muscular anomalies have been described in the chapter on "Method of Examination," to which the reader is referred.

ABUSE OF THE EYES

The eye, like any other organ of the body, and in the same manner as any delicate instrument, may become the subject of abuse, the bad effects of which are most noticeable during its growing period. The coats of the eye-ball do not reach their full measure of firmness and power of resistance until adult age, about the twentieth year of life, the time when the rest of the body arrives at maturity.

Consequently before this age, and particularly between the ages of six and sixteen, during what may be called the school years, the eye is liable to injury from overwork. This results (as has been stated earlier in the chapter) in the production of myopia. After the twentieth year of life the eyes may be abused in many ways by overwork and insufficient or improper light without much danger of causing myopia. One-fourth of the same application of the eyes at the age of ten, with its coats and contents soft and yielding, would cause the posterior wall to give way and bulge and bring about the defect of myopia. Whereas when the eye is well hardened by full growth a much greater amount of eye application can be borne continuously without the fear of causing the walls of the eye to stretch and injuriously changing the shape of the organ. Hence the fact obtains that the danger of the production of myopia by abuse of the eyes is peculiar to youth and to its growing state.

We sometimes meet persons having a slight degree of myopia who are so little inconvenienced by it that they are not conscious of being near-sighted; in fact, consider their vision as up to the normal standard. The existence of the defect may be accidentally discovered by contrast with the sharper sight of some friend, or by casually trying on a pair of concave glasses which happened to be in their way, and which brightened up distant vision to such an extent as they never before believed possible.

Others may complain of their near-sightedness, calling attention only to the fact that they are compelled to hold their book very close, but never making mention of their inability to see distant objects.

CORRECTION OF MYOPIA

The correction of myopia is by means of concave lenses properly adapted, and the manner in which they act can be readily understood. It will be remembered that in this defect parallel rays of light meet in front of the retina; if now the focus can be thrown back just far enough to correspond exactly to the location of the retina, then, and only then, does clear distant vision become possible. This is accomplished by means of concave lenses, which spread the rays of light and cause them to enter the eye divergently, and then (the refractive power of the eye remaining the same) they will not meet in focus so soon as the parallel rays; this is equivalent to throwing the focus farther back, and if the concave lens corresponds with the degree of myopia the focus will be exactly upon the retinal surface.

PRACTICAL POINTS

In myopia, up to a certain degree, there is usually no disturbance of close vision, but when it exceeds 5 D. then there is apt to be some trouble in reading.

In the higher degrees there is no distinct vision beyond a few inches from the eyes, and consequently as such a myope cannot fix objects, his eyes assume a peculiar far-away look.

In the slighter degrees the only inconvenience suffered is a limitation of distant vision, so that if the person does not wish to wear glasses no very great harm is done, only the loss of pleasure of seeing the world quite as distinctly as other people see it. The reading limit is not interfered with, as the measure of the myopia (say 2 D.) indicates that the person is able to read as far away as twenty inches, and therefore in these cases there is no occasion to hold the book close, but it may be kept at the usual reading distance where there is no very great demand made upon either the accommodation or convergence. But it is just in this class of cases that the precaution should be taken to guard against any inclination to hold the book too close or to read by any kind of insufficient light on account of the imminent danger of increasing the myopia by these means.

Floating specks before the eyes, sparks, flashes of light, white or colored rings, are not uncommon in this defect, and they are apt to cause the patient a great deal of uneasiness; but they are not usually of any special pathological import.

BENJAMIN FRANKLIN, THE ORIGINAL BIFOCAL MAN

In myopia the effects of presbyopia are not felt at the usual time, perhaps not until the age of fifty-five or sixty; but when it does manifest itself, there is the double inconvenience of needing glasses for both distance and reading. This annoyance would be felt by clergymen, lecturers and others who might desire to look at the book in their hand one moment, and then to look at the audience, some of whom might be at a distance of fifty feet or more. This was the case of Benjamin Franklin, and as he was a very busy man and could not afford to waste so much time as might be required to constantly change his glasses if he wore separate pairs for reading and distance, he had made to his order a pair of spectacles which contained in the one frame both pairs of glasses, known as divided or double focus spectacles, and he was the first to wear this form of spectacles, which are so common at the present day.

The eyes should be examined at intervals, perhaps once a year, to determine the degree of myopia, so that if there is any tendency to an increase of the defect, it may be at once detected. Spectacles should be worn for distance, or for distance and reading, as may be indicated, with the proviso that the book be kept well away from the eyes, not allowing it to get any nearer than eighteen inches, except in aggravated cases where such a reading distance is impossible even with the most suitable lenses.

STRAIN ON THE ACCOMMODATION

When a near-sighted person is given a pair of concave lenses of sufficient strength to completely correct his defect, the eyes are thereby rendered emmetropic, and when reading is attempted with these glasses the accommodation is called upon for the same amount of effort as in a normal eye. But as has already been stated the accommodation in myopic eyes is always feeble, the more so the higher the degree of defect. and hence it is not equal to the task; so that to ask such a person to read through concave glasses of full correction is to expect an impossibility; or else it is accomplished at the expense of a great strain upon the accommodation, which is lessened if the book be held at an inconveniently great distance from the eyes.

There is one thing about concave glasses of which patients frequently complain, and that is they make everything seem smaller. This is partly real and partly comparative. Concave lenses have the property of making objects smaller just as convex lenses magnify them. But besides this, to the uncorrected myopic eye on account of its increased refractive power objects appear larger than they really are and their outlines imperfect; concave lenses concentrate the sight, make the outlines of objects distinct, and in contrast with the former vision, smaller.

SURGICAL TREATMENT OF MYOPIA

This chapter would be incomplete without some reference to the surgical treatment of myopia; that is, the removal of the crystalline lens for the purpose of reducing the excessive refraction. It cannot be denied that in theory this method of treatment is most excellent, and forms an ideal way of neutralizing the defect. While it is sound in theory and feasible in practice, and attractive to the ophthalmic surgeon who is making a brilliant reputation by skillful operations, yet when it is considered entirely from the patient's standpoint it will scarcely become a popular procedure.

Unlike a strabismus operation, which does not open the cavity of the eye-ball, the removal of the crystalline lens is a most serious matter and violently disturbs the normal condition of the organ of vision. The parts most affected are the ciliary region and adjoining portions, a region which is particularly liable to inflammatory reaction after injury or operation. This is shown in the history of cataract operations, where an occasional eye will go wrong without any apparent cause and in spite of every precaution being taken to avoid such a calamity.

A case of myopia and one of cataract have no points in common. The latter has practically lost his sight and there is only one means by which it can be restored, and hence while he has everything to gain by an operation, he has nothing to lose in case it is unsuccessful, as he is a blind man in either case. In myopia, on the other hand, even in the highest degrees of defect, a fair amount of vision is always obtainable by means of properly adjusted glasses, which might be entirely lost by the failure of the operation. Besides, there is some risk that the operation might give rise to detachment of the retina, and the possibility of such a disastrous sequence might well make the boldest surgeon hesitate.

Many hundreds of cases of removal of a normal crystalline lens for the relief of high myopia have been reported in

Europe, particularly in Germany. But so far this country has furnished very few such cases, and in view of the readiness of our surgeons to take up new operations, this certainly speaks well for their conservatism. Perhaps an additional reason may be found in the fact that we have given more attention to the correction of extreme myopia by lenses than is the case abroad.

The writer neither commends nor condemns this operation, nor do we think our readers should ever assume the responsibility of advising for or against it, but such grave cases should rather be referred to the ophthalmic surgeon for advice and such treatment as he may deem necessary. At the same time we feel the optometrist should be kept advised of the latest knowledge on this subject and of the optical principles involved.

DEGREE OF MYOPIA CALLING FOR OPERATION

The first thought that arises in the consideration of this subject is as to the amount of myopia that would suggest the advisability of removing the crystalline lens. Some operators would place the limit at 10 D., others at 14 D., while still others would extend it to 16 D. Of course the higher the degree the greater might be considered the need for the operation. It seems reasonable to place the lower limit at about 14 D., because the reduction in the amount of myopia by the extraction of the lens, while it varies in different eyes, will scarcely be less than 14 D. and may extend to 20 D. Therefore, in a case of 10 D. the removal of the crystalline lens would leave the patient markedly hypermetropic, so that there would scarcely be any advantage in its removal, unless possibly in the hope of preventing an increase in the defect, if the same seemed imminent. But it is an error to suppose that every case of myopia of 8 D. or 10 D. is progressive, or that there is danger of approaching blindness.

THE REFRACTION OF APHAKIAL EYES

This leads to a consideration of the changes brought about in the refraction of an eye by the loss of its crystalline lens, concerning which there has been much misunderstanding and many misstatements in the current literature of the subject. In the ordinary cases of aphakia after cataract operation, the previously emmetropic eye calls for a lens of about + 10 D., from which it might be inferred that the extraction of the crystalline lens in myopia would lessen the defect by about 10 D. But a clear understanding of the optical principles involved shows that it does more than this, which is also corroborated by experience.

A + 10 D. cataract lens, placed as it usually is, about half-inch in front of the eye, would be equal to about 16 D. of refractive power of a crystalline lens in its place. This fact is in accord with the principles of optics, and partly accounts for the wonderful refractive changes which aphakia produces in high degrees of myopia. But the arguments in favor of this operation rest not alone upon a neutralization of the myopia or a reduction in the strength of the concave lenses, but also upon the probability of checking an increasing myopia and the retino-choroiditis that accompanies it. In this direction the operation promises much, not in the positive improvement of every eye any more than every cataract operation can be guaranteed to be successful, but a satisfactory result in a fairly good proportion of cases.

AGE FOR OPERATION

When the operation is performed on cases between the ages of ten and twenty-five years the best results are attained. Under ten years of age it is rare to find myopia sufficiently high to justify an operation, while in those older than twenty-five the myopia has ceased to progress, or else the changes at the fundus are such as to contra-indicate an operation. This latter is really an important factor; a very careful ophthalmoscopic examination must be made to determine the amount of retinal and choroidal change, on which will depend the benefit that can be expected and by which the surgeon will be guided in arriving at a conclusion as to the advisability of the procedure. The limit of age has been placed as high as fifty years, but the fact is that patients past thirty years of age will rarely submit to an operation, because they have become accustomed to their condition and their vision does not grow any worse.

SHOULD BOTH EYES BE OPERATED ON?

This is a question about which there is a good deal of difference of opinion. The truth is that if one eye was fairly good the operation would be scarcely justifiable, and it would only be resorted to in case both eyes were equally bad, in which case it would seem as if the binocular operation was proper.

DONDERS' WORDS

In this connection it is interesting to read the words of Donders, uttered many years ago. He says, "When in a case of highly myopic structure of an eye, a lens affected with cataract has been successfully extracted and a nearly emmetropic condition has been obtained, the operator has been exposed to the temptation of endeavoring, by the abstraction of a normal lens, to remove the myopia. A patient who was an amateur in dioptrics endeavored to induce me to perform this operation.

"But I need not say that such a momentous undertaking, doubly dangerous where a myopic and a transparent lens are concerned, without that, even in the most favorable cases, any real advantage is to be expected, would exhibit culpable rashness. Not only would the staphyloma posticum continue equally threatening, but we should also have sacrificed the accommodation—an advantage which that of somewhat larger images than would be obtainable by neutralizing glasses, could by no means counterbalance."

RESULTS OF THE OPERATION

The amount of vision to be obtained by an operation will depend upon the fundus changes, modified by the surgeon's skill in performing his work. Cases have been reported where it was impossible by any glasses to raise the vision to 20/200, or in other words to enable the patient to see even the largest letter on the test card at a distance of twenty feet, where a vision of 20/30 was secured after the extraction of the crystalline lens. This is certainly a remarkable result, which cannot be accounted for by a simple reduction in the amount of myopia; but there are in addition three factors that enter into the question:

First, the size of the retinal image is increased. This varies with the amount of ametropia remaining after the operation, it being one and a half times larger when the aphakial condition is emmetropic.

Second, the retinal illumination is greater. In a highly myopic eye the strong concave lens that is required diverges or scatters the rays of light, and hence fewer of them can enter the eye than in emmetropic aphakia, where the rays would be nearly parallel.

Third, the dispersion of light is less. If a case of corrected myopia is compared with a case of emmetropic aphakia, it will be seen that there are at least five refracting surfaces in the former condition, as against one in the latter, or against three in a case of aphakia that requires glasses; with the advantage in the latter case that the glasses required would be much weaker than the strong concave lenses used before the operation, and therefore there is less reflection and less aberration.

THE LOSS OF ACCOMMODATION AFTER OPERATION

One of the points used against the advisability of the operation under consideration is that the increased acuteness of vision is nullified by the loss of accommodation, but a close consideration of this argument robs it of some of its strength. After the usual cataract extraction the glasses required for distance and reading may range from + 10 D. to + 20 D. Such strong glasses focus the rays of light upon the retina at a very acute angle, and hence a slight displacement of the object quickly throws the retinal image out of focus. On the other hand, in the elongated eye of myopic aphakia the rays reach the retina at a greatly reduced angle, which admits of considerable variation in the position of the object viewed without throwing it much out of focus.

Besides, even if lenses are required in myopic aphakia, they are of such low refractive power that they can be made up as bifocals, and if accurately prescribed and carefully adjusted, will prove of great convenience and secure for the patient the brightest degree of vision which surgical skill has rendered possible.

OPACITIES OF THE CORNEA

Opacities of the cornea, which have resulted from some preceding inflammation, may seriously impair the vision, and yet escape notice on a casual examination. Inasmuch as a clouded cornea lessens the visual acuteness and causes the patient to hold his book close to his eyes, thus simulating myopia, the optometrist who fits glasses for the correction of this defect should be on his guard, and must be able to exclude a defective cornea as a cause of the impaired vision. The transparency of the cornea is best determined by oblique illumination by a convex lens, as described and illustrated in the chapter on "Method of Examination." It would be rather embarrassing for the optometrist, after putting the patient through a tedious and fruitless examination with the trial case, to learn that the so-called myopia was due to scars on the cornea, and hence could not be remedied by glasses.

CAUTION IN PRESCRIBING CONCAVE LENSES FOR YOUNG PEOPLE

In the early part of the chapter reference was made to apparent or accommodative or false myopia, and the necessity for its recognition in order to avoid falling into the danger of giving concave glasses when myopia was not really present. Such a condition results from spasm of the accommodation, and is most apt to occur in youth; therefore, it is not always proper and safe to give concave glasses to all young persons indiscriminately, simply because their vision was improved by them. This is a truth that is universally recognized, as is evidenced by the following question taken from those given at the written examination for the diploma of the Worshipful Company of Spectacle Makers of England, November 1, 1898.

"Question No. 9.—A boy aged twelve has vision = 6/9, but with a concave lens of 1.25 D. he has vision 6/6. What tests would you employ to ascertain the nature of his defect?"

The answer, as prepared by the examiners in charge, is: "It is very unlikely that this is true myopia. I should test for astigmatism in the usual way, and also for hyperopia, by taking the place of the near point, and by these means ascertain the real nature of the defect. It is almost certainly astigmatism, either myopic, or perhaps hyperopic."

The serious condition of an eye affected with high myopia and the responsibility involved in prescribing glasses in such cases is emphasized by the following question taken from the same examination:

"Question No. 11.—A youth aged twelve sees best with — 14 D. Would you give him this correction on your own responsibility? And if not, state your reasons."

The answer prepared was: "On my own responsibility I would not give glasses in this case. I should look upon it as a diseased condition, and as one that is likely to increase seriously unless proper medical treatment be obtained."

VALUE OF CONCAVE GLASSES

Roosa says: "Gustavus Adolphus was near-sighted and it is said that he lost his life at the battle of Lutzen because he had no correcting lenses and got among the soldiers of the enemy, thinking them to be his own." One of the most successful Union generals of the late war, more fortunate than the great Swedish commander, was wise enough to recognize the fact that he was astigmatic and ordered a pair of cylindrical glasses to be ground for himself, with which he said he was enabled to be a much better soldier than without them.

Yet a great many people—and by no means are they always unintelligent and uneducated—prefer to see as they have always done, "in a beautiful haze," as one lady once described her short-sighted vision to me, than to be startled by seeing distant objects with distinctness. But there are myopic persons who appreciate the delight of seeing well. One of my New York patients, a full-grown woman, after her eyes had been fitted with a pair of concave cylindrics, with which she probably saw clearly at a distance for the first time in her life, told me that after passing down Broadway she turned and walked up, because, to use her graphic language, "I never had seen the street before, although I was born very near it."

"It has been said that the Jews have more myopia than other people. There seems to be no valid ground for this assumption other than can be found in the fact that Jewish vocations the world over are usually those of shop-keepers, money-changers, etc., which necessitates close application to books and textures. In countries where the great mass of the inhabitants turn to open-air employments, and the Jew, naturally, gravitates toward commercial life, no surprise need be experienced if an examination of scholars shows a wide discrepancy in the development of myopia. Proof, however, fails to demonstrate the same variance where Jew and Christian are reared alike, and where inherited tendencies from one generation to another can be estimated upon a basis of similarity."

A CASE OF HIGH MYOPIA

Mrs. E. S.——. Aged thirty years. Complains that eyes pain her and she is compelled to hold everything so very close to her eyes in order to see. Has always been near-sighted, but never wore glasses. She is not able to see the test card across the room, much less any letters on it. — 18 D. lenses gave her the best vision, with which, however, she could read only the No. 70 line, and there was no other glass that enabled her to read any lower. But although an emmetrope would consider this very poor sight, yet it is so very, very much better than she has been able to see at any time in her life, that she thinks the glasses are splendid. According to the rule given in this chapter, we would deduct about 3 D. for the reading glasses, but a trial shows that — 14 D. gives her the best vision for close work. Hence — 18 D. was ordered for general wear and distant vision and — 14 D. for close use. Six weeks later her husband reported glasses as very satisfactory and couldn't do without them.

There are two conclusions that can be pretty certainly drawn from this case, and the first is that if she had commenced to wear glasses in youth, as she should have done, a much weaker glass would have sufficed, and the defect would not have increased to such a serious degree. The second is that the failure of the present glasses to raise the visual acuteness to normal is due to a partial amblyopia, or a blunted sensibility of the retina, which in turn was caused by the circles of diffusion which have been formed on this membrane for the past thirty years. Rays of light did not focus upon the retina naturally, nor were they made to do so artificially, and hence a focal point was unknown upon this membrane and clear vision had never been experienced, and as a consequence its impressibility was markedly lessened.

MYOPIA IN RELATION TO EYE-STRAIN

There is no power an eye possesses that will overcome myopia or improve the defect in vision except by compressing the eye-ball slightly in squinting or half closing the lids; hence myopic persons are not subject to the muscular strain which hypermetropes constantly and unconsciously exert in order to be able to enjoy clear vision. As soon as the latter opens his lids the accommodation instinctively contracts, to prevent the diffusion circles that would otherwise be formed upon the retina; whereas in myopia these circles cannot be dissipated by any amount of muscular effort, a tension of the accommodation only serving to make them more pronounced.

Besides, a myopic eye can read and perform all the functions required of it, when book or paper is held sufficiently close to the eyes, with less accommodative effort than in a normal eye. In contrast with which the hypermetropic eye is called upon to exert an unnatural effort of accommodation even for distant vision, which is much intensified when engaged in close work; hence the fatigue, the blurring of letters upon a printed page, the watering of eyes, the pain in head and eyes, and the many other ills that have been described in the previous chapter.

Myopes can scarcely help being aware of some defect in their vision, because of their inability to see across the room distinctly or to recognize friends on the street. Thus they naturally gravitate to occupations where the work is brought close to the eyes, because they have no difficulty in seeing near objects. Near-sighted children are liable to be considered precocious beyond their years, because they prefer to read rather than to play out-of-doors. It is generally safe to conclude that a child is near-sighted when it avoids the usual games of childhood in order to gratify a taste for reading and indoor amusements.

Myopia is less liable to cause nervous disturbances, except it leads to muscular insufficiency and asthenopia. And yet the number of myopes applying for relief is not small, because the defect of vision is so apparent and cannot be concealed by an effort of the eye, as in hypermetropia.

The writer can speak of myopia from a personal standpoint. When a student in the medical department of the University of Pennsylvania his eyes were examined under atropine by Dr. Risley at the commencement of the course, twenty-six years ago, and were found slightly hypermetropic and weak convex glasses prescribed. The excessive demands upon the eyes in pursuing the prescribed studies resulted in asthenopia and a continued trouble with eyes all through the course, until at graduation in 1878 a myopia of 2 D. was found to be present, and Dr. Risley considered the case of sufficient interest and importance to make and publish a report of it, as illustrating the production of myopia. At that time this subject was being generally discussed, and examinations of school children were being made on a large scale in this country and abroad in order to determine the exact relation between school life and study, and the causation of near-sightedness; and the writer's case formed an apt illustration, and was one among many which proved the dire effects of excessive application in causing an elongation of eye-ball.

CHAPTER XIII.

ASTIGMATISM

This subject has always been a bugbear and stumbling-block to the average optician. The word conveys to his mind the idea of some complicated defect shrouded in great mystery, difficult or impossible of explanation and comprehension, refusing to be discovered or corrected except by the expert touch of the oculist, and therefore the jeweler-optician concludes it is beyond his reach. While it must be admitted that this defect is more complicated and difficult of study than those which have so far been described, yet the same laws and principles are applicable in both cases, and a close study will rob the subject of much of its mystery and make it plain and easily understood, so that we feel like assuring the student that its difficulties lie rather on the surface and in the imagination.

At the same time we would add that the detection and correction of astigmatism will be a severe test of the optometrist's knowledge and understanding of the subject, as well as of his patience and forbearance. But experience is the great teacher and assistant in refraction work, as in many other things, and in connection with a proper knowledge of the defect, soon enables the educated optometrist to accurately adjust the necessary combination of glasses for its correction.

HISTORY OF ASTIGMATISM

The discovery of this defect dates back a hundred years and more, the credit for which is unanimously given to Thomas Young, but the exact date is somewhat a matter of dispute, some authors placing it at 1793, others at 1800, and still others at 1801. His own description of his case is as follows: "His eye in the state of relaxation collected to a focus on the retina those rays which diverge vertically from an object at the distance of ten inches from the cornea, and the rays which diverge horizontally from an object at seven inches distance." This would indicate a case of compound myopic astigmatism, the refraction of the vertical meridian being — 4 D. and of the horizontal meridian — 5.50 D. It is recorded that the astigmatism in this case was *lental,* that it was due to an irregularity in the curvature of the crystalline lens, and that while Young stated his observations and described the condition of his sight, he does not seem to have discovered or had the means at hand for its correction.

The next case reported appears to have been in 1827, when a Mr. Airy published an account of a similar condition in his own eye, in which the farthest point of distinct vision for vertical rays was three and one-half inches and for horizontal ones six inches, showing an astigmatism of 4.50 D. engrafted on a myopia of 6.50 D., which is a very considerable degree of defect and markedly impairs the acuteness of vision. This observer proved that his cornea was not a perfect surface of revolution, but that the curvature was greater in the vertical meridian than in the horizontal, and that both meridians were more convex than normal. This gentleman is given the credit for being the first to apply cylindrical lenses for the correction of astigmatism.

Although the history of this defect dates back a whole century, it was not understood, nor did its correction become common until within the past thirty-five years, until after Donders had completed his investigations and published his views on the nature and causes of astigmatism. This was in 1862, and the statement is made that up to that date only eleven cases of astigmatism had been recorded, the strict correctness of which we are inclined to question.

At any rate the credit for the preparation of the first charts for the detection and correction of astigmatism is given to a certain Colonel Goulier, professor of topography at the Military School of Metz, who noticed the frequency of the defect among the soldiers under his command. He ordered cylindrical glasses to be made for them and reported the result of his observations to the Academy of Sciences in 1852. This was about the time that Donders was pursuing his investigations, of which Goulier seems to have known nothing. A facsimile is given of the diagram which the latter used in the measurement of astigmatism, the value of which is enhanced by the lines which he wrote upon it when placing it in the hands of the illustrious Javal.

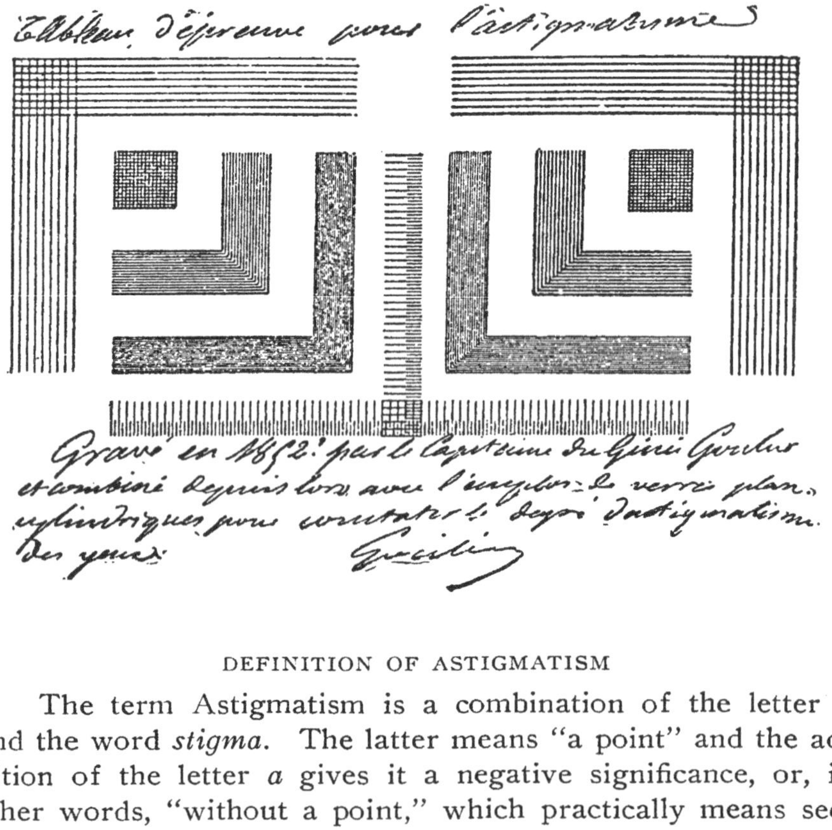

DEFINITION OF ASTIGMATISM

The term Astigmatism is a combination of the letter *a* and the word *stigma*. The latter means "a point" and the addition of the letter *a* gives it a negative significance, or, in other words, "without a point," which practically means seeing in line. In a symmetrical eye the rays of light are brought to a focus in a point from the union of the rays from a given point of the object, the visibility of which depends upon the impressions of these points being carried to the brain. A number of these points causes an accurate reproduction of the object. In astigmatic vision the rays of light proceeding from the points of an object cannot be reunited in points, but instead, are extended in the form of lines, causing blurred vision. The points are distorted by being spread out. A series of such distorted points adjacent to each other gives the impression of a blurred line.

Every point of light throws out diverging rays in the form of a cone, which, by the action of the refracting media of the eye, are again united in a point. Thus we have a divergent cone and a convergent one with their bases together, when the eye is symmetrical and emmetropic. In asymmetry of the eye, on the other hand, when there is a difference in the curvature of the several meridians, the second or convergent cone will be altered in shape and will no longer form a simple point, but an extended one or a blurred line. This makes the difference between the image formed in a normal eye and one affected with astigmatism, which will be more fully described and illustrated later on.

De Schweinitz defines astigmatism as follows: "The term Astigmatism is applied to that refractive condition of the eye in which a luminous point, for example, a star, forms an image on the retina, the shape of which image is a line, an oval or a circle, according to the situation of the retina, but never a point."

SEAT OF ASTIGMATISM

Usually the seat of astigmatism is located in the cornea, which then differs from the normal in that it is no longer spherical in shape, but the curvature of one meridian is greater or less than another at right angles to it. The emmetropic cornea is assumed to be a surface of revolution about the visual axis; but this is not strictly exact, as the use of a keratoscopic disk shows it to have an ovoid configuration, the radius of curvature being less at the center than towards the periphery.

THE KERATOSCOPE

The simplest and quickest way of determining the curvatures of the cornea is by the use of the method devised by Placido, who advised a disk of cardboard or metal about nine inches in diameter, with a central aperture of one-quarter of an inch, to which is attached a handle of suitable size. On one surface of the disk is painted a series of concentric circles, alternately black and white. Out of compliment to its inventor this keratoscope is known as *Placido's Disk.*

In the use of this instrument the patient is placed with his back to the window where a good light is entering room,

and the optometrist facing him with the keratoscope in his hand reflects the light from the window into the eye under examination, when the images of the circles can be seen upon the cornea by looking through the central aperture, which is usually supplied with a convex lens of 4 D. refractive power.

If the curvatures of the cornea are normal the reflected rings will be perfectly circular and of regular shape; but if astigmatism be present; that is, if the curvature of the cornea be greater in one meridian than another, the rings will appear of oval shape, with the longest diameter in the meridian having the longest radius. If the cornea be the seat of irregular astigmatism, the rings will appear very much distorted and out of shape, and portions of them will even be entirely invisible.

While we cannot recommend the keratoscope as an instrument of precision in the detection and correction of astigmatism, because it does not definitely locate the impaired meridian, nor does it indicate the degree of defect, yet it forms an interesting method of examination and affords instant information of any departure of the cornea from its normal curves.

But astigmatism may also be located in any other of the refractive media, especially the crystalline lens, and this naturally leads to the division of astigmatism into *corneal* and *lental*, the total being the sum of the two.

The horizontal meridian of the cornea is normally a little flatter than the vertical on account of the pressure exerted in this direction by the closure of the eye-lids, which affect slightly the former meridian, while the latter is free from any such pressure.

This will explain the significance of the terms "astigmatism according to (or with) the rule" and "astigmatism contrary to (or against) the rule." In the first case the vertical meridian has the sharper curvature, which condition would be corrected by a + cyl. axis 90°, or a — cyl. axis 180°. In the second condition the excess of curvature is in the horizontal meridian, and then the correcting cylinder must be placed axis at 180° if convex, and axis at 90° if concave.

REGULAR AND IRREGULAR ASTIGMATISM

When the meridians of the cornea progress evenly in their refraction from the lowest to the highest, or, in other words, when the meridians of least and greatest curvature are just at right angles to each other, the astigmatism is termed *regular*. But when the curvature varies in different parts of the same meridian and the meridians vary irregularly in their curvature, as the result of cicatrices from ulcers or distention of the cornea from inflammation, it is known as *irregular* astigmatism.

Almost all eyes are said to possess more or less irregular astigmatism, the seat of the defect in these cases being located in the crystalline lens. It is only slight, giving rise to no inconvenience, but it tends to cause stars, street lamps, etc., to shoot out rays and twinkle. The crystalline lens of young people is made up of several sectors, which may present different degrees of density, and the union of which is visible by three faint lines, this appearance giving rise to the name of "the lens-star."

When irregular astigmatism is spoken of, reference is usually had to that form where, as the result of disease, the corneal surface is irregular in certain parts; as, for instance, in the healing process of ulceration, where the outer surface of the cornea presents small facets, which will materially interfere with the refraction of the rays of light that enter the eye in that meridian. It is also found in conical cornea and in that condition of the crystalline lens in which there is a marked difference in the refraction of its various sections.

IRREGULAR ASTIGMATISM BEYOND OPTICAL ASSISTANCE

The condition of vision resulting from irregular astigmatism is very annoying to the individual, because nothing appears clear, but objects are seen blurred, distorted and irregular in all their parts. The means at our command for its relief are very limited, because it is obvious that such a condition is not correctible by the usual forms of lenses. The only possible method of improving vision is to cut off all the peripheral rays and allow the light to pass only through a small portion of the cornea, where the curvature is most even and the transparency greatest, thus presenting the most regular refraction and affording the best vision. This can be accomplished by means of an opaque diaphragm, with a small opening about 1 or 2 mm. in diameter, placed in that position before the cornea that has been found to be the most favorable.

Although by this means the larger portion of the rays of light proceeding from an object are shot off and the illumination correspondingly lessened, there is at least gained a perfect focus for those few rays which are allowed to pass through the hole and enter the eye at the most suitable portion of the cornea. The disk must be placed as close to the eye as possible, because the farther it is removed the smaller will be the field of vision.

Those who have had the most experience with these cases bear testimony to the great benefit that is often derived from even approximately correcting irregular astigmatism, which may be done by careful testing, assisted by the use of the ophthalmometer. It is surprising how much the sight of some of these individuals can be improved by the methods mentioned above. Valk records a case in his practice of a patient who was almost blind and unable to perceive any object clearly, and yet with a small aperture in a diaphragm of metal could readily discern the figures on the face of a small watch. Therefore, the importance of the correction of these forms of astigmatism, even if it cannot be done with any great degree of precision, cannot be over-estimated.

If one meridian of the cornea can be found that presents a regular curvature, the application of a cylindrical lens is a comparatively simple matter and raises the acuteness of vision very considerably. Sometimes a great improvement of vision can be secured by the operation of iridectomy (removal of a piece of the iris) which displaces the pupil towards a more regular portion of the cornea.

NORMAL AND ABNORMAL IRREGULAR ASTIGMATISM

Irregular astigmatism may be divided into two classes: the *normal* or physiological, and the *abnormal* or pathological.

The former, as has already been pointed out, is due to irregularities in the structure and density of different portions of the crystalline lens, and in spite of the accommodation is responsible for an imperfect coincidence of the rays of light that traverse its different sectors. Besides, there may be also astigmatism of each sector in itself. It is obvious that this form of astigmatism is not found in those eyes in which the crystalline lens has been removed. One of the chief symptoms of this form of irregular astigmatism is polyopia (multiple vision), without, however, any impairment of the acuteness of vision; when this occurs, the case must then be classed under the head of abnormal irregular astigmatism.

Abnormal irregular astigmatism, having its seat in the curvature of the cornea, has already been mentioned.

THE OPHTHALMOSCOPE IN IRREGULAR ASTIGMATISM

One of the best methods for the detection of the last-mentioned form is by the use of the ophthalmoscope. The eye is illuminated with the instrument at a distance of ten or twelve inches, when it will be noticed that the reflex from the fundus is not clear in all its parts, but that certain portions of it will be cut off and appear as dark spots on the cornea. The cause of which is that the return rays of light, as they are reflected from the retina, are refracted in such a direction that they cannot enter the eye of the observer. Conical cornea by this method will present dark rings inside the periphery of the cornea, changing their position and shape as the light is moved to one side or the other.

When the ophthalmoscope is approached close to the eye, as in the direct method, in order to examine the condition of the fundus, although the eye can be illuminated, the blood-vessels and optic disk will appear distorted and indistinct in certain parts.

RETINOSCOPY IN IRREGULAR ASTIGMATISM

The pupil should be well dilated, when it will be found that the refraction of the eye varies in different portions, as shown by direct and reversed movements of the shadow being visible at the same time in the same pupil. The center of the pupil is the place of most interest, and usually the area immediately surrounding it has the same refraction; if it is possible to gain any definite results, this is the part to which attention should be given, as the refraction in the peripheral portions of the pupil is of less practical importance.

In cases like the above, the eye is said to present *aberration*, which is called *positive* when the center of the pupil has less curvature than the portion immediately surrounding it, and *negative* when the opposite condition prevails.

As irregular astigmatism is beyond the reach of optical assistance, and therefore outside the province of the optometrist, it will not receive any further consideration, and the balance of the chapter will have reference to the defect as it exists in a *regular* form, which may be defined as that condition in which the refraction varies in different meridians of the eye at right angles to each other, but each meridian possessing the same curvature throughout its extent.

THE OPTICS OF ASTIGMATISM

The difference in the curvature of the two principal meridians as found in astigmatism, has been illustrated by comparing it with the bowl of a spoon, where the curvature is sharper and more pronounced crosswise than lengthwise, and the convex surface of which affords a very good idea of the shape of an astigmatic cornea.

It should be remarked in passing that in astigmatism we study the curvature and refraction of only two meridians, and that these are called the *principal meridians* and are always located at right angles to each other. The intermediate meridians having no focal points, can be ignored and left out of the calculation.

When the two chief meridians are measured, the whole refracting surface of the eye is calculated for. This may be illustrated and perhaps be better understood by those just commencing the study of these subjects, by referring to the fact that when two cylinders of the same curvature are placed together with their axes at right angles, the resulting lens is a sphere of the same number as each of the cylinders. For instance, when a + 1 cyl. axis 90° is placed over a + 1 cyl. axis 180° the optical equivalent of the combination is a + 1 spherical.

In considering the two principal meridians in regular astigmatism it is found that the cornea presents one meridian with the shortest radius of curvature causing the greatest refraction, and another meridian at right angles to it with the longest radius of curvature producing the least refraction. These meridians may be situated at any angle on the cornea, but the natural tendency is for the meridian of greatest curvature to lie in or near a vertical position, and for the meridian of least refraction to be located in a horizontal direction.

In order to simplify the study of the two principal meridians in astigmatism they may be considered as running vertically and horizontally, with the greatest refraction in the former and the least refraction in the latter, which conditions are found in astigmatism "with the rule." It should be borne in mind, however, that these meridians may be inclined at any angle, or may even be reversed as in astigmatism "against the rule."

FORM OF A PENCIL OF RAYS AS REFRACTED BY AN ASTIGMATIC EYE

Rays of light entering an eye with refracting surfaces, such as have been described above, are more sharply refracted and brought to a sooner focus by the vertical meridian. This is well illustrated by the following diagram:

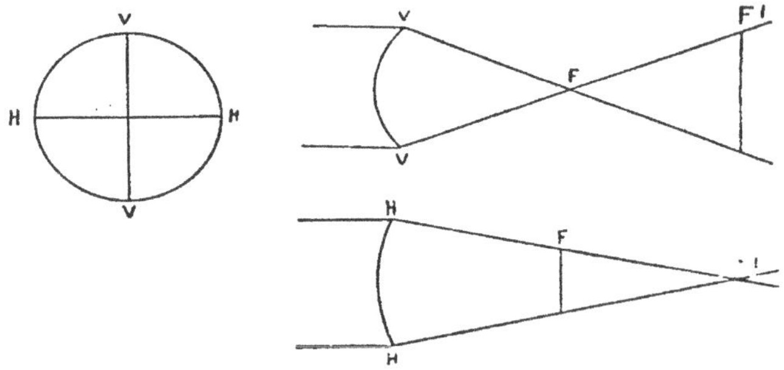

Antero-Posterior Section of Rays

V H V H represents the anterior surface of the cornea receiving a beam or bundle of parallel rays, *V V* being the vertical meridian and *H H* the horizontal. On account of the sharper curve of the former the rays of light passing through that section will be more quickly converged than those passing through the horizontal meridian. Therefore the focus of the vertical meridian will be at *F*, and of the horizontal meridian at *F*1. Hence, at the position of *F*, the principal focus of the vertical meridian, the rays entering in this meridian, have united in a point, while those entering horizontally will be spread out in a line. In the first instance they then begin to diverge, while in the second case they continue to converge, until at the location of *F*1 the vertical rays are spread out in a line and the horizontal have just united in a point, which is the principal focus of the horizontal meridian.

The space between the foci of these two meridians is called the *focal interval* or the *interval of Sturm*. The greater this interval the more pronounced the astigmatism; the less this interval the slighter the degree of astigmatism, until when the curvatures in the two meridians become equal and the foci are both located at the same point, astigmatism is no longer present.

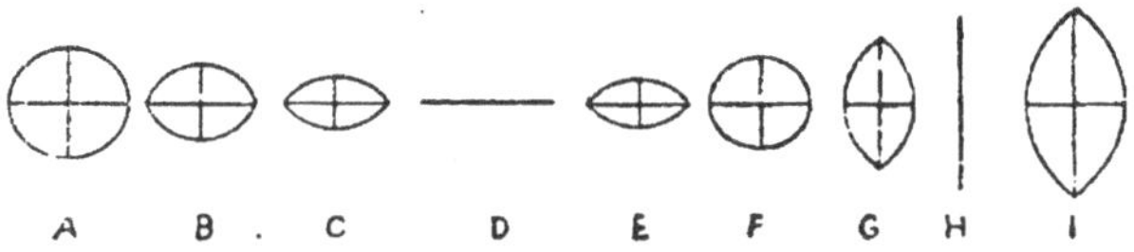

Transverse Section of Rays

The bundle of rays, as they strike the external surface of the cornea, represent a circle, as shown at *A*. After entering the eye and becoming subject to the action of its refracting surfaces, on account of the sharper curve of the vertical meridian, a section of the rays will show that the vertical have converged much more than the horizontal and thus form a horizontal oval, as shown at *B*. Both meridians gradually become smaller, the vertical more rapidly than the horizontal, as illustrated at *C*, until finally the vertical have united in a line, as shown as figure *D*, which is said to be the focus of the vertical meridian, because the rays passing in this direction are brought to one level, while the horizontal remain diffused. Then the vertical rays begin to diverge, while the horizontal continue to converge, and the figure again assumes the form of a horizontal oval, as shown by *E*. Beyond this point, nearer the retina, the divergence of the vertical rays and the convergence of the horizontal rays, has brought the two meridians to an equality as to size, and the form of the rays is in the shape of a circle, as illustrated at *F*. Still farther on the continued divergence vertically and convergence horizontally causes the figure to assume the shape of a vertical oval, as at *G*. Finally, the spreading out of the vertical meridian and the approximation of the horizontal produces a vertical line (as at *H*), which is the focus of the horizontal lines. Beyond this point both sets of rays diverge and a large vertical oval is formed, as shown at *I*.

D is the *anterior focal line* and *H* the *posterior focal line*, and it is evident that no matter what position the retina would occupy, no distinct image can be formed upon it, but there will always be an overlapping of the images at the different points of an object, causing a blur or a wrong impression of its outline. Such a person will bring his accommodation into action so as to lessen as much as possible the diffusion circles, but there can be no true focus for both meridians and therefore the image cannot be made sharp and distinct; but the best vision is secured at the middle of the focal interval. The greater the difference in the refraction of the two meridians, the more pronounced will be the circles of diffusion and, consequently, the greater the impairment of vision.

The shape of a point as formed on the retina in the different forms of astigmatism is as follows:

B C: Compound hypermetropic astigmatism.
D: Simple hypermetropic astigmatism.
E F G: Mixed astigmatism.
H: Simple myopic astigmatism.
I: Compound myopic astigmatism.

ASTIGMATIC REFRACTION ILLUSTRATED BY A COMPOUND CYLINDRICAL LENS

A sphero-cylindrical lens is practically a spherical and a cylindrical lens placed together with their surfaces in contact, and rays of light passing through such a combination will be acted upon by both lenses to the full extent of the refractive power of each, and instead of bringing all the rays to a focus at one place, will result in the formation of two focal points, each represented by a short focal line.

The second of these is situated at the focal distance of the spherical lens alone, and is formed by the rays that pass in the meridian of the axis of the cylinder. The first focal line is located at the principal focus of the combined lenses, and is produced by the rays that pass in a meridian at right angles to the axis of the cylinder. These two focal lines can be easily shown by passing parallel rays of light through the lenses in front of a suitable screen, and moving them to the proper distances. At all other points there will be no distinct images, but only various shapes of illumination formed by the circles of diffusion, as the rays pass to meet before and beyond the focal points. One of these focal lines is parallel with the axis of the cylinder, and the other at right angles to it.

If a + 5 D. cylinder axis 90° be placed over a + 5 D. spherical, then the rays that pass through the lenses in the vertical meridian will be refracted by the spherical lens only, and would meet in focus at a point eight inches away. While the rays that pass in the horizontal meridian would be subject to the refractive action of both lenses and would be converged to a focus four inches away.

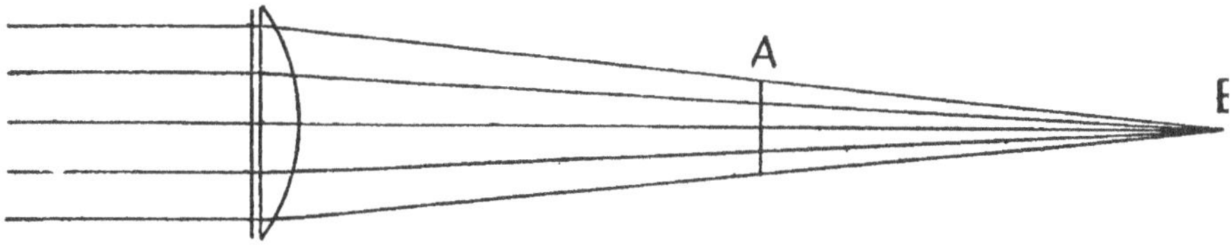

This is illustrated in the above diagram where the rays pass through the axis of the cylinder (which is as plane glass) and are refracted only by the spherical lens.

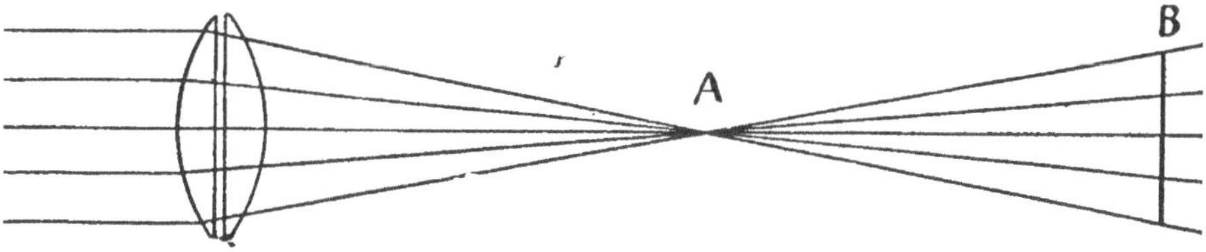

This drawing illustrates the effect upon rays of light when passing through the horizontal meridian of the two lenses, where they are bent by the combined action of both lenses, which causes the focus to be located much nearer the lenses.

If a screen should be placed at *A*, the horizontal rays will meet in focus there, while the vertical rays will strike it in the form of a vertical line or an ellipse. If the screen is removed to the position of *B*, there the vertical rays will focus, while the horizontal will have crossed over and form a horizontal line or ellipse. It is evident that the screen cannot be placed at any one point where both sets of rays can be focused, but when it is in focus for the rays of one meridian, it is out of focus for the other.

APPEARANCE OF LINES TO AN ASTIGMATIC EYE

Consideration will now be given to the question as to how points and lines will be seen by an eye affected with astigmatism, their appearance, of course, depending upon their directon in relation to the meridians of least and greatest curvature. A line must be regarded as consisting of a succession of points, each of which makes its own impression upon the retina, and the aggregation of these impressions constitutes the perception of a line. In order to make the subject more easily understood, we have arranged a succession of points vertically and a similar number horizontally.

Rays of light proceeding from a single point are focused to a point in the emmetropic eye and will make a distinct impression, separate from and without overlapping the adjacent points. In the astigmatic eye, however, the rays from a point cannot be again united in a point, but those that pass through the defective meridian are all out of focus, as shown by a blurring of the image, which will then present an appearance like this  or this  each overlapping the others adjoining it in the same direction. In the first case the rays

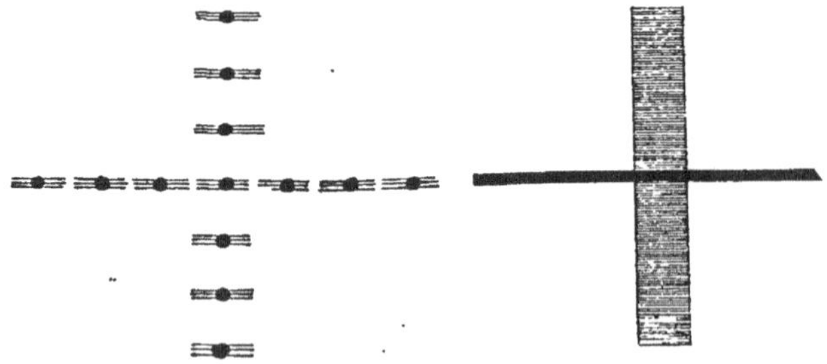

Vertical Meridian Emmetropic

entering in the vertical meridian, which is emmetropic, will be focused and distinctly defined above and below, while those passing through the horizontal meridian, which is ametropic, will be blurred and diffused on each side.

In the second case, where the horizontal meridian is emmetropic, the rays entering in this plane will be accurately focused upon the retina, thus affording distinct definition of each side of the object, while those entering the vertical meridian, which is astigmatic, cannot be brought to a focus, but will be blurred and diffused above and below.

An inspection of these two diagrams, in connection with the explanation given, makes it evident that the horizontal

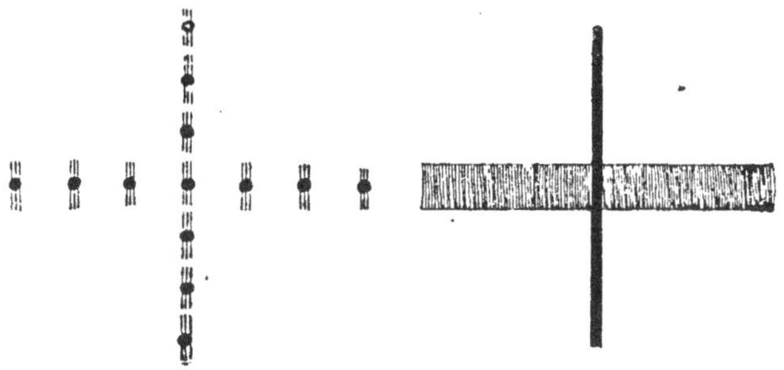

Vertical Meridian Astigmatic

line is distinct, because the rays which diverge from each of its component points in a direction at right angles to the course of the line, are focused upon the retina, affording clear definition above and below, and thus making a distinct horizontal line. While the rays diverging in a horizontal plane from each of the points of the line; that is, in the same direction as the line, cannot be focused upon the retina; but they do not disturb the distinctness of the line, because their diffusion effects, which result from the imperfect focus of this meridian, exist in the same direction as the line we are considering, and, consequently, overlap each other in the same direction, and hence are not visible, except slightly at each end of the line, where the diffusion images cause a slight fuzziness and make the line appear a little longer than it really is.

In this condition the vertical line appears fuzzy and indistinct and loses its natural sharpness of outline, because the rays proceeding from each of the points of the vertical line are focused only in the vertical meridian and are diffused in the horizontal, and thus become very noticeable in a vertical line because they cannot overlap. This causes the horizontal line to appear black and clear, and the vertical gray and diffused. Hence the corollary that naturally follows is that the horizontal line is clear because the vertical meridian is emmetropic, and the vertical line is indistinct because the horizontal meridian of the eye is out of focus.

On the other hand, in those cases where the horizontal meridian is emmetropic and the vertical is the defective one, the line running vertically will appear clear, because the rays diverging horizontally from the points of this line will enter the eye in its emmetropic meridian, and being brought to a focus will afford distinct definition of the vertical sides of the line. While the rays proceeding from the points of the line in a vertical direction will diffuse and overlap, but as this occurs in the direction of the line it is not noticeable, nor does it interfere with its distinctness.

But the rays that diverge vertically from the points of a horizontal line and enter the eye through its defective meridian cannot unite upon the retina, but form diffusion circles and overlap one another, and as this overlapping is at right angles to the line, it is very perceptible and causes a spreading out of the line in this direction. The distinct definition of outline being thus destroyed, the line appears blurred and indistinct.

WHAT DISTINCT PERCEPTION OF A LINE DEPENDS UPON

The whole matter may be summed up by saying that the distinctness of a line depends upon the correct focusing of its edges; so that in order to see a vertical line clearly, it is necessary that the rays proceeding from its edges and entering the horizontal meridian of the eye should be focused upon the retina. And in order that a horizontal line should appear distinct, the rays diverging from its edges and passing through the vertical meridian of the eye, must be united upon the retina.

Thus is explained the well-known fact that when a patient affected with simple astigmatism looks at the card of radiating lines and says the vertical lines are indistinct, the examiner knows the horizontal is the defective meridian; or, in other words, that the impaired line is at right angles to the defective meridian and the line seen clearly is at right angles to the emmetropic meridian and not parallel to each other, as at first sight might be supposed. If the distinct line is oblique, then the indistinct line will also be oblique at right angles to it, and will indicate the location of the two chief meridians, or the meridians of least and greatest curvature. Points are drawn into lines and circles are elongated into ovals in the direction of the ametropic meridian.

Although the correction of astigmatism will be considered in detail later on in the chapter, it might be remarked in connection with the foregoing explanation that the axis of the cylinder is placed in the same direction as the indistinct lines.

A FURTHER ILLUSTRATION OF THE CROSSING OF LINES IN ASTIGMATISM

This subject is one so difficult of comprehension by the average optical student that a variation of the form of illustration may serve to make it more intelligible to the beginner, even at the risk of being wearisome to the older optometrists of advanced standing. The refracting media of the eye may be regarded as equivalent to a strong convex spherical lens, which, in turn, may be regarded as made up of convex cylindrical lenses of indefinite number with their axis crossing each other at right angles in every meridian. To simplify the matter we will select the two that run vertically and horizontally.

If a strong convex cylindrical lens be held with its axis vertical in front of a screen in such a position as to allow rays of light to pass through it, a bright vertical line will be seen upon the screen, as a result of the action of the lens. This seems proper and on first thought does not call for an explanation; but when it is remembered that the axis of the lens is plane and incapable of bending the rays of light, and that the power is located in the horizontal meridian of the lens, which is at right angles to the bright line, then at once the inquiring mind is set to thinking and reasoning out the why and wherefore.

If the axis of the cylinder is held horizontally, a bright horizontal line of light will be formed upon the screen, because it is the vertical meridian of the lens that bends the rays of light, and in spite of the fact that the horizontal meridian is plano. Therefore, we say that the direction of the bright line is at right angles to the meridian of perfect refraction, and contrariwise the course of the blurred line is at right angles to the meridian of imperfect refraction.

ACTION OF CYLINDERS COMPARED WITH THE REFRACTIVE SURFACES OF THE EYE

Suppose the cylinders were made to represent the refractive media of the eye and that the one with its axis horizontal had the greater refractive power, while the vertical cylinder caused the rays to unite upon the retina. In such a case the vertical meridian would be myopic and the horizontal emmetropic. Rays passing through the vertical meridian would be refracted too much, and by crossing over would produce a blurred line, which, for the reasons mentioned above, would be in the horizontal direction. The real defect is vertical, at right angles to the apparent defect, which is shown in the indistinct horizontal line.

On the other hand, the horizontal meridian being normal and the rays passing through it being focused on the retina, for similar reasons causes the vertical line to appear clear and bright.

It should be noted that in passing from one meridian to the other there is no sharp variation, but a gradual increase or diminution of curvature. In the above example, where the maximum curvature was at 90°, there is a gradual shading off in each direction. At 89° and at 91° the rays would meet in front of the retina, just as they do at 90°, but not quite so far from it. Every additional degree removed from the vertical on either side would bring the focus of rays a little nearer to the retina, until finally, when the horizontal meridian is reached, the rays will exactly meet upon the retina, and this will be the point of maximum clearness. As soon as this meridian is departed from the lines begin to be blurred and each additional degree of departure makes them more and more indistinct.

Any one can demonstrate these facts for himself by making his eye artifically astigmatic by means of a convex cylinder and then using a concave cylinder to neutralize the artificial defect, and rotating it near to and beyond the desired meridian, and noting the effect upon the clearness of vision as the axis approaches and departs from this meridian.

FORMS OF ASTIGMATISM

Astigmatism may be divided into two great classes:

I. Irregular.
II. Regular.

The first form has already been described at such length as the importance of the subject seemed to demand, in view of the fact that it is not correctible by glasses.

Of the second form there are three varieties: *Simple, compound* and *mixed.*

In *simple astigmatism* one of the principal meridians is emmetropic (focuses on the retina) and the other at right angles is ametropic (focuses before or behind the retina).

In *compound astigmatism* both of the principal meridians are ametropic (neither of them focusing on the retina), but the focus of one meridian is farther away than that of the other.

In *mixed astigmatism* both of the principal meridians are ametropic, the focus of one being in front of the retina and of the other behind it.

With this general description the five forms of regular astigmatism may be mentioned as follows:

1. *Simple Hypermetropic Astigmatism.* In this variety one meridian is emmetropic and the other principal meridian is hypermetropic. If the focus of parallel rays passing through the vertical meridian is on the retina, the focus of the horizontal meridian would be behind it. The retinal image is in the form of a horizontal line, and by the subjective examination the horizontal line would appear the most distinct. The correcting lens would be a convex cylinder with its axis in or near a vertical position; for example: + 1 D. cyl. axis 90°.

2. *Simple Myopic Astigmatism.* This is a condition where one principal meridian is emmetropic and the other at right

angles is myopic. If the focus of the horizontal meridian is on the retina, that of the vertical meridian would be in front of it. The retinal image in this condition is in the form of a vertical line, and when the patient looks at the card of radiating lines the vertical appear to him the most distinct. The correcting lens would be a concave cylinder with its axis in or near a horizontal position; for example: — 2 cyl. axis 180°. This is the least common form of astigmatism, scarcely more than one person out of every hundred being affected with it.

3. *Compound Hypermetropic Astigmatism.* In this form both principal meridians are hypermetropic, one being more so than the other, usually the horizontal. The focus of both meridians is back of the retina, that of the horizontal being farthest from it. The retinal image is neither a line nor a circle, but a horizontal oval. Usually the patient says the horizontal lines are the most distinct.

This condition may be regarded as a combination of hypermetropia and simple hypermetropic astigmatism, the former due to a flattened eye-ball and the latter depending upon a lessened curvature of the cornea in the horizontal meridian. This is the most common of all the varieties of astigmatism, it having been estimated as representing nearly one-half of all errors of refraction. The correcting lens is a compound one, a convex spherical combined with a convex cylinder; for example: + 1 D. Sph. ⊃ + .50 D. cyl. axis 90°.

4. *Compound Myopic Astigmatism.* In this condition both principal meridians are myopic, one being more defective than the other, usually the vertical. This causes parallel rays passing through both meridians to come to a focus in front of the retina, but that of the horizontal will lie closer to it. The retinal image is neither a line nor a circle, but a vertical oval, and to such a person vertical lines will appear the plainest.

This form of astigmatism may be considered as a myopia with a simple myopic astigmatism engrafted upon it; in fact, most myopic eyes have more or less astigmatism in addition. The correcting lens is a compound one, a concave sphere combined with a concave cylinder; for example: — 1.50 D. sph. ⊃ — 1.25 cyl. axis 180°.

5. *Mixed Astigmatism.* This form of defect may be due to either one of the three following combinations:

1. Simple hypermetropic astigmatism with simple myopic astigmatism.
2. Hypermetropia with simple myopic astigmatism.
3. Myopia with simple hypermetropic astigmatism.

In any case the retina lies between the foci of the two principal meridians, one being before it and the other behind it. The retinal image is never a line, but may be an oval or a circle, and neither vertical nor horizontal lines will appear very distinct.

The correcting lens is a compound one, with a convex and a concave element. It may be one of the three following combinations, corresponding to the forms of the defect mentioned above:

1. + 1.25 D. cyl. axis 90° ⊃ — 1.50 D. cyl. axis 180°.
2. + 1.25 D. sph. ⊃ — 2.75 D. cyl. axis 180°.
3. — 1.50 D. sph. ⊃ + 2.75 D. cyl. axis 90°.

FURTHER SUBDIVISIONS OF ASTIGMATISM

A—*Astigmatism with the rule.*

B—*Astigmatism against the rule.*

These have already been sufficiently described.

C—*Symmetrical Astigmatism.* When the axis of the cylinder of each eye is at 90° or 180°. Or when the axis of the cylinder in one eye inclines as much to the right as the other does to the left. Or when the axis on the right and left side is an equal number of degrees above the horizontal. In other words, when the sum of the two axes exactly equals 180°. For example: if the axis inclines 30° to the right and left of the vertical, in the one eye it would be 60° and in the other 120°, and these combined equal 180°. Again, if the axis on the right and left was 45° above the horizontal, in the one eye it would be 45° and in the other 135°, the sum of the two amounting to 180°. Symmetrical astigmatism occurs when the features are regular and the center of each pupil at an equal distance from the median line of the face.

D—*Asymmetrical Astigmatism.* When the direction of the axis of one cylinder bears no relation to the direction of the axis of the other, or their combined values do not make 180°. As an example: if the axis of one was at 80° and of the other at 120°, these added together would make 200°, which is more than 180°. Or if one axis was at 50° and the other at 100°, the sum of these would equal 150°, which is less than 180°. Asymmetrical astigmatism usually occurs when the features are not regular and the pupillary center in one eye is farther from the median line of the face than the other; and, in addition, muscular insufficiency is much more common, in fact, it should always be suspected in this form of astigmatism.

In addition to the above, the following terms have also been employed:

Homonymous astigmatism, in which the axis of the cylinder is the same in each eye.

Heteronymous astigmatism, a condition in which the defect in one eye is with the rule and in the other eye against it.

CAUSES OF ASTIGMATISM

Astigmatism, which depends upon irregularity of the cornea and if of high degree may be part of a general malformation of the face, is usually regarded as congenital, and in many cases hereditary, although not necessarily so. In other words, the child is born with astigmatic eyes, which, however, cannot always be blamed upon the parents. The degree of defect and the meridians of curvature may vary somewhat at different periods of life.

Acquired astigmatism may result from traction on the cornea, as seen in the cicatrices that occur in the healing of wounds of this membrane, either produced by accident or purposely made in the operation for the extraction of cataract or in iridectomy (especially if there has been imperfect coaptation of the lips of the wound), as well as after the repair of ulcers. In fact, anything that causes an increase or diminution of the curvature of one or both meridians of the cornea will develop an astigmatism.

When astigmatism occurs after the removal of the

crystalline lens, it is usually due to changes in the curvature of the cornea from the union of the wound, as mentioned above. But it may depend upon the fact that the lens while in position was itself astigmatic, but just the opposite of that existing in the cornea, so that the latter was neutralized by the former. In another class of cases the astigmatism which had existed prior to the formation of the cataract, disappeared after the extraction of the crystalline lens, which would tend to prove that the defect was located in the latter rather than in the cornea.

Pressure on the cornea or sclerotic from superficial tumor growths situated in the orbit or in the eye-lids may give rise to corneal astigmatism, as may also spasmodic contraction of the orbicularis muscle. Astigmatism may also be caused by intraocular pressure and by a continued contraction of some of the extraocular muscles, as is sometimes seen in forms of nervous disease.

In the production of astigmatism there are four surfaces to be considered, the anterior and posterior faces of both the cornea and crystalline lens, as well as the density of the different portions of these structures, and of the aqueous and vitreous humors, especially in the path of the axial line.

Differences in the curvature of the meridians of the cornea may be neutralized or partly changed by irregularities in the lens surfaces dependent upon unequal contraction of the ciliary muscle. Lental astigmatism may, in some cases, be due to an oblique position of the lens as a result of injury, although it has also been observed as a condition of congenital origin.

Astigmatic effects may be produced by spherical lenses placed obliquely or tilted before the eye, thus changing their optical value.

PHYSIOLOGICAL ASTIGMATISM

This variety is produced by lid-pressure, and as the cause is under the control of the will, the defect is temporary and not constant. It does not occur in all eyes, but is rather the exception. In approximating the lids, as in the act of frowning and squinting, some amount of pressure is made upon the eye from above and below. This causes the horizontal meridian of the cornea to have a longer radius of curvature and the vertical meridian a shorter radius. This can sometimes be beautifully illustrated by the ophthalmometer, which will show a difference in the position of the two mires when the patient is asked to open his eye widely as he looks into the telescope of the instrument, occasionally to the extent of .50 D. to 1 D. It is almost superfluous to say that no attempt should be made to correct this temporary astigmatism with glasses.

A PECULIARITY OF ASTIGMATISM

It is always customary to determine the refraction of each eye separately, and when this is done in astigmatism and the amount measured and the principal meridians located, it will sometimes be found that not only will there be a variation in the relative angles of the meridians, but also in the degree of defect, when an examination is made of both eyes simultaneously. This can be explained only by the action of the external muscles in producing different degrees of tension on the eye-balls, and thus causing a difference in the corneal curves during the combined use of the eyes in binocular vision.

SYMPTOMS OF ASTIGMATISM

There are really no positive and definite symptoms by which the presence of astigmatism can be surely determined simply by the patient's recital of the history of his case. Neither can it be diagnosed by the appearance of the face and eyes, nor by any of the external evidences of eye-strain.

In young persons, and especially if the astigmatism is not of high degree, few symptoms may manifest themselves. The acuteness of vision may be practically up to the normal standard and no great difficulty may be experienced in the use of the eyes. This is especially the case in slight hypermetropic astigmatism (when with the rule), which may then be considered as existing in a latent form and may remain unsuspected until the patient approaches the presbyopic period of life.

Usually, however, the vision is impaired, sometimes slightly and sometimes very markedly. In hypermetropia the near vision suffers most, while the distant vision oftentimes remains fairly good. In myopia, on the other hand, the distant vision is very much reduced, while the near vision is rather improved than impaired. But in astigmatism both near and distant vision are affected.

In myopic astigmatism the patient gives evidence of being near-sighted. But even in hypermetropic astigmatism the book is very often brought quite close to the eyes, in order to increase the size of the visual angle and thus compensate for the indistinctness of the retinal image. Astigmatic persons often get into the habit of contracting their lids into a stenopaic apparatus in their efforts to overcome their defect.

Asthenopia is one of the most important symptoms of astigmatism and manifests itself chiefly in the form of *headache*. The cases of astigmatism that do not suffer with headache are exceptional, and the further fact may be stated that more than one-half the cases of functional headaches are caused by this type of refractive error. The assertion has been made that the tendency to headache reaches its highest point in compound hypermetropic astigmatism, eighty-five per cent. of the cases of which suffer from headache. Even where the error is so slight that the visual acuity is not impaired, it may still be the cause of very severe headaches. One writer states that when vision is normal and headache follows use of the eyes, astigmatism of low degree is indicated, and the less the degree the more severe the headache. The same authority reports that during one year he prescribed six hundred pairs of cylinders of only .25 D., all of which patients suffered from headache and eye pains and the majority of whom were cured by the glasses. Astigmatism causes least trouble when "with the rule" and when the principal meridians are at 90° and 180°; somewhat more inconvenience when "against the rule" with meridians vertical and horizontal, and still more so when oblique.

In astigmatism there is confusion of the images (worse in the hypermetropic variety), which the ciliary muscle makes a constant effort to remove, and which it does, even if successful, at the expense of severe headaches. In the effort to overcome the astigmatism of the cornea, an artificial astigmatism of the lens (the inverse of that of the cornea) is produced by an unequal contraction of the ciliary muscle, such partial and unnatural use being productive of headache.

In testing the vision of an astigmatic person it is sometimes noticed that the patient sees better when he holds his head to one side, and this has come to be regarded almost as a distinctive symptom of this defect; so that when a patient has acquired the habit of tilting his head, astigmatism may be suspected.

In simple hypermetropic astigmatism "with the rule," if the vertical meridian is emmetropic the horizontal must be hypermetropic. In these cases there is a contraction not only of the ciliary muscle, but also of the eye-lids. The latter has somewhat the effect of a horizontal stenopaic slit, and by shutting off the emmetropic meridian and allowing rays to pass only in the hypermetropic meridian, practically reduces the case to one of simple hypermetropia. The normal use of the ciliary muscle to correct the horizontal meridian would, at the same time, render the vertical myopic, unless, as is probably the case, he has acquired the faculty of a partial or unequal contraction of this muscle, as mentioned above.

Astigmatism has also been regarded as playing some part in the causation of epilepsy and chorea, where there is a twitching and jerking of the face and clonic spasms of the facial muscles. Nervousness, irritability and discontent are sometimes symptoms of astigmatism.

The question has recently arisen and has been discussed as to whether errors of refraction, as astigmatism, are capable of producing disease in organs remote from the eyes? In diabetes, insanity and consumption there usually occur various forms of accommodative and asthenopic troubles, which have always been regarded as results of the disease. But the suggestion has been advanced that perhaps we have been "putting the cart before the horse" all these years, and that possibly the eye symptoms have been the cause of the disease instead of the result of it. It will probably take a long time and a vast aggregation of facts by different observers to prove the truth or falsity of these suggestions; and while the writer is very skeptical, yet we are all seekers after the truth and must admit it

> "Wheresoever found,
> On heathen or on Christian ground."

It would vastly enlarge the sphere of optometry if it were found that these diseases, which are so intractable to medical treatment, should become amenable to the optometrist's specially ground lenses.

RECOGNITION OF ASTIGMATISM

The diagnosis of astigmatism is one of the most interesting and important questions that confronts the optometrist early in his career. In the higher grades of the defect this is not usually a matter of any great difficulty, but the hard nut to crack is rather the determination of its nature, its degree and the exact location of the principal meridians. The slighter forms will be more of a test of the examiner's skill in his discovering its presence.

It may be suspected when the vision is slightly impaired and patient complains of headache and difficulty in using eyes; if he has contracted the habit of holding his head sideways, and if some letters are seen more clearly than others. Also, when the refraction is tested, if spherical lenses fail to afford a satisfactory acuteness of vision, and if several glasses seem to produce the same degree of improvement and patient is unable to decide between them. As astigmatism is such a frequent defect and plays such an important part in the every-day work of the optometrist, making or marring his reputation and affording relief or disappointment to the patient, as it is properly or improperly corrected, a distinctly marked line of examination should be adhered to, and to that end we will mention and explain all the various tests that are of any value in the detection of this defect.

TESTS FOR ASTIGMATISM

1. Test Cards.
2. Trial Case.
3. Stenopaic Slit.
4. Keratoscope.

5. Scheiner's Test.
6. Chromatic Test.
7. Ophthalmometer.
8. Ophthalmoscope.
9. Retinoscope.

TEST CARDS

Radiating Lines.—One of the commonest tests for astigmatism, and one that can be made use of even by the patient himself, is the card of radiating lines. First, the patient is requested to read the smallest and lowest line on the card of letters, when it is discovered that he is unable to make out the No. 20 line at all or perhaps only one or two words on it. The test for hypermetropia is then made by convex lenses, after which the person's attention is directed to the clock dial or any card with lines running in different directions, for the purpose of determining by his answers whether or not astigmatism is present, and if so the location of the defective meridian. The chart should be well illuminated, either naturally or artificially, and should hang at right angles to the axis of vision. One eye is to be covered while the other is being tested.

If all the different lines appear equally clear and black, the natural presumption is that no astigmatism is present, or at least of inconsiderable amount. But if any contrast in the distinctness of the various lines is noticeable and the patient selects one series as plainer, or another set as dimmer, than others, then the presence of astigmatism is proven. In higher degrees of the defect the contrast is very marked, in some cases the three lines running into one confused black line without interspaces, and in others these lines being almost invisible.

An illustration of this fact is found in the report of a case of "Periodic Obscuration of Vision." The patient seated in his office could see the hands on the clock and tell the time at certain hours of the day, while at other hours it was an utter impossibility for him to do so. An examination by an oculist revealed the fact that the man was highly astigmatic, and when the hands of the clock reached his normal meridian they were clearly seen, and when they passed to his abnormal meridian they became invisible. Of course, the adaptation of the proper glasses removed the periodic obscuration and rendered his vision equal at all times.

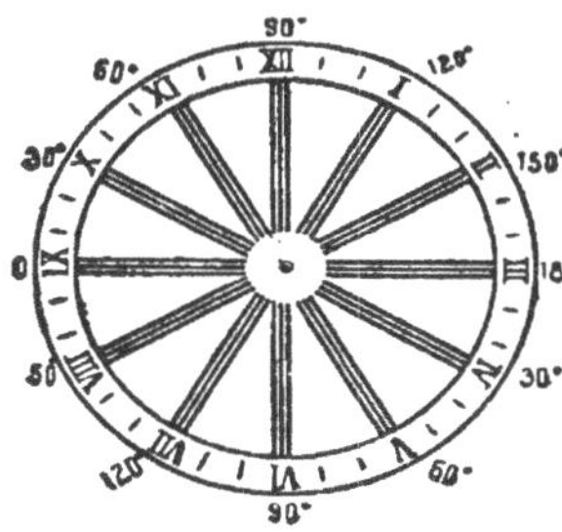

Having then diagnosed astigmatism, the next thing is to determine the direction of the defective meridian, or the meridians of least and greatest curvature, which is accomplished by asking the patient which series of lines are plainest and which are dimmest. Whichever one he names, we know the other is at right angles to it. If he says the horizontal lines are most distinct, we infer the vertical are least clear, in which case the horizontal meridian of the eye is the defective one, most probably hypermetropic, because this is naturally the direction of least curvature, from which may be deduced the following axioms:

The direction of the lines that appear plainest on the card corresponds to the defective meridian of the eye.

The direction of the lines that appear most blurred on the card, corresponds to the emmetropic meridian of the eye.

The axis of the cylinder that is prescribed for correction is placed in the same direction as the indistinct lines, which in the above case would be a convex cylindrical axis vertical or 90°.

Those patients who select the lines at or near the horizontal as plainest, are usually hypermetropic in their astigmatism, while those who select the lines at or near the vertical are likely to have myopic astigmatism.

Pray's Astigmatic Letters.—These are striped letters composed of strokes running in different directions. They constitute what has always been considered as one of the standard tests for astigmatism. The patient indicates which letter or row of letters is most distinct, and the direction of the lines

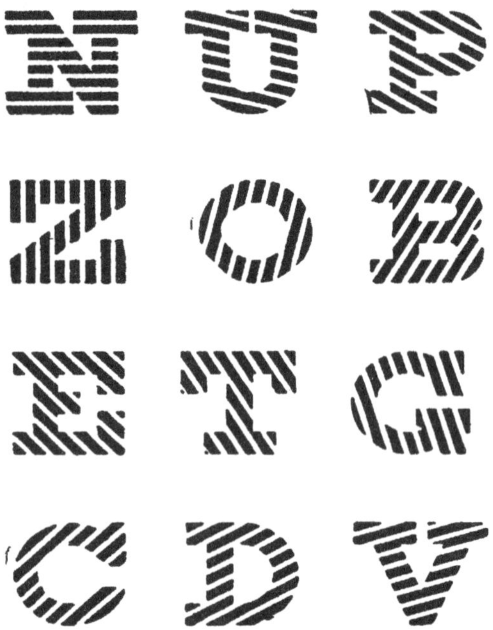

that make up the letter or letters would correspond to the meridian of greatest defect. This test is sometimes confusing as the blackness may vary from one letter to another.

Confusion Letters.—These are letters which bear a marked resemblance to each other, in deciphering which the patient is likely to be confused and miscall them. For instance, X and K, L and E, O and D, C and G, B and H, P and F, V and Y, etc. While some of these letters may appear plainer than others, on account of the direction of their lines as seen by an astigmatic eye, yet it can hardly be classed as a distinctive test for astigmatism, because a person with impaired vision from other causes may make similar mistakes in naming these letters.

TRIAL CASE

Cylindrical Lenses.—The test for astigmatism by means of the lenses from the trial case is the "old reliable," with which the average optometrist is most familiar and on which he principally depends, and when carefully and patiently carried out yields very satisfactory results. Spherical lenses are always tried first, commencing with convex. If a weak one is accepted (say, + .50 D.) a stronger is tried, the preference being given to the strongest one which the patient will accept at a distance of twenty feet.

If astigmatism is present, it may be either simple or compound. If simple, the spherical lens will probably be accepted, which would indicate that the refraction of the eye is hypermetropic. Then it is removed and a convex cylinder is put in its place with its axis at 90°, which, in the majority of cases, is at the proper position. It is then slowly rotated to ascertain if there is any other meridian at which vision is better, or if a removal of the axis from the vertical impairs the clearness of sight. In the large proportion of cases the answers of the patient are so decided that the location of the defective meridian can be quickly and accurately determined. And then stronger cylinders are tried until that one is found that feels the most comfortable to the patient and affords the most satisfactory vision.

In the trial with cylindrical lenses, the optometrist has two objects in view; to find that lens which will cause all the radiating lines to appear equally plain, and also which will afford the clearest vision as the patient looks at the card of test letters. Sometimes the number of the lens or the position of its axis, that equalizes all the lines, will not seem so good for the letters and vice versa; in such cases where the examiner is in doubt which glass to prescribe or which meridian to select, preference may safely be given to the results obtained while the patient looks at the card of letters.

If the astigmatism is compound, the convex spherical lens which was first tried corrects whatever amount of hypermetropia there may be present, and with this lens in the trial frame before the eye, a cylinder is placed in front of it just as in simple astigmatism, and rotated to that position and increased to that number that affords the best vision on the cards at twenty feet.

If a convex spherical and a convex cylindrical lens have been tried with negative results, and if the acuteness of vision is very greatly impaired, then a concave sphere is placed before the eye, alternated with a concave cylinder. The effect upon the sight will indicate whether the refraction is myopic or not, and whether astigmatism is present in a simple or compound form. If the former, the sphere is supplanted by a cylinder, which is rotated to ascertain the proper angle and increased to determine the correct strength. If the latter, the cylinder is placed over the sphere and rotated as before, while each is gradually increased until the best visual result is attained. It is customary in placing the concave cylinder in the trial frame, to insert it with its axis horizontal (which corresponds to astigmatism with the rule), and then if necessary, to rotate to right or left.

This method of testing is very simple, and an experienced operator can obtain very speedy and accurate results. But it is scarcely safe to prescribe glasses based on a single examination. Wherever possible the test should be repeated on several days, in order to determine on the proper glasses with a reasonable degree of certainty. Not only may the number of the glass that is accepted vary from day to day, but also the location of the axis. If the results obtained at each examination correspond, one can feel pretty sure that the glasses are right. Whereas, if different days produce different results, one must strike an average and thus arrive at a glass that can be depended upon.

CYLINDRICAL LENSES

As cylindrical lenses play such an important part in the detection and correction of astigmatism, we have thought that space could be profitably given to a description of them and of their action on light, as this is a subject that is not always clear in the minds of beginners.

In writing a prescription a cylindrical lens is represented by the letter C or the abbreviation Cyl. The name is derived from the fact that such a lens is a segment of a cylinder parallel to its axis. A concave cylinder is ground on the outer surface of a revolving cylinder, and a convex on the inside of a hollow cylinder. The meridian of the lens on which it is ground is plane and possesses no refracting power; this is the summit of curvature and is called the *axis of the cylinder.* In the cylindrical lenses of the trial case this is indicated by a short diamond scratched on each edge, or by having the

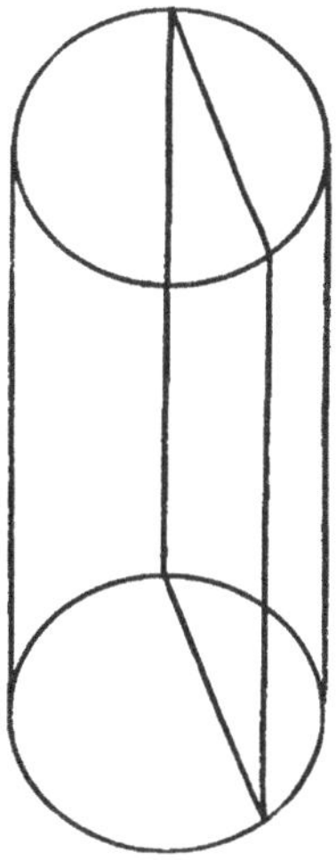

transparency of the lens ground off on each side parallel to the axis.

It will be seen that the curvature and hence the refractive power of a cylindrical lens lies in the meridian at right angles to its axis, and here it has the same action as a spherical lens of like radius of curvature and index of refraction would have in this meridian. Rays of light passing in the meridian of the axis would continue in straight lines, while those entering the meridian at right angles to axis would be converged until they meet in a line where they intersect the rays first mentioned, the distance of which from the lens would be the same as the focal length of a spherical lens of the same number. This line is called the *focal line* of the lens, and the distance its *focal distance.* In like manner a concave cylindrical lens would act upon the rays of light passing through it, except that in this case the rays would be diverged as if they had proceeded from a line behind the lens, representing its negative focal line. From what has been said it will be understood that the system of numbering cylindrical lenses is the same as applies to sphericals, with the knowledge kept constantly

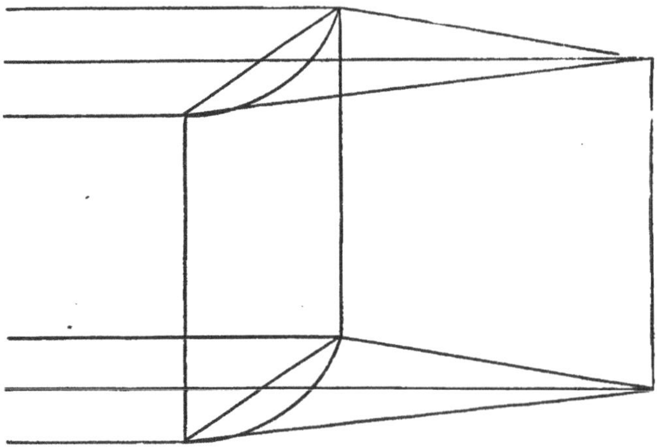

in mind that the action of the former is confined entirely to the meridian at right angles to the axis of the lens.

For instance, a + 4 D. cylinder will converge parallel rays of light so as to bring them together in a straight line at a distance of ten inches from the lens, while a — 4 D. cylinder will diverge them as though they came from a line ten inches back of the lens. If the axis of the cylinder be placed at 90° the focal line will be vertical, while if the axis be at 180° the focal line will be horizontal. Or, in other words, recalling that the refractive power lies in a meridian at right angles to the axis a vertical line appears distinct at the focus of the horizontal meridian of the lens, and a horizontal is clear at the focal distance of the vertical meridian.

RECOGNITION OF CYLINDRICAL LENSES

When a cylinder is held before the eye and moved in the direction of its axis there is no motion or apparent change in position of the object looked at, because this is the meridian of plane glass having no refractive power. But when the lens is moved in any other direction, there is evident motion in the object seen through it. If the movement is in a direction at right angles to its axis, the effect is the same as that caused by a spherical lens, that is, *opposite* for *convex* and *with* for *concave*.

The effect of a convex cylinder upon a circle is to elongate it in a direction at right angles to its axis. If the lens be held with its axis vertical, the circle will appear as a horizontal oval, and when the axis is horizontal, a vertical oval. The effect of a concave cylinder on a circle is also to elongate it in one direction, in this case corresponding to its axis. If the lens be held with its axis vertical, a circle view through it will appear as a vertical oval, and if held horizontally as a horizontal oval.

If a cylindrical lens be held before the eye and a distant object looked at through it of rectangular shape, such as a picture frame or a test card, there will be a change in its shape and a distortion which will vary with every turn in the position of the axis of the lens. If this be parallel to either the vertical or horizontal sides of the object, its rectangular form will not be disturbed, but the length of one side in relation to the other will be altered. In the case of a concave cylinder the sides that are parallel to its axis will be elongated and the sides at right angles to it will be shortened, while in the case of a convex cylinder the lengthening and shortening will be in the reverse sides. If now the lens be rotated, there will be not only a change in the shape of the object, but a very marked distortion will become evident, affecting the lines that form the sides, which will become oblique instead of straight.

These phenomena are made use of in determining the location of the axis of a cylinder. Looking through such a lens at a distant straight line, of sufficient length to extend above and below it, sometimes the line will appear continuous and at other times it will be broken. In the first case the axis of the lens is either parallel to the line or exactly at right angles to it, and in the second case it is oblique in relation to it.

If we take a convex cylindrical lens and hold it at arm's length from the eye and look through it at a vertical line. there will be no apparent deviation when the axis is at 90°; but if the lens is rotated to one side or the other the line is immediately broken and the portion seen through the lens turns in a direction away from the axis, increasing until an angle of 45° is reached, when it begins to approach it again, and when the axis arrives at the horizontal plane the line is again an unbroken one.

If a concave cylinder is taken and used in the same way, the broken portion of the line seen through the lens will move in the same direction as the axis, increasing until the maximum deviation is reached at an angle of 45° and then diminishing again until the 180th meridian is arrived at, when the line once more assumes its original continuous form. This to and fro deviation is familiar to all opticians who use the trial case and handle cylindrical lenses.

Under certain conditions exceptions may be noted to the above statements. If we take a moderately-strong convex cylinder (say + 3 D.) and hold it at arm's length as we rotate it, the effect upon the straight line will be quite different; it no longer moves away, and then back, but as the axis is turned to the extent of 90°, or a quarter of a circle, the line travels twice as far, to 180°, or half a circle. This can be explained by comparing the action of a cylindrical lens with that of a spherical lens of the same refractive power. If a + 3 D. sphere be held within a short distance from the eye, a distant object viewed through it will be blurred; as the lens is moved

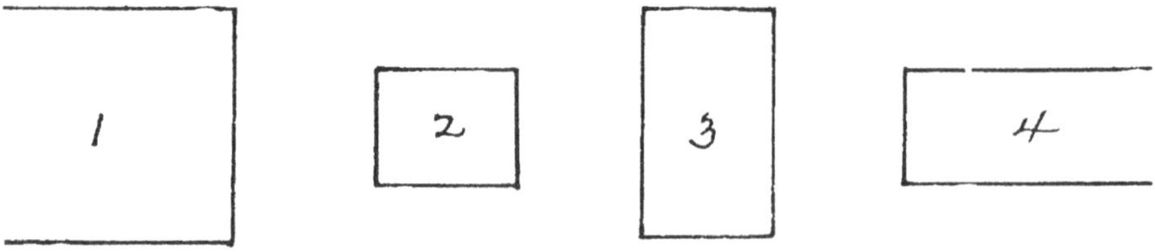

farther away the object grows more and more indistinct, until finally it is entirely lost. If the lens is extended still farther, to arm's length, the object again becomes visible, but now in an inverted position.

Suppose *1* to represent a rectangular object hanging on the wall across the room. If it be viewed through a spherical lens it will be reduced in size equally in both directions, as shown by *2*. If viewed through a cylindrical lens of similar focal power the effect of the lens will be evident only in one meridian. This is represented by *3*, where the axis of the lens is vertical, and by *4*, where the axis is horizontal. These figures are diagrammatic, the aim being illustration of the subject rather than mathematical accuracy.

SPHERO-CYLINDRICAL LENSES

A sphero-cylindrical lens is a combination of sphere and cylinder, the piece of glass being ground with a spherical tool on one surface and a cylindrical tool on the other. These may be variously curved; both may be convex or both concave, or either one convex and the other concave. The refraction of a convex sphero-cylinder has been fully described in the earlier part of this chapter, showing its two focal points and the location of each.

THE SPHERO-CYLINDRICAL EQUIVALENT OF BI-CYLINDRICAL LENSES

1. *When two cylinders of the same sign but of different power are combined with their axis at right angles to each other.* Take the smaller of the two for the spherical, and the difference between the two for the cylindrical, retaining the same sign and axis of the greater. For instance, a + 2 D. cyl. axis 90° and a + 3 D. cyl. axis 180° combined will equal a + 2 D. sph. ⊃ + 1 D. cyl. axis 180°. The 2 D. convex supplies that amount of refractive power in all meridians; this is just right in one meridian, but in the other meridian an additional + 1 D. is required, which is furnished by the + 1 D. cyl. which is combined with the spherical.

2. *When two cylinders with dissimilar signs are combined with their axis at right angles to each other.* This is commonly known as a cross cylinder and is written + 1.25 D. cyl. axis 90° T — 2.50 cyl. Take either one of the cylinders for the spherical, and the sum of the two for the cylinder with the sign and axis of the latter. By following this rule we can get two transpositions of the above formula, as follows: + 1.25 D. sph. ⊃ — 3.75 D. cyl. axis 180°; or — 2.50 D. sph. ⊃ + 3.75 D. cyl. axis 90°. It must be remembered that

a refractive power of + 1.25 D. is desired in the horizontal meridian and — 2.50 D. in the vertical, which is maintained in the second and third formulæ, as proven by an analysis of them. In one case the + 1.25 D. sphere supplies the necessary power in the horizontal meridian, but in the vertical, where a concave is desired, the sphere must first be neutralized, and then the desired concavity supplied, which is accomplished by means of a — 3.75 D. cyl. axis 180°. In the other formula the — 2.50 D. sphere is just right for the vertical meridian, but in the horizontal where a convex is called for, this sphere must first be neutralized and then the desired convexity supplied, which is accomplished by means of a + 3.75 D. cyl. axis 90°.

In a sphero-cylindrical lens the meridian of the axis of the cylinder possesses the refractive power of the sphere alone, while the meridian at right angles to the axis possesses the combined power of both sphere and cylinder. All cross cylinders, whether combined at right angles or at oblique angles, can be transposed to an equivalent in sphero-cylinders.

3. *When two cylinders are combined whose axes are not at right angles.* The fact that a combination of two cylindrical lenses obliquely inclined to each other is equal to a sphero-cylindrical lens, was first demonstrated by Sir G. G. Stokes, an English investigator in physics, and since then the problem has been described and solved by other authorities; but these methods cannot be understood except by those who are familiar with the higher mathematics and, unfortunately, a large number of intelligent optometrists have not received the necessary training in algebra and geometry.

With the methods of examination that are in use at the present day, it will scarcely be necessary in testing the vision of an eye to use two cylindrical lenses with their axes obliquely inclined to each other, because we naturally arrive at a sphero-cylindrical combination. But if perchance we should get two cylinders with their axes placed as above described, the sphero-cylindrical equivalent can be found by the following practical method, without making use of any algebraic formula or calculation.

Two cylinders are taken from the test case of the same

number and denomination as those that are to be transposed and placed in the trial frame with their axes to correspond, They are then held about twelve or thirteen inches in front of the eye, while the observer looks through them at the corner of a test card or rectangular picture frame hanging twenty feet away. The trial frame is then rotated until a position is found in which there is no break in the vertical and horizontal sides of the card as seen through the lenses and beyond them. Or, as can be more easily accomplished, by confining attention to the vertical line alone and noting the position on the dial of the trial frame where this line is uninterrupted, which will indicate the location of one of the principal meridians of the equivalent lens, and then the other meridian will be at right angles to it.

Having in this way located the two principal meridians, the next step is to determine the refraction of each one. The lesser one is measured by a spherical lens; this will be the position for the axis of the new cylinder; and the lens found will be the spherical element of the new combination. Then a cylinder is added with its axis in this meridian, which will neutralize the opposite meridian of greatest refraction. A sphero-cylinder of the same number and axis, but of opposite signs, will then represent the equivalent of the bi-cylinder with oblique axes.

This method is sufficiently accurate for all practical purposes; in fact, the exact equivalent is obtained as closely as the intervals between the lenses in the observer's trial case will allow, and after a little practice can be arrived at in a few moments.

TO DETERMINE THE AMOUNT OF LENTICULAR ASTIGMATISM

The total amount of astigmatism is found by the usual objective and subjective tests; then the measure of the corneal astigmatism as shown by the ophthalmometer, and the latter subtracted from the former will represent the lenticular astigmatism. When the axes of the two defects are at oblique angles the problem can be solved by the above methods.

Suppose, for instance, the entire astigmatism as revealed

by the usual methods was two and one-half diopters, with the meridian of least curvature halfway between the vertical and horizontal meridians. This would be represented and corrected by a + 2.50 D. cyl. axis 135°. The ophthalmometer is then employed and the corneal astigmatism is found to be one and one-half diopters, with the meridian of least curvature at 155°, which would be represented and corrected by a + 1.50 D. cyl. axis 65°. We then place the first-named cylinder in the trial frame with its axis at the proper position, and the lens that neutralizes the second-named cylinder in the other groove of the frame, the effect of which is to subtract the glass which represents the corneal astigmatism from that which represents the total defect, and the result will evidently be the lenticular astigmatism.

The trial frame now contains a + 2.50 D. cyl. axis 135° and — 1.50 D. cyl. axis 65°, which combination of cylindrical lenses with their axes obliquely inclined, represents the amount of astigmatism existing in the crystalline lens, the measurement of which can be determined by neutralizing this combination, in accordance with the methods just described.

STENOPAIC DISK

Every trial case contains a stenopaic slit. It is made of black metal and is fitted in a ring of the same size as the test lenses, so that it can be placed in the trial frame. There is an oblong opening across its center about 1 mm. wide and 20 mm. long. This is made of various widths by different manufacturers, while some are adjustable, having a small plate which can be moved and then fastened by a screw, in this way increasing or diminishing the width of the opening. If it is too wide it allows too many rays to enter, while, if it is too narrow, the patient experiences difficulty in seeing through it. The writer recommends the 1 mm. size as most satisfactory.

The purpose of the slit is to allow the rays of light to enter the eye only in one meridian. When placed at 90°, the vertical meridian alone is used and the horizontal is excluded. When at 180°, the horizontal meridian only is brought into use and the vertical is shut out from vision.

In any error of refraction where rays of light are not accurately focused on the retina, diffusion circles are formed there; in astigmatism the diffusion areas on the retina are wider in the direction of one principal meridian than in the direction of the other. The stenopaic slit does not lessen them in the direction of its length, but limits them in the direc-

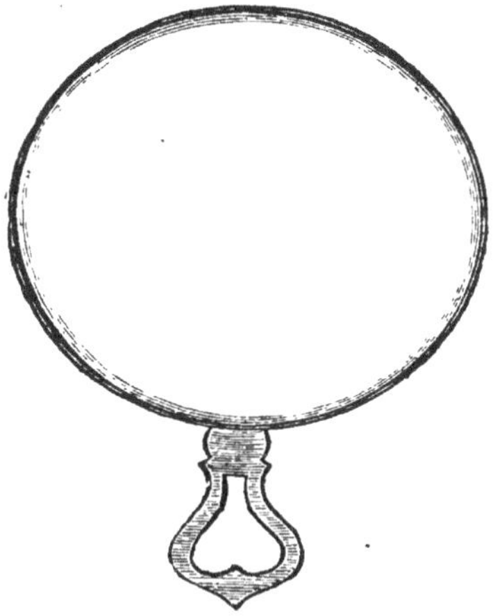

tion at right angles. When, therefore, it is placed before the eye in the proper direction, the diffusion area is reduced in its larger dimension, thus affording the greatest improvement in vision. In the meridian at right angles where the diffusion area is naturally the least extended, it yields the least improvement in vision.

The stenopaic disk is placed in the trial frame in front of the eye to be examined, while the other is excluded from the act of vision by the opaque disk. As the patient looks at the letters on the test card hanging twenty feet away, the disk is slowly rotated to the right and to the left, and the question is asked if the vision gets better or worse as the slit is brought successively in front of the different meridians of the eye. If there is no change in the acuteness of vision in any of the meridians, it is safe to presume that no astigmatism is present; while if the vision grows alternately clearer or dimmer as the slit passes from one meridian to another, then the case can be diagnosed as one of astigmatism.

The slit is then rotated to that meridian which affords

the best vision, and if this is equal to 20/20 then the meridian is assumed to be emmetropic, which diagnosis is confirmed if a weak convex lens placed before the opening in this position renders the vision indistinct. The slit is then rotated a quarter of a circle, and if the vision in this meridian is below normal, the case is one of simple astigmatism, and the number of the convex or concave lens that is necessary to raise the vision to normal will be the measure of the astigmatism, the correction of which is made by placing the axis of the cylinder over the emmetropic meridian.

It might be well to remark, in passing, that the lenses which are placed in front of the slit in the different positions in order to measure the refraction of the various meridians, are spheres, not cylinders, because a sphere is really converted into a cylinder when such a disk is placed over it.

For example, if the patient says that the slit at 90° affords the best vision and that he is able to read all the letters on the No. 20 line clearly, but they are blurred and made indistinct by a + .25 D. sphere, then we know the vertical meridian is emmetropic. The slit is then turned to 180°, when the patient says he can scarcely make out the line he formerly read through the other meridian. A + .25 D. improves it a little, a + .50 D. brings it out clear and sharp, while a + .75 D. destroys the distinctness. This proves the refraction of this meridian to be hypermetropic to the extent of .50 D. This is a case of simple hypermetropic astigmatism, the defect being in the horizontal meridian, and the correcting lens would be + .50 cyl. axis 90°.

The stenopaic slit thus enables the examiner to locate the two principal meridians, and by means of spherical lenses placed in front of it to determine the refraction of each.

If one meridian is emmetropic and the other shows an impaired vision which is raised to normal by a *concave* sphere, then the case is one of simple myopic astigmatism. The examiner must be on his guard in cases like this where a weak concave lens improves vision, lest he be misled by a spasm of the accommodation into the error of diagnosing the refraction as myopic when hypermetropia really is present. This question was discussed in detail in the previous chapter.

If no meridian can be found in which the vision is normal through the slit, then the case is presumably one of compound or mixed astigmatism. In such a condition the slit must be rotated to the meridian of best vision (there is always one meridian that affords better vision than another), and then the strongest convex or weakest concave spherical lens must be found which gives the greatest amount of vision in this meridian. If convex lenses, varying in strength, improve both meridians, the case is one of compound hypermetropic astigmatism. If concave lenses, one stronger than the other are required, it is compound myopic astigmatism. While if one meridian is corrected by a convex lens and the other by a concave, a case of mixed astigmatism is made out.

For example, if a + 1 D. lens is required in the vertical meridian, and a + 2 D. in the horizontal, compound hypermetropic astigmatism is present, the excess of defect being in the horizontal meridian, and the literal correction would be + 1 cyl. axis 180° ⊃ + 2 cyl. axis 90°, which, however, should be transposed to a sphero-cylinder as follows: + 1 sph. ⊃ + 1 cyl. axis 90°.

If the horizontal meridian was found to be the better of the two, both being very indistinct, and a — 1.50 sph. raised vision to normal, while a — 3 sph. was required in the vertical meridian, the defect is a compound myopic astigmatism, with the excess of refraction in the vertical meridian. The literal correction would be — 1.50 cyl. axis 90° ⊃ — 3 cyl. axis 180°, which should be transposed to the following sphero-cylinder: — 1.50 sph. ⊃ — 1.50 cyl. axis 180°. Both of the above instances are cases of astigmatism with the rule.

If none of the meridians afford distinct vision, but the horizontal is found to be the better of the two, and here a + 1.25 sph. is required, while the vertical takes a — 1.50 sph. to yield good vision, the refraction of the meridians differing, the case is one of mixed astigmatism, which would be corrected by the following cross-cylinder: + 1.25 cyl. axis 90° ⊃ — 1.50 cyl. axis 180°, which can be transposed to a sphero cylinder in two ways:

+ 1.25 sph. ⊃ — 2.75 cyl. axis 180° or
— 1.50 sph. ⊃ + 2.75 cyl. axis 90°.

The writer finds in his experience that confusion exists in the minds of some optometrists as to which card should be used in connection with the stenopaic disk. Not a few have tried the radiating lines, and as a consequence have failed to get satisfactory results. Hence it seems proper to make special mention of the fact that the card of letters is the one to be employed, the same as is used in the determination of the acuteness of vision, for the reason that we wish to ascertain the vision and the refraction in each meridian separately, instead of with the whole refracting surface of the eye.

KERATOSCOPE

This instrument enables the observer to determine whether the surface of the cornea is spherical, or whether its curvature varies in different meridians, and thus discloses the presence of corneal astigmatism. It was illustrated and its method of use described in the earlier part of this chapter.

SCHEINER'S TEST

This test, as applied to the detection of hypermetropia and myopia, has been described in Chapters XI and XII. A card is used with two small holes in it, or a piece of metal which can be cut to the exact size of a trial lens. The distance between the openings should be about 2 mm., and the disk must be placed close enough to the eye so that the rays passing through each shall enter the pupil at one and the same time. The patient looks through these holes at a distant point of light, which appears single if the eye is emmetropic. In hypermetropia and myopia two lights are seen; in the first case because the two lines of light strike the retina before meeting, and in the second case they have already met and continued as divergent lines.

Inasmuch as two lights are visible in both hypermetropia and myopia, in order to make the test discriminative, it is customary to cover one of the openings in the disk with a red glass, and then the relation of the white light to the red light will indicate the nature of the refraction. If the disk is placed before the eye with the red glass below, in hypermetropia it will appear as the upper of the two lights, and in myopia as the lower. This phenomenon depends upon the law of projection, by means of which rays that fall upon the lower part of the retina are referred to as coming from an object above, those falling upon the upper part of the retina as coming from below, those falling upon the temporal side of the retina as coming from the nasal side, and those upon the nasal side are referred towards the temple.

As the disk is gradually rotated the two lights are made to move, and in simple hypermetropia or myopia they maintain the same relative positions and distance apart. But if in any one meridian they approximate or separate, then astigmatism is known to be present.

In *simple hypermetropic astigmatism* one meridian shows but one light, while at right angles two lights would be seen, separated as in hypermetropia, and the convex lens that fuses the two lights in this meridian is the measure of the astigmatism, and the axis of the correcting cylinder is placed in the emmetropic meridian.

In *simple myopic astigmatism* one meridian is normal as shown by the single light, and at right angles two lights are seen, separated as in myopia, and the concave lens that fuses these two lights in this meridian will be the measure of the astigmatism, and the axis of the correcting concave cylinder is placed in the meridian of emmetropia.

In *compound hypermetropic astigmatism* two lights are visible in all the meridians, the red light appearing in the direction of the clear opening of the disk, but there will be a difference in the amount of separation in the different meridians. The position is found where the lights are nearest together, and then the convex lens that fuses them will be the measure of the defect in this meridian, and should be used as the sphere. The disk is then turned 90° where the lights are the most widely separated, and the convex lens that fuses them will be the measure of the defect in this meridian, and then the difference between the two lenses will represent the strength of the cylinder which should be combined with the sphere with its axis in the direction of the least defective meridian.

In *compound myopic astigmatism* two lights are seen in all meridians, this time the red light appearing in the same direction as the colored glass, and the amount of separation varying in the different meridians. The location is found where the lights are nearest together, and then the concave lens that fuses them will be the measure of the defect in this

The Ophthalmometer

meridian, and will represent the sphere of the correcting lens. The meridian at right angles is measured by the concave lens that fuses the lights, and the difference between the two lenses will represent the cylinder of the correcting lens, the axis of which is placed over the meridian first tested.

In *mixed astigmatism* one meridian will be like a simple hypermetropic astigmatism, and that at right angles like a simple myopic astigmatism, each of which meridians is measured and corrected as described. The resulting lens is a cross-cylinder, which can be transposed into a sphero-cylinder, the method of doing which has already been explained in detail.

CHROMATIC TEST

This test has been described at some length and illustrated in the chapter on "Method of Examination," Volume I. The cobalt blue lens that is made use of excludes all the colors except blue and red, the former being the more refrangible are brought to a focus sooner than the latter. In the *emme-*

tropic eye the retina is located midway between the foci of the blue and red rays, resulting in the appearance of a diffused violet color. In the *hypermetropic* eye, the retina being farther front, approaches the location of the blue focus, resulting in the appearance of a blue center with a red border. In the *myopic* eye, the retina being farther back, approaches the location of the red focus, resulting in the appearance of a red center with a blue border.

In *astigmatism* the light will appear elongated instead of circular. In the hypermetropic and myopic forms, the centers and borders corresponding to hypermetropia and myopia.

THE OPHTHALMOMETER

This instrument was invented by Helmholtz, who published a description of it in 1854. But the primitive ophthalmometer was hardly a practical one and did not come into general use.

About twenty years ago Javal and Schiötz commenced to alter and improve the instrument so as to adapt it for office use, but it is only about ten years ago that the present model was perfected, and as now constructed it seems almost to have reached the limit of improvement. The word "Ophthalmometer" literally means an "eye measure," and, strictly speaking, should be applied only to an instrument which measures the refractive condition of the whole eye; whereas, this instrument is designed only to measure the radius of curvature of the cornea in its various meridians, to which the term "Keratometer" would be more applicable.

The essential parts of the ophthalmometer are a *telescope,* which contains an arrangement for doubling the images seen through it; and a set of *mires* or reflectors, which are capable of approximation and separation. The *telescope* contains an eye-piece, two objectives, and a bi-refracting prism, the latter being made from the best mountain crystal quartz, which possesses the power of doubling objects when ground in a certain direction with regard to the axis of the quartz. This prism is in reality composed of two prisms, the base of one placed over the apex of the other, in such a way as to cause the deviation to take place from each side, and as each prism produces a certain degree of deviation, twice the amount of separation is secured, and at the same time the doubled images can be kept nearer the center of the field. And the prisms are placed in the telescope in such a way that their plane of doubling is in exact line with the plane of the graduated arc.

The prisms are so adjusted as to produce a separation of three millimeters when the telescope is properly focused. When, therefore, the cornea is viewed through it there is the appearance of two corneæ, and every object reflected from its surface is displaced 3 mm. as well as doubled. If the image of such object happened to be 3 mm. in length, the two images seen would have their edges just in contact.

The two *mires* that are used are illustrated in the above diagram. One is a simple white block and the other has a series of steps, arranged in groups, so that they can be readily counted, both of the mires having a black line running directly in the middle, which may be called the guide line, and is parallel with the plane of the arc. These lines serve to show when the arc is in one of the chief meridians of curvature of the cornea, that is, when in the meridian of longest or shortest radius of curvature. When in either of these meridians, the two lines are straight, opposite each other and apparently continuous. In all other meridians the lines run somewhat obliquely and are separated one above or below the other. If the cornea had the same curvature in all meridians, the lines would remain straight and continuous, no matter in what position they were rotated.

As the determination of the two chief meridians in any case of astigmatism is one of the first and most necessary points, and as this is accomplished by means of these guide lines it is obvious that they are of much importance. The location of the principal meridians is shown by an indicator which is movable with the mires and points to figures on a dial, where the meridians are marked in degrees of a circle.

The curvature of the cornea is measured by determining how large an object is required to give a reflection from the cornea just equal to the separation of the doubled images It is evident that the images reflected from the cornea will vary in size according to its curvature, being larger when the radius of curvature is longer, and grows smaller as the radius is shorter. Hence, it follows that the size of the images reflected from the cornea bears a direct relation to its radius of curvature, and when the first is measured and known the second can be calculated.

The distance of the object is maintained fixed and constant by means of the arc, and the size of the corneal reflection is also a constant quantity, because it is measured by the amount which the prism separates the two images at the fixed distance. From these two factors a scale has been calculated by which a certain sized object will correspond to a certain radius of curvature of cornea.

The graduated arc, which carries the mires, is concentric with the cornea. It is graduated into equal spaces and numbered, commencing at the center and extending outward in each direction. Each of these divisions represents one diopter. For example, when the cornea is in focus and the arc in the horizontal position, and the reflections of the mires show them to be just in contact when they are standing on each side of the arc at 20, then the horizontal meridian of the cornea represents a refractive power of 40 D. Now the arc is turned to the vertical meridian, and the reflections overlap, then the mires must be moved outward until the images are simply touching again. If the mires are then located at number 21 on each side of the arc, the refractive power of the vertical meridian of the cornea is equal to 42 D., which is an excess of 2 D. over the horizontal, and indicates an astigmatism of that amount.

The images of the mires as reflected from the cornea are farther apart on one of longer curvature, and nearer together on a cornea of shorter curvature, and therefore when the mires are set in such a position as to correspond to the normal or average radius of curvature, if the mires must be approximated there is evidence of less refractive power and a presumption of a hypermetropic condition. Whereas, if the mires would need to be separated, in order to allow of simple contact, there is evidence of an increase of refractive power and a presumption of myopia.

PRINCIPLE OF THE OPHTHALMOMETER

The principle on which the ophthalmometer acts in measuring the radius of curvature of the cornea in its various meridians, and thereby revealing the existence of corneal astigmatism, depends on the measurement of the size of an image reflected from the surface of the cornea.

In order that this may be the more readily accomplished, it is first doubled by the bi-refracting prism in the telescope of the instrument. The inner edges of the two mires furnish the objects of observation. As everything is doubled, it must be remembered that four mires are visible. *A* and *a* are the

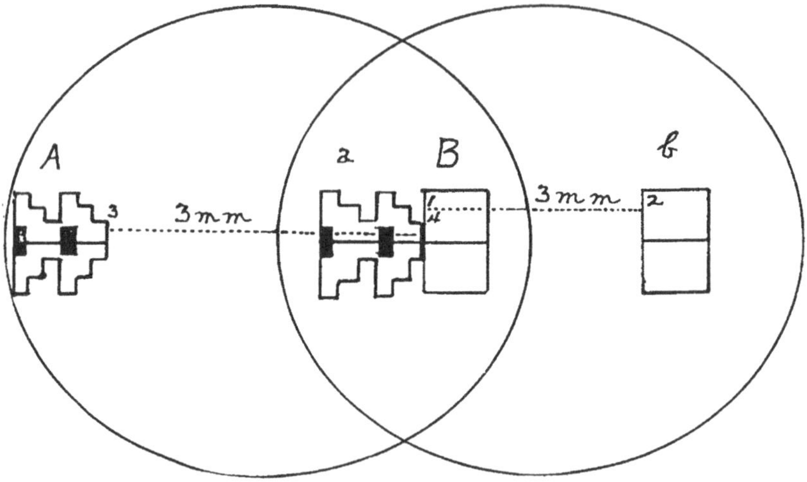

images of the stepped mire and *B* and *b* the images of the plain mire. In practice, the two outer images *A* and *b* are disregarded, the whole attention being fixed on the central images *a* and *B*. The distance *1* to *2* between the inner edges of the plain mire, and the distance *3* to *4* between the inner edges of the stepped mire, each represent the amount of deviation caused by the prism, which is 3 mm. (The diagram is incorrect in that it does not show these two distances exactly the same.)

It might be well to repeat that the ophthalmometer is not intended to determine the nature of the refraction, whether hypermetropic or myopic, except in the indirect way, which has already been referred to, and which is not to be relied upon. The scope of the instrument is to measure the anterior surface of the cornea, and to reveal any differences of curvature in its various meridians, which is essentially astigmatism. Hence, the stepped mire is provided, which indicates the amount of astigmatism by the overlapping or separation of the mires in the several meridians, the mires being so constructed that each step represents one diopter. If the cornea is uniformly curved in all of its meridians, there is no change in the relative positions of the two mires as they are moved through the different meridians.

METHOD OF USING THE OPHTHALMOMETER

A good *light* is essential. Daylight from a large window with a northern exposure will answer the purpose, but artificial light is better. Four electric lamps surrounding the face of the patient are preferable on account of their convenience, although two Welsbach gas burners with suitable reflectors, one on each side, afford just as good an illumination.

The patient is seated with his chair drawn up close to the table, with his chin upon the rest provided for that purpose, his forehead pressed firmly against the head-rest and his face in comparative shadow. The eyes should be wide open, the one under examination being directed into the opening of the telescope, while the other may be covered with the metal shade. The patient's head should be in such a position that the eyes are horizontal, because if the head was tilted and one eye higher than the other, the apparent location of the meridians would not be true, but might be 5° or 10° off from what they really are, and hence would not correspond with other tests and could not be relied upon.

The mires are placed at those points which indicate the normal radius of corneal curvature, and the graduated arc must be exactly in the horizontal position. The operator looks along the telescope to see that it is turned towards the patient's eye, and its height is adjusted to correspond by means of a large hand-screw. Then he looks through the telescope and brings it into focus, which is accomplished by sliding it backwards and forwards on the stand, and perhaps to one side or the other, until the cornea of the patient occupies the field of view, and the reflections of the mires will appear sharp and clear. Attention is directed solely to the two central images, which should be exactly in the center of the field.

Then what is called the "primary position" should be obtained, which is that position in which the black lines which bisect the mires are opposite each other and form a continuous straight line, which indicates that this is the location of one of the principal meridians. In a majority of cases this is at the 180th meridian, but if not the instrument is slowly revolved until this primary position is found. The horizontal position is selected as the one from which to make the start for another reason, and that is because it is usually the meridian of least refraction, but if it is not, then the meridian of least refraction is found by rotating the instrument to that position where the mires appear the most widely separated.

For sake of illustration we will suppose that when the mires are placed at the indicated points and the arc is in a horizontal position the central images just touch each other and one continuous line runs through the middle of each. The other principal meridian will be at right angles to this, to which the instrument must be turned, where, on account of the excess of refraction, there will be an overlapping of the mires, the extent of which will be the measure of the difference in refraction of the two meridians and thus an indication of the amount of astigmatism.

When the primary position is horizontal, as above, and the images overlap when turned to the secondary position, the condition is astigmatism with the rule; while in astigmatism against the rule they are separated in the secondary position. These changes are due to the fact that in the first condition the excess of curvature is in the vertical meridian, while in the second the horizontal possesses the greater curvature.

In order to intelligently interpret the readings of the ophthalmometer, there are two points to be constantly borne in mind:

1. There is a small amount of lenticular astigmatism which is nearly always present and which is against the rule.

2. There is a small amount of corneal astigmatism which is nearly always present and which is with the rule.

These conditions neutralize each other; that is, they cause the two principal meridians to have the same degree of curvature, thus removing the astigmatic element in the case.

Therefore, when there is no change in the relative positions of the two mires as they are moved through the different meridians, when they neither overlap nor separate on turning from the primary to the secondary position, the cornea is shown to be spherical in form and without astigmatism. But in such cases, on account of the lental astigmatism, the patient will often take a weak cylindrical lens with its axis set against the rule; that is, a + .50 cyl. axis 180° if the refraction is hypermetropic, or a — .50 cyl. axis 90° if the patient is myopic.

This leads to the enunciation of the following rules:

Deduct one-half diopter from the reading of the instrument in astigmatism with the rule.

Add one-half diopter to the reading of the instrument in astigmatism against the rule.

Examples: In the horizontal meridian the mires are simply in contact, while in the vertical they overlap one-half a step; this shows astigmatism with the rule of the normal amount, and when allowance is made, as above, no glass is required. If the overlapping in the vertical meridian amounts to two steps, by making the deduction that is necessary, the glass prescribed would be either + 1.50 cyl. axis 90°, or — 1.50 cyl. axis 180°.

Suppose the optometrist finds the vertical meridian to have the least curvature, which is known to an experienced observer as soon as he looks through the instrument, then he takes this for his primary position and moves the mires so as to bring them together, and then when they are rotated to the horizontal meridian there will be an overlapping. If this should amount to one step, by making the necessary addition, the glass prescribed would be either + 1.50 cyl. axis 180° or — 1.50 cyl. axis 90°.

In astigmatism with the rule the lental astigmatism is in the *same* meridian as the corneal, but is of the *opposite* refraction; while in astigmatism against the rule, the lental and corneal astigmatism agree both in meridian and in kind.

In case the two chief meridians should be at 45° and 135°, we have neither astigmatism with or against the rule, and in such cases the above directions are scarcely applicable. The method of procedure is to find the primary position by rotating the telescope to that meridian where the bisecting line of each meridian is straight, opposite each other and continuous. In the usual position of the mires horizontally, these lines would be broken and separated, but as the instrument is turned they approach each other until when 45° is reached they become straight and continuous. If they are not in exact contact the movable mire is made to slide until their edges simply touch. Presuming this is the meridian of least refraction, then at 135°, where the lines are again opposite each other, there will be an overlapping, the extent of which will indicate the degree of astigmatism. If, in making the change from the primary to the secondary position, the mires should separate, then the optometrist would know that he has made the start from the wrong position and he will change the secondary position so as to make it the primary one.

When it is found that one meridian has a greater refractive power than the other the object is to equalize them, which can be accomplished in two ways. If the refraction of the eye is hypermetropic, a convex cylinder is used to build up the meridian of least refraction. If the refraction is myopic, a concave cylinder is employed to diminish the meridian of excessive refraction. In both cases the same result is obtained, viz., a uniformity of the two meridians. If the ophthalmometer showed an overlapping equal to 1.50 D. in the vertical meridian, after making the necessary allowance, the case might be corrected by one of the following formulæ: + 1 D. cyl. axis 90°, or — 1 D. cyl. axis 180°.

OPHTHALMOSCOPE AS A TEST FOR ASTIGMATISM

Direct Method.—In the use of the ophthalmoscope the presence of astigmatism is revealed by the view of the fundus appearing more or less blurred, and by the inability of the observer to make it perfectly clear by rotating into the sight-hole the various spherical lenses of the instrument. The disks of the ophthalmoscope do not contain cylindrical lenses, and hence the refraction of the two chief meridians must be measured by spheres.

In the ophthalmoscopic examination of an astigmatic eye the first thing that attracts the attention of the optometrist is that the optic disk, instead of being circular, as it usually appears, presents an oval shape, the long axis of which corresponds to the meridian of greatest refraction.

But it is the difference in degree of the clearness of the retinal blood-vessels and of the margins of the disk, that is to be noticed as indicating the presence or absence of astigmatism, and the lenses required to equalize them as the measure of the defect. The vessels running horizontally and the upper and lower sides of the disk are focused, and the lens noted that is necessary to give them clearest definition. Then the blood-vessels running upwards and downwards and the inner and outer sides of the disk are focused and measured in like manner. Thus the refraction of the two chief meridians is determined, and any difference that may be shown between them will indicate the presence and amount of astigmatism. For example, if the horizontal vessels are seen best with a + 2 D. while the vertical vessels are blurred with any lens stronger than + 1 D., astigmatism would be proven to exist to the amount of 1 D. The rule is to select the strongest convex or the weakest concave lens, through which these vessels are most distinctly seen. When the chief meridians are not vertical and horizontal, but in some oblique position, an effort must be made to find a vessel running upwards and outwards from the disk that will coincide with one of the principal meridians, which is focused and measured; after which one at right angles is sought and estimated in the same way.

In these examinations it is very necessary that the accommodation of both patient and optometrist be as nearly at rest as possible. Directions for the best methods of accomplishing this result without atropine were given in the previous chapter. It is also desirable that the observer approach his ophthalmoscope close to the eye under examination, as the strength of the indicated lens varies with the distance, a concave lens being weakened and a convex lens strengthened by removal from the eye, which might lead to an under-correction in myopia and an over-correction in hypermetropia.

In using the ophthalmoscope for these purposes it must be remembered that the vertical vessels are seen through the horizontal meridian of the eye, and the horizontal vessels through the vertical meridian. Hence, when a vessel running upwards or downwards is measured, it is the refraction of the horizontal meridian that is being estimated; when a horizontal vessel is focused, the refraction of the vertical meridian is measured.

ILLUSTRATIVE EXAMPLES

If the vertical vessels are seen with a + 1 D. while the horizontal vessels are clear without any lens and are blurred by the weakest convex lens in the ophthalmoscope, the case is one of *simple hypermetropic astigmatism*, the defect being in the horizontal meridian, and the correcting lens + 1 cyl. axis 90°.

If the vertical vessels are clearly seen without any lens and are blurred by the weakest convex, while the horizontal vessels are indistinct and require a — 2 D. to make them clear, the case is one of *simple myopic astigmatism*, the defect being located in the vertical meridian, and a — 2 cyl. axis 180° is the lens required to correct.

Even though the vessels are seen distinctly, hypermetropia is still possibly present, being concealed by the accommodation of patient or observer. Hence, a convex lens is always rotated into the sight-hole, and if the vessels are made clearer, or at least if they are made no worse, the refraction is proven to be hypermetropic. Following this method, if the vertical vessels will bear + 2 D. and the horizontal + 1 D., the diagnosis is *compound hypermetropic astigmatism*, the excess of hypermetropia being in horizontal meridian, and the formula would be written: + 1 S. ⊃ + 1 cyl. axis 90°.

If it is impossible to obtain a view of any of the vessels of the fundus, and a — 1.50 D. suffices to render the vertical vessels clear, while — 3 D. is required for the horizontal, the case is one of *compound myopic astigmatism*, the excess of refraction being in the vertical meridian, and the correcting lens would be — 1.50 S. ⊃ — 1.50 cyl. axis 180°.

If the vertical vessels will bear + 1 D., while the horizontal require — 2 D., *mixed astigmatism* is present, the horizontal meridian being hypermetropic and the vertical myopic, which calls for the following cross-cylinder: + 1 cyl. axis 90° ⊃ — 2 cyl. axis 180°, which may be transposed to + 1 S. ⊃ — 3 cyl. axis 180°.

Indirect Method.—On withdrawing the lens from the eye, an increase in the size of the disk indicates myopia; while a diminution in its size, hypermetropia; or a change more noticeable in one meridian than another, astigmatism. If it grows larger in one direction, that meridian is myopic; if smaller, hypermetropic; if no change, emmetropic. In this way it may be possible to determine the refraction of the several meridians and thus calculate the necessary correcting lens; but this method does not yield accurate results and is not one to be depended upon.

RETINOSCOPY

One of the characteristic appearances met with in astigmatism is the streak or band of bright illumination. It is not always present, but when it is observed it may be regarded as distinctive of this defect. But dependence is more to be placed on the measurement of the several meridians by the same methods that are pursued in hypermetropia and myopia. Astigmatism is determined by a difference in motion in the two principal meridians. This is evident even if the motion is the same in both meridians, varying only in degree; but still more manifest if the direction of the movement differs in the two meridians, in the one moving with and in the other against the mirror.

It is not always an easy matter to detect slight differences in the two meridians, and hence the better way is first to determine by the direction of the movements whether the refraction is myopic or hypermetropic, and then commence with the indicated lens, whether concave or convex, gradually increasing until a lens is found that stops all movements in one meridian. If this lens fails to correct the other meridian,

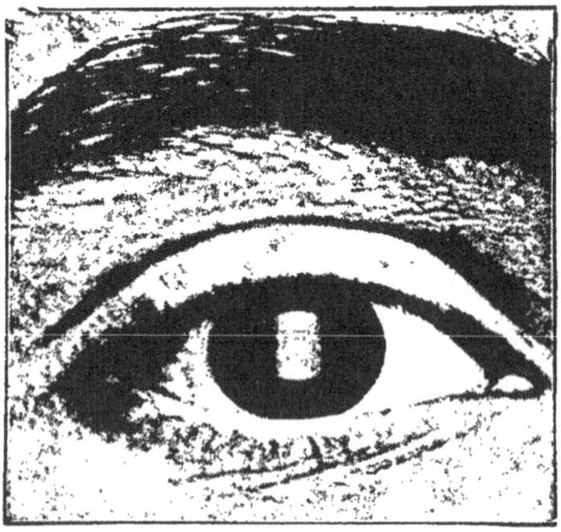

The Banded Appearance

then a cylinder may be placed over it with its axis in the direction of the first meridian, gradually increasing in strength until one is found that neutralizes the second meridian; and then the two principal meridians being measured, the nature of the refraction and degree of astigmatism become evident.

Or spherical lenses may be used to determine the refraction of the two principal meridians, just as in the use of the stenopaic slit, and calculations made in the same way to figure out the glasses required. The weakest lens is found that neutralizes any one meridian, and this will represent the sphere of the correcting combination, and then the lens is determined that is required in the opposite meridian and the difference between the two will be the number of the cylinder that must be combined with the sphere.

THE CROSS-CYLINDER TEST

The use of a cross cylinder forms a valuable test for corroborating or disproving the results of the trial case, and for determining with greater accuracy the cylinder required in cases of astigmatism. Weak cylinders only are desired, the two in most common use being

— .25 cyl. ⌐ + .25 cyl.

and — .50 cyl. ⌐ + .50 cyl.

These are equivalent to a .25 sphere combined with a .50 cylinder and a .50 sphere combined with a 1 cylinder.

The correcting glass is determined as nearly as possible by the usual tests, and is placed in the trial frame and a weak convex and weak concave lens held over it to determine if the sphere can be changed to any advantage. Then the cross cylinder is made use of as the crucial and final test, being so fixed that the axis of one of its cylinders shall be directly over the axis of the cylinder in the frame, and then turned a quarter of a circle, so that the axis of the other cylinder may occupy the same position. This is done to enable the patient to determine which position affords the better vision, when the axis of the convex or the concave cylinder is parallel to the axis of the trial cylinder, and the optometrist is guided in his choice of lenses by the patient's statement.

If the cylinder in the trial frame is convex and vision is improved when the convex axis of the cross cylinder coincides with it, then a stronger cylinder may be borne. If the concave axis of the cross cylinder is preferred, a weaker cylinder is indicated. If, on the other hand, the trial cylinder is concave and improvement is afforded when the concave axis of the cross cylinder coincides with it, the cylinder may be strengthened. If preference is given to the convex axis of the cross cylinder, then the cylinder must be weakened.

If any change is indicated and made in the strength of the cylinder, the position of its axis must also be re-tested, and then a weak convex and concave sphere used to determine if any change is necessary in the sphere of the combination.

The estimated correction may be assumed to be correct:

1. When no improvement is caused by the cross cylinder in either position.

2. When the change indicated and made in one direction is afterwards reversed.

Even in cases of simple hypermetropia or myopia with apparently no evidence of astigmatism, the cross cylinder may be of value by developing a latent defect, as it is placed in front of the indicated sphere and rotated to different positions.

By way of example, an imaginary case of compound hypermetropic astigmatism may be taken, the exact correction of which is represented in the following formula:

+ 1.50 S. ⊃ + .75 cyl. axis 90°.

If this case was examined by a number of optometrists of average skill, their prescriptions would vary something like this:

+ 1.25 S. ⊃ + 1 cyl. axis 90°.
+ 1.75 S. ⊃ + .50 cyl. axis 90°.
+ 1 S. ⊃ + 1.25 cyl. axis 90°.
+ 2 S. ⊃ + .25 cyl. axis 90°.
+ .75 S. ⊃ + 1.50 cyl. axis 90°.

While none of these five formulæ is correct, neither the sphere nor the cylinder being of the proper strength, yet in every one of them the horizontal shows the correct measure of refraction, while the vertical meridian as represented by

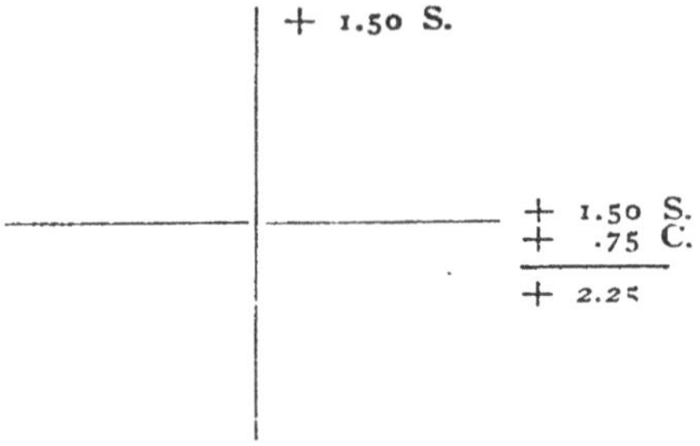

the spherical departs from the desired power and varies in every case. This can be readily seen by comparing each formula with the diagram, which represents the necessary number in the vertical and horizontal meridians. Any one of these prescriptions might afford a reasonable amount of satisfaction and apparently seem to the patient to be all that could be desired, and yet they are not strictly correct.

The conscientious optometrist, before ordering a pair of sphero-cylinders, wants to be satisfied of their exactness. Some men may think an approximate correction will suffice, but accuracy should always be the aim, which requires attention to all the minutest details. And in many cases this makes the difference between relief or dissatisfaction for the patient, and between success and failure for the optometrist.

After the optometrist has decided on what seems to be the proper combination, the cross cylinder can be employed to test its faultlessness. Referring to the imaginary case, the formula for which was mentioned above, suppose the third prescription be taken and submitted to this test. The weaker of the cross cylinders is preferred in this case, the stronger of the two being reserved for those cases where the astigmatism is of high degree. The patient is asked to note whether the vision is improved or made worse and which of the positions is the better.

When the cross cylinder is held with the axis of its convex surface vertical, the resulting lens is as follows:

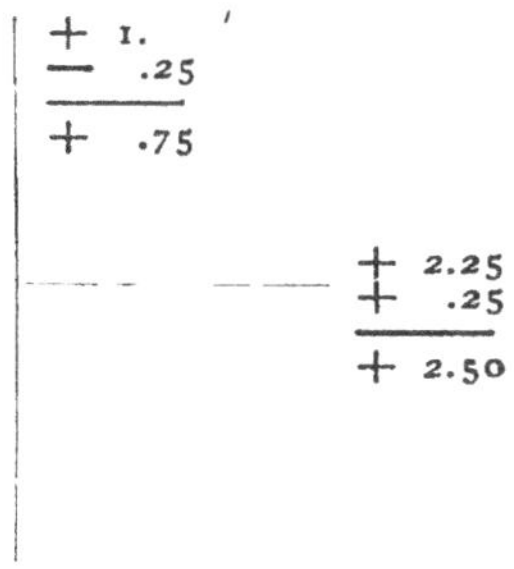

$$+ .75 \text{ S.} \supset + 1.75 \text{ cyl. axis } 90^\circ,$$

which the patient would probably reject as making vision worse. Then the lens is rotated a quarter of a circle, when the following combination results:

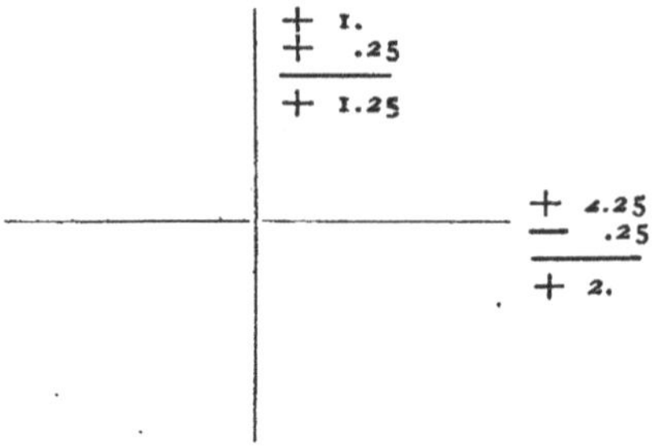

+ 1.25 S. ⊃ + .75 cyl. axis 90°,

which the patient will doubtless accept as an improvement, because it more clearly approaches the real correction. Spherical lenses held before this combination will show that the sphere will bear an increase of .25 D., and when the + 1.25 S. is replaced by + 1.50 S. the exact measurement of the refraction is reached. Neither the cross cylinder nor sphere will now show that further improvement is possible.

After each change in either sphere or cylinder the position for the axis of the latter should be again determined, in order to detect any possible alteration that may be necessary. This is so important a piece of advice that it will bear repetition.

TREATMENT OF ASTIGMATISM

The remedy for astigmatism consists in the adaptation of the proper lenses that will correct the refractive error existing in each particular meridian. This is accomplished by means of cylindrical lenses, which supply the necessary refractive power in the abnormal meridian, and leave the emmetropic meridian unaffected. In simple hypermetropic astigmatism the convex cylinder adds sufficient refractive power to the hypermetropic meridian to make it equal to the emmetropic meridian, which is not changed by the axis of the cylinder that is located over it. In simple myopic astigmatism the concave cylinder reduces the excessive refraction in the myopic meridian, thus equalizing the two meridians.

Simple astigmatism is corrected by a *plano-cylinder, compound astigmatism* by a *sphero-cylinder*, and *mixed astigmatism* by a *crossed cylinder*, which can be reduced to a sphero-cylinder.

Rays of light passing through the axis of a cylindrical lens are not refracted, because it is like a plate of plane glass with parallel surfaces. All the other portions of the lens refract the light, those nearest the axis the least, but with gradually increasing power until the maximum is reached in the meridian at right angles to the axis. The same gradations of refractive power precisely are found in the surfaces of an astigmatic eye, where one meridian may be taken as normal, from which there will be a gradual increase or diminution of refractive power as the meridian at right angles is approached, where the maximum degree of deviation is found, and which is the location of the full extent of the astigmatism. Therefore in simple astigmatism, when a suitable cylindrical lens is placed before the eye with its axis over the normal meridian, there will be such a correspondence between the gradually decreasing curvature of the eye and the gradually increasing curves of the lens, or *vice-versa*, as to make all the meridians have the same refractive power, and thus neutralize the astigmatism, and raise the acuteness of vision to normal.

In the mild cases of astigmatism which are commonly met with, there is usually no great difficulty in securing normal vision. But in the higher degrees of the defect, on account of the distance of the correcting lens from the refracting surfaces of the eye, the neutralization cannot be perfect, although the improvement in vision they afford is very noticeable. If the cylindrical lens could be cemented to the astigmatic cornea, the correction would be ideally complete and perfect vision might be expected. But no matter how carefully the cylinder is adjusted, the correction can approximate perfection only when the eyes are in one certain position directed straight ahead. Therefore, on account of the mobility of the eyeball, and the inability of the lenses to change their position and follow the ocular movements, there must be a large portion of the time when cylindrical curvature and the eye curvature do not accurately correspond, and the planes of light passing through the different portions of the lens do not enter the meridians of the eye for which they were intended. This displacement of adjustment between the defective surfaces and the correcting ones is not noticeable in the lower grades of astigmatism; but in the higher degrees of the defect it becomes a source of great disturbance and interferes considerably with the clearness of vision.

The optometrist need therefore not be discouraged when he fails to raise the acuteness of vision to 20/20, if he has given the case careful examination and feels that the glasses have been properly chosen. The patient will probably be satisfied because he has never known normal vision, and the glasses make it so much better than that to which he has been accustomed. It frequently happens that after they have been worn for a time the vision will gradually improve. The explanation of this can be found in the fact that the retina of the uncorrected astigmatic eye becomes blunted by the imperfect and indistinct images and circles of diffusion that are formed upon it, which gradually changes to a more sensitive condition as the sharply defined images are now impressed upon it by means of the cylindrical lenses.

SPHERE OR CYLINDER FIRST?

In testing eyes with trial lenses it is customary to commence with spheres, first convex and then concave, and if these fail to improve vision, to resort to cylinders. In compound astigmatism the rule has been to use the spheres first and correct whatever there is of hypermetropia or myopia, thus reducing the case to one of simple astigmatism, which is then to be corrected by a plane cylinder placed over or in front of the spherical. The cylinder to be increased or diminished as necessary, and rotated to that position which affords the best vision, just as is done in correcting a case of simple astigmatism.

But this is not an iron-clad rule that is to be blindly followed in every case, but common sense and judgment must be used to interpret any and all rules. If the astigmatic element is the more pronounced of the two, while the axial defect is but slight, the vision is probably so much impaired and so little improvement is afforded by spherical lenses, that it becomes necessary to use the cylinders and correct the astigmatism first, after which the spheres can be added and increased as the vision is raised.

In those cases where the two defects are nearly equal, the best results can be obtained by changing first one and then the other. For instance, a spherical lens is placed in the trial frame, which is accepted as an improvement over the naked eye vision. Then instead of trying a stronger sphere, a cylinder is dropped in front of the first lens, which, when rotated to its proper position, affords a still greater betterment of vision. Then the sphere is changed, afterwards the cylinder, alternating from one to the other until a combination of sphere and cylinder is found which cannot be further improved upon.

A recent author says: "Here again I wish to emphasize the importance of correcting the astigmatism first; for if there happens to be only a simple astigmatism present, we have gone to the root of the trouble at once; and if a spherical error is present in addition to the astigmatism, we have disposed of the astigmatism and have only the spherical error left to deal with, as in simple hypermetropia and myopia. This method of procedure is of great advantage when there is a tendency to spasm of accommodation; for after the astigmatism has been corrected in each eye separately, we can then put spherical glasses before both eyes at once. In this way, as is well known, the tendency to spasm of accommodation is overcome and the patient many times accepts stronger plus, or weaker minus, glasses than when one eye is tested at a time. However, it should not be forgotten that spherical glasses should be tried in addition to the cylindrical glasses on each eye separately, before both eyes are tried together, for there may be more spherical in one eye than the other.

"For example, say the patient accepts in the right eye $+ 1$ S. $\supset$ $+ 2$ cyl. axis 90°, and in the left eye $+ .50$ S. $\supset$ $+ 2$ cyl. axis 90°, when each eye is tested separately. If we suspect spasm of accommodation, we should leave the cylindrical glasses as they are, and place in front of them at the same time a $+ .25$ D. stronger spherical glass than they accepted singly. In this instance, in front of the right eye $+ 1.25$ D. and in front of the left $+ .75$ D. If these are accepted, add $+ .25$ D. stronger sphere yet, and continue until the vision begins to be made worse. Where the patient does not accept as strong a cylindrical glass as indicated by the ophthalmometer, I often try both eyes at the same time with cylindrical glasses. Of course, this is after the eyes have been tried separately, when both cylindrical glasses can be increased proportionately in strength, just as in the case of spherical glasses."

This author takes the view of correcting the astigmatism first, no matter how much or how litttle. While his advice is not by any means to be despised, yet we cannot entirely agree with him that this is the proper procedure in every case. We have found by experience that better results can be obtained by varying the method as we have outlined.

SPASM OF ACCOMMODATION

Spasm of accommodation (by which is meant a tonic contraction of the ciliary muscle) may occur in any form of error of refraction, and even in emmetropia, which is thus transformed into an apparent myopia. But it is most commonly found in hypermetropia and hypermetropic astigmatism, either simple or compound. In this way simple hypermetropic astigmatism is made to appear as simple myopic astigmatism, the defective meridian in the latter case appearing at right angles to that in the former.

Spasm of the accommodation has been the bugbear of refraction and the nightmare of the optometrist, largely because of the idea that prevails that it can be detected and combatted only by a mydriatic. The statement can safely be made that it is not necessary to use a drug in every case of ciliary spasm, because in many instances, if the cause can be discovered and remedied, the spasm will gradually disappear. Therefore we may say there is a point which the expert optometrist may reach, where he will find that spasm of the accommodation is a thing that is not to be so much dreaded after all, because a mydriatic is not the only weapon with which it can be fought, although we must admit that there are occasional cases where it has to be called into requisition as a last resort.

SYMPTOMS OF SPASM OF ACCOMMODATION

The patient affected with the spasm of accommodation will usually complain of more or less pain in and around the eye, and a feeling of strain with drawing or contraction in the ball.

In testing his vision the optometrist may find great variability in its acuteness. When first looking at the test card the patient may say he can read only the larger letters, but after intently looking at it the other letters may come into view, until the vision may reach 20/40, or 20/30, or even 20/20. The writer has had this experience frequently; he has entered the acuteness of vision in his record book according to the patient's first statement at 20/100 or 20/70 perhaps, which he has had to cross out because the patient afterwards was able to read a lower and smaller line. These may again fade out and only the larger letters remain legible. This condition when present is usually found in both eyes, although there may be occasional cases where, on account of the difference in the refraction of the two eyes, it is present in only one. The patient may be allowed to rest his eyes a few moments by closing them, but when the examination is repeated the same thing is likely to happen again.

A case like the one we have just cited is evidently affected with a marked degree of hypermetropia or hypermetropic astigmatism, which reduces the acuteness of the vision very perceptibly, and the improvement in vision which temporarily occurs is due to a spasmodic contraction of the ciliary muscle, which neutralizes the defect but cannot in every case be maintained for a length of time.

In other cases, the spasm of accommodation by causing the crystalline lens to become more convex and increasing the refractive power of the eye, brings the parallel rays of light to a focus in front of the retina, which is exactly the condition found in myopia, and is known as *simulated, false or accommodative myopia,* which, of course, makes distant vision very indistinct.

Another evidence of spasm of accommodation is a variableness in the appearance of the radiating lines on the clock-dial card, at one time the patient saying one set of lines appear clear and distinct, and a moment later these become dim and another set of lines take their place as being plainer.

In simple hypermetropic astigmatism there is always a tendency to ciliary contraction, which then transposes the case into one of apparent simple myopic astigmatism, with the defect in the meridian at right angles.

For instance, in a case of simple hypermetropic astigmatism "with the rule," the hypermetropia lies in the horizontal meridian, and, if the accommodation is passive, the vertical lines will seem the least plain. But the ciliary muscle unconsciously and automatically comes into action, and in doing so it neutralizes the deficiency of refraction in the horizontal meridian, thus making this meridian normal, and at the same time increases the refraction in the vertical meridian, thus rendering it myopic. Now, instead of the horizontal meridian being defective (hypermetropic) and the vertical lines indistinct, the vertical meridian will be defective (in this case myopic) and the horizontal lines become indistinct. In this way it will be readily seen that the location of the indistinct lines will vary according to the contraction or relaxation of the ciliary muscle.

Another evidence of ciliary activity is a variability in the glasses accepted by the patient at different examinations or, perhaps, even during the same test. One day, or one minute, the patient will accept a convex lens, and the next it will be refused, and nothing but a concave will answer. Or at one time a strong convex lens will be borne, and at another time only a very much weaker one will be accepted.

Corroborative evidence of accommodative spasm is found when the retinoscope shows the refraction of the eye to differ greatly from the glasses accepted by the test with the trial case. For instance, the strongest convex glasses the patient will accept when viewing the test card hanging twenty feet away, may be + 1 D., and yet the retinoscope will show a hypermetropia of possibly 4 D. or 5 D. Or perhaps in some cases the patient will positively reject all convex lenses and accept only concaves, when the retinoscope will show the actual condition of the refraction to be hypermetropic.

The circumstances under which the retinoscopic examination is made are necessarily such as to favor a relaxation of the accommodation. The room is darkened, and the patient requested to look off without fixing the sight on any one object, and without trying to see anything; in contrast to the subjective examination where the test card is brightly illuminated and the patient looks at it intently in the effort to see the smaller letters, thus exciting the ciliary muscle to action.

In those cases of astigmatism where there is a wide variance between the glasses accepted by the patient in the subjective examination and those indicated by the ophthalmometer, ciliary contraction may be suspected.

CAUSES OF SPASM OF ACCOMMODATION

The more pronounced causes of accommodative spasm may be mentioned as follows:

1. Overwork or abuse of the eyes.
2. Unusual sensitiveness of retina.
3. A systemic tendency to spasmodic affections.
4. A superficial inflammatory condition.
5. Muscular insufficiency.
6. Reflex irritation.
7. Commencing the test with concave lenses.

REMOVAL OF SPASM OF ACCOMMODATION

In endeavoring to overcome spasm of accommodation the first step is to look for the cause and try to remove that if possible. This is certainly much better than a hasty resort to the use of a mydriatic, as being more in the line of the optometrist's legitimate work, and also more in accord with the patient's desire in the matter. Even though the drug is employed, and the spasm relaxed by this means, as long as the cause remains in operation, it is apt to return as soon as the effects of the mydriatic wear off. Some oculists have recommended a continuance of the atropine for a few weeks after the glasses have been fitted, in the hope that the effect of the glasses will be to prevent a return of the trouble, but this is a practice that is hardly likely to become popular. The only rational plan is to seek for and remove the cause; and if this fails, then mydriatics may be reserved as a last resort.

When the eyes have been used to excess, it is well to have them rested or used quietly for a day or two before the examination is made.

Where the retina is hyperæsthetic, shaded glasses of light smoke may be worn for a few days, which will place the eyes in better condition for examination.

In those nervous cases with spinal or cerebral irritation, causing a tendency to spasmodic diseases, a consultation should be had with the family physician and his services availed of in the treatment of such condition.

Where the cause of accommodation spasm may be thought to lie in an insufficiency of the internal recti muscles, the optometrist will employ the usual means for the correction of such trouble.

Sometimes a conjunctivitis, even in a mild form, will cause sufficient irritation of the ciliary muscle and of the eye itself to render the examination unsatisfactory. In such cases a few days' treatment with a weak astringent collyrium, will allay the inflammation and place the eyes in a condition favorable for a satisfactory test.

TESTING WITH CONCAVE LENSES A CAUSE OF SPASM OF ACCOMMODATION

As soon as a concave lens is placed in front of an eye, whether a sphere or cylinder, the accommodation is at once called into action, and when this occurs it is always more or less difficult to produce a relaxation of the muscle. Therefore, the rule is to always commence the test with convex lenses, spheres first, and afterwards cylinders, if there is any evidence of astigmatism.

When a patient is first examined, the optometrist presumably has no knowledge of the condition of the refraction, whether it is hypermetropic or myopic. If the patient happens to be hypermetropic, the convex glasses are accepted and the diagnosis of hypermetropia is definitely determined, and the examination is completed with convex lenses alone.

But if concave lenses are tried first, the patient will almost invariably accept them, even if hypermetropia is actually present, and this is especially true when the error is slight, as so frequently happens. The contraction of the ciliary muscle, which instinctively occurs, with the accompanying diminution in the size of the pupil, apparently for the moment improves the distant vision.

The fact that a patient accepts concave lenses should not by itself be regarded as positive evidence of the existence of myopia, because almost any eye with approximately normal vision will take weak concave lenses for distance if they are placed before it. This is a fact that is so generally known that it seems almost superfluous to refer to it, and yet it is so often disregarded that we feel that emphasis should be placed upon its importance.

When a concave lens is placed before an eye that is really hypermetropic, and it is accepted, the case is then masked and the optometrist is led into error by regarding it as myopic, or is perhaps in a quandary as to the exact refraction. The reason of this is that the ciliary muscle, which is stimulated to action by the concave lens, cannot readily relax, and hence a convex lens, which may be tried next, will be positively rejected. Therefore, concave lenses should not be tried until the optometrist, by the negative results obtained by convex lenses and by other methods, is pretty sure the case is one of myopia.

Another piece of valuable advice is to commence the test with the weakest convex lens, and when that is accepted to increase gradually, .25 D. at a time. In this way the ciliary muscle may be coaxed to relax more effectively than if a stronger lens is put on at once, for then the change is so sudden and marked that the eye will not so readily adjust itself to it.

By the means mentioned above, spasm of accommodation can usually be detected if present, and in the majority of cases con be overcome, or, at least, will not be likely to lead the optometrist into error.

AN ILLUSTRATIVE CASE OF SPASM OF ACCOMMODATION IN HYPERMETROPIC ASTIGMATISM

Margaret M., aged thirteen years. Her eyes have troubled her more or less ever since she has been attending school. She is nervous, as shown by her inability to sit still for any great length of time. She cannot see the blackboard very well and complains of headache and pain in eyes whenever she reads or studies. On directing her attention to the card of radiating lines, she could give no definite answers, because first one set of lines would appear plainest, and these would fade and another set would take their place; this at once gave rise to a suspicion of ciliary spasm. With each eye she could barely see the largest letters on the test card. Convex lenses were rejected and a concave sphero-cylinder, with its axis horizontal, was selected, but afforded only a slight improvement in vision. The ophthalmometer was used and showed an excess of curvature in the vertical meridian of 1.50 D. (the same in both eyes), thus indicating the presence of astigmatism with the rule.

In cases like this oftentimes more satisfactory results are obtained in the use of the trial case if both eyes can be tested together. Therefore, guided by the reading of the ophthalmometer, a + .25 cyl. axis 90° was placed before each eye, which was not only accepted, but which caused a notable improvement in the letters. The strength of the cylinders was gradually increased and then diminished, until finally + 1 cyl. axis 90° was decided on as most satisfactory. With these cylinders in the trial frame, weak convex spheres were tried and accepted and increased, until + 1 was found to be the strongest borne; the correcting lenses were now: + 1 D. sph. ⊃ + 1 D. cyl. axis 90°, with which vision was raised to 20/50.

In this girl's case, her poor vision and the desire of her parents that everything possible should be done, led to the employment of atropine, under which the glasses accepted were + 2 S. ⊃ + 1.25 cyl. axis 90°. A week later, when the atropine had worn off, another test was made, when she accepted +. 1 S. ⊃ + 1.25 cyl. axis 90°, which were the glasses prescribed.

There are three morals to be drawn or lessons to be learned from this case.

1. The ease with which one might be led into a diagnosis of myopia and concave lenses prescribed, when hypermetropia is really present and convex lenses required. In this case, when each eye was tested separately, convex lenses were rejected and the optometrist might almost have been justified in excluding hypermetropia; but the careful man will realize the fact that the symptoms do not point to myopia, while the inability to obtain anything near normal vision with the concave lenses would also disprove it. But the superficial examiner (of whom there are too many), seeing convex lenses rejected and concaves accepted, would confidently prescribe the latter and imagine himself a scientific optometrist.

2. The advantage in cases of suspected spasm of accommodation or latent hypermetropia, of trying both eyes together.

3. That the value of atropine in cases of this kind has been to a great extent overestimated. The full amount of defect as developed under atropine can never be corrected anyhow, and in this case it will be noticed that the glasses prescribed differ but slightly from those accepted before the mydriatic was used; so little that it is almost fair to conclude that the latter would have yielded as much satisfaction as the former. This is certainly a source of gratification to the examiner, who should endeavor to correct his cases without recourse to drugs.

We have made no mention of the results of skiascopy and ophthalmoscopy in this case, because the majority of optometrists depend upon the test case, and we desired to exemplify how much could be accomplished by its use in skilled hands, even in a difficult and obscure case like this.

FITTING ASTIGMATISM

In the correction of astigmatism, our principal test and our main reliance in fitting glasses is by means of trial lenses. In simple astigmatism, the spherical lenses which should be tried first are usually rejected, and cylindrical lenses are unhesitatingly accepted. In compound astigmatism the test is commenced with convex spherical lenses, which are accepted and increased until the hypermetropia in the case is corrected. If astigmatism is present, it is found to be impossible to secure the full normal vision of 20/20. If the astigmatism be not of high degree the patient may perhaps be able to name some of the letters on this line only with evident difficulty, but many of the letters will be miscalled and some of them will be entirely indistinguishable.

If the strongest convex lens which the eye will bear for the distant test has been selected, it may be replaced by one slightly weaker, and then the convex cylindrical lenses placed in front of it, rotated to the meridian affording the best vision and increased as the eye will accept. This combination of convex sphere and cylinder would indicate a case of compound hypermetropic astigmatism.

If the convex spheres are rejected, concaves may be tried; but in this connection it is necessary to utter a word of caution and that is, never to place concave spheres before the eye unless the acuteness of vision is markedly impaired. If the vision is 20/30, or if some of the letters on the No. 20 line can be read, as in the instance mentioned above of compound hypermetropic astigmatism, myopia could scarcely be present and the concave spheres should not be made use of. If they are, they will most likely be accepted and then the diagnosis of the case will be in doubt.

In cases like the foregoing, when the strongest convex sphere has been found and when convex cylinders placed in front of it afford no improvement or are rejected, a concave cylinder may be tried over the convex sphere, with its axis at 180°, and if this causes a notable improvement in vision, or if it can be rotated to any meridian that does, astigmatism is shown to be present and the cylinder should be increased until perfect vision is obtained. If the convex sphere and the concave cylinder have the same refractive number, the case is one of simple hypermetropic astigmatism. For instance, if + 1 D. spherical is accepted as affording some improvement, and a — 1 D. cyl. axis 180° placed before it is still better and gives the highest vision, the cylinder neutralizes the sphere in the vertical meridian, while the 1 D. remains in the horizontal meridian, which would be equivalent to a + 1 D. cyl. axis 90°. This plane cylinder has the same refractive power as the sphero-cylinder, and may be substituted for it, and will produce the same improvement in vision.

If it is found that the concave cylinder accepted is weaker than the convex sphere, the case may be regarded as one of compound hypermetropic astigmatism. For instance, if + 1 D. sph. and — .50 D. cyl. axis 180° are combined in

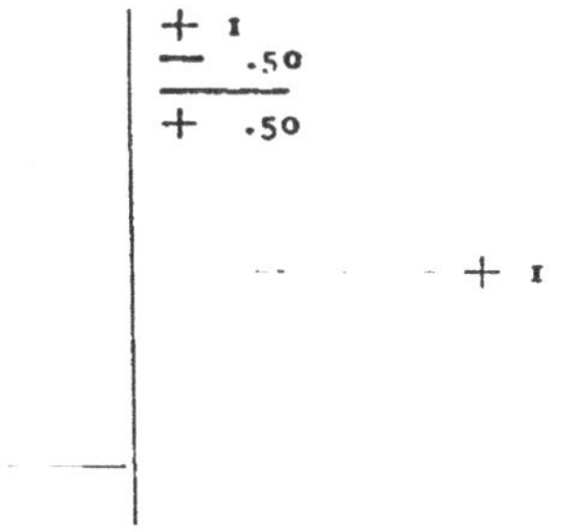

the trial frame, the cylinder will partially neutralize the sphere in the vertical meridian, while the horizontal meridian is unaffected, and the resulting lens would be as follows: + .50 S. ⊂ + .50 cyl. axis 90°.

If the concave cylinder should happen to be stronger than the convex sphere, a case of mixed astigmatism is indicated. For instance, if a — 2 cyl. axis 180° is required in connection with a + 1 sphere, the refraction of the vertical

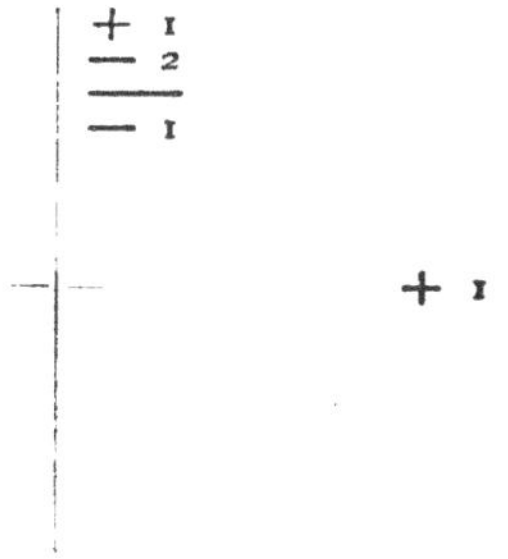

meridian would be myopic to the extent of 1 D., and the horizontal meridian hypermetropic to the same degree. The error can be corrected by a cross-cylinder or a sphero-cylinder, the choice being made from the three following combinations:

+ 1 D. cyl. axis 90° $\supset$ — 1 D. cyl. axis 180°.
+ 1 D. S. $\supset$ — 2 D. cyl. axis 180°.
—1 D. S. $\supset$ + 2 D. cyl. axis 90°.

Following along these same lines in the use of concave lenses, the weakest sphere is selected that affords the best distant vision. If this is not quite up to the standard a weak convex cylinder may be placed before it with its axis at 90°. If this improves vision, a stronger one may be tried, or it may be rotated to some other meridian in the hope of securing still better vision and then increased.

If the convex cylinder makes vision worse, a concave cylinder may be tried with its axis at 180° and slowly rotated to determine the proper meridian. If this yields an improvement it may be carefully increased as indicated.

If the convex cylinder and the concave sphere are of the same number, there is neutralization in one meridian and the equivalent is a concave cylinder, which indicates a case of simple myopic astigmatism.

If the convex cylinder is weaker than the concave sphere, there is partial neutralization in one meridian only, both of which still remain concave, and the case is shown to be one of compound myopic astigmatism.

If a convex cylinder is stronger than the concave sphere, the convex element predominates in one meridian, while the concave remains unaffected in the other, and the cross-cylinder that results indicates a case of mixed astigmatism.

When a concave cylinder is combined with a concave sphere, no matter which is the stronger, or if they are both of the same number, the case is always one of compound myopic astigmatism.

SUNDRY POINTS

The advice is usually given to observe the shape of the face and head, and any irregularity in their conformation is supposed to indicate the possible existence of astigmatism. But this cannot be relied upon, and the beginner must not be misled into trying to establish a case of this defect, simply because he sees some apparent abnormality in the contour of the features. Astigmatism is to be determined by the tests of the refraction of the eye as outlined in this chapter, and not by the appearances of the face.

Inasmuch as hypermetropia is the prevailing error of refraction, astigmatism is more often associated with it than with myopia, and hence hypermetropic astigmatism is the most common variety.

Astigmatism may be classed as a congenital defect, and hence one may naturally infer that the symptoms to which it gives rise would manifest themselves early in life. The scholar may be troubled with a blurring of vision at times, occasional headaches and show a peculiar tilting of the head. In some cases these symptoms are so noticeable that they cannot be ignored, and the child receives the attention which his eyes need. In other cases the suffering is not severe, and the child passes through school and the man enters on a business life with scarcely a suspicion of any defect of the eyes. Finally, business cares, or impaired health, or excessive use, or advancing age, bring to the surface an unmistakable error of refraction, which, on examination, proves to be astigmatism, and which now receives the proper attention.

But there are numerous other cases where there are no symptoms of trouble during childhood and where it is fair to presume the eyes are emmetropic. Later in life, from the causes mentioned above, eye symptoms begin to manifest themselves and increase until they demand attention, when it is found that astigmatism is unquestionably present, and the correction of the same affords the desired relief. This is contrary to the accepted view of the congenital origin of astigmatism, and yet it is scarcely more improbable than that astigmatism should arise *de novo*, and that the defective meridians should alter in location and degree.

When the radiating lines are used as a test for astigmatism, the amount of the defect can be measured by spherical lenses alone, although the correction can be made only by cylinders. For instance, if the patient says the vertical lines are clear and distinct, while the horizontal lines are blurred and misty, the case is presumably one of simple astigmatism, and the spherical lens that will make the horizontal lines clear will be the measure of the defect.

For this purpose the patient's attention must be directed to these lines, and convex spheres tried first; these make the lines decidedly worse, and then a weak concave is tried, which causes a noticeable improvement. This is gradually increased until it is found that a — 1 D. sphere is the weakest lens and makes the lines distinct. This proves a myopia of 1 D. in the vertical meridian alone, because it is evident that the horizontal meridian cannot be myopic, else the vertical lines could not be clearly seen.

Now the correction cannot be made by this sphere, because while it neutralizes the myopia in the vertical meridian of the eye, it at the same time places a concave lens before the horizontal emmetropic meridian, which is contrary to all teaching. Therefore a lens must be sought that will diminish the excess of refraction in the vertical meridian, and that will at the same time leave the horizontal meridian unaffected, which is found in a concave cylinder with its axis horizontal; hence the correcting lens in this case would be — 1 D. cyl. axis 180°.

Suppose the patient says the horizontal lines are clear and the vertical lines indistinct. A convex spherical lens will clear up the latter, but will make the former indistinct. This, then, is a case of simple hypermetropic astigmatism; the deficiency of refraction being in the horizontal meridian. A convex sphere cannot be prescribed, because while it adds sufficient refractive power to the horizontal meridian to make it normal, it at the same time increases the vertical meridian which was normal, but is now made myopic. A convex cylinder with its axis at 90° will not disturb the normal vertical meridian, but will supply the needed assistance in the hypermetropic horizontal meridian.

CHANGES IN THE CURVATURE OF THE CORNEA

There is no doubt that the curvatures of the cornea may vary from time to time, thus changing the degree of astigmatism and altering the location of the two principal meridians.

This happens more often than was formerly thought possible, and may be due to general (as of the system) or local conditions (as of the eye itself).

With patients in good health when astigmatism is present, it is usually found to be with the rule. As the condition of the system and of the eye changes, and the general or local vitality and nutrition becomes impaired, the normal form of astigmatism gives way to other varieties.

A recent writer has noticed a connection between patients with the uric acid diathesis and astigmatism against the rule, and he argues that this is too constant to be accidental, and that there must be some causative relation existing between the former and the latter. In some of the cases which received treatment to eliminate the excess of uric acid, the abnormal form of astigmatism lessened or disappeared, to be replaced by the normal variety. After a lapse of time, if the lithæmic condition again became pronounced, there was a return to the form of astigmatism against the rule.

We do not assume that the connection between these two conditions has been actually proven to exist as an invariable rule, but it is interesting to know that it occurs at times, and further investigations may throw light on a class of cases that have heretofore been inexplicable.

COMPLAINTS WHEN GLASSES ARE FIRST WORN

The glasses that are prescribed for the correction of astigmatism, even when most carefully fitted, are not always satisfactory and comfortable at first. The most common complaints are that the ground or floor does not seem level, but appears to slant, and the patient feels that he is walking up or down hill, and that there is more or less distortion in the shape of objects. A square object will show slanting sides, and the top and bottom will not be of equal width. If the astigmatism has been correctly measured and the axis of the cylinder set at the proper angle, the patient can be assured that these unpleasant appearances will gradually pass away if the wearing of the glasses is persisted in, and in the course of two or three weeks the vision will become natural and comfortable.

IMPORTANCE OF THE CORRECTION OF ASTIGMATISM

The general teaching is that astigmatism should be corrected fully, and that the glasses should be worn constantly, but it cannot be denied that frequent cases are met where the eyes are used without any evidence of discomfort in the presence of an uncorrected astigmatism, sometimes even of quite a marked degree. This is really only what is to be expected when it is remembered that there is great variation in the condition of the nervous system of different individuals, and its ability to bear a certain amount of strain. Some are so sensitive as to be unpleasantly affected by the slightest irritation, while others are apparently unconscious of any amount of strain.

This has led to a discussion of the question whether any harm is done if astigmatism is not corrected, and if it is apt to increase more rapidly when glasses are not worn? To arrive at a satisfactory solution of this question, all the features of a case must be taken into account, and each patient must be considered separately; in other words, there can be no general rule to apply to every case.

If the patient suffers from headache or any other symptom of eye-strain, there can be no question as to the propriety of prescribing glasses for constant wear. But in those cases where it exists without giving rise to any symptoms, and where it is only accidentally discovered, it is scarcely proper to force glasses on a patient and insist on him wearing them, under a penalty of possible blindness if he fails or refuses to follow the advice given.

This question frequently occurs in connection with patients who are being fitted for presbyopia. The examination of the eyes, when made along the indicated lines, discloses the presence of an astigmatism which had never before been suspected. Should such patients have a correction for both distance and for reading, and advised never to be without glasses? This certainly would not be a proper rule to lay down for all cases, and in fact many patients not feeling the need of glasses for constant use will refuse to wear them for distance. Of course, it is only reasonable that the indicated cylinders should be added to the spheres that are necessary for the correction of the presbyopia, and yet even here it is found in very many cases that the spheres alone are sufficient for the purpose and are even sometimes more satisfactory than the sphero-cylindrical combination.

Notwithstanding the importance of the correction of astigmatism, and the relief afforded to cases of asthenopia by cylindrical lenses, there have been cases reported, strange to say, where the same relief has been obtained from simple spheres. A person wearing cylinders with entire satisfaction, breaks or loses them; instead of returning to the optometrist who gave the original glasses, another one is consulted, who prescribes spherical lenses, with the result that the patient gets along just as well as before. Such an experience is exceptional, however, and should not be allowed to influence the optometrist to depart from the custom of correcting astigmatism when present with cylinders.

ASTIGMATISM AGAINST THE RULE

Some new views of this form of astigmatism have recently been advanced, which are of sufficient interest to justify a notice of them. It is stated that astigmatism against the rule is not a congenital defect, as is astigmatism with the rule, but that it is due to a change in the corneal curves, which appears with the advance of age, and consists in a flattening of the vertical meridian. The cause of this change is found in the diminished resistance of the cornea from general disturbances of nutrition, and from senile degeneration. When the horizontal meridian of the cornea shows the greater curvature early in life, it is looked upon as a pathological condition, being usually of high degree and causing a marked impairment in the acuteness of vision.

CHANGE IN FORM OF ASTIGMATISM AFTER TENOTOMY OF EXTRA-OCULAR MUSCLES

It is interesting and important for the optometrist to know that the curvatures of the cornea may be altered by an operation on the muscles, and thus the form and degree of astigmatism may be changed. The cutting of a muscle is likely to cause a lessening of muscular tension, which in some cases (not in all) may produce or allow a change in the curves of the cornea and a consequent variation in the condition of the refraction. Cases have been reported where one meridian has changed from hypermetropia to myopia, most likely due to a bulging of the cornea in this location.

MYOPIC ASTIGMATISM

In cases of high myopic astigmatism it sometimes happens that the vision is but little improved by the correcting lenses. The cause of the difficulty in these cases is mostly a matter of conjecture, possibly the eyes are poorly developed, or the functions of the retina have never been properly established. However that may be, cases not infrequently occur in which there is no discoverable abnormality of the eye-ground and yet the concave cylinders do not afford the desired improvement in vision. The proper procedure is to prescribe the glasses for constant wear, in the hope that the sensibility of the retina will increase, and the acuteness of vision likewise.

In low degrees of myopic astigmatism, there may be reflex inflammatory conditions such as conjunctivitis and blepharitis, with asthenopia and photophobia, aggravated by near work. In these conditions there is a tax on the accommodation, and perhaps a spasm of the orbicularis muscle. This latter condition more often results when the defective meridian is vertical, as then the patient, by half closing his lids, can obtain a clear image through the more normal horizontal meridian, a thing which would be impossible if the defect existed at or near the 180th degree.

There can scarcely be any doubt that the symptoms are caused by muscular strain, as they disappear very rapidly when it is relieved. There is a contraction of the ciliary muscle in the emmetropic meridian to afford clear vision for near work, which can be accomplished only in the lower degrees of astigmatism (2 D. and less). In the higher degrees these symptoms of asthenopia are less likely to occur; the patient cannot see clearly and he holds his near work closer in order to secure the benefit of the larger retinal image.

It is an interesting fact that the ophthalmometer is not

as satisfactory a test in the low degrees of myopic astigmatism as in the hypermetropic form, as it is found that the amount and axis shown by this instrument differs from that found by other tests. The reason for this is probably that the ciliary muscle does not adapt the shape of the lens to the cornea in myopic as it does in hypermetropic astigmatism.

CHOICE BETWEEN A CONVEX AND A CONCAVE CYLINDER

On account of the tendency to a contraction of the ciliary muscle in the slight forms of hypermetropic astigmatism, thus changing it into an apparent myopic defect, there is constant danger that a concave cylinder may be prescribed when a convex is really needed. In consideration of this fact it has become a widespread custom among intelligent optometrists to lean to the safe side and prescribe a weak convex cylinder with its axis at right angles.

But this matter may be viewed from several standpoints, and especially should the physical condition of the patient be taken into account, as well as the equilibrium of the ocular muscles and the amplitude of accommodation. It is manifest that a delicate, nervous woman cannot be treated the same as a strong, hearty man. In the latter there would be but little risk in reversing the cylinder, whereas the former must receive much more consideration. The condition of the muscular equilibrium must be determined, and if exophoria was found to be present the concave cylinder may be employed, and if esophoria the convex cylinder. If the glasses were desired only for distance to improve a blurred vision, it would be proper to give the concave cylinders; whereas if they were to be used only for near work, convex cylinders should be preferred. These remarks apply to the slight defects where it is difficult to choose between a weak convex and a weak concave cylinder.

TORIC LENSES

In this connection it may not be out of place to make mention of the so-called toric lenses, which have recently come into notice, and of which there may be some optometrists who have not a clear idea.

A toric surface is one in which there are two meridians at right angles to each other, presenting a difference of curvature and of refractive power in contrast with

1. A spherical surface, where these two meridians have the same curvature.

2. A cylindrical surface where one meridian is plane and the other curved.

Therefore a toric lens possesses the properties of a sphero-cylinder, the necessary curves for which are all on one surface.

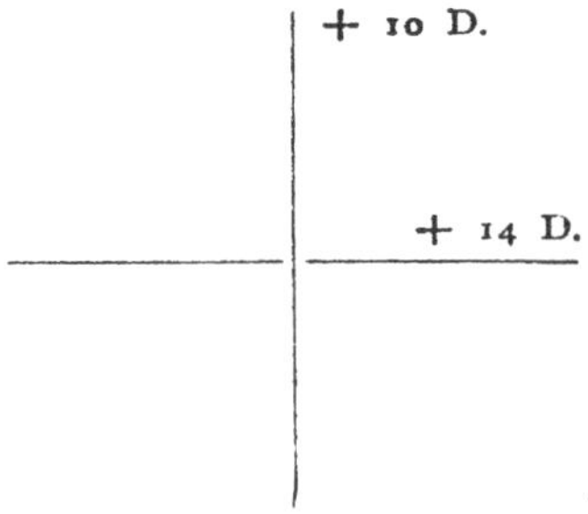

A sphero-toric lens is one in which one surface is spherical and the other toric. This can perhaps be best understood by analysis and comparison with a sphero-cylinder. For instance, we may have a lens ground according to the following formula: + 10 D. S. ⊃ + 4 D. cyl. axis 90°. This is a sphero-cylinder, one surface spherical to the extent of 10 D. and the other surface cylindrical 4 D. more. This shows a refractive power of 10 D. in the vertical meridian and 14 D. in the horizontal, and can be transposed to a sphero-toric lens of the following formula: + 5 D. S. ⊃ + 5 D. cyl. axis 180° ⊃ + 9 D. cyl. axis 90°. The spherical surface has a curve of + 5 D. and the toric surface a similar curve in the vertical meridian with a curve of 9 D. in the horizontal meridian; the result being a refraction of 10 D. vertically and 14 D. horizontally as desired.

In the toric lens the spherical curvature of 10 D. in the sphero-cylinder is divided, half being supplied by the spherical surface and the balance by the toric surface in one meridian and the additional curvature that is desired in the other meridian.

The sphero-toric lens is especially applicable in cases of aphakia, but will answer equally well in high degrees of compound myopic astigmatism. It can be made thinner and is therefore lighter, and avoids many reflections which are apt to occur in the sphero-cylinder. The toric lens can also be made in more of a periscopic form than is possible with a sphero-cylinder, and hence can be brought nearer and conforms more to the convex surface of the eye, thus affording a wider and more satisfactory field of vision.

Until recently it was thought that there could be only one kind of curvature on each surface of a lens; and as a lens can have but two surfaces, there was place only for a sphere and cylinder, one on each side. When the toric lens was introduced it was announced that it was now possible to grind a double curvature on the one surface, giving the effect of a sphero-cylindrical surface, and the impression was created among many optometrists that it was really ground spherical and cylindrical, but this is not strictly true.

A toric surface may be represented by the pneumatic tire of a bicycle, in which there are two diameters involved, that of the wheel and that of the tire itself, the one differing greatly from the other. Thus there are two distinct curvatures at right angles to each other. If a gauge is taken that has the same radius of curvature as the tire, it will not fit when applied to the circumference of the wheel; and likewise if a gauge is used that has the radius of curvature of the wheel, it will not fit when applied crosswise on the tire. For sake of illustration we might say that the curvature of the wheel was equal to 4 D., and the curvature of the tire being much sharper was equal to 8 D. Then such a lens would have a refractive power of 4 D. in the vertical meridian and 8 D. in the horizontal, and would be equivalent to the following sphero-cylinder: $+$ 4 D. S. $\supset$ $+$ 4 D. cyl. axis 90°.

It should be remembered that it is not ground as a spherical surface and a cylindrical, but that it has two radii of curvature at right angles to each other, which give the refractive effect of a sphero-cylindrical surface.

In making a comparison between sphero-cylinders and sphero-toric lenses, there is one point that must not be lost sight of. The lenses from the trial case with which the patient is fitted are bi-convex or bi-concave, that is, the necessary curvature is equally divided between the two surfaces. The cylinder is placed in front of this lens and a certain acuteness of vision is obtained, which the patient naturally has a right to expect from his glasses. But if the latter be ground with a great spherical curve on one surface, and a weak cylindrical curve on the other, in the usual sphero-cylindrical form, a very one-sided lens is the result, which is not identical with the test lens combination, and which consequently does not afford as satisfactory vision. In such a condition the toric lens possesses all the advantages; the strong spherical curve is divided between the two surfaces and the cylinder added, thus insuring the conditions necessary to obtain the best vision.

RULES FOR CONVERTING A SPHERO-CYLINDER INTO A SPHERO-TORIC LENS

Divide the greatest meridian in half for the sphere.

Subtract this from each of the meridians in turn for the strength of the two toric curvatures. We will take, for example, the following sphero-cylindrical formula: + 7 D. S. ⊃ + 3 D. cyl. axis 90°.

If we divide the greatest meridian in half, we will get 5 D. as the power for the spherical surface.

Subtract 5 D. from 7 D., and + 2 D. will be the strength of the one toric curve; subtract 5 D. from 10 D., and 5 D. will be the strength of the other toric curve. The lens will be + 5 D. S. ⊃ toric + 2 vertically and + 5 horizontally.

When the cylindrical element is the strongest, as in the following: + 6 D. S. ⊃ + 8 D. cyl. axis 90°, the strongest meridian is divided in half for the one surface, which in this case will be cylindrical; the other half will be the strength of the one toric curve, and the weaker meridian the other toric curve. Such a lens would be a cylindro-toric lens, as follows: + 7 D. cyl. axis 90° ⊃ toric + 7 D. horizontal and + 6 D. vertical.

ROUTINE METHOD OF EXAMINATION

The patient is seated at the customary distance from the test card (twenty feet if possible), and the acuteness of vision is ascertained by the line which he is able to read with ease. A vision of 20/20 ordinarily implies emmetropia, and yet there is possibility of the presence of hypermetropia or hypermetropic astigmatism concealed by the accommodation.

In cases like this the radiating lines are of but little value in determining the existence of a slight hypermetropic astigmatism, because being masked by the ciliary spasm, no difference will be discernible in the clearness of the lines running in different directions. Instead, a weak convex cylinder may be made use of, a + .25 D. or a + .50 D., and in some of the cases this will suffice to afford definite information. The axis is placed first at 90° (corresponding to astigmatism with the rule), which will possibly afford a slight improvement in vision; if not, the axis may be rotated through all the meridians until the location is found where vision is most satisfactory, and the strength of the cylinder increased as the eye will accept.

But in a large number of cases the result of the trial with convex cylinders is negative, or they may even be rejected. If the symptoms of which the patient complains point towards astigmatism, or in any case in order to exclude this defect, a + .50 D. sphere is placed before the eye and the patient directed to look at the card of test letters instead of the clock dial card. He will probably say that he cannot see so clearly; now a — .50 D. cylinder is placed in front of the sphere with its axis horizontal, which at once is likely to improve vision; if not, perhaps it can be rotated to some other meridian where it will be accepted. If a concave cylinder over a convex sphere improves vision, astigmatism is shown to be present of the hypermetropic variety; and conversely if hypermetropic astigmatism is present, it can more likely be detected by this means than by the use of the convex cylinders.

A person with normal vision who is emmetropic will be able to see as well with the concave cylinder in one position as another. A person with normal vision who is astigmatic will quickly see a difference, as the cylinder is rotated, and will be able to designate which position affords the best vision, and which causes the most blurring. It is almost superfluous to say that if a — .50 D. cyl. ax. 180° is accepted over a + .50 D. sphere, the vertical meridian is neutralized and the hypermetropic meridian is the horizontal one; in such a case the correcting cylinder is + .50 D. cyl. ax. 90°.

If the acuteness of vision is below normal, then the astigmatism may be either hypermetropic or myopic. If the vision is but little impaired, as for instance if it equals 20/30 or perhaps an occasional letter in the No. 20 line, it is most probably hypermetropic; whereas if it is markedly lessened, and reduced to 20/40 or less, if astigmatism is present at all, it is more likely of the myopic variety.

In these cases the radiating lines may be made use of, as there is enough astigmatism, or at least it is not concealed by the accommodation, to cause a difference in the appearance of these lines. If the vertical lines are indistinct, the horizontal meridian of the eye is the defective one; and as the refractive power of the cylinder is located in the meridian at right angles to its axis, therefore the latter is placed over the normal meridian of the eye and in the same direction as the indistinct lines which in this case would be axis at 90°.

A + .50 cyl. is tried and if accepted the defect is proven to be hypermetropic, and the lens is increased until all the lines appear equally clear. If the convex cylinder is rejected, a — .50 cylinder is placed in front of the eye, and if accepted the defect is shown to be myopic and the lens is slowly increased until the indistinct lines are made to appear as clear as the others.

Or the card of letters may be used, and the convex or concave cylinder placed in front of the eye as indicated, rotated to the proper meridian, and increased as necessary, until the greatest improvement in the acuteness of vision is obtained.

The correction of astigmatism has become common only within the last thirty years. At first it was not considered necessary to correct anything under 1 D. Afterwards the limit was lowered to .50 D., ignoring any less amount, and correcting only the spherical error, but not always with the relief and satisfaction desired. Within recent years among accomplished refractionists it is customary to take note of .25 D., or even .12 D. of astigmatism, because it has been found that even these slight degrees are often accompanied by the most distressing symptoms.

CHAPTER XIV

ANOMALIES OF THE OCULAR MUSCLES

ANATOMY

The eyeball, as it lies in the cavity of the orbit, is capable of motion in different directions, by means of six slender muscles, which are named as follows:

Internal rectus.
External rectus.
Superior rectus.
Inferior rectus.
Superior oblique.
Inferior oblique.

It might be stated in parenthesis that the term "rectus" is the Latin word for straight, and that "recti" is simply the plural of rectus.

At the posterior portion of the cavity of the orbit is the optic foramen, which is a circular opening in the sphenoid bone, for the passage of the optic nerve and ophthalmic artery. Immediately surrounding this opening is a ring or band of fibrous tissue, known by anatomists as the *ligament of Zinn,* from which arise the four recti muscles. The tendinous origins of these muscles are so closely connected that they seem almost continuous, and apparently form a short tube, which soon separates into the individual tendons of each muscle.

The *internal rectus* muscle arises from the inner margin of the optic foramen, having a common tendon with the inferior rectus, runs forward along the inner side of the eyeball, and is inserted in the sclerotic 5.5 mm. from the cornea. This muscle leads all the others in size and strength, and length of tendon, and being attached nearest to the cornea, has a decided mechanical advantage. The internal recti are the muscles concerned in the function of convergence, and are the ones usually affected in muscular asthenopia. On this account they are of special interest to the optometrist. They are supplied by the third cranial nerve, known as the oculomotor.

The *external rectus* has two origins, from the outer border of the sphenoidal fissure and the optic foramen. It is therefore called two-headed, although the muscular fibres really arise in an unbroken series, and there is no gap between them. The muscle runs forward along the outer wall of the orbit, and is attached to the sclerotic 6.9 mm. from the cornea. The external is the longest of the four straight muscles, although its tendon is the shortest, being only 3.7 mm. in length. Its

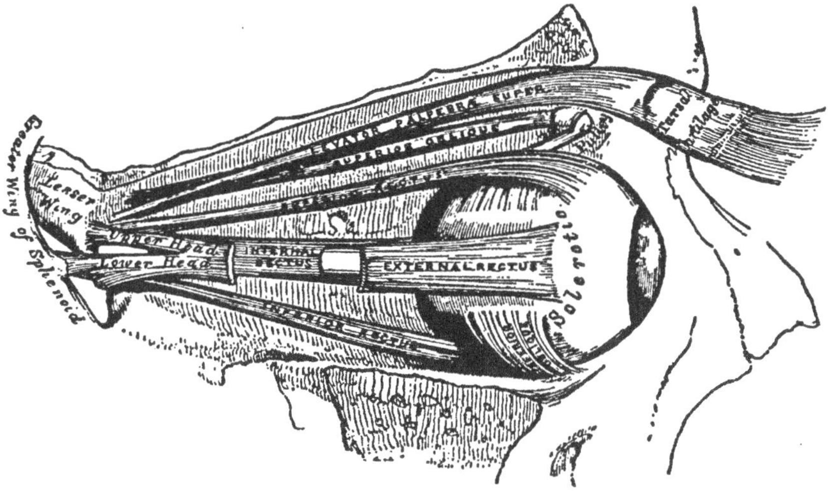

Muscles of the Right Orbit

nervous supply is derived from the sixth cranial nerve, known as the abducens.

The *superior rectus* arises from the upper border of the optic foramen, passes under the levator palpebræ, and is inserted in the sclerotic 7.7 mm. from the cornea. This muscle is the thinnest and narrowest, and therefore the weakest of the recti, and having its insertion farthest from the cornea, acts at a greater disadvantage. There is, therefore, an anatomical hindrance that discourages the habit of "looking up," and great fatigue of the eye is soon manifect when looking at pictures hung high in a gallery. The superior rectus is supplied by the third or oculo-motor nerve.

The *inferior rectus* springs from the lower border of the optic foramen, having the same tendon as the internal. It runs along the floor of the orbit, and is inserted in the sclerotic 6.5 mm. from the cornea. This muscle is next in length to the external rectus. The nervous supply is derived from the third cranial or motor-oculi nerve.

The *superior oblique* muscle arises from a point a little in front of the inner margin of the optic foramen, passes forward and upward in close relation to the wall of the orbit, and as it gets to the upper and inner part it becomes a small, round, fibrous band, which passes through and is supported by a short tube or ring of fibro-cartilaginous tissue, which serves as a pulley for its action. It then expands into a tendon, which passes backward, downward and outward, beneath the superior rectus, and is inserted in the sclerotic midway between the optic nerve and the margin of the cornea. The superior oblique is supplied by the fourth cranial or pathetic nerve.

The *inferior oblique* muscle arises from the floor of the orbit, close to its anterior portion, in a slight depression in the maxillary bone. Its fibres are almost entirely muscular, and it passes along the floor of the orbit under the inferior rectus, curving outward, backward and upward, and terminating in a tendon which becomes attached to the sclerotic in the outer and inferior region of the back of the eye, between the inferior and external recti muscles. The third cranial nerve furnishes its nervous supply.

The *levator palpebrae* can scarcely be included in the extra-ocular muscles that control the movements of the ball, and yet it is so closely allied and associated with them, as to deserve a slight description. It originates from a point above and in front of the optic foramen in close association with the superior rectus, so that one muscle cannot be used without more or less contraction of the other. The levator muscle grows broader as it passes along the roof of the orbit, and is finally attached as a broad membranous expansion to the tarsal cartilage of the upper eyelid.

ACTION OF THE MUSCLES

The individual action of the several muscles may be summarized as follows:

Internal rectus rotates eyeball horizontally towards nose, known as adduction.

External rectus rotates eyeball horizontally towards temple, known as abduction.

Superior rectus rotates the eyeball vertically upward, and giving the upper portion of the vertical meridian of the cornea a slight inclination inward.

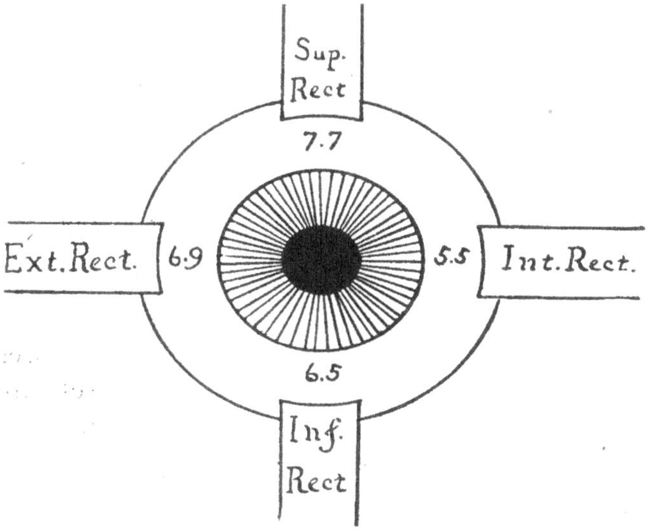

This diagram shows the insertion of the four recti muscles upon the sclerotic as viewed from the front. The exact distance of each from the cornea is marked in millimeters.

Inferior rectus rotates the eyeball vertically downward, and giving the lower portion of the vertical meridian a slight inclination inward.

The axis of rotation of the superior and inferior recti is horizontal, and of the internal and external recti vertical, with the inner extremity more forward than the outer.

The superior oblique moves the eyeball downward and outward, and at the same time rotates the upper part of the vertical meridian inward.

The inferior oblique moves the eyeball upward and outward, and rotates the lower part of the vertical meridian inward.

The outward rotation of the cornea, caused by the action of the oblique muscles, takes place in opposite directions; when produced by the superior oblique the movement of the cornea is at its lower portion from within outward, while, when produced by the inferior oblique, the upper portion of the cornea is displaced outward, at the same time that the lower half is deflected inward.

Oblique movements are the result of the associated action of the recti and oblique muscles, as the superior rectus and

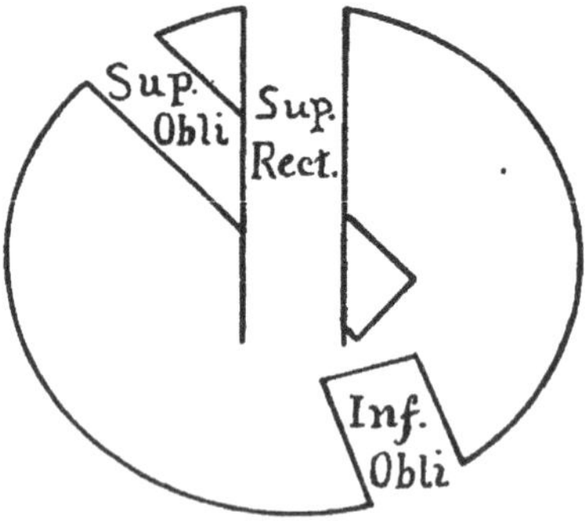

This diagram shows the insertion of the two oblique muscles from the rear. The lines of their insertion are directed diagonally across the meridians, that of the superior oblique forming an angle of 45° with the vertical meridian, and that of the inferior oblique an angle of about 20° with the horizontal meridian. There is an impression that their insertions are parallel, which, however, is erroneous.

the inferior oblique act together, and the inferior rectus with the superior oblique.

Elevation and depression of the eyeball is effected by the superior and inferior recti muscles only when the eye is turned out, and by the superior and inferior oblique when the eye is turned in.

Abduction of the eye is accomplished mainly by the external rectus muscle, which, however, is reinforced later in the act by the two obliques. Adduction is principally due to the action of the internal recti muscles, which is likewise reinforced later in the act by the superior and inferior recti, which are of appreciable value in extreme adduction.

The ocular muscles as a whole, with the single exception of the inferior oblique, form an irregularly-shaped cone, corresponding to the shape of the orbit, the muscles diverging from the apex of the orbit and proceeding to their insertions on the anterior portion of the eyeball. The divergence of the axes of the orbits determines the direction of the muscular cone as well as of the optic axes, and this bears an important relation to the function of convergence, because the greater the divergence the more the internal recti muscles are put upon a strain to maintain binocular vision.

The orbit was evidently made of a conical shape in order to accommodate the cone of muscles, and of sufficient size to allow of it being padded with soft cushions of oily fat for the better protection of the eye. The ball, therefore, does not come in contact with the walls of the orbit, but is really enclosed in the capsule of Tenon, which is a *cone of fascia,* enclosing a *cone of muscles,* and contained within a *cone of bone.* This membrane, covering as it does everything within the orbit except the cornea, necessarily modifies the actions of the ocular muscles and goes to form the check ligaments, which serve to prevent excessive rotation of the eyeball in either direction.

MOVEMENTS OF THE EYES

The movements of the eye are quick, and the popular estimation of the rapidity of these movements is shown in the expression "the twinkling of an eye," which is regarded as the shortest space of time that can be measured. Yet they are no less swift than they are precise; there is no wobbling as the vision is changed from one object to another, but the line of vision of each eye is kept steadily fixed on an object which may be in constant motion, without ever losing its distinctiveness or its singleness.

By the movements of the eyes is understood the various rotations of the organ in different directions. Some of the lower animals possess a muscle by which they are enabled to draw the eye deeper into the orbit; but man is not thus endowed, doubtless because there is no necessity for it, and when the eye protrudes or recedes some abnormal condition is suspected.

In *the primary position* the head is held erect and the eyes are directed straight forward towards the horizon, the muscles are all balanced, being passive or at rest.

Motion of the eyeball directly outward is accomplished by the external rectus alone, and directly inward by the internal rectus alone.

Motion directly upward and directly downward is effected chiefly by the superior and inferior recti. But these muscles also rotate the eyeball slightly inward, giving an inclination to the vertical meridian which should be upright.

Therefore, if a motion directly upward is desired, how can it be obtained? Dependence cannot be placed entirely upon the superior rectus, because this muscle, if left alone,

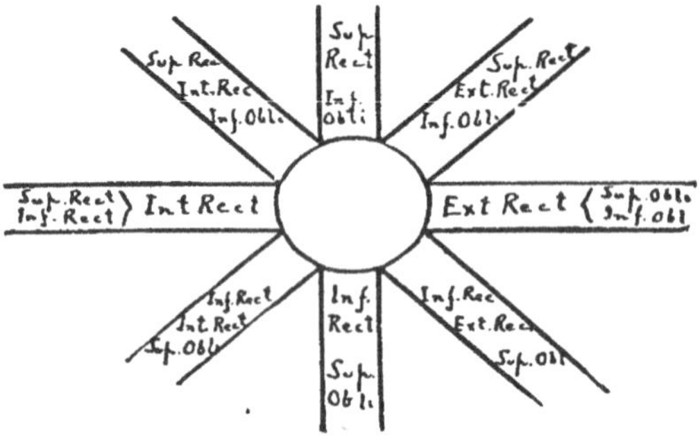

Diagram showing the muscles concerned in the act of moving the eye in different directions. This is a view of the right eye from behind, or as it would appear to the person who was making the movements. As this diagrammatic form shows at a glance the muscles required to produce the various movements, it may serve to supplement the descriptive text, in fixing this somewhat complicated subject in the student's mind clearly and definitely.

will also rotate the ball slightly inward. In the production of this movement the inferior oblique is associated with the superior rectus. The former assists the latter in the upper movement, and the outward tendency of the one neutralizes the inward tendency of the other, thus maintaining the ball in the upright vertical position.

In rotation of the ball directly downward, the inferior rectus alone will not accomplish the purpose on account of its inward tendency, but the superior oblique must be associated with it. Both muscles act in unison in the downward movement, while the inward tendency of the rectus is counteracted by the outward tendency of the oblique, thus preventing any undesired twisting of the eyeball on its axis.

Rotation of the ball *upward* and *outward* is effected chiefly by the action of the superior and external recti, assisted by the inferior oblique. The external rectus draws it outward, the superior rectus upward and inward, the latter motion being more than counterbalanced by the inferior oblique, which draws it upward and strongly outward.

Rotation *upward* and *inward* is effected chiefly by the superior and internal recti, assisted by the inferior oblique. The latter not only helps in the upward movement, but also counteracts the inward twisting produced by the superior rectus, which would otherwise destroy the parallelism of the vertical meridians of the two eyes, because that of the other eye could not be inclined outward to a corresponding degree.

Rotation *downward* and *outward* is effected chiefly by the action of the inferior and external recti, supplemented by the action of the superior oblique. The external rectus draws the ball outward, the inferior rectus downward and inward, but this latter motion is more than counterbalanced by the superior oblique, which, while drawing it downward, also turns it strongly outward.

Rotation *downward* and *inward* is accomplished chiefly by the action of the inferior and internal recti, supplemented by the superior oblique. The internal rectus draws the ball inward, the inferior rectus downward and inward, while the superior oblique muscle assists in the depression.

The eyeball may be moved in any direction desired by the combined action of two or more of its muscles. In oblique movements up or down, three muscles are always called into action, two recti and an oblique, or in other words of expression, the two elevators or the two depressors combined with either the internal or external rectus. It should be remembered that the superior oblique is a depressor muscle, as much so as the inferior rectus; and the inferior oblique an elevator, as much so as the superior rectus. But these differences are to be noted: when the gaze is upward and inward, the action of the superior rectus will predominate; when upward and outward, the inferior oblique; when downward and outward, the superior oblique; when downward and inward, the inferior rectus.

When the sight is turned upward and inward, the upper part of the vertical meridian inclines towards the nose; when upward and outward, towards the temple; when the gaze is directed downward and inward, it is the lower portion of the vertical meridian that is inclined nasalwards; when downward and outward, templewards. . An analysis of these movements will show that the inclination of the vertical meridian is the same when we look up and in as when we look down and out, viz., tilting towards the nose; and the same when we look up and out as when we look down and in, viz., tilting towards the temple. When we look straight up or down, in or out, there is no rotation because the tilting action of the oblique and of the recti muscles neutralize each other, the one tending to turn out and the other in.

FIELD OF VISION OR FIELD OF FIXATION

In passing from the primary to all the various secondary positions that are possible, the eye is able to see a great number of objects by causing the images of these objects to fall successively upon the yellow spot. The portion of space within which objects can be seen by the various movements of the eye, while the head remains stationary, is known as the *field of vision or field of fixation.* The boundaries of this field represent the extreme limits of movement of which the eye is capable.

Various methods of determining the limits of the field of vision have been employed, the most satisfactory of which is the perimeter.

The limits of the field have been variously stated by different observers, the average being somewhat as follows:

Upward	47°
Upward and outward	65°
Outward	90°
Downward and outward	90°
Downward	65°
Downward and inward	50°
Inward	55°
Upward and inward	60°

All the movements of the eye start from the primary position, which is the position of rest. In this position the muscles are all balanced, and if all of them contracted simultaneously to an equal extent, the antagonistic actions of the various muscles would prevent a turning of the eye in any direction. In all the secondary positions of the eye, one muscle or set of muscles exerts greater power than its antagonistic muscle or set, thus drawing the eye in the direction of the more active muscle. When any tests are to be made to determine the muscular equilibrium, the eyes should always be placed in the primary position, that is, straight ahead.

INNERVATION

The third, fourth and sixth cranial nerves, known as the oculo-motor, pathetic and abducens nerves, supply the external ocular muscles. In considering the innervation of these muscles, two facts are to be taken for granted:

1. Every contraction of a muscle or set of muscles to produce ocular movement in a given direction, is accompanied by a corresponding relaxation of the antagonistic muscle or set of muscles.

2. The nervous impulse is sent to the muscles in pairs; it seems impossible to separate them and innervate one muscle without affecting the corresponding muscle of the other eye. As a consequence the two eyes work together as a single organ. Every movement of one eye is accompanied by a corresponding movement of the other. It is not possible for us to turn one eye to the right and the other to the left, or one eye up and the other down, but each muscle has a fellow associated with it in the other eye. The superior rectus of one eye is associated with the inferior oblique of the other; and the inferior rectus of one with the superior oblique of the other.

The associated movements of the eyes are five in number, as follows:

1. The two sets of elevating muscles acting together turn both eyes upward.

2. The two sets of depressing muscles acting together turn both eyes downward.

3. The right external rectus and the left internal rectus acting together turn both eyes to the right.

4. The left external rectus and the right internal rectus acting together turn both eyes to the left.

In all four of the movements just mentioned the axes of vision continue parallel.

5. The two internal recti acting together turn both eyes inward, constituting the function of convergence, and destroying the parallel condition which otherwise naturally exists.

The association between accommodation and convergence is a well-established fact. The nervous impulse is sent to the two ciliary muscles just as to the two internal recti. At a distance these two functions are at rest, and they increase in equal proportion as the object to which the sight is directed approaches the eyes. The muscles concerned in the act of convergence are chiefly the internal recti, supplemented by the inferior and superior recti, rotating the eyeball inward, while the function of accommodation is controlled by the ciliary muscle increasing the convexity of the crystalline lens. All of these muscles (the former being extra-ocular and the latter intra-ocular) are supplied by the third nerve, which when called into action can make no discrimination, but must carry the nervous impression to all its terminations, and thus cause a contraction of the accommodation and convergence muscles in equal proportion, as well as of the sphincter muscle of the pupil.

CONVERGENCE

When a distant object is viewed, the visual axes of the two eyes are parallel. In this condition C (the letter used to represent the power of convergence) = O. When an object at a distance of one meter in the median line is fixed, the two internal recti contract and the eyes converge to that point, and then C = 1. This meter angle is the unit of convergence. If the eyes be fixed on an object at a distance of half a meter (or 50 cm.) the angle of convergence must be correspondingly increased, and then C = 2. If the object approaches to 33 cm. C. = 3; and to 25 cm. C = 4.

The amplitude of convergence is the amount or power

of convergence required to change the visual axes from a condition of parallelism and direct them simultaneously to the punctum proximum of convergence.

The punctum remotum of convergence is the expression of the condition of the eyes when at rest, that is, when the impulse for fusion as required by binocular vision is removed; just as the punctum remotum of accommodation is the expression of the refraction of the eye when completely at rest. In order to determine the punctum remotum, we test the muscular equilibrium at a distance, and if there is no deviation, the convergence is at rest, corresponding to the refraction of the emmetropic eye at a distance. If there is a divergence, the punctum remotum of convergence is negative, corresponding to the hypermetropic condition of the refraction; whereas if there is convergence at a distance, the punctum remotum is positive, corresponding to the myopic condition of refraction.

In order to determine the punctum proximum of convergence, a small test object is held at reading distance, in the median line in front of the eyes and on a horizontal plane with them. The best test object is a hair or fine wire stretched vertically in a frame, which is gradually approached to the eyes until it appears double, when the distance can be read off in inches or centimeters. If the latter is used, it can be divided into 100 in order to find the number of meter-angles. For instance, if the punctum proximum was 10 cm., then C = 10 (100/10 = 10).

This test can be used to determine both the punctum proximum of convergence and of accommodation, but the two should not be confused. When the hair or wire becomes hazy or indistinct, it is closer than the point from which the accommodation is able to focus the rays. When it becomes double, it is within the person's near point of convergence. Usually the object becomes blurred before appearing double, showing that the punctum proximum of convergence is apt to be closer than that of accommodation.

This principle is made use of in the ophthal-dynameter devised by Dr. C. H. Brown, which has two test objects; a card of small block letters and a hair dynameter. The latter consists of a metal frame on which are stretched two hairs, two millimeters apart, which is placed in the carrier traveling along a horizontal spiral rod, the movements of which are controlled by a milled head at the far end. As this is turned the hairs are caused to approach the eye, and the punctum proximum of accommodation and of convergence can be read off the scale.

Although accommodation and convergence are so intimately yoked together, yet the connection is not absolute Using both eyes together and looking through weak convex or weak concave lenses, the accommodation is thereby lessened or increased without any change of convergence. In like manner a weak prism can be held before the eye, with its base in or out, and the convergence be lessened or increased slightly without modifying the accommodation.

The extent of this variation is limited and differs with the individual, but it can be increased by practice. This is a most fortunate condition for ametropes; as, otherwise, a hypermetrope would always use his convergence to excess, and convergent strabismus would be the unavoidable accompaniment of hypermetropia.

In an emmetrope looking at an object 13 inches away, the accommodation and convergence are used in equal proportion, viz.: 3 D. of accommodation and 3 m. a. of convergence. A hypermetrope of 2 D. looking at the same distance would need 5 D. of accommodation because he must use the additional accommodation to overcome his hypermetropia. If the association between accommodation and convergence were absolute, one of two things would necessarily happen—either he would have to increase his convergence to 5 m. a., which is more than is necessary and would destroy binocular vision and produce strabismus; or he would reduce his accommodation to 3 D., which is not sufficient for clear sight, but would permit binocular vision to be retained. His two alternatives would be clear vision and squint, or blurred letters with binocular vision. The former is what occurs in certain cases of hypermetropia, as has already been explained in the chapter on hypermetropia.

But, fortunately, there is more or less flexibility in the association between these two functions, and the person learns to dissociate them by practice and by nerve education. Many hypermetropes are endowed by nature with the faculty of increasing their accommodation without changing their convergence, this power, of course, being limited. Such a condition calls for an increased nervous supply and symptoms of eyestrain are apt to result, because the two functions are not working in harmony; whereas, in the emmetropic eye a minimum amount of effort is required, since they act together and one assists and supports the other.

Those hypermetropes who do not acquire this faculty of using their accommodation in excess of their convergence, are not so likely to suffer from strain, but a no less evil befalls them—they become strabismic.

BINOCULAR VISION AND DIPLOPIA

Binocular vision may be briefly defined as "single vision with two eyes." The placing of the two eyes in such a position that the image of the object looked at shall fall upon the yellow spot of each, is as voluntary as the adjustment of the accommodation. Vision is single, because the image impresses corresponding portions of the two retinæ and is received by the brain as one.

When the image is focused upon portions of the retinæ that do not correspond, the brain is unable to fuse them, and two objects are seen, a condition known as diplopia. In some cases where the two eyes fail to fix the object simultaneously, diplopia does not occur, because nature, desiring to avoid such a condition, allows the one image to be ignored or suppressed.

Diplopia may be removed by placing a prism before the eye and thus causing the rays that pass through it to deflect to such an extent as to fall upon the yellow spot of this eye, which then corresponds to the other eye and two objects are no longer seen. On the other hand, an artificial diplopia may be produced by placing a prism before the eye, which deflects the rays in such a way as to prevent them from falling upon the yellow spot. In this case if the prism is not too strong, the eye may turn and overcome it, thus keeping the image upon the yellow spot and maintaining single vision.

FORMS OF DIPLOPIA

There are two varieties of diplopia—homonymous and heteronymous or crossed.

In *homonymous diplopia* the right image belongs to the right eye, and the left image to the left eye. It is caused by

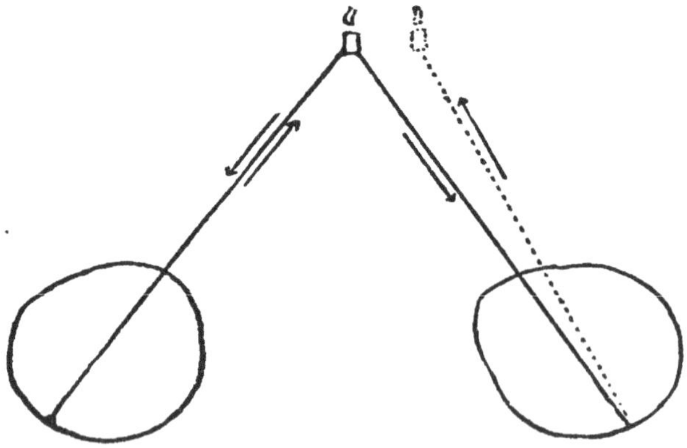

Homonymous

an inward deviation of the eye, as in esophoria. On first thought it would seem as if the appearance of the object would be in the same direction as the deviation, and that therefore in esophoria the diplopia would be crossed. This is a matter concerning which many optometrists are confused, and over which the optical student ponders long and hard before it becomes clear to him.

When an image is formed upon the retina at either side of the yellow spot, it is referred outward in the opposite direction. An object situated in the outer portion of the field of vision impresses its image upon the inner portion of the retina; an object situated below impresses the upper portion of the retina, and so on. Therefore, when an impression is received upon a portion of the retina inside of the yellow spot, it is referred by the brain to the outer part of the field; when received above the yellow spot, it is referred below. This is the law of projection, by which is explained the fact that our vision is erect in spite of the fact that the retinal image is inverted. The brain sees not this retinal image but its projection outward, and as the inner portion of the retina carries to the brain the impression of the outer part of the object, and the upper portion of the retina the lower part of the object, the latter is in this way righted and appears as erect.

In convergent strabismus, and sometimes in esophoria, one eye fixes the object and the other eye turns in. In the first eye the rays of light from a candle strike the retina at the yellow spot and are reflected back to the source of light, which appears in its proper position. In the squinting eye which turns inward the fundus with the yellow spot is at the same time necessarily moved outward, and the ray of light strikes the retina inside the yellow spot, when, according to

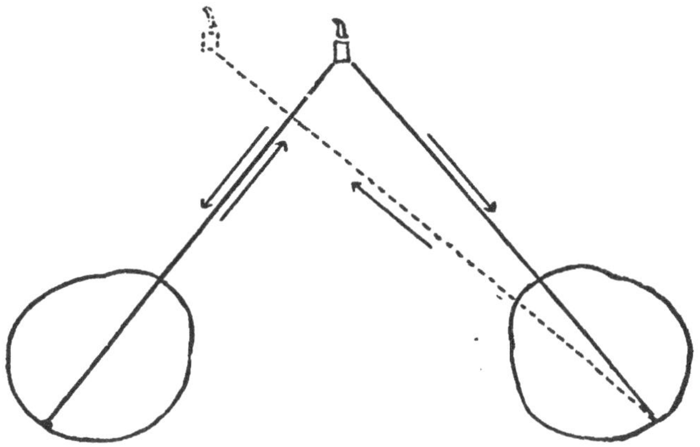

Heteronymous

the law of projection, it is referred outward in a straight line. Diplopia is produced, the two images being seen side by side, and since the right image belongs to the right eye, it is known as homonymous diplopia.

In divergent strabismus, and sometimes in exophoria, one eye fixes the object and the other turns out. In the first eye the rays of light are referred back to the candle, which therefore appears in its proper place. The other eye, since its visual line is turned outward, has its fundus moved inward, and therefore the ray of light entering the eye strikes the retina outside of the yellow spot, when, according to the law of projection, it is referred nasalward in a straight line. The diplopia produced is of the heteronymous kind, because of the two images seen side by side it is the left one that belongs to the right eye.

Binocular vision depends upon the blending or fusion of the image formed in each eye, and the natural desire to preserve it is the origin of the impulse which directs the movements of the eyes and keeps them in association in the same direction.

POINT OF FIXATION

The object of all ocular movements is to place the eyes in such a position that the rays from an object will fall upon the best part of the retina, viz.: the yellow spot, in order that the clearest vision may be obtained of whatever object engages the attention at that particular moment. When attention is directed to any point, the eyes unconsciously and simultaneously follow, and as we glance from point to point a series of pictures is formed, from which is gained a conception of the shape, size, solidity and position of objects. At times the eyes may wander aimlessly, without the attention being called to any particular object.

The "point of fixation" is the point which for the moment engages the eye. In the dark the eyes are apt to be in constant motion, while blind eyes are scarcely ever quiet in one position. The object of fixation is to retain the image upon the yellow spot, thus affording a small area of acute vision, which constitutes *direct vision.*

Immediately outside of this spot *indirect vision* is located, in which the perception of light and motion is but little lessened; the former serves the astronomer in good stead by enabling him to see a star better by looking a little to one side of it; and the latter opens an avenue of escape from danger under many circumstances.

PARALYSES OF OCULAR MUSCLES

The term paralysis is used to indicate a loss of power in one or more of the orbital muscles, and should be regarded not as a disease of itself, but rather as a symptom. The lesion producing this symptom may be located either in the orbit or in some portion of the brain.

The *symptoms* produced by ocular paralyses may be mentioned as follows:

1. *Diplopia.*—This is usually the first symptom of which the patient is conscious, and is apt to be the most constant, persistent and annoying. Two objects are seen because the image cannot be formed upon identical portions of the retina of each eye. One image is true and the other false; some patients in the course of time learn to ignore the latter, resulting in monocular vision and the disappearance of the diplopia.

2. *Impaired Vision.*—If the paralysis be slight there may be no real diplopia, but an overlapping of the two images causing indistinct vision.

3. *Dizziness.*—This symptom is the result of the foregoing and is also partly due to faulty projection, and the result is an uncertain gait. It is most noticeable in cases where the depressor muscles are affected, because these are the ones most used for work, for reading and for walking.

4. *Impaired Movement.*—There is a noticeable inability of the eye to move in the direction of the paralyzed muscle as shown when a test object is moved towards this side. The normal eye easily follows the movement, while the affected eye cannot turn beyond the median line. The "primary" deviation is that shown in the affected eye when the normal eye is open and fixing an object. The "secondary" deviation is produced when the working eye is covered, thus compelling the paralyzed eye, if possible, to take up fixation. The deviation is now in the good eye, and if it be examined under cover, it will be seen to be much more pronounced than the primary, since the effort to cause the paralyzed muscle to contract requires such a strong innervation, which also goes to the normal muscle where it produces an excessive action.

5. *Vicarious Inclination of the Head.*—In order to avoid the annoyance of the diplopia, the head may be turned in such a way as to cause the true and false image to fuse into one. When the eyes turn in the direction of the paralyzed muscle, diplopia manifests itself, to avoid which the individual turns his head in the same direction. In paralysis of the right external or left internal rectus, the face turns to the right; if

the right internal or the left external be affected, to the left; if the depressor muscles, down; and if the elevator muscles, the face is turned up. These compensatory movements furnish valuable (but not infallible) indications in determining the muscle affected, it being necessary to remember only that the patient's face turns in the direction of the paralyzed muscle.

STRABISMUS

Strabismus is a departure from the normal parallel condition of the eyes, and may be defined as that condition in which the two eyes do not fix the same object, or in other words, in which there is a deviation of one fixation line from the other. In regard to the nature of the strabismus, it may be said to be either *paralytic* or *concomitant*. When the deviation is in or out, it is known as *convergent* or *divergent* strabismus, which are the two most common forms. In addition to which there may be a *vertical* squint, one eye turning above or below its fellow. Strabismus may be either *fixed, intermittent* or *alternating*, terms which are sufficiently descriptive of the conditions they are intended to represent.

PARALYTIC STRABISMUS

This form of strabismus being due to a palsy of one or more of the muscles, occurs only when the affected muscle is called upon to perform its function, that is, when an attempt is made to look in this direction, in which there is an actual limitation of movement.

The characteristic of this form of strabismus is that when the eyes are in certain positions, no deviation is noticeable. This is in the direction of the normal muscle; but when the effort is made to turn them in the other direction, one eye moves normally while the other is unable to turn at all. This inability to follow the movements of the other eye constitutes a deviation from the normal position.

Any one of the six ocular muscles may be paralyzed by itself and give rise to its own form of diplopia. Or two or more of the muscles may be paralyzed at the same time. Paralysis of all the rotary muscles of the eye is known as *ophthalmoplegia externa.*

The *causes* of paralytic strabismus may be located in the muscles themselves, in the nerves that supply the muscles, or in the brain. These may occur from wounds, suppuration, tumors, hemorrhage, or from constitutional disorders, such as syphilis, diseases of kidneys, etc. Alcohol and tobacco may produce degeneration of the nerves leading to strabismus of the paralytic variety.

Paralysis of the third or oculo-motor nerve will affect the superior, inferior and internal recti and the inferior oblique.

Paralysis of the fourth or pathetic nerve affects only the superior oblique muscle.

Paralysis of the sixth or abducens nerve affects only the external rectus muscle.

Paralytic strabismus may occur suddenly, sometimes coming on during the night. More frequently it is a gradual process, the patient being conscious of some difficulty in using the eyes, with occasional appearance of double images, the trouble increasing from week to week, until the condition becomes fully established.

The *symptoms* of paralytic strabismus have already been enumerated. The patient falls into the habit of closing one eye or turning the head in order to prevent diplopia. After a time the eye instead of remaining straight when at rest turns away from the paralyzed muscle, on account of the secondary contraction of the opposite muscle, which can no longer be restrained by the affected muscle.

The *diagnosis* of paralytic strabismus depends on the following conditions:

Limitation of the movements of the eye.

Diplopia, which is confined to one portion of the field of vision, and which increases the more the eyes are turned in this direction.

The secondary deviation of the sound eye exceeding the primary deviation of the affected eye, is a characteristic sign of paralytic strabismus.

When the good eye is covered by the hand or a screen, it becomes the squinting eye and the uncovered eye is compelled to take up the work of fixation; the strabismus is thus transferred from the affected eye to the sound one. The displacement of the affected eye is called the *primary deviation* and of the sound eye (when covered) the *secondary deviation.* The first is the natural deviation; and the second the deviation that is caused artificially, which gives place again to the primary as soon as the cover is removed.

The amount of each deviation is a matter of easy determination and must be carefully noted. In concomitant strabismus the primary and secondary deviations are equal, but in the paralytic form of strabismus the secondary deviation is very much greater than the primary, the more so as the attention is directed to the extreme limit of the field on the side of the paralyzed muscle. The reason for this is found in the fact that the affected muscle is unable to respond to the usual impulse, but is able to fix the object only under the stimulus of an excessive nerve impulse; and to the further fact that the nerve supply goes to associated muscles in equal proportion, and hence the muscle of the sound eye receives such a preponderating impulse as to cause an excessive deviation.

Paralysis of the Internal Rectus limits the inward movement of the eye, and creates a tendency for the eye to deviate outward, thus causing a crossed diplopia.

Paralysis of the External Rectus limits the outward movement of the eye, thus favoring a convergent strabismus. The diplopia produced in such a case is homonymous.

Paralysis of the Inferior Rectus limits the downward movement of the eye, causing a vertical diplopia which increases as the gaze is directed downward.

Paralysis of the Superior Rectus limits upward movement, causing a diplopia which increases on looking up.

Paralysis of the Inferior Oblique limits upward and outward movement, and of the *Superior Oblique,* downward and outward movement.

TREATMENT OF PARALYTIC STRABISMUS

These cases should usually be referred to a physician, as the treatment is largely medical. After the benefit from such treatment has been exhausted and the case becomes chronic, prisms may be prescribed. The base of the prism is always toward the paralyzed muscle, and over the other eye in a corresponding position. Diplopia may thus be removed and binocular vision restored. The eyes should be examined from time to time so that the prism can be varied to correspond to any change in deviation.

The weakened muscle can sometimes be strengthened by gymnastic exercises conducted as follows: A small object is to be held in that portion of the field of vision where there is no diplopia, and then slowly moved towards that portion where diplopia commences to manifest itself, the effort being made to keep the object single as long as possible. When diplopia finally occurs, the effort is to be discontinued and the eye allowed to rest for a few minutes. In a little while the exercise may be repeated, continuing it for only the fraction of a second.

When the diplopia is beyond the correction of a prism and becomes a source of much annoyance to the patient, he may wear glasses with the deviating eye covered by a ground glass.

Paralytic strabismus when given early attention is curable in the great majority of cases, depending, of course, on the cause, or there may be a partial recovery, which enables the patient to use his eyes without diplopia or inconvenience. In the advanced stages an operation will be of benefit to lessen the diplopia, and sometimes to improve the patient's appearance.

CONCOMITANT STRABISMUS

This term is used in contradistinction to paralytic strabismus, and implies that the squinting eye accompanies the straight eye in all its movements; and hence there is always the same amount of deviation no matter in which direction the eyes are turned. Since both eyes cannot be turned toward the same point, it is evident that only one can *fix* the object while the other must *deviate*. Naturally the patient gives preference to the eye with the best vision, which then becomes the fixing eye, and the eye with the poorer vision the deviating eye. But this does not actually indicate that the strabismus belongs to the latter eye any more than to the other. Either eye alone is normal as regards its muscular movements; but when the two eyes act together, strabismus occurs because there is not a perfect co-ordination.

Man is distinguished from the animal world in the possession of binocular vision, which is dependent upon the accurate co-ordination of the movements of the eyes, or rather they are mutually dependent one on the other. While binocular vision is not possible in the absence of muscular co-ordination, at the same time the latter is most easily accomplished under the guidance of binocular vision. The two functions seem to develop together in childhood, and it is during this period of life that they are most easily disturbed. Hence concomitant squint most frequently occurs among children.

When the controlling influence of binocular vision is lost, the perfection of co-ordination of movement is impaired. This is shown in cases where the sight of one eye is lost, or even when the acuteness of vision is lessened by injury or disease of the cornea, when strabismus of the affected eye is likely to supervene.

CONVERGENT CONCOMITANT STRABISMUS

This is the most common form of strabismus. It is the condition that is popularly known as inward "cast" or "squint" or "cross-eyes." There is convergence of the visual axes at all times, which is least noticeable when looking at a distance and most so when engaged in close vision.

It makes its appearance in children when they first begin to evince an interest in toys and picture books, which amounts to the same thing as saying when they begin to use their accommodation and convergence, which is usually between the ages of three and six. It is understood, of course, that both eyes do not squint at the same time, as is so often stated by the anxious mother.

It may be well to state here that this condition is not due, as is popularly thought, to fright, imitation, naughtiness, or by looking at a lock of hair hanging down over one side of the eye; but the fact was long ago pointed out by Donders that it was connected with hypermetropia, and that in the great majority of such cases the refraction was hypermetropic, and therefore he arrived at the logical conclusion that hypermetropia was the predominant cause of convergent strabismus.

This subject has been discussed in the chapter on Hypermetropia, where it was shown that an intimate relation exists between accommodation and convergence, and that for every effort of accommodation there was a corresponding effort of convergence, and that by an abnormal amount of the latter, a greater effort of accommodation was possible. This physiological fact is unconsciously taken advantage of by the hypermetrope in order to overcome his error of refraction, as Nature prefers clear sight even at the expense of binocular vision. The convergence is therefore brought strongly into action which causes one eye to turn in, and by this means an additional amount of accommodation is made possible in the other eye and thus the hypermetropia is overcome and clear vision secured. It must not be understood that all cases of convergent strabismus are due to hypermetropia, nor that all cases of hypermetropia result in convergent strabismus. Without any reference to the refractive condition of the eyes, there may be a contraction or shortening of the internal recti, or a preponderance of power of these muscles or a lack of strength of the external recti or a surplus of nervous supply to the function of convergence, or an impaired acuteness of vision in one eye.

SINGLE VISION IN CONVERGENT STRABISMUS

While diplopia usually occurs under certain conditions in paralytic strabismus, and in fact may be said to be the rule, in concomitant convergent strabismus on the other hand it is seldom present, the patient enjoying single vision although, of course, not binocular vision. In both cases the image is formed in the squinting eye on the retina at some distance from the yellow spot, and on this account cannot be fused by the brain into the impression of a single object. The conditions then being similar, the question naturally arises why diplopia should occur in one case and not in another.

Concomitant convergent strabismus does not seem to be

so much of a pathological or abnormal condition, as does the paralytic form, and hence Nature's abhorrence of a diplopia leads the mind of the patient to ignore and suppress the annoying image belonging to the deviating eye, very much as when engaged in an interesting conversation we become oblivious to all other sounds that enter the ear. The suppression of this image is rendered all the easier on account of its indistinctness, being formed on a peripheral portion of the retina, as compared with the perfect image of the fixing eye that is formed upon the yellow spot.

But in many cases, even from the beginning, the vision of the squinting eye has been more defective than its fellow, which also assists in paving the way for the suppression that follows. Or it might be said that diplopia is actually present, but that having become habitual to the patient it passes unnoticed by him.

AMBLYOPIA EX ANOPSIA

In the great majority of cases of convergent strabismus, even where the refracting media are clear and the retina apparently normal, the deviating eye is amblyopic. The generally accepted opinion is that this condition is due to the lack of use of the eye or its non-participation in the act of vision, to which the term amblyopia ex anopsia is applied. After a tenotomy of the shortened muscle and a correction of any existing refractive error, patient and continued systematic exercise of the eye separately from the other may result in much improvement of sight or even a return to normal vision, in which case the amblyopia would be classed as functional. Where, however, it is impossible to produce any improvement, we are forced to conclude that the trouble is organic, and that some structural change exists, possibly in some portion of the nervous apparatus beyond the reach of the ophthalmoscope.

The nervous impulse is sent to both eyes equally, and hence in these cases there is a tendency for both eyes to converge. The natural desire for fixation prevents the two eyes from squinting, but when one looks straight forward to fix the object, the deviation in the other eye is doubled, so that one eye bears the blame for the squint of both.

In some cases, instead of an intermittent exercise of the affected eye, the good eye may be entirely occluded, thus imposing the burden of vision entirely and continuously on the amblyopic organ. Sometimes in a few days a very great improvement is manifest, which progresses in some cases in jumps, as in learning to swim, because there is an awkwardness of sight which requires practice to remedy, and which after a time, is overcome suddenly.

Convergent concomitant strabismus may be *periodic* (occurring only when some great effort of accommodation is put forth, and which may remain so or which may pass over into permanent); *permanent*, which is constant and confined to one eye; and *alternating*, in which the patient has the faculty of squinting either eye at pleasure, and as soon as one eye squints the other becomes straight and fixes the object. In these cases the vision of both eyes is usually good, and hence the patient has no preference as to which one to use. Although in most cases of strabismus the patient has a decided preference for one eye as the working eye (usually because its vision is better), still alternating strabismus is not uncommon. In order to determine to which class a case belongs, the fixing eye is screened, thus throwing the burden of vision on the other eye. The screen is then removed, and if the latter eye continues fixation, the strabismus is alternating; whereas if the squint returns to the original eye it is fixed.

DEFICIENCY OF ABDUCTION

In concomitant convergent strabismus there is always more or less impairment of the outward movement, not only in the squinting eye but also even in the straight eye, although this restriction of abduction is always much less than the inward squint. There may be some affection of the sixth nerve to account for this restriction, but it is mostly due simply to want of habit and has no pathological significance, the external rectus being weak from want of use.

DIVERGENT STRABISMUS

When the eyes are removed from the active control of the brain there is a tendency to divergence, as is shown under anæsthesia and during sleep. This would seem to indicate that the production of divergent strabismus partakes rather of a passive nature, in contrast with the convergent form, which is an active process. Divergent strabismus is most noticeable when the eyes are directed at a distance, while when looking at near objects, they may become parallel, but they cannot converge enough to meet at the object looked at.

It seems to be a well-established fact that divergent strabismus usually occurs in connection with myopia, and as the latter defect is acquired in contrast with hypermetropia, which is congenital, divergent strabismus makes its appearance later in life than the convergent form.

The elongated shape of the eyeball in myopia tends to make convergence somewhat more difficult, and thus favors a divergence of the visual axes. But the cause of the divergent strabismus in myopia is rather to be found in the fact that in this condition of refraction the eye is naturally adapted for near vision requiring little or no accommodative effort, and the accommodation being thus passive, there is a lack of the natural aid or stimulus to convergence.

Another reason why divergent strabismus is less frequent in youth, is the natural divergence of the orbital axes, which is an accompaniment of adolescence and age, which also serves to account for the presence of exotropia in the face of emmetropia and even hypermetropia. Therefore, a divergent strabismus which makes its appearance in youth only becomes more pronounced as the years pass by.

It is partly for the same reason that convergent strabismus oftentimes diminishes with the advance of years. But in this condition there is an additional factor, and that is the physiological growth of the eye, which, by increasing the antero-posterior diameter, lessens the hypermetropia.

NOMENCLATURE

The following terms have been suggested and introduced:

Esotropia, internal or convergent strabismus.

Exotropia, external or divergent strabismus.

Hypertropia, upward strabismus of one eye above the other.

Heterotropia, a generic term for strabismus.

These terms, while very expressive, have not as yet come into general use, and it is doubtful if they ever will entirely supplant the familiar word strabismus.

Convergent strabismus is an active condition, dependent upon an overaction of the muscles controlled by the third cranial nerve; while divergent strabismus, on the other hand, is rather a passive condition, dependent upon a relaxation of the muscles governed by the same nerve.

CAUSES OF STRABISMUS

These may be *intrinsic* and *extrinsic*. The intrinsic causes of strabismus are:

1. *Ametropia*, as evidenced by the convergent strabismus of hypermetropia and the divergent strabismus of myopia.

2. *Impaired Vision*, as shown by the number of cases of strabismus that follow amblyopia and opacities of the cornea and of any of the refracting media.

The extrinsic causes of strabismus are:

1. A difference in the length and strength of the several extra-ocular muscles.

2. Variations in the inter-pupillary distance, in the shape of the eyeball and in the divergence of the orbits.

SYMPTOMS OR EVIDENCES OF STRABISMUS

Usually the first and always the most decisive evidence of strabismus is the appearance of a manifest deviation of one eye. This may be variable, intermittent or constant. It may be productive of no discomfort and may be borne for years without any apparent inconvenience to the patient, until he himself, as well as his family and friends, become so accustomed to it as to often fail to realize the disadvantages of such an unpleasant deformity.

Diplopia is rarely complained of, because even if present at the commencement of the strabismus, it soon disappears; in fact, in a well-established strabismus it is usually impossible to produce even an artificial diplopia.

DIAGNOSIS OF STRABISMUS

Inspection.—Simple inspection will, in most cases, not only determine the presence of strabismus, but will also locate the fixing eye and show the probable degree of deviation. It is thus seen that the sclerotic on the temporal side of one eye is exposed to a greater extent than that on the nasal side, or vice versa, and that the cornea of one eye is deflected inward or outward. Still the obvious appearance of squint may be misleading, and, therefore, the diagnosis of this condition must be confirmed by careful tests. Sometimes the eye will appear to squint when both eyes really have their visual lines properly directed to the same point; or they may both appear to fix the object when really one squints.

The Cover Test.—In any case of strabismus, whether manifest or latent, one eye fixes the object and the other deviates. The patient's attention may be directed to some small but distinct object at some distance away. If the fixing eye be excluded from vision, the patient is compelled to rotate his deviating eye into the proper position to fix the object, and at the same time what was formerly the straight eye now becomes the squinting one; in other words, by covering the fixing eye the strabismus can be transferred from one to the other, shifting it back and forth as often as the cover is moved. The cover may be the optometrist's hand or a piece of cardboard, and must be held far enough in front of the eye to allow the observer to watch the movements that occur behind it; but of course care must be taken to entirely obstruct the view of the eye that it is desired to cover.

If the right eye be covered and the left eye remains perfectly immobile, the latter cannot be accused of squinting, but this does not acquit the right eye, which may possibly be strabismic; therefore, after waiting a moment in order to insure that the patient has his gaze steadily fixed upon the object, the left eye is now covered, and if the right remains immobile it must be declared innocent of any strabismus.

If the cornea of either eye makes an excursion inward when its fellow is covered, it must previously have been deviating outward; and if the excursion should be outward, the previous deviation must have been inward. In alternating strabismus, when the squint is transferred from one eye to the other, it remains after the withdrawal of the screen, because the patient has no preference as to which eye he uses for fixation. But in a fixed, monolateral strabismus, when the strabismus has been shifted to the good eye by covering it, it immediately returns to the other eye as soon as the cover is removed.

The "primary deviation" is that which the squinting eye assumes under ordinary conditions. When the straight eye is covered by a screen and the squinting eye compelled to fix the object, thus transferring the strabismus from one eye to the other, the deviation of the eye behind the screen is called the "secondary deviation."

The extent of these two deviations should be observed for purposes of clinical diagnosis. In paralytic strabismus the secondary deviation is always greater than the primary; so infallible is this test, that it has come to be regarded as the one on which the determination of a paralytic element depends. In concomitant strabismus, on the other hand, the secondary deviation is the same as the primary, no greater and no less, and maintains the same relation over the whole motor field.

STRABISMOMETRY

After having ascertained the presence of a strabismus and its variety, the next step is to measure the degree or amount of the deviation of the squinting eye from its normal position, which, as a matter of course, is not the same in all cases. This can be done by one of the following methods:

Linear Method of Measuring Strabismus.—This takes account of the displacement of the pupil by measuring the amount of deviation in millimeters or fractions of an inch, and was at one time the popular method. The accepted theory was that the displacement of the pupil, measured in lines or millimeters, could be rectified by setting back the tendon the same number of lines or millimeters; but this was not found to be practicable.

The strabismometer is made of bone or ivory, with a concavity to fit the shape of the ball and lower lid, and graduated in fractions of an inch or millimeters. The patient may sit facing a window and his attention directed to some distant object in the median line, when the good eye is to be screened. This causes the squinting eye to fix the object, when the instrument is placed gently against its lower lid, so that the zero (o) mark corresponds to the center of the pupil. Now the good eye is uncovered, when it immediately fixes the object and the defective eye resumes its squint, and the amount of its deviation can be measured by noting the position of the center of the pupil over the millimeter line of the instrument.

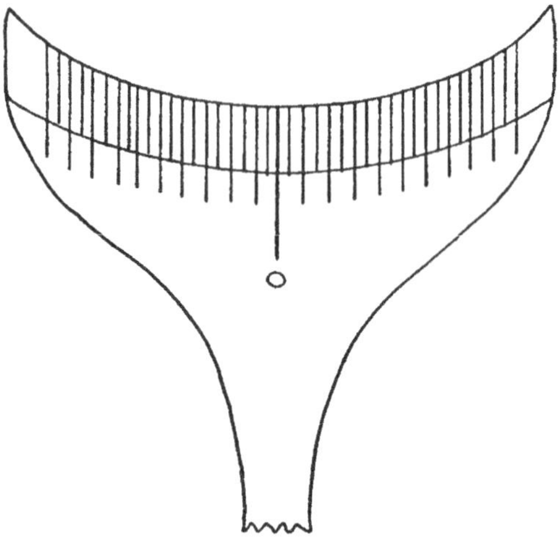

Strabismometer

This method of measuring strabismus is but little used, although it deserves mention because of its historical interest.

Hirschberg's Method.—This consists in estimating the degree of deviation by the location of the corneal reflex of a candle flame held in front of the eye. The candle should be about one foot in front of the patient's face, and the observer stands near to it and looks over it at the eyes of the patient, who is also told to fix his gaze in the same direction; in other words, the eye of the optometrist, the flame and the squinting eye must all be in one line. The position of the reflection from the cornea of the squinting eye indicates approximately the degree of strabismus. When the eye is straight the reflex is situated at the center of the pupil, or perhaps slightly to its inner side. In convergent strabismus it would be displaced outward, and in divergent strabismus inward.

According to Hirschberg, if the reflex is moved a little from the center, but is still closer to it than to the margin of the pupil, a strabismus of less than 10° is indicated, which is not enough to call for an operation. If the reflex is at the margin of the pupil (3 mm. in diameter), strabismus of 12° to 15° is indicated, which may require a simple tenotomy. A reflex situated half way between the center of the pupil and the corneal margin represents a strabismus of about 25°, and calls for a tenotomy of the internal rectus and possibly an advancement of the external. When the reflex occupies the margin of the cornea, a strabismus of 45° is indicated, which requires a tenotomy of the internal rectus, an advancement of the external and possibly a later tenotomy of the other internal rectus. If the reflex is on the sclerotic, away off from the margin of the cornea, this represents a strabismus of 60° to 80° and calls for a tenotomy of both internal recti and the strongest possible advancement of the external.

Perimeter Method.—The most reliable method of measuring the degree of strabismus is by means of the arc of a perimeter. The patient is placed at the instrument in the same way as if his field of vision was to be mapped out, and with the squinting eye in the center of the arc. He is then requested to look at some distant object across the room, which, of course, is fixed with the good eye. This is shown in the diagram, where the visual axis of the left eye is directed towards the candle flame. If the eyes were straight the visual line of the right eye would be similarly directed and would pass through the point *A*; but instead it passes through the point *B*. The latter is determined by moving another lighted candle along the arc of the perimeter, until the reflection of the flame appears to occupy that portion of the cornea which is directly over the center of the pupil when the eye of the observer is behind the flame. This indicates the optical axis of the eye, and the extent of the strabismus can be measured and read off from the scale.

Method by Double Images.—When diplopia can be excited, it affords one of the most valuable tests of the measure of the strabismus. In cases where the squinting eye is amblyopic, there is always difficulty in getting the patient to recognize the image belonging to this eye, because it has always been suppressed, or at least he has never been conscious of it, thus avoiding the diplopia which it is now desired temporarily to produce. At first the patient is unable to catch the false image, but if he is intelligent persistent efforts usually accomplish the desired end. Strong prisms are used,

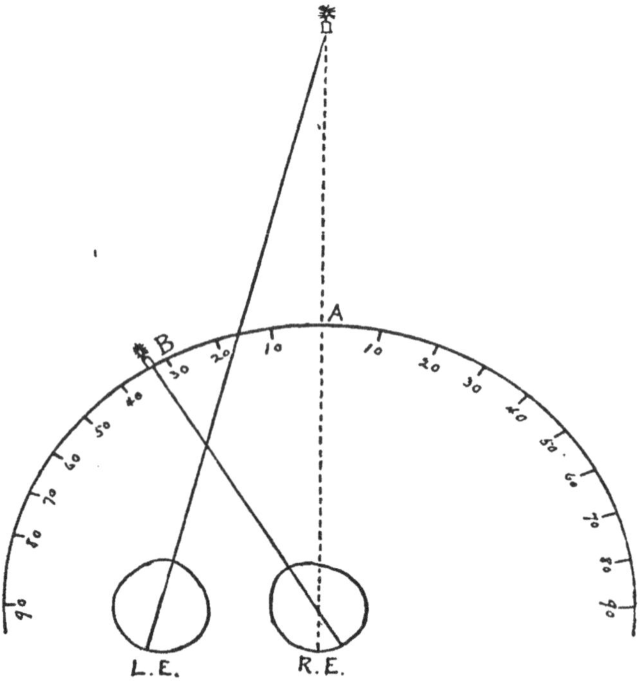

Diagram Showing the Perimeter Method

with their bases in the direction opposite to the deviation, and placed before the squinting eye. The rays of light, being bent by the prism, are focused on the retina nearer the yellow spot, in a position where they can be more easily noticed. A colored glass may be placed over the good eye in order to dull the light and make the image in this eye less distinct. By thus favoring the squinting eye at the expense of the good one, the patient will soon be able to discern two objects; and when once this occurs the subsequent steps of the test present no further difficulties. The prisms are increased before the squinting eye until the two images are brought so near together that they can be fused into one. The prism that accomplishes this will represent the measure of the deviation. In convergent strabismus the base of the prism is out, and in divergent strabismus the base of the prism is in.

TREATMENT OF STRABISMUS

The treatment of strabismus may be divided into *operative* and *non-operative.*

The operative treatment may consist in a *tenotomy* of the muscle that turns the eye too strongly in this direction, or an *advancement* of the muscle which does not possess sufficient power to keep the eyeball straight, or a combination of both. Thus in convergent strabismus there may be a tenotomy of the internal rectus or an advancement of the external rectus, or both operations may be performed on the same eye.

The operative treatment of strabismus, as a matter of course, lies outside the domain of the optometrist; but in spite of this, as a man educated in visual optics, he should be in position to justify the public confidence in him as such, and should, therefore, have some definite knowledge of this treatment, as he should of many other matters which are at present beyond his province.

The effect produced by a tenotomy varies with different operators and in different cases, ranging from 15° to 20°, with an average of about 16°, which is to be considered a very satisfactory result. If the deviation to be corrected is less than this, an advancement is to be preferred; if the deviation is greater, an advancement and a tenotomy may both be performed. The rule is to aim at a slight undercorrection in convergent strabismus; while in divergent strabismus a slight overcorrection is not undesirable.

The object of a tenotomy is to alter the tendinous attachments of a muscle, which changes its mechanical relations to the eyeball and lessens its power, thus tending to restore a muscular equilibrium and to equalize the nerve supply

Before a tenotomy is performed, there are several points that must be carefully determined:

1. The measurement of the angle of the strabismus. If this does not exceed 15° or 20° (in a case of convergent strabismus), a division of the internal rectus muscle will suffice. If the strabismus be greater than this, a free separation of the conjunctiva and capsule of Tenon will be required; if the deviation be less than this, such separation should be avoided as much as possible. The effect of the tenotomy can be increased by a suture passed through a fold of conjunctiva at the outer side of the ball and tied tightly; or it can be lessened by drawing the conjunctival wound together after the operation. The result is naturally more satisfactory if the external rectus muscle of the squinting eye be of normal strength, and also if its vision be fairly good.

Total anæsthesia is inadmissible, especially in heterophoria, where the success of the operation depends on an accurately measured tenotomy, and where the patient must be able to give intelligent answers during the progress of the operation. The necessary local anæsthetic effect is produced by a class of drugs, of which cocaine is the type. It is generally used in solution of two per cent. strength (about ten grains of the drug to an ounce of water), although some operators prefer a four per cent. solution, and a few employ it as strong as five per cent.; in fact, the preference of different operators varies considerably.

A description of the preparation of the eye, of the instruments required and of the various steps of the operation, as well as the after-treatment, scarcely come within the scope of this work.

THE NON-OPERATIVE TREATMENT OF STRABISMUS

Under the non-operative treatment of strabismus, the following methods are included:

1. Correction of the refraction.
2. Prisms.
3. Cycloplegics.
4. Exclusion of good eye.
5. Bar reading.
6. Stereoscope.

These means have been designated the *orthoptic* or *educative* treatment of strabismus. One or more of them may be used at a time, as the nature of the case seems to indicate.

Much of the success of the non-operative treatment of strabismus will depend on the nature of the amblyopia, which is usually present to a greater or less extent in all squinting eyes; if it is congenital and, therefore, presumably organic, the outlook for improvement is not very encouraging; but if the amblyopia is acquired and, therefore, probably only functional, the possibilities of this method of treatment are wide and the final result very hopeful.

There has been much argument on this question as to the character of the amblyopia, and there are able authorities on each side. The adherents of the theory of congenital amblyopia are able to present evidence mainly of a negative character, because the convergent strabismus usually develops at such an early age that it is almost impossible to decide whether the amblyopia was present or not before the appearance of the squint. But one of the points on which they base their claim is that there is not as much improvement in vision after the eye is straightened as could reasonably be expected if the amblyopia was only functional and congenital; and they further assert that an eye that once possesses good vision is not likely to lose it through strabismus. But this last assertion has been disproved by cases that have been reported in which the eyes were straight and vision in each eye normal in early life, and later, after the development of a strabismus, the vision of the squinting eye has been very much reduced; and doubtless this has been the experience of many observers.

1. *Correction of the Refraction.*—The first step should be the careful correction of any existing error of refraction, and the constant wearing of the prescribed glasses. Believing, as we do, that hypermetropia and hypermetropic astigmatism are the foundation causes of convergent strabismus, and as the rational treatment of any disease or defect calls for the removal or amelioration of the cause, convex lenses (either spheres or cylinders, or both) play an important part in the treatment and cure of this form of strabismus. The glasses should be prescribed early, just as soon as the deviation

makes itself manifest, when there is little doubt that they will effect a cure. But even if the strabismus be of several years' standing, the full correction for the refractive error constantly worn is likely to cure it.

In these cases glasses serve a double purpose; they not only improve vision by correcting the refractive error and affording a stimulus to binocular vision, but by lessening the need for accommodation they at the same time diminish the convergence, and thus allow the visual axes to return to their normal parallel condition.

Divergent strabismus is often connected with myopia, and if the patient's vision is not so greatly impaired as to interfere with reading and work at ordinary distances, concave glasses will often effect a cure. In many of these cases there is an anisometropia, and the equalization of the vision of the two eyes by means of the correcting lenses is an important factor in the cure. The placing of the effort of the accommodation of the two eyes on the same basis and the favoring of binocular vision may be essential points, without attention to which all other measures will prove insufficient.

In this connection the question often arises as to what age children should commence to wear glasses. Since so much more good can be accomplished by these means in youth, and at the time when the strabismus first develops, it is important that the wearing of glasses should not be postponed after the need for them is clearly indicated. Cases are reported where glasses have been placed upon children three years of age, and even younger, with the greatest benefit; but there are many difficulties in the way of such young children wearing glasses, and, therefore, as a rule, it is more satisfactory to wait until the child has reached his fourth year. In those cases where the need of glasses is urgent to improve the vision, as in high degrees of hypermetropia, the child can readily be induced to wear them.

It seems almost superfluous to say that such young children can be of no assistance to the optometrist in selecting the glasses, but which must be determined by some purely objective method, such as skiascopy. Sometimes the use of a cycloplegic will render the glasses more acceptable at first.

because with the accommodation placed at rest, they afford a noticeable improvement in vision. The drug can then be gradually discontinued, and the eyes by this time having become accustomed to them, there will be no further objection.

2. *Prisms*—strictly speaking—do not correct strabismus; they simply aid in procuring binocular vision in spite of the deviation. The base of the prism is placed opposite to the deviation.

In convergent strabismus one eye turns in and the image necessarily falls upon a portion of the retina to the inside of the yellow spot, and is thence referred outward as in homonymous diplopia. If now a prism is placed before such an eye with its base out, the rays of light passing through it and entering the eye are turned outward, and instead of impressing the retina in the same position as before, are focused nearer the yellow spot, and if the prism is of the proper degree exactly on the yellow spot, thus restoring binocular vision.

In divergent strabismus one eye turns out and the image is formed upon a portion of the retina to the outside of the macula, and is thence referred inward as in crossed diplopia. A prism placed before such an eye with its base in, turns the rays of light passing through it and entering the eye inward and nearer the yellow spot; and if of the right degree exactly on the yellow spot, thus restoring binocular vision.

If diplopia occurs at any time, or if it can be artificially produced, the case assumes a hopeful aspect, and prisms will prove of advantage. In order to bring the deviating eye into the act of vision the normal eye is covered. The faulty eye then fixes the flame, which should be the one bright object in an otherwise darkened room. Then the opaque disk over the normal eye is replaced by a colored glass, so dark as to lower its acuteness of vision considerably. In this way the good eye is dethroned from its predominancy, and the two eyes placed more nearly on a level as regards their retinal sensibility, and the false image then becomes recognizable when both eyes are uncovered and the patient is conscious of a diplopia.

When once a distinctive diplopia is produced, the most difficult part of the task has been accomplished. Then it remains to determine the character of the diplopia, whether homonymous or heteronymous, and the degree of prism required to fuse the two images into one, which latter procedure sometimes calls for much patience.

If the strabismus is convergent and the diplopia homonymous, the apex of the prism is placed *in*, which displaces the false image inward and brings the two lights close together. A stronger prism is then tried, bringing the two lights still nearer, until finally one is found that enables the eyes to fuse them and thus restore binocular vision.

Sometimes the two lights seem to refuse to be blended; we find a prism that brings them close, and think a slightly stronger one will accomplish the purpose, but instead they glide past each other. With the weaker prism they fall short of each other, and when it is slightly increased they jump past each other in the opposite direction. It is possible that this apparent contrariness on the part of the eyes may be overcome by repeated trials; but if not, prisms are worse than useless and any attempt to correct the strabismus by this means should be discontinued.

Cycloplegics.—These are drugs which paralyze the accommodation, and should be employed with the concurrence of a physician. They are applicable in that large class of cases of convergent strabismus occurring in young children and dependent upon hypermetropia. Atropine sulphate is the type of drugs of this class, and may be applied once daily. The drops suspend all effort of accommodation, and inasmuch as the excessive convergence is dependent upon the unnatural amount of accommodation that is required to overcome the hypermetropia, the suspension of the latter will tend to a relaxation of the former. The child will, of course, be unable to see anything clearly, which can be remedied to some extent by glasses which may be prescribed as soon as the child is old enough to wear them. The glasses should be strong enough to correct the total hypermetropia, which will afford the child good vision for general purposes, but on account of the enforced rest of the accommodation will not allow close use of the eyes for small objects, such as reading, writing or sewing, which, however, is small deprivation for a child.

The suggestion has recently been made that the drug be applied to one eye only and that the good one. The child would still continue to use this eye for distant vision as before, but on account of the accommodation being abolished he would not be able to use it for close vision. For this purpose he would practically be compelled to bring into use the squinting eye in which the function of accommodation has not been interfered with. In this way the vision of the eye is improved, fixation preserved and amblyopia from disuse avoided.

This method of treatment has somewhat the same effect as covering up the good eye, but few parents take the trouble to do this every day and continue it for a year or more, while few children are willing to bear the inconvenience. A point of difference is that when the eye is simply covered it will still be able to accommodate in sympathy with the uncovered eye.

If it is considered advisable, glasses to correct the hypermetropia may be prescribed in connection with the atropine. The atropinized eye would be adjusted for distance by means of the glass, but would be unable to accommodate for near objects. The other eye would have its refraction corrected and its accommodation assisted to the same extent. The latter would, therefore, be used for close vision, while both eyes would come into play for distant vision.

Exclusion of good eye consists in covering the eye by tying a patch over it or by placing an opaque lens before it, and thus compelling the patient to use the squinting eye for all purposes of vision. This not only preserves for the eye the faculty of fixation, but develops and increases its vision. In alternating strabismus, where first one eye is used and then the other, each eye is able to maintain its vision and power of fixation unimpaired. When nature points the way in this decided manner we cannot but follow, and transpose every case of fixed unilateral squint into an artificially-made alternating one by excluding the good eye for several hours each day and compelling it to assume the squint for that period.

Children are apt to rebel against the pad being tied over the eye, and will at first tear it off when unobserved. But it should at once be replaced and the child given to understand that it must be worn for a certain period each day.

The exclusion pad is not very comfortable at any age, but in the case of children it can scarcely be dispensed with. Adults, however, may use a "blinder," which is made of black rubber and may be clamped upon the spectacle or eyeglass the patient is wearing.

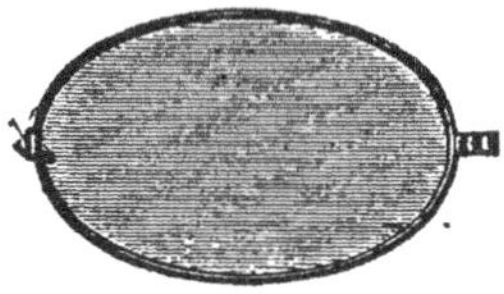

Blinder for Monocular Exercise

Bar Reading.—This consists in holding a pencil or ruler in front of the eyes in a vertical position while looking at a printed page which the patient is instructed to read. If he does not possess binocular vision, but is making use of only one eye, when the line of vision of this eye comes to the pencil or ruler, a certain portion of the page will be cut off and the patient will be compelled to skip a word. Whereas, if the two eyes are being used together, no portion of the page will be occluded and there will be no interruption or hesitation in the reading.

By persistent practice with this method, in order to avoid or remove the obstruction to the reading, the patient may be taught to use the eyes together. This may require considerable effort at first, but gradually the sense of effort diminishes or is entirely lost, and the function of binocular vision has been established. It may be remarked in parenthesis that in such a condition of vision an obstruction before one eye does not interfere with vision, because the uncovered eye takes up and continues the function where the obstructed eye left off.

In the cases of young children this method would be of no value, as it requires a certain amount of intelligence for its successful application.

Stereoscope.—The stereoscope, by affording the perception of form and outline, furnishes a great stimulus to binocular vision. Partial pictures may be placed in the two sides of the instrument in such a way that the complete image can be obtained only by combining them. An ordinary stereoscope can be used by removing the prisms and substituting a pair of strong convex lenses. The two portions of a picture should at first be placed in such positions that their images can be easily focused, and then slowly moved, and thus the fusion effort is increased. This may be continued for a few minutes at a time and repeated several times daily, care being taken not to exercise the muscles at any time to the point of exhaustion.

PROGNOSIS OF THE NON-OPERATIVE TREATMENT OF STRABISMUS

The prospect of the benefit to be derived from the treatment of strabismus depends on the nature of the strabismus, the possibility of the restoration of binocular vision and the age of the patient. It is a well-known fact that strabismus occurring in early childhood sometimes disappears with the growth of the child. He "outgrows" it, as the expression goes. This fact constitutes a strong argument for the postponement of operative measures until all other measures have been tried and is at the same time a good reason why some of the methods described above should be recommended. The natural tendency on the part of parents is to delay bringing the child, and hence the chance for improvement by this form of treatment is greatly reduced. When the public are educated up to the recognition of the importance of early treatment in these cases, the best results can be expected in the removal of the disfigurement and the restoration of binocular vision.

But little can be accomplished during the first year of life, even in those cases where the strabismus exists at birth or develops immediately thereafter. During the second year the exclusion pad can be made use of, covering the good eye at intervals during the day. A few years later atropine may be employed and continued for several weeks at a time, with intervals of rest between. Then any existing error of refraction may be corrected and the necessary glasses prescribed for constant wear. The patient has now probably arrived at an age when bar-reading and the stereoscope can be brought into play.

The method of treatment as outlined may be continued as long as the conditions improve. Even after the eyes become apparently straight, the treatment should not be discontinued at once, but the eyes should be exercised with the different procedures from time to time, and the wearing of glasses persisted in. In order to determine what progress the case is making, the amount of strabismus can be measured at intervals, according to the method already determined.

HETEROPHORIA

Synonyms: *Muscular Insufficiency, Latent Squint, Superable Squint.*

With the dawn of modern ophthalmology but a few decades ago, attention was first drawn to the latent or suppressed affections of the ocular muscles. Von Graefe was the first great authority to give them prominence and to call attention to this class of cases, and while he furnished many valuable ideas and apparently solved many of the problems presented by these cases, yet he scarcely did more than lay the foundation upon which his successors have builded a great storehouse of facts, and pointed the way along which the more recent investigators have worked.

Donders' labors were rather in the study of refractive errors, and he thought he had discovered the cause of all cases of asthenopia in the strain placed upon the accommodation by hypermetropia, to a great extent overlooking that large and troublesome class of cases now known to arise from muscular asthenopia.

Coming down to the men of the present day, those best known as original workers in this field are Maddox in England and Stevens in this country, names which have become familiar to every optometrist in connection with the rod and phorometer which bear their names.

The anomalies of the ocular muscles still continue to furnish a fruitful field for investigation, and the literature upon the subject grows rapidly. And yet with all the knowledge that has been accumulated on this subject, and the various methods that have been devised for the determination of the presence of these anomalies, a feeling of uncertainty or incompleteness impresses the careful student, and it is quite within the range of possibility that further research may vary materially change the views that are at present generally accepted.

In the study of the relations of the muscles to each other, sometimes contracted and again relaxed, we enter a field in which the symptoms are uncertain and vague. There are no demonstrable lesions of the muscular or nervous system which would be recognized by certain logical manifestations in life, or which could be discovered on the dissecting table by the knife or microscope of the pathologist. We have to deal rather with the peculiarities of an unbalanced nervous system, showing themselves in *tendencies* to inco-ordination of the ocular muscles. The examination and treatment of every such case is attended with difficulty, and calls for repeated tests by the latest methods of diagnosis.

Muscular anomalies are closely associated with refractive errors, although they may also occur in connection with emmetropia. But in either condition there is no case of muscular trouble that may not be modified or complicated in some way by the action of the ciliary muscle. This relation is universally recognized as so close that some authorities claim that all cases of heterophoria are dependent upon errors of refraction, and that the proper correction of the latter will cause the former to disappear. While others go so far as to maintain that the nervous disturbance caused by muscular imbalance reacts upon the accommodation and the refraction of the eye, and that the first step in the management of these cases should be attention to the condition of the muscles.

Functional deviations of the eye are not so simple as they may seem, but are influenced by the individuality of the patient and by his environments. They are not to be considered as dependent upon a weakness of the nervous system, but rather as a cause of this condition; being reflex or symptomatic of troubles elsewhere. A minority of the cases of heterophoria are due to substantial changes and are attended by a train of symptoms of their own.

MUSCULAR EQUILIBRIUM

The movements of the eyeballs in the orbit are under the direction of the brain, which controls them by means of a delicate muscular harness, and a sensitive nervous bridle. The four recti muscles acting in combination *tend* to draw the ball backward into the orbit, which tendency is neutralized or opposed by the superior and inferior oblique muscles whose action is to draw the eyeball forward. This backward or forward movement is very slight; practically we may say the movements of the eye are limited to those of rotation. A slight degree of contraction of all the muscles holds the ball taut in the orbit and maintains it in its proper position during our waking hours.

This process is simultaneous in the two eyes, so that when the two eyes are directed towards an object, their axes will meet; this is co-ordination of the eyes with perfect muscular balance, and is governed to a great extent by the natural desire to see the object single. When attention is directed to another object situated at about the same distance, both eyes turn to the right or to the left, or up or down, to an equal extent; these are called the associated movements of the eyes. If the objects looked at are directly in front, but one closer than the other, it is simply a matter of increased convergence, both turning inward to the same extent. While if the two objects are not only at different distances but in different directions, the eyes must make both the associated movement and also that of convergence. It is impossible for one eye to move and the other to remain stationary. This is a wise provision of nature, as otherwise we would be annoyed and vision distressed by a more or less constant diplopia.

The conical shape of the two orbits, the axes of which diverge from the median line, and the natural length of the muscles when passive, favor a position of divergence of the optic axes, and this probably obtains when the eyes are closed in sleep. But when the eyes are opened the parallel position that is required for binocular vision must be maintained, and the driver (the brain) through his reins (the nerves) pulls the eyes from the normal divergence to the equally normal functional condition of parallelism; this is accomplished without any special act of volition on the part of the individual; and being free from exertion, may be considered as the position of rest.

This results in normal and comfortable binocular vision, but it does not follow that a muscular imbalance will destroy this condition of parallelism or prevent binocular vision. In the majority of cases an increased innervation is sent to the insufficient muscle in order to maintain the desired positions of the eyes; and thus the nervous supply of the eyes being in excess of the amount to which they are entitled, some other organ is robbed and the general nervous system is bankrupted.

Functional muscular anomalies may be manifest or latent, or at one time assume one form and again the other. There may be an actual deviation of one optic axis from the other, or there may be simply a tendency to deviation. It should be remembered that the corresponding muscles of the two eyes must be considered together, and we do not speak of the defect of a single muscle of either eye. For instance, we recognize insufficiency of the internal recti, and not of the internal rectus of one eye. Nor can we consider the external rectus of one eye as possessing more power than the external rectus of the other, when measured by prisms, but rather that the strength of the external recti is 6°, or 7°, or 8°, as the case may be. Therefore, in heterophoria, we have a disturbance of the normal relation that should exist between two sets of opposing muscles, rather than an insufficiency or overaction of any individual muscle.

The causes which tend to disturb the natural muscular equilibrium do not always act with the same force or produce the same result, but they are modified by the individuality of the patient, or by the personal equation, as it is aptly expressed. This is well illustrated in the tendency to convergence of the visual axes that is dependent upon the hypermetropic condition of refraction. In some cases a high degree of defect is unaccompanied with any muscular imbalance, while in other cases a slight hypermetropia is productive of marked muscular disturbance. Everything depends on the nervous susceptibility of the individual; a person of a highly wrought nervous temperament will suffer from a low degree of hypermetropia, while a strong, robust individual will not be disturbed or inconvenienced by even a much greater degree of defect. Outside of this difference in temperament it is possible for a high degree of hypermetropia to exist with a perfect muscular equilibrium, while in other cases it is the cause of a decided strabismus. There is a factor in these cases that is not susceptible of explanation; it is a neurosis, or it occurs in a neurotic individual, that is, one in which there is an exaggeration of the reflex excitability.

NOMENCLATURE AND CLASSIFICATION OF MUSCULAR ANOMALIES

The nomenclature and classification of the muscular anomalies of the eye has been passing through certain stages of evolution. The first classification of any group of diseases has always been based upon the outward appearances presented, without any reference to the underlying cause. For instance, not many years ago dropsy figured as a disease and was treated as such. But as knowledge increased it soon became evident that dropsy was merely a symptom, and that the proper procedure was to search for the cause of the dropsy (it might be hepatic, renal or cardiac) and direct the treatment to the removal of that cause, rather than to the dropsy itself. This led to a classification based upon the pathological condition that was found instead of the symptoms presented.

Similarly the muscular anomalies of the eye were formerly named (and still are) simply in accord with the apparent deviation, whether upward, downward, outward or inward. The first great step in advance was taken when it was demonstrated that convergent strabismus was usually dependent upon hypermetropia, and divergent strabismus upon myopia. Thus was indicated the proper treatment, viz., the removal of the cause by the correction of the hypermetropia by convex lenses.

Then followed the discovery, by von Graefe, of what are

known as the "insufficiencies," and of the method of determining them, and of the relation existing between them and strabismus. The time soon came when the term insufficiency began to be regarded as an improper one, because it implied a condition that was not always present. This was supplanted by the "phorias," with the prefixes hetero-, exo-, eso- and hyper-, to designate the general condition and the outward, inward and upward tendencies. This nomenclature has the merit of convenience, and hence has been generally accepted in this country. But it is open to the objection that it groups the deviations according to their anatomical characters and is silent in regard to the etiological factors, classifying these anomalies according to their visible appearance and not according to their cause. In this one respect it is perhaps not much of an improvement over the term insufficiency, but it has come into general use and is likely to continue in favor on account of its convenience for purposes of record, and because in many cases it is not always possible even after a careful examination to determine the underlying causative condition, and, therefore, we must be content with this anatomical diagnosis.

It is unreasonable to expect too much of a mere term, but its employment should not lead anyone to adopt erroneous views of the matter. For instance, the statement that in a given case so many degrees of exophoria were found, should be regarded as only a partial presentation of the facts, the final diagnosis not being reached until the cause of the exophoria has been determined.

Thus the term "exophoria" comprises some half dozen or more conditions, differing in anatomical or physiological character, and requiring more or less different treatment. It may arise from one or more of the following conditions:

1. Over-action of one or more of the external recti, due to structural or functional anomalies.

2. Under-action of one or more of the internal recti, due to structural or functional anomalies.

3. Over-action of the divergence center.

4. Under-action of the convergent center, which may be accommodative or non-accommodative.

5. Two of these causes, acting together, as for instance, insufficiency of convergence with excess of divergence.

In a similar manner the causes or conditions under which the other forms of heterophoria may arise can be outlined. For example, if a case of esophoria was found to be due to excess of accommodative convergence, the indicated remedy would be the proper convex lenses. Whereas, if it was dependent upon an under-action of the external rectus, convex lenses would prove of no benefit, but instead prisms may be prescribed or possibly a tenotomy of the internal rectus may be necessary. In this way an etiological classification may lead out at once to the proper indications for treatment, but unfortunately this is not always found to be possible.

Cases are met with in which the power of convergence is weak; naturally this might be attributed to inherent weakness of the internal recti muscles. But if it was found that they worked normally in associated parallel movements, then we must consider that it is the function of convergence that is at fault, and not the action of the internal recti *per se*. Other cases may present an excess of divergence, which cannot be attributed to weakness of the internal recti if the latter act normally in convergence and in lateral movements, nor to excessive strength of the external recti as such if they do not carry the eye too far outward in the associated parallel movements. In such a case we must conclude that it is the function of divergence that is at fault, and not the external recti *per se*.

In both the above cases there is the one common symptom of divergence in fixation, and both would be classed under exophoria, but it is evident that this is naming only the symptom and not the disease. We are interested not only in the movements and disorders of the individual muscles as such, but also in the associated movements of the eyes together as produced by the co-ordinated actions of the muscles; and hence, as mentioned above, we must take into consideration faults of the functions of convergence and divergence, as well as the insufficiencies of the muscles themselves.

The nomenclature suggested by Stevens is as follows:

ORTHOPHORIA (Greek word *orthos*, meaning right). A condition of the muscular system of the eyes where there is perfect binocular balance.

HETEROPHORIA (Greek word *heteros*, meaning other). That condition of the muscular system of the eyes where there is some departure from the normal binocular balance.

ESOPHORIA (Greek word *eso*, meaning in). That condition of the muscular system of the eyes which favors or allows a tendency of the visual axes to turn inward.

EXOPHORIA (Greek word *exo*, meaning out). That condition of the muscular system of the eyes which favors or allows a tendency of the visual axes to deviate outward.

HYPERPHORIA (Greek word *huper*, meaning over). That condition of the muscular system of the eyes which favors or allows a tendency of the visual axes of one eye to deviate above that of the other, and may be either *right* or *left hyperphoria*, as the case may be.

In addition there are a number of compound terms, as *hyper-esophoria, hyper-exophoria*, etc., the meaning of which is evident.

It should be borne in mind constantly that these functional anomalies are named with reference to binocular vision. In esophoria we recognize a tendency of the visual lines inward, and in exophoria outward. In hyperphoria there is not necessarily a tendency of the visual line of the eye upward, but there may be a tendency of the visual line of the other eye downward. Therefore, in right hyperphoria we recognize a tendency of the visual line of this eye to place itself above that of the other, without indicating whether the right eye turns up or the left eye down.

To this classification Savage would add:

CYCLOPHORIA (Greek word *kuklos*, meaning a circle). That condition of the muscular system of the eye where the oblique muscles are at fault.

Duane, of New York, introduces the following terms:

HYPOKINESIS, inadequate action of a muscle, or no action at all.

HYPERKINESIS, excessive action of a muscle.

PARAKINESIS, irregular action of a muscle, sometimes inadequate and again excessive.

ESOPHORIA

Symptoms.—The symptoms of esophoria are not distinctive, and they vary according to the degree of defect and the nervous susceptibility of the patient. There may be pain in and around the eyes, conjunctival congestion, photophobia; lachrymation, blurring of the print, and drowsiness coming on after any use of the eyes. But these same symptoms may also arise from hypermetropia, astigmatism, or from some other form of heterophoria. One symptom of esophoria that is somewhat peculiar to it, is that the patient sometimes complains of seeing his nose when engaged in close work; but the fact is, that this symptom is to a great extent an imaginary one.

The headache of esophoria is periodic and accompanied by dizziness and nausea. It comes on after prolonged use of the eyes in distant vision, as after attendance at a theater, where it is apt to be attributed to the close air; after bicycle riding, and the like. During the attacks the esophoria may become manifest and result in diplopia, which is, of course, of the homonymous variety. Headaches depending upon esophoria tend to diminish in severity and frequency with the advance of age, on account of the weakening of the internal recti, by which means the esophoria spontaneously disappears.

There seems to be ground for believing that the symptoms above mentioned are not directly due to the internal recti muscles, but rather to the strain placed upon the external recti to prevent undue convergence. If the latter are unequal to the task of maintaining co-ordination of the visual axes, one eye will deviate inward; this will probably relieve the urgent symptoms, but the patient will complain of double vision. It can be readily understood that this constant strain on the external recti muscles may give rise in susceptible patients to serious reflex nervous disturbances. In fact, no set of muscles in any part of the body can bear such an unending strain without bankrupting the nervous system. The patients who suffer most are not necessarily those who possess the highest degree of defect, but rather those who are the most sensitive to abnormal impressions.

Dizziness, either with or without nausea, is to be especially mentioned as one of the probable symptoms of esophoria, and it is stated on authority that more cases of vertigo occur in this than in any other form of heterophoria.

ACCOMMODATIVE ESOPHORIA

Esophoria with Hypermetropia.—The well-known close connection existing between the functions of accommodation and convergence will furnish the explanation for the existence of esophoria in a majority of cases. A certain amount of contraction of the ciliary muscle is accompanied by an equal contraction of the internal recti, and therefore a stimulus that affects the accommodation, is bound to act on the convergence to an equal extent. If an undue amount of accommodation is called for, a corresponding demand is made upon the convergence.

In the emmetropic eye the accommodation and the convergence are used in the same proportion at the customary reading point. In a condition of hypermetropia, in order to maintain clear vision, an extra amount of accommodation must be used equal in extent to the degree of the refractive error; this causes an extra effort of convergence. Now the extra accommodation is just sufficient to focus the rays of light sharply upon the retina, but the extra convergence is more than is required to bring the visual axes together at the same point, one of which necessarily tends to turn inward.

If notwithstanding this disturbance of the natural relation between the two functions, binocular vision is maintained without any apparent excess of convergence, it can be only at the expense of a great strain upon the divergence, as already mentioned. If the relative range of adaptation of the accommodation and convergence is not exceeded, there is no production of esophoria, and this affords an explanation why it does not occur in every case of hypermetropia.

Accommodative esophoria in young people can usually be recognized without any great difficulty. The power of divergence is not below normal, and when the proper correction for the hypermetropia is placed before the eyes the esophoria disappears, sometimes at once and again after the glasses have been worn for some time.

But as time goes on in these cases, if the refractive error is not corrected, the power of divergence gradually lessens and falls to about 5°. If it should fall below this, the presumption is that the case does not belong under the head of accommodative esophoria. It may, perhaps, be asked why this is the case, and the reason is not hard to find. Ordinarily the effort of accommodation that is put forth to overcome the hypermetropia, stimulates the convergence to such an extent as to cause convergent strabismus; if now the natural desire for binocular vision is so strong as to avoid this and allow only esophoria to result, it must be because the power of divergence remains sufficiently strong to prevent the inward deviation.

Therefore, if the divergence falls below 5°, instead of the esophoria being due to an overaction of the internal recti, we must consider it as rather dependent upon an *insufficiency* of the external recti.

Because contraction of the ciliary muscle causes esophoria, it is naturally to be expected that relaxation of the muscle by the application of atropine would diminish its amount or correct it entirely. But there are occasional cases where more esophoria is shown while the eyes are under the influence of the drug than before its use. This has been explained by attributing it to the increased (but ineffective) efforts of the accommodation to overcome the action of the cycloplegic. But although this is a most reasonable explanation, a recent writer disputes it and claims that the increase of the esophoria is really due to excitement, and cites several cases in support of his view.

In the case of a child with convergent squint, where atropine increased the deformity, the mother stated that there was a noticeable increase of the strabismus whenever the child was excited or agitated, and that there was an exhibition of anger when the drops were about to be instilled, which resulted in a greater crossing of the eyes than ever. In another case a middle-aged woman of nervous temperament was worried and excited because the atropine had caused dryness of her throat and kept her awake at night, with the result of showing a great increase of esophoria at the commencement of the examination. But after her fears had been calmed and her excitement abated, it was found at the close of the examination that the muscular anomaly had very much lessened.

Accommodative esophoria is more apt to occur in young persons and is seldom found after fifty years of age on account of the natural failure of accommodation. In accommodative esophoria a tenotomy is contraindicated. Unfortunately the operation is frequently performed, doing more harm than good, and thus tending to bring the operation into disrepute. If the symptoms are not relieved by correction of the refraction, prisms may be combined to assist and increase the divergence.

ESOPHORIA WITH MYOPIA

This form of esophoria is attributed to the habit of fixing near objects, which, on account of the myopia, are held closer and call for more convergence than normal. It is apt to occur in those persons who have not had their refractive error corrected in early life, and then the symptoms make their appearance as soon as the glasses are worn, in some cases passing off as the eyes become adapted to the new conditions.

The most common symptoms are dizziness with the glasses at a distance, and headache.

When myopic esophoria is recognized, it is usually amenable to treatment by properly prescribed lenses. When overlooked the strain on the external recti continues and the symptoms go from bad to worse. The amount of esophoria is not always in proportion to the weakness of divergence. and is usually increased when concave glasses are worn on account of the stimulation to the accommodation.

MUSCULAR ESOPHORIA

This form of esophoria may be due to excessive action of the internal recti or to insufficient action of the external recti, and may occur either with or without an accompanying error of refraction. The majority of cases of muscular esophoria are probably due to an insufficiency of the external recti; divergence falls to 4°, or even less, but the convergence is not excessive.

In measuring the power of divergence, it may be well to note that occasionally cases where the external recti are weak can for the moment overcome prisms placed bases in much stronger than would represent their real muscular power; but if the prisms are kept before the eyes diplopia soon results, and the prisms must be reduced. Whereas, if the external recti are not weak, a comparatively light prism may at first produce diplopia, which, however, soon disappears, and stronger prisms be substituted, thus proving the divergence to be much in excess of that amount which a hasty examination would have shown. Therefore, in order to discover these latent deviations, the endeavor must be made to favor a relaxation of the strain under which the weak muscle is laboring, by means of our tests. The eyes are practically forced into binocular fixation, and hence there is a tendency to a concealment of the heterophoria from the very nature of the case. The prisms should not be removed too quickly, because, in attempting to measure the muscular power, momentary strength is not so much to be considered as endurance.

TREATMENT OF ESOPHORIA

The treatment of esophoria may be mentioned under the following heads:

1. Correction of any existing error of refraction.

2. Use of prisms; *a*, for exercise of weak muscles; *b*, for correction of the defect.

3. Tenotomy.

The estimation of the refractive error and the prescription of the proper lenses is the first step, and is a most essential one. No other method of treatment should be considered until the indicated glasses had been worn long enough for the eyes to become thoroughly accustomed to them, and in order to note what results follow from this assistance to the overtaxed accommodation. There is no dissenting opinion among ophthalmological authorities on this point, and hence no optometrist should attempt to influence the muscles directly until all the benefit that could possibly follow from the glasses has been exhausted. During this period the patient should be cautioned not to overtax the eyes in reading or other close work.

Prisms may be used to develop the strength of the muscles by exercising them, and in many cases the power of divergence may be strengthened and its range increased by this means. The normal power of divergence when tested with a light at 20 feet equals about 8°. In esophoria this is much lessened and sometimes falls to 2° or 3°, and in this way the normal ratio that should exist between divergence and convergence is destroyed.

In these exercises square prisms are really preferable, because they can the more easily be placed in a strictly horizontal position, and any departure therefrom can the more quickly be detected. As they are not always available, the circular prisms from the trial case will be more often used, when care must be taken that the base does not deviate from the horizontal position. A prism of 2° is placed over one eye with its base in while the patient looks at the light; this may cause nothing that is noticeable to the patient. Then a similar prism is placed in a like position over the other eye; this will probably cause two lights to be seen at first, but they may quickly run together into one. Then one or both of the prisms are increased to 3°, and now a diplopia is produced which the patient cannot overcome. He is asked to approach the light, and as he does so the lights get closer and closer until when within a few feet only one will be noticeable. He is now requested to recede from the light, making the effort to maintain it single as long as possible. When two lights are again seen he approaches until they are once more fused. This may be repeated a number of times, but must not be continued too long, else the muscles become fatigued and the object of the exercise be defeated. About two to three minutes is sufficiently long at first, and perhaps five minutes as long as it should be continued at any one time.

These exercises may be repeated daily, and on the second

or third day the patient will notice that the lights fuse easier than at first, and in the course of a few days the eyes will probably be able to overcome the prisms at the full distance of 20 feet. The prisms may be slightly increased in the judgment of the optometrist, and the exercises continued for several weeks.

Fusion of the lights is accomplished not by the contraction of one external rectus, nor even by both of them, but by the forced action of all the muscles concerned in the act of divergence.

Prisms may also be worn constantly for the correction of the esophoria, the amount of which must first be carefully measured. If the esophoria is not greater than 2° it will scarcely call for correction by prisms. If it exceeds 12° or 14° it is too high for prisms, and then a tenotomy is indicated. The proportion of the insufficiency that should be corrected by prisms varies in different cases, but as a rule it should not be more than one-half to two-thirds. For instance, if the amount of esophoria was found to be 6° the extent of prism assistance should be from 3° to 4°, which may be divided and placed 1½° or 2° over each eye bases out.

It will be remembered that esophoria does not give rise to much trouble in using the eyes for near vision, but that the symptoms manifest themselves when looking at a distance, as in a church, or theater, or looking out of the window of a moving train. Therefore, the prisms should be worn constantly, instead of only for reading, as on first thought might seem sufficient. In some cases the prisms may need to be increased from time to time, in order to afford relief to the symptoms, until finally perhaps the operation point is reached. As long as the patient is comfortable and the glasses seem satisfactory, the prisms may be worn without change.

In those cases where an increase in the strength of the prisms is called for, the question arises whether the prism is responsible for the increase of the insufficiency? This does not necessarily follow, because the effect of the prisms may be rather to make manifest a certain amount of defect which had formerly been latent.

Prisms have been aptly compared to crutches, on which the eyes can depend for assistance, but the former cannot be considered any more a means of cure than the latter. They afford relief when placed in the position of rest, because comfortable binocular fixation is maintained by the bending power of the prisms, rather than by the undue effort of the external recti muscles. The visual axes being converged, the yellow spot in each eye is moved from the median line; the prisms with their bases out turn the rays of light outward so that they fall upon each yellow spot in its new position, instead of calling upon the external recti to make an excessive effort to overcome the convergence and keep the maculæ in their normal positions.

In esophoria the position of rest is one of convergence, instead of parallelism, as is the normal condition.

If the full measure of esophoria is corrected, or the prisms prescribed are stronger than two-thirds of the defect, the external recti muscles are called upon to make little or no effort to maintain equilibrium, and on account of this disuse they will naturally become weaker and weaker and thus cause the esophoria to increase.

Tenotomy should be held in reserve as a last resort after all other means have been tried and failed to effect a cure. If the procedures mentioned above are faithfully carried out the number of cases that seem to require an operation will be reduced to a minimum. There is a great diversity of opinion among ophthalmic surgeons as to the benefits to be derived from an operation; some assert that it is entirely useless, while others are enthusiastic in praise of it and probably operate on cases that could be improved by less radical methods.

The aim of any and all methods of treatment is to relieve the symptoms and restore the muscles to a normal equilibrium, which latter is proven when the Maddox rod is made use of and the line of light passes directly through the center of the flame vertically and horizontally.

While an operation on the ocular muscles is a procedure entirely outside of the optometrist's sphere, yet it is so closely allied to his legitimate work that he should at least have some intelligent knowledge regarding it.

It is not possible to state definitely the exact amount of esophoria that calls for operation, as this will vary greatly in different cases according to the severity of the symptoms and the effect of the treatment previously instituted.

If the correction of the refraction and the use of prisms ameliorates the symptoms, even though the degree of esophoria is but little diminished, an operation is not to be thought of. But if in spite of glasses and prisms, both for correction and exercise, the severity of the symptoms continues unabated, then an operation may become advisable.

A tenotomy is scarcely necessary unless the esophoria exceeds 12°. In slighter degrees the use of prisms will generally suffice, but more than 5° over each eye can seldom be worn with comfort. It should be borne in mind that the degree of esophoria varies on different days and even at different times on the same day; in other words, it is a variable quantity, a fact that must not be lost sight of in determining the degree of prism correction.

The operation may consist either of an advancement of the external recti or a tenotomy of the internal, depending on whether there is an insufficiency of divergence or an excess of convergence. In esophoria, division of the internal recti is the operation that is most often performed.

The question that arises for the surgeon to solve is whether the operation should be confined to one eye, or whether both should be included? Theoretically, it would seem proper to divide the operation between the two eyes, because we are dealing with defective divergence or excessive convergence, which is an act not of one eye or of one muscle, but of both eyes and both muscles. In the same way when prisms are prescribed, they should be divided between the two eyes. Esophoria is not a monocular affection, but a binocular defect. Some surgeons prefer to cut only one eye at a time, deferring the second operation for several days after the first.

During the progress of the operation its effect must be noted by testing the eyes with the light at twenty feet, in order that the operator may be guided in his efforts to produce an equilibrium of the ocular muscles, and that an excessive effect may be avoided, as otherwise the final result may be a divergence of the visual axes.

EXOPHORIA

The outward tendency of the visual axes as occurring in exophoria, is rather to be regarded as a lack of convergence than an excess of divergence, and hence is a passive and not an active condition. It is a deficient innervation of the function of convergence. This contrasts with the conditions found in esophoria, where it was shown that the stimulation of the accommodation caused an innervation of the convergence; whereas, in exophoria there is relaxation of the convergence, which may arise from the lessened call on the accommodation, as in myopia. This insufficiency of convergence may also be caused by a lowered vitality of the general system.

SYMPTOMS

The headache of exophoria is likely to occur only when near work is done, or at least it is aggravated by close use of the eyes. It may be a general headache, or it may be localized in the frontal or occipital region, and is sometimes accompanied by dizziness and nausea. Or the eyes may quickly become tired from near work, even without headache.

These symptoms may also be produced by prisms bases out; this may happen in any other condition when prisms are placed in such a way as to cause a strain upon the weak muscles, but it is particularly noticeable in exophoria, which for this reason was the first of the insufficiencies to be recognized, and is the one to which perhaps the most attention has been given.

Exophoria indicates that the divergence exceeds the convergence at least comparatively, but it must be understood that there is a slight (but appreciable) difference between twenty feet and infinite distance in making a test of the ocular muscles with weak prisms. If the visual axes could be made to assume the position of parallelism suitable for infinity, and then the test light be placed at the usual distance of twenty feet, a prism of about 1° base in will probably be required to restore equilibrium. Therefore an exophoria of 1° at twenty feet should not always be considered abnormal without other corroborative tests, but any greater amount would represent a real defect.

CAUSE OF EXOPHORIA

The most common and active cause is a myopic condition of refraction. The myopic eye is adapted for the divergent rays proceeding from near objects, and hence there is but little need for accommodation in reading and close work. This deprives the function of convergence of the customary innervation which is associated with accommodation for near objects, the effect of which in the course of time becomes manifest in a lessening of convergence and the appearance of exophoria. Following out this line of reasoning it would seem probable that the amount of exophoria would bear a definite and constant relation to the degree of myopia, but this does not always follow, because it may be modified by individual peculiarities.

In young myopes the full correction may be prescribed, which increases the demand on the accommodation and at the same time stimulates the convergence, thus tending to a natural correction of the exophoria. When middle age is reached and the insufficiency has become permanent it will no longer yield to a correction of the refraction.

In exophoria dependent upon a loss of accommodation impulse, there may be but little increase of divergence for distance, but the convergence power is below the standard; it is at the reading or working point that the exophoria manifests itself and may be out of all proportion to that shown at a distance.

The tests indicate less power of convergence, while the divergence may or may not be increased, but in any case there is no indication as to whether the fault is located in the external or internal recti muscles. A case might be assumed in which the convergence and divergence were equal at twenty feet, say 10° for each; this shows the convergence to be less and the divergence more than the normal standard. In such a case the question for solution is whether the exophoria is due to the diminution of convergence or to the excess of divergence. It is more than likely the former, and it is probable that the excess of divergence which is shown is only relative and depends upon the greatly diminished power of adduction which is unable to resist a divergence that is not above normal.

If, however, the convergence was equal to 20° and the divergence to 10°, the conditions would be quite different and the same reasoning woud not apply. Here it would be only fair to conclude that the divergence was really in excess, which is a proper inference in any case where the divergence reaches a high degree, while the convergence remains of nearly normal strength.

There may be other cases in which the power of convergence is reduced almost to nothing, and the power of divergence also much below normal, but as this shifts the preponderance of strength from the internal to the external recti, a condition of exophoria results.

EXOPHORIA IN HYPERMETROPIA

It is a not uncommon occurrence for exophoria to be produced by convex glasses, which could in many cases be avoided. It happens when a hypermetrope is given the full correction found under atropine, or when by the fogging system the eyes are coaxed to accept what may be called an over-correction of their hypermetropia; that is, after the strongest lens is found that each eye separately will accept, the two eyes together will sometimes suffer still stronger convexes. These lenses remove to a great extent the need for accommodation, and in this way diminish or stop the nervous supply to the convergence, which is manifested by a condition of exophoria.

In these cases of exophoria which are due to an over-correction of hypermetropia, the optrometrist might be led to combine prisms with the spheres for the correction of the deviation, but such a course is only likely to increase the trouble. The proper plan would be to restore the harmony between accommodation and convergence by a lessening of the strength of the convex lenses and a removal of the prisms.

Accommodative exophoria from glasses may also occur in cases of presbyopia, where the convergence power is usually weak; convex lenses accentuate this weakness by their effect upon the accommodation as mentioned before. In addition, the optical centers are often too wide, thus adding an adverse prismatic effect of the other difficulties. Whereas in these cases if the glasses are ordered decentered inwards for reading, the slight prismatic effect that is produced will be such as to assist the convergence and lessen the tax upon it. But it would scarcely be proper to wear such glasses for distance, as they would then impose a tax upon the divergence which would really do more harm than the strain upon the convergence in the first place, because the latter is more easily exercised than the former.

After all is said and done, it is sometimes a difficult or impossible matter for an optometrist to give satisfaction to his presbyopic patients. Many of them expect glasses with which they can see both far and near, and are apt to regard the optometrist as obstinate or incompetent when he fails to fulfil what they consider a reasonable request. Therefore the man who tries to satisfy these patients by attention to all the proper details will often find himself sadly disappointed.

There is no definite standard as to what should be considered the normal balance for the ocular muscles at the near point. In healthy persons with good muscular tone and with no great error of refraction, orthophoria is the rule at close distances. This is, of course, the ideal condition; but many exceptions will be found among persons applying for glasses. A slight amount of exophoria at a close point must not always be considered abnormal, because it may easily occur simply from a lack of proper contraction of the accommodation and convergence. If, however, the tests should show an exophoria of 2° or more at twelve inches, then the muscular equilibrium can no longer be considered normal, although some authorities maintain that an exophoria of 3° at the reading distance has no special significance.

While there can be no doubt that heterophoria may be produced by glasses, it must not be forgotten that the eyes are sometimes forced to maintain an equilibrium in spite of the adverse prismatic effect of improperly decentered lenses, on account of the natural desire for binocular vision, which is favored by the ability of these ocular muscles to adapt and adjust themselves to differences in muscle power.

EXOPHORIA FROM EXCESS OF DIVERGENCE

This condition may be discovered by the usual tests with prisms bases in and the light at a distance of twenty feet. The average normal power of divergence is about 8°, and therefore a divergence of 9° and over may be considered as constituting an excess. Convergence is apt to grow less with age, and if now divergence should increase, the disproportion between the two would be the more strongly marked, and asthenopia be the probable result, calling for careful attention.

A tenotomy of one external rectus, and sometimes of both, may become necessary. During the first few days after the operation, the patient is instructed to practice forced convergence, in order to put the divided muscle upon the stretch, in which case the immediate effect of the operation will diminish but little with time. The result of the operation is not only a decrease of divergence, but an actual increase in the power of convergence, which latter is less apt to occur in myopic eyes or in persons in whom the muscular system is not well developed.

EXOPHORIA FROM INSUFFICIENCY OF CONVERGENCE

"Insufficiency of the internal recti" is the type of muscular weakness which belongs to neurasthenic patients, and may properly be called insufficient amplitude of convergence. In such cases good food, fresh air, exercise and tonics like strychnia are indicated.

It is possible that this condition may be due to simple inaction of the convergence, or may be a sign of constitutional laziness; in such cases, however, it is not likely to cause pain or discomfort. An operation is not indicated and is apt to do more harm than good; the external recti may be injured by a tenotomy, while the internal cannot be much strengthened by an advancement.

Common sense and judgment are necessary in these cases, in order to determine the proper proportion that should be observed between rest and exercise. It seems only reasonable that abstention from that which fatigues or irritates the nervous system, or rest of an overworked organ, would afford relief. Since the eyes are constantly in use during our working hours, it is impossible to obtain absolute rest without closure of the lids, which is scarcely practicable for any length of time. But inasmuch as a rational treatment of an eye with structural or functional weakness, suffering from symptoms brought on by strain of the affected part, includes rest for the weary organ, the indications are met by a correction of the refraction, which, at least, partially rests the ciliary muscle, and by means of prisms to rest the extra-ocular muscles, while the effort is made to restore the muscular balance by the various methods. It is really not the insufficiency itself that causes the asthenopia, but rather the use of the insufficient muscles. Therefore the general rule should be that the use of the eyes for near work must not be continued after evidences of fatigue begin to manifest themselves. The function of vision, like that of digestion or any other function of the body, should be carried on without the consciousness of the individual; as soon as one is conscious of his eyes or his stomach, there is evidence that something is wrong, and it may be considered as a request of Nature for relief.

EXOPHORIA IN ACCOMMODATION

The tests for muscular anomalies are made at a distance of twenty feet, and therefore when a patient is said to have an exophoria of 4°, it is understood that this amount of insufficiency has shown itself at a distance of twenty feet. But the tests can and should be repeated at the reading distance, where the "dot and line" is very useful. A vertical prism is placed over one eye, and if the diplopia that is produced is of the crossed variety, insufficiency of the internal recti is proven to exist at the reading point, to which condition has been applied the term *exophoria in accommodation.*

DIAGNOSIS OF EXOPHORIA

A prism of 8° is placed before one eye in a vertical position, while the patient looks at the light twenty feet away. A vertical diplopia is thus produced, and if the image belonging to the eye over which the prism is placed is on the opposite side. exophoria is shown to exist, and the prism base in placed over the other eye which brings the two lights on the same vertical plane will be the measure of the exophoria.

Maddox Rod.—This is placed in a horizontal position before one eye, producing the appearance of a vertical streak of light, which in exophoria will be on the opposite of the light seen by the uncovered eye. The strength of the prism base in that is required to bring the streak directly over the flame, will be the measure of the exophoria.

TREATMENT OF EXOPHORIA

After the existence of exophoria has been definitely determined by the various tests, and by a repetition of the examination on several different days, the question occurs as to what shall be done to overcome the tendency to excessive divergence, and what means are available to afford relief of the annoying symptoms?

It may be stated that exophoria of quite a marked degree is sometimes accidentally discovered in persons who present no symptoms traceable to it; while others may suffer severely from slight insufficiencies.

1. Correction of refraction.
2. Exercise of convergence.
3. Prisms for correction.
4. Medical treatment.
5. Operation.

Inasmuch as the larger number of muscular anomalies are conceded to be directly or indirectly dependent upon some condition of ametropia, it cannot be too strongly insisted upon that the first step in the treatment should always be the correction of any existing error of refraction. A cure will follow if this is the cause of the insufficiency; but at any rate this disturbing factor should be removed before we can expect a restoration of muscular balance.

As previously stated, exophoria is usually dependent upon or, at least, associated with myopia; because the little need for accommodation deprives the convergence of its customary innervation. It is a manifest proposition that if concave lenses are employed to neutralize the myopia, the eyes will then be made artificially emmetropic and the accommodation be called upon to exert itself in the normal manner; this will restore to the convergence the natural stimulant to which it is accustomed and entitled. By this means the tendency to divergence is overcome, and oftentimes concave glasses alone will suffice to cure the exophoria. At any rate they should be given a fair trial for several months, and worn constantly both for near work as well as for distance. If they should fail to afford relief and the symptoms should continue, then some other form of treatment must be added.

Exercise of Convergence.—There is no doubt that the power or amplitude of convergence can be increased by exercise with prisms, which are placed before the eyes with their bases outward. The strongest prisms which the patient can overcome and maintain singleness of vision, should be placed in a frame and worn for a few minutes, lifting them several times during this period while gazing at the light across the room. The maximum length of this exercise should not exceed five minutes, and it may be repeated daily. The prisms may gradually be increased and in the course of a month or two will easily reach 40° or 50°. The statement has been made on authority that the convergence power can in this way be increased as high as 100°.

The rationale of this method of treatment should be explained to the patient, so that he may be made to realize the necessity for and the importance of it, to the end that his co-operation may be secured, as otherwise but little result can be obtained. Many cases of painful asthenopia can be entirely relieved in this way. The improvement is more noticeable in a lessening of the exophoria at the reading point than at twenty feet.

Prisms may also be set in frames with their bases out

and given to the patient for home use. They should not be too strong, not more than half what the eyes can overcome, and may be worn for fifteen minutes to a half hour each day, while the patient goes about his customary duties. These exercises are of most value in young and growing subjects, and in convalescence from exhausting illness, and their effect is increased by outdoor exercise and a nourishing diet.

CORRECTING PRISMS

Sometimes it becomes necessary in order to relieve the emergency of the symptoms, to prescribe prisms in the position of assistance, which in exophoria would be bases in, and thus lessen the strain under which the convergence is laboring. This allows the visual axes to diverge slightly, and the eyes assume those positions which are most restful to them. The convergence effort is lessened, and binocular vision is maintained by the converging power of the prisms bases in.

Exophoria is almost invariably greater at the reading distance than at twenty feet; there is no definite proportion existing between the two points, but it varies in every case. This complicates the case, and prevents the wearing of one pair of glasses constantly and for all purposes. If prisms are needed for distant wear a stronger pair is usually necessary for close use. Slight degrees of exophoria found by the test at twenty feet (2° to 3°, or sometimes even more) may be left to themselves without assisting prisms, and only such lenses be worn for distance as may be called for by any existing error of refraction. In higher degrees of exophoria, if the symptoms are such as seem to demand it, prisms can be prescribed for constant wear, in which case a stronger pair may be necessary for reading and close use.

It is not considered proper to give prisms strong enough to correct the full amount of the exophoria, as otherwise there would be such a limited need for convergence that the function would suffer from disuse. In an exophoria of 8°, a prism of 2° may be placed over each eye base in, and after a fair trial this may be increased to 3° for each eye, if found necessary for a relief of the symptoms.

There is a limit to the strength of prismatic correction,

beyond which no practical benefit is likely to result. The writer has had a case in his practice in which 8° prisms were worn over each eye; and while the limit will vary according to the circumstances of the case, it may usually be placed at about 12°, divided between the two eyes.

Some authorities claim that when prisms are given to an exophoric patient, by this act all prospect of cure is abandoned, and that the glasses can never be laid aside without a return of the previous symptoms, and that in fact they must be increased in strength from time to time. With this view the writer is compelled to disagree, and on what he considers are sufficient grounds.

The use of prisms of the proper strength removes the great burden of strain from the convergence, which is then called upon for only so much work as it can comfortably accomplish. Now it is a well-known fact that a proper and rational amount of use is necessary and conducive to the healthy development of any organ or muscle. While the eyes may break down under the tremendous strain of an uncorrected exophoria, does it require any stretch of imagination to see that the function of convergence, when intelligently assisted, may be placed in such a position not only to regain its lost power but even to develop unusual strength?

Medical treatment is mentioned here, not for the purpose of advising the optometrist to carry it out himself, but in order that he may have knowledge of this as one of the means of cure of exophoria, and that he may be able to give intelligent advice to such of his patients as suffer from this defect. The muscles of convergence are weak, and there is also in most cases a lack of tone of the general system, which condition is met by the internal administration of nerve tonics, such as "nux vomica."

OPERATION FOR EXOPHORIA

If all the other methods of treatment fail and an operation is deemed advisable, the surgeon has choice between tenotomy of the external recti and advancement of the internal recti. The aim to be kept in mind should be rather to strengthen the convergence than to weaken the divergence, and therefore the operation to be preferred in most cases of exophoria is an advancement instead of tenotomy. The former operation is more difficult for the surgeon and more trying to the patient, but the results in most cases are likely to be more satisfactory.

The number of prism degrees of convergence that can be gained by an operation varies greatly. It oftentimes will not exceed 4° or 5°, and therefore in high degrees of defect, such as usually call for operative interference, both internal recti should be advanced. This is preferable to a tenotomy of one external rectus in connection with an advancement of one internal rectus, because whatever benefit would result in the lessening of the exophoria would be at the expense of a diminished power of rotating the eyes outward. It is the custom of most operators to advance both internal recti at the same sitting, rather than make two operations at different times, and thus duplicate the dread and anxiety with which a patient anticipates an operation.

HYPERPHORIA

Hyperphoria is that condition of the muscular equilibrium in which there is a tendency of the visual line of one eye to place itself above that of the other. The eye does not actually deviate upward, but only the tendency to this deviation exists, and hence binocular vision is still maintained. The statement has been made that one-third of the patients who apply for treatment of their eyes show some degree of hyperphoria, either alone or in connection with some other form of heterophoria, and yet it does not necessarily follow that the vertical imbalance calls for special attention, or that it may not exist even when the eyes are comfortable and apparently healthy.

SYMPTOMS OF HYPERPHORIA

The symptoms of hyperphoria do not specifically differ from those of other forms of heterophoria.

Headache is not uncommon and is situated in the back of the neck, or it may affect the whole head. It varies in intensity, getting worse towards evening and passing away during sleep. Dizziness may also occur, sometimes with nausea and vomiting. The headache is aggravated not only by close work, but also by watching a crowd or any moving objects.

Congestion of the eyeball is noticed, showing itself in a redness of the conjunctiva and of the edges of the lids. The latter may be partly due to the irritation caused by an increased secretion of tears. These cases of conjunctivitis, and blepharitis are not amenable to the usual collyria and ointments, but are apt to be aggravated by any except the mildest applications.

The position of the head, if tilted toward the shoulder, will excite suspicion of hyperphoria. This tilting is usually toward the shoulder opposite to the hyperphoric eye, that is in left hyperphoria the head is inclined towards the right shoulder, in order that the images of the two eyes may be brought to the same level and binocular vision be maintained with less effort.

There is usually some hyperesthesia of the retina, as evidenced by photophobia and a painful condition of the eyes.

It is not unreasonable to assume that vertically decentered lenses are a common cause of hyperphoria. This is especially noticeable when the frame is crooked and the spectacles sag on one side, or when the right lens of eyeglasses is pulled down by the weight of a chain. But even when the frames are straight and perfectly adjusted, we cannot be sure that there is no vertical decentering of the lenses themselves; this is perhaps more apt to occur when one of the lenses is broken and is replaced by a different manufacturer.

The right shoulder is apt to be a little lower than the left in right-handed people, and similarly the right ear, which must be kept in mind in the adjustment of spectacles, in order to prevent a sagging on this side.

Hyperphoria may be latent, as hypermetropia oftentimes is. It is that portion of the defect which is concealed and which the observer fails to find; but what is latent at one time or to one observer, may be manifest at another time or to another observer. Hyperphoria does not always remain stationary, but may show a tendency to appear or disappear, to increase or decrease, but it is more apt to increase as some of the latent defect becomes manifest. For the reasons mentioned above, the examination for hyperphoria should be repeated on different days and under different conditions in order that it may not escape detection.

DIAGNOSIS OF HYPERPHORIA

The diagnosis of hyperphoria should not be based upon any single test, but should be verified by every test at the optometrist's command. The detection and measurement of hyperphoria calls perhaps for greater accuracy and precision than in any other form of heterophoria.

A prism of 8° or 10° is placed before one eye with its base in, and great care must be taken to see that the base is strictly horizontal. This produces a horizontal artificial diplopia, and if the two lights are on the same plane, the superior and inferior recti are assumed to be equally balanced; but if one of the lights is higher or lower than the other, then hyperphoria is proven to be present. If the right light is lower, it is a case of right hyperphoria; if the left image is lower, left hyperphoria. The first is corrected by a prism base down before the right eye, and the second by a prism base down before the left eye; the degree of hyperphoria being measured by that prism that restores the lights to the same horizontal plane.

A Maddox rod may be placed before one eye (say the right) in a vertical position; this causes the streak of light to be seen horizontally by this eye. If this streak passes through the flame as seen by the other eye, the superior and inferior recti are assumed to be equally balanced. If the streak is seen above the flame, it is a case of left hyperphoria; if below the flame, right hyperphoria. The prism that is required base up or down to bring the streak into the flame, will be the measure of the hyperphoria.

TESTS FOR SUPRA- AND INFRA-DUCTION

The tests just mentioned indicate only that the visual axis of one eye tends to deviate above that of the other, but the defect has not been located in either eye, nor is there any evidence as to whether it is due to excessive strength of the muscle of one eye or weakness of the corresponding muscle of the other eye. In order to determine these points, the power of upward and downward rotation of each eye must be measured by means of a vertical prism.

A very slight prism, when held with its base vertical, is sufficient to destroy binocular vision, averaging from 2° to 3°. When the prism is placed before an eye base up, the inferior rectus muscle of this eye is brought into action in the effort to maintain binocular vision, and the strongest prism the muscle is able to overcome will represent its power. The strength of the superior rectus is measured in the same way by a prism over the eye with its base down. The extent of the downward rotation of the eye is greater than the upward, the power of the inferior rectus being equivalent to a 3° prism, while the superior rectus seldom exceeds 2°. Therefore, if there is a difference of more than 1° between the power of supraduction and infraduction of the same eye, the existence of hyperphoria is to be suspected. Or if either supraduction or infraduction exceeds the figures mentioned above, there is indication, or at least suspicion of hyperphoria.

In such cases a perimeter may be made use of to measure the limits of upward and downward rotation. In the normal eye this would show about 40° for the former and about 60° for the latter. If in any case the result greatly exceeds or falls short of these figures, we are in position to locate the cause of the trouble in either the superior or inferior rectus, and determine whether there is excessive or deficient action in one or the other.

THE RELATION BETWEEN VERTICAL AND LATERAL DEVIATIONS

Some authorities make the claim that esophoria and exophoria are dependent upon hyperphoria, while others claim that the latter is caused by the former. Both are right to a certain extent, because when there is a muscular imbalance of any variety, all the rotary muscles are put upon a strain to fuse the images and maintain binocular vision. Cases have occurred where lateral deviations have been cured by a restoration of the vertical equilibrium, and others where the hyperphoria disappeared after the correction of an exophoria or esophoria.

In the determination of the relative importance of vertical and lateral imbalances, in any given case, the power of the various muscles to overcome a prism must be measured. The normal power of ad- ab- supra- and infra-duction being known, any departure either in the direction of excess or deficiency, is at once detected, and the offending muscles picked out in their several degrees of departure from normal conditions.

HYPERPHORIA WITH ASTIGMATISM

It can scarcely be doubted that the action of the various muscles may affect the cornea in such a way as to change the defective meridian in a case of astigmatism. On the other hand, a recent writer finds that an imbalance of the vertical muscles occurs very frequently in cases of astigmatism where the axis of the correcting cylinder is at some other angle than vertical and horizontal, and concludes that there is a direct connection between oblique astigmatism and the production of hyperphoria, explaining it on three grounds, as follows:

1. By inco-ordination of muscular action.

2. By an attempt on the part of the rotating muscles to change the axis to a better position.

3. By a supposition that in some of these cases the muscles are normal, but the deflection of light caused by a difference in the height of the corneal centers shows a vertical displacement, which is really optical and not muscular. Cylinders set at an oblique angle can sometimes be adjusted in such a way as to remove a hyperphoria, which tends to emphasize the importance of accuracy in determining the proper angle for the axis of the correcting cylinder.

LATENT HYPERPHORIA

Hyperphoria may exist in a latent form, as does hypermetropia, and represents that portion of defect which the observer is unable to discover. What is latent one day, may be manifest the next; or what is latent to one optometrist, may be manifest to another possessing more skill in examination. When the amount of hyperphoria that is discovered is equal to the difference between right and left sursumduction, it may usually be considered as all manifest. But when it is less than this difference, there is probably some additional defect that is latent, and which may become manifest at a later examination or under different tests. Or it may become necessary to correct with vertical prisms what little hyperphoria can be discovered, the symptoms thereby being more or less relieved. After wearing these glasses for a time, more of the defect becomes manifest, calling for an increase in the strength of the prisms, with the result of a cessation of all the troublesome symptoms.

Hyperphoria, like some of the other defects, may vary from time to time; it may increase or diminish, it may disappear and reappear, or it may remain constant. It is, however, more likely to get worse than better, and it is scarcely possible for marked degrees of hyperphoria to disappear except by operation.

SLIGHT DEGREES OF HYPERPHORIA NOT TO BE IGNORED

When astigmatism was first brought to notice, it was scarcely thought necessary to correct it unless it equaled or exceeded 1 D. Later the amount was reduced to .50 D., and soon many cases were reported where great relief was experienced from the correction of .25 D. of astigmatic defect; and now the fact is recognized that a cylinder of + .12 D. may often be prescribed with advantage.

The correction of muscular insufficiencies is passing through similar changes, and especially in the treatment of hyperphoria have weak prisms proven of great value. In many cases, depending of course upon the sensitiveness of the patient, a half degree (in expressing fractions decimals are preferable, and hence we write it .50) of hyperphoria may cause sufficient trouble to call for correction. The weaker the power of the vertical muscles, the greater the trouble that may be expected from a slight degree of hyperphoria; for instance, in a case where supra- and infra-duction did not exceed 1 and 1.50, a deficiency of .50 is likely to cause more discomfort than if the upward and downward rotation was equal to 2 and 3, respectively. The greater the hyperphoria, the more urgent the symptoms that will be produced by it, until in the higher grades binocular vision is no longer possible and vertical strabismus may occur, in which cases symptoms of asthenopia are unknown.

TREATMENT OF HYPERPHORIA

It goes without saying, in this as in any other form of muscular imbalance, that an accurate correction of any existing error of refraction is always first in order, which sometimes suffices after a time to cure the hyperphoria, or at least to relieve the symptoms caused by it, so that no further attention need be given to it. But if the persistent wearing of such lenses fails to afford the desired relief, or if the refractive error is slight and appears to be subordinate to the muscular insufficiency, then it will be proper to correct the latter by means of vertical prisms.

Hyperphoria is the one form of muscular imbalance in which it is desirable to prescribe prisms strong enough for the full correction of the manifest error, or at least within .25 or .50 of it. This refers to the degree of hyperphoria as usually found. If it equals or exceeds 3°, a correction of two-thirds will probably suffice, although these are the cases in which a tenotomy is recommended.

In following the rule which has already been enunciated that the base of the prism should be placed over the weak muscle, in hyperphoria the base of the prism must be down, because this is a tendency to upward deviation due to insufficiency of the inferior rectus muscle. Therefore, in right hyperphoria the prism is base down over right eye, and in left hyperphoria base down over left eye; or the prism may be divided between the two eyes, in the first case base down over right eye and base up over left, and in the second case base down over left eye and base up over right.

In order that the student may thoroughly understand the foregoing statements, we will pause for a few words of explanation. In right hyperphoria, on account of the upward tendency of this eye, the image would naturally be formed upon the retina above the yellow spot, while in the normal eye the image falls upon the yellow spot; in other words, the image formed in the hyperphoric eye is always above that of the normal eye, and the asthenopia results from the muscular effort required to place them on the same plane, in order that binocular vision may be preserved. A prism base down over the hyperphoric eye deflects the rays downward and lowers the retinal image of this eye to the same plane as that of the normal eye; while a prism base up over the good eye bends the rays upward and raises the retinal image of this eye to the same plane as that of the hyperphoric eye. In either case the retinal images are placed on the same horizontal plane, which is the great desideratum. Or when the prism is divided and placed base down over one eye and base up over the other, the retinal image of one eye is raised and of the other lowered, so as to bring them to the same level.

In these conditions the apparent position of the objects seen by the two eyes, is the reverse of that mentioned above. The object seen by the hyperphoric eye, according to the law of projection, appears to be below that of the normal eye. Objects viewed through a prism are displaced in the direction of its apex, and therefore a prism base down before a hyperphoric eye raises the object to the plane of the good eye; or base up before the normal eye lowers its image to the plane of the hyperphoric eye, in either case restoring the images to the same level.

If the hyperphoria does not exceed 1°, a prism of that degree should be placed over one eye with its base in the position indicated. If the defect equals or exceeds 2°, the prism may be divided between the two eyes as suggested above, unless it can be seen that the deviation is positively limited to one eye.

In cases where a single prism is prescribed, unless there are distinct indications to the contrary, it should be placed over the left eye for the following reason: the right eye is usually the fixing eye, and the left eye deviates downward in right hyperphoria and upward in left hyperphoria. Now, for obvious reasons, a prism placed over the right and fixing eye to change it to the level of the left and deviating eye, would not be so well borne as one placed over the deviating eye to bring it to the level of the fixing eye.

The value of a vertical prism can often be demonstrated to the patient. When placed in its proper position, while the patient looks at the distant test card, it affords a sense of comfort and satisfaction, while a reversal of its base will be instantly rejected.

In spite of this, in cases where there is no error of refraction, patients cannot always be depended upon to wear the glasses, because they do not afford any material improvement in the acuteness of vision. As soon as the urgent symptoms are relieved they begin to grow careless in wearing their glasses, inasmuch as vision is as good without as with them. In this class of cases an operation would be advisable if the case is otherwise a suitable one for this procedure.

Cases have been reported where the glasses seemed to be of the greatest benefit for a time, and later the patient would return with the complaint that the eyes were worse and they believed the glasses were doing more harm than good. An investigation would result in discovering that the prismatic lens had dropped out of the frame and had been replaced with its base in the wrong direction, which resulted only in adding fuel to the fire.

When hyperphoria is present it is apt to be greater at the reading point than at a distance. In young persons, where one pair of glasses is used for all purposes, this discrepancy cannot be taken into account; but in presbyopic hyperphorics advantage can be taken of the additional glasses required for reading to incorporate a slightly stronger prism as seems indicated.

Some refractionists prefer to order the needed prisms in an extra front, or grab front or hook front, as they are sometimes called, when they are indicated in connection with the regular glasses. This enables them to be used tentatively, and increased or diminished in strength as necessary at the least possible expense.

The prisms prescribed in hyperphoria should be placed in the position of rest or assistance to the muscle. Some authorities have recommended exercise of the muscles, but while this would be good advice in exo- or esophoria, it is of doubtful value in hyperphoria. The experience of the writer in this class of cases has been such as to lead him to expect but little benefit from exercise of the vertical muscles.

In some cases the hyperphoria is secondary to or dependent upon a lateral deviation, and disappears when the exo- or esophoria is corrected by prisms, or when the internal or external recti have been invigorated and strengthened by a course of prism gymnastics.

When a vertical and a lateral deviation exists in the same case, there is diversity of opinion among authorities as to which should receive attention first. Some would ignore hyperphoria altogether, while others would correct it first, arguing that the symptoms produced by it are more troublesome and annoying and less capable of removal by any effort of the eye itself, than in the case of esophoria or exophoria.

If the amount of hyperphoria equaled or exceeded 2°, we would make the attempt to correct it first and note the effect on the lateral muscles. Or if the deviation of the latter was great enough to call for attention, it would be proper to order a vertical prism for one eye and a horizontal prism for the other, or the two may be combined in the form of an oblique prism.

When a case of hyperphoria gets beyond the help of prisms, or when a radical cure is desired, an operation may be resorted to, and the one that is most often preferred is tenotomy of the stronger superior rectus. In well-selected cases the relief of the annoying symptoms that follow an operation is sometimes wonderful, and is apt to tempt the surgeon to apply the same treatment to cases in which it is not so suitable, and the disappointment that follows may cast operative measures into undeserved disrepute.

CYCLOPHORIA

This is a condition in which there is an imbalance of the oblique muscles, and as yet is not so clearly defined or well recognized as the vertical and lateral deviations. It is detected by means of a double prism, and a horizontal straight line on a card, as described and illustrated in the chapter on

Method of Examination. The treatment consists in "rythmic exercise" of the weak oblique muscle by means of cylindrical lenses which are rotated before the eye. This exercise should be repeated daily and continued for several weeks.

METHODS OF DIAGNOSIS OF MUSCULAR ANOMALIES

The objects of the various tests for the detection of muscular imbalance may be mentioned under two heads:

1. Those which displace the image in one eye from the yellow spot, destroying binocular vision and producing an artificial diplopia; the natural instinct for the maintenance of binocular vision being removed, the eye is given over to the action of its several muscles, and a weakness of any one of them in this way becomes manifest by a deviation in the direction of the antagonistic muscle.

2. Those in which the image formed on the retina of one eye is changed in color, shape or size, so that the images of the two eyes on account of their dissimilarity cannot be fused into one. The fusion instinct being no longer called into play, any unnatural strain upon a muscle is removed, and if there is a tendency to deviation it will at once manifest itself.

It would seem as if the latter test, which changes the appearance of the image, but does not displace it from the macula, ought to be the most accurate and trustworthy one. It allows a comparison of the images formed on the yellow spot of each eye, both of which possess the same degree of retinal sensibility, in contrast with the first test, where one of the images is extra-macular and therefore less vivid.

The "dissociation" of the eyes does not mean an entire cessation of innervation to either one of them, but simply on account of binocular vision being made impossible and the desire for it removed, the eyes assume their position of equilibrium or that which is most restful for them, and a tendency to deviation develops into an actual deviation, and becomes subject to detection and measurement.

A slight physiological heterophoria is not incompatible with normality, because although the accommodation and convergence are closely connected and share the same nervous supply, yet they are not indissolubly one. The unconscious effort that is made to maintain binocular vision in the presence of a normal amount of deviation is so slight that no inconvenience is experienced. But when the heterophoria is greater, the effort required is sufficient to cause symptoms of asthenopia, which will be all the more marked in a neurasthenic or debilitated patient.

TESTS FOR HETEROPHORIA

1. Screen test: *a, objective.*
   b, subjective.
2. Prism tests.
3. Phorometer.
4. Maddox rod.
5. Maddox double prism.
6. A strong convex sphere.
7. A Cobalt blue lens.
8. The tropometer.
9. The clinometer.
10. The perimeter.
11. Tests for convergence.
12. Tests for divergence.
13. Tests for sursumvergence.

THE COVER OR SCREEN TEST

Objective Test.—This is an interesting test that can be easily made and requires no instruments. It depends on the fact that in the condition of normal muscular equilibrium, the instinct of binocular fixation is so strong that it continues even after one eye is excluded from vision. The patient is asked to look at a test object (a light or a round black spot on a white card) twenty feet away. A screen or a card is placed before one eye, which will still look straight in the direction of the object the same as if it was yet visible. The card is then shifted to the other eye, and as the eye that was first covered is already in position to fix the object, no change will be required and it will remain stationary. This indicates a condition of orthophoria.

But if the first eye when covered deviates in any direction it will, when the card is transferred to the other eye, turn in the opposite direction, and the amount of one movement will be exactly the same as the other.

The card should be kept before the eye for an appreciable length of time, at least thirty seconds, and then suddenly withdrawn while the eye is closely watched for any "corrective" movement that may take place and which indicates some form of heterophoria.

If the corrective movement is *inward*, the presumption is that there had been a tendency to an outward deviation which would indicate a condition of *exophoria*.

If the corrective movement is *outward*, the inference is that there has been a tendency to deviation inward, from which we diagnose a condition of *esophoria*.

The prism base in or base out that stops this movement will be the approximate measure of the exo- or esophoria, although this method is scarcely applicable in slight degrees of heterophoria.

This test will also determine which of the two eyes habitually fixes the object.

Before making the above tests it has been recommended that both eyes be closed for a short time.

SUBJECTIVE COVER TEST OR PARALLAX TEST

In the former test the observer determines the existence of heterophoria without asking the patient any questions, but in the parallax test the co-operation of the patient is necessary. The test depends upon the fact that when any muscular imbalance is present, a sudden screening of the fixing eye makes the flame appear to the patient to move, as it becomes necessary for the deviating eye to make a corrective movement in order to assume the task of fixation, and this movement manifests itself by an apparent displacement of its field of vision.

The perception of this movement depends upon a momentary diplopia, which is quickly corrected as fixation is shifted from one eye to the other. This is a form of diplopia in which the images are not both seen at the same time, but in succession, and thus give the impression of moving from one place to another.

If the right eye is screened and then uncovered, and the object appears to move from left to right, *esophoria* is indicated. This can easily be understood when it is remembered that in esophoria the diplopia is of the homonymous variety and the right image is seen by the right eye, which accounts for the apparent movement from left to right.

If, on the other hand, when the cover is removed from the right eye, the light appears to move toward the left, *exophoria* is indicated. In this condition the diplopia is crossed, and the left image belongs to the right eye, which accounts for the apparent movement from right to left.

This test possesses the advantage of requiring no special apparatus. Its usefulness depends upon the intelligence of the patient, but after a few trials the movement of the light and its direction can be quickly determined.

The movement of the light can be controlled by prisms, and the amount of heterophoria measured by the strength of the prism which, when placed before the eyes, will cause the movement to cease. The following statement in tabular form may serve to emphasize the above facts and present them in a form that can easily be remembered:

GUIDE IN PARALLAX TEST

	INDICATES	CORRECTED BY
Light moves out	Esophoria	Prism base out
Light moves in	Exophoria	Prism base in

PRISM TESTS

These are the time-honored tests introduced by von Graefe. An artificial diplopia is produced by placing before one eye a prism strong enough to prevent fusion, and the positions assumed by the two images will indicate whether the muscles are in or out of balance.

The testing prism must be strong enough to produce an

insuperable diplopia and to separate the two images sufficiently to make slight deviation tendencies easily perceptible. On the other hand, it should not be too strong, or else the false image is formed on the retina at a point so far distant from the yellow spot, that it does not allow a proper and accurate comparison to be made with the true image. In the production of vertical diplopia, the writer recommends a prism of 6°; and for the production of horizontal diplopia, a prism of 10°, although it may be necessary in some cases to increase this to 12°.

The first is placed in a vertical position and it is a matter of indifference whether the base be up or down. The second is placed in a horizontal position, and it is of importance that the base be placed in, as that is the position in which diplopia can be more quickly obtained and with the weakest prism. The reason is that in this position the diplopia results from an overpowering of the external recti muscles, the weaker of the lateral muscles; whereas if placed base out a prism of 30° to 40° might be required to vanquish the internal recti.

The importance of the base line of the prism being in a strictly vertical or horizontal position cannot be too strongly insisted upon, because a slight turning of the prism will introduce new prismatic values that will vitiate the result, and the stronger the test prism the greater the vitiation.

A vertical prism is used to determine the equilibrium of the lateral muscles. Two lights are seen, and if they occupy the same vertical plane the external and internal recti are assumed to be equally balanced.

If the false image deviates outward, esophoria is indicated; if inward, exophoria.

The amount of defect is measured by the prism, base out or base in, that is required to restore the two images to the same vertical plane.

A horizontal prism is used to determine the equilibrium of the vertical muscles. The prism is placed base in before one eye, and an insuperable homonymous diplopia is produced. If the two images that are seen are on the same level, the visual lines themselves are assumed to be on a level, and the superior and inferior recti properly balanced.

If, however, the right-hand image should be lower, we know that the right visual line is directed above the left, and a condition of *right hyperphoria* is indicated, the amount of which is measured by the degree of prism that is required, placed base down before the eye, to restore the two images to the same level.

If the right image should be higher, we know that the right visual line is below that of the left eye, or amounting to the same thing, that the left visual line is directed above the right, which indicates a condition of *left hyperphoria*, the amount of which is measured by the prism that is required, base down before this eye or base up before the right eye, to restore the two images to the same level.

This is called the "equilibrium test" by some authors.

THE PHOROMETER (STEVENS)

The use of the instrument is simply a variation of the prism test, and overcomes the difficulty of ensuring that the base line of the prism is in a strictly vertical or horizontal

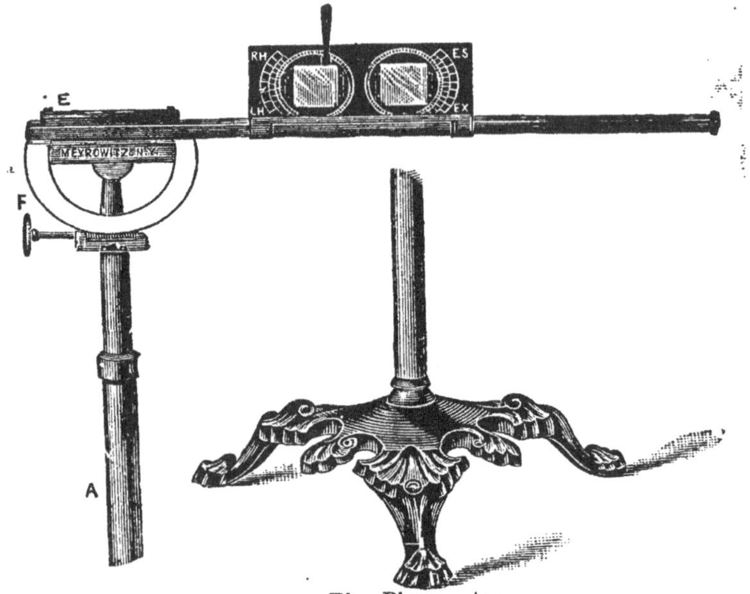

The Phorometer

position and thus prevents the inaccuracies that might be introduced by a slight departure from the proper position.

There are two cells, each of which holds a rotating disk, and each disk carries a prism of 5°, which affords a prismatic value of 10° in any meridian. The edge of the disk is furnished with a border of teeth or cogs. A small gear wheel placed between them communicates the movements from one disk to the other.

Around the border of each cell there is a scale marked in degrees, increasing from the center each way from 0 to 9°, the numbers representing the refracting angles of the correcting prism. The scale before the right eye shows the value of the prism with its base up or down, and before the left eye with its base in or out.

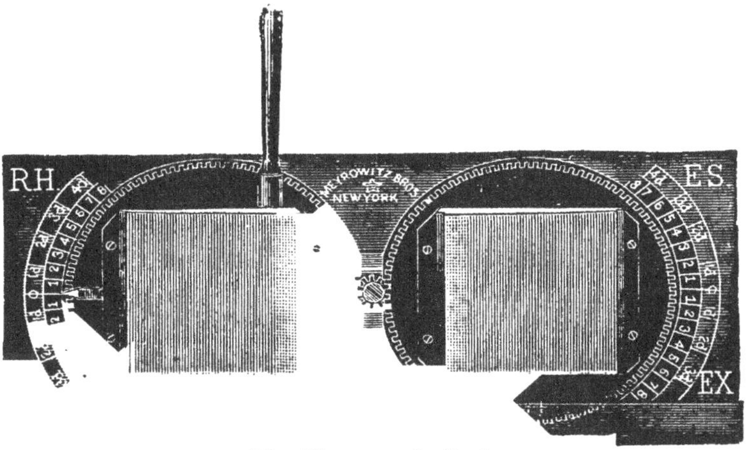

The Phorometric Scale

The principle of the phorometer depends upon the fact that when a prism is rotated, it introduces prismatic values in the meridian at right angles. For instance, if a prism of 12° is placed in a horizontal position and then rotated up or down, each rotation of 5° from the horizontal will represent 1° of vertical prism. If the same prism of 12° be placed in a vertical position, each rotation of 5° from the vertical will represent 1° of prism base in or out.

The phoromoter, therefore. permits of measurement of the deviation by simply revolving the prisms that had been used to produce the artificial diplopia, until the two images occupy the same vertical or horizontal plane, when the amount and character of the heterophoria is read off the scale.

When it is desired to test the lateral muscles, the disks are rotated until the pointer is at o on the scale of the left eye, when it will be seen that the prism before this eye is base down, and before the right eye base up. This produces a vertical diplopia, the two images being the same distance apart as if a single prism of 10° had been placed over either eye.

If the two images are in a vertical line, the external and internal recti are assumed to be of normal strength and equally balanced. But if the two images are not vertical, heterophoria is indicated, and the lever is turned and the prisms rotated until the images are restored to a vertical plane, when the position of the pointer will indicate the character and degree of the defect, whether esophoria or exophoria, and how much.

When it is desired to test for hyperphoria, the disks are rotated until the pointer is at o on the scale of the right eye, when the two prisms will be before the eyes with their bases in. This produces a horizontal diplopia, the two images being the same distance apart as if a single prism of 10° had been placed over either eye.

If the two images are on the same level, the superior and inferior recti are assumed to be of normal strength and equally balanced. But if one is higher or lower than the other, hyperphoria is indicated and the lever is turned and the prisms rotated until the images are made perfectly level, when the position of the pointer will indicate the character and degree of the defect, whether right or left hyperphoria, and how much.

In these tests it must be borne in mind that we are dealing with both eyes, and not with a single eye. In esophoria and exophoria we study the strength or weakness of the power of convergence and of divergence, as exerted by the associated action of the pair of internal or external recti muscles.

MADDOX ROD

This consists of a glass rod, transparent or colored, fitted in a disk of hard rubber, which is mounted in a metal rim of the size of a trial lens, so as to easily fit in the trial frame.

The effect of this rod is to cause a point of light viewed through it to be drawn out and elongated into a streak or line of light, at right angles to the position of the rod, the reason being that the light is thrown so greatly out of focus by the sharp curvature of the rod in the meridian at right angles to its axis. This might be called a "diffusion line." similar to the "diffusion circles" formed on the retina in uncorrected myopia, or that may be formed in any eye by a strong convex spherical lens.

The length of the diffusion line formed on the retina by the cylinder is exactly the same as the diameter of the diffusion circle formed by a spherical lens of the same strength.

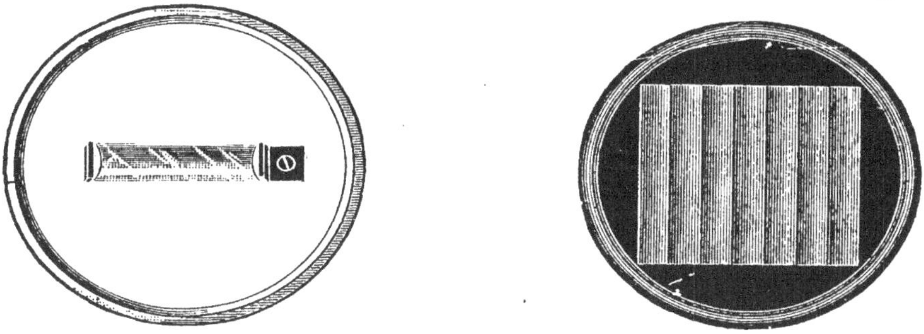

The Maddox Rod

Inasmuch as it is desired to have a line of some length, a strong cylinder must be used to produce it, which is found in the simple glass rod, and which should be free from flaws, and mounted as already described and as shown in the cut. Some authorities prefer the compound or multiple rod, as affording a longer total line of light and requiring less care in placing before the eye.

When the rod is placed before one eye, the line perceived by it, and the normal flame as seen by the uncovered eye, are so dissimilar that they cannot be conceived to be double images of the same object, and consequently there is no desire to unite them into one. This unlikeness is accentuated by using a rod of red glass, and still more so by placing a blue glass over the other eye.

Inasmuch as the line of light is always at right angles to the axis of the cylinder, in order to produce a vertical streak with which to test lateral deviations, the rod is placed horizontally; and in order to produce a horizontal streak with which to test the vertical muscles, the rod is placed in a vertical position. In other words, the axis of the cylinder should be in the same direction as the muscles to be tested.

The light should be at a distance of fifteen or twenty feet, and the rod placed over one eye. If the streak passes directly through the light, orthophoria is indicated; if removed from the light, some form of heterophoria.

The rod is usually placed first in a horizontal position to determine the equilibrium of the lateral muscles.

If the line of light appears to pass through the flame,	Orthophoria
If the line of light appears on same side as rod,	Esophoria
If the line of light appears on the other side,	Exophoria

The prism base out or base in that combines the line of light and the flame, will be the measure of the esophoria or exophoria.

The rod is then turned to the vertical position to determine the presence of any vertical deviation. In the great majority of cases the line will pass in a horizontal position directly through the flame.

Rod before right eye, line below flame,	Right Hyperphoria
Rod before right eye, line above flame,	Left Hyperphoria
Rod before left eye, line below flame,	Left Hyperphoria
Rod before left eye, line above flame,	Right Hyperphoria

The prism that is necessary to change the streak from its faulty position and bring it into the light, will be the measure of the hyperphoria. The correcting prism is placed as follows:

Right Hyperphoria	Base down right eye, Base up left eye.
Left Hyperphoria	Base down left eye, Base up right eye.

MADDOX DOUBLE PRISM

This consists of two prisms of 4° each fitted base to base, and mounted in a trial-lens rim, and will cause diplopia in the eye over which it is placed (monocular diplopia). The other eye, being uncovered, sees a single light, which in orthophoria will appear midway between the two and directly on a line with them; otherwise, heterophoria is indicated.

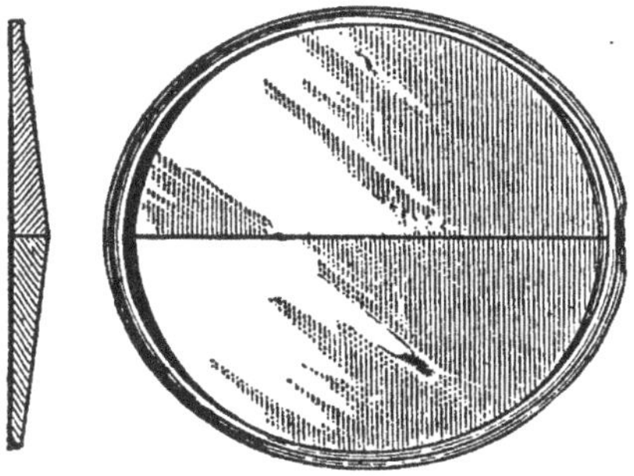

Maddox Double Prism

This test was described in detail and illustrated in the chapter on Method of Examination, to which the reader is referred.

STRONG CONVEX SPHERE

A strong convex lens (from 10 D. to 20 D.) is held before one eye, in which it produces diffusion of light. The slightest movement of such a lens, in or out, up or down, calls into action its prismatic effect and moves the light in the opposite direction, and thus vitiates the accuracy of the test. If, however, the lens be covered in all parts except its center, the adjustment of the lens as a prism is prevented and the periphery of the diffusion is cut off in such a manner as to give the impression of an exact disk or patch of light. One of the pin-hole disks contained in the trial case, if the opening be not too small, can be conveniently placed in the trial frame over the convex lens for this purpose. In orthophoria the natural light seen by the uncovered eye will be located in the center of the diffusion patch of the other eye; whereas, if it is removed from it to one side or the other, above or below, heterophoria is indicated, and the greater the interval between the two the higher the degree of defect.

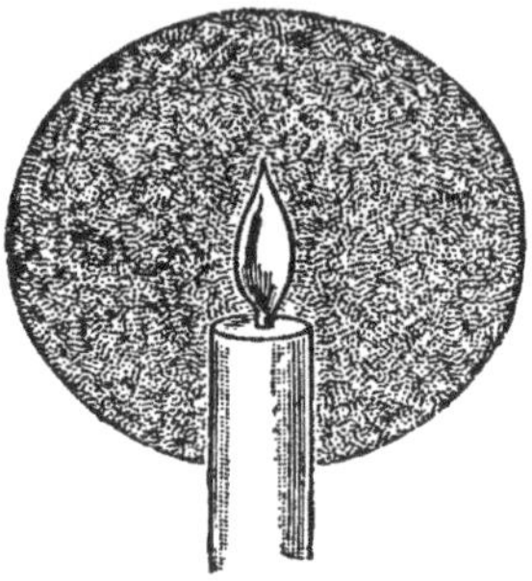
Orthophoria

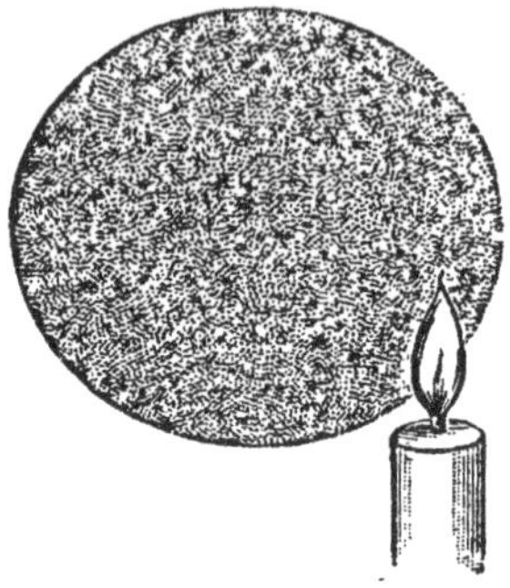
Heterophoria

Diffusion patch deviates inward indicates exophoria.

Diffusion patch deviates outward indicates esophoria.

Diffusion patch deviates downward indicates hyperphoria of that eye.

Diffusion patch deviates upward indicates hyperphoria of other eye.

The prism base in, out, down or up, that is required to combine the images will be the measure of the insufficiency.

COBALT BLUE LENS

This lens produces a colored image in the eye over which it is placed, and may be used as an indication for myopia, hypermetropia and astigmatism, as has been already described. But it may be employed in the detection of muscular troubles, because the image it forms is so dissimilar to the clear light that fusion is to a great extent destroyed, and heterophoria if present manifests itself by an interval between the clear and the colored flame. The position assumed by the latter affords the same indications as when a strong convex sphere is employed, as previously mentioned.

THE TROPOMETER

This instrument has been devised by Dr. Stevens for the measurement of the various rotations of the eye. This gentleman, who is an acknowledged authority on muscular troubles, attaches great importance to the determination, absolute as well as comparative, of the rotations of the eyes, arguing that excessive tension upon the vertical muscles often causes converging or diverging deviations, independent of any anomaly of the lateral muscles, and that many cases of heterophoria may be explained in a similar manner.

The instrument consists essentially of a telescope in which an inverted image of the eye is formed at the eye-piece where

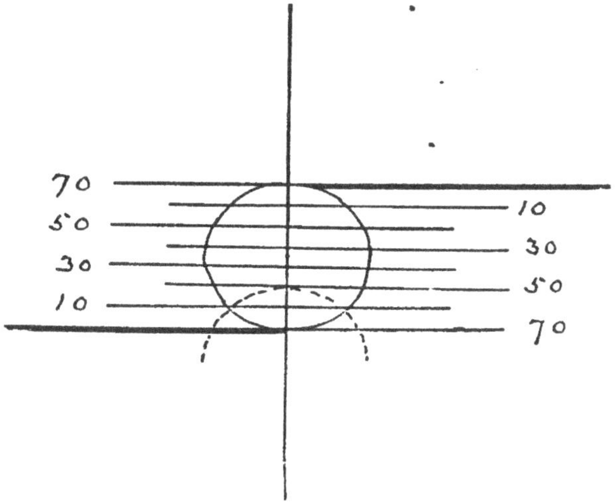

Scale for Tropometer

its movements can be observed upon a graduated scale, permitting rotations in any direction to be measured. A prism or a diagonal mirror at the objective end of the telescope, permits the observer to sit at the side of the observed. By means of a head-rest and an adjustable stirrup with a wooden bar, which the patient holds closely between his teeth, the head may be held firmly in the primary position. This position is indicated by the two buttons at the extremities of the guiding rods.

The vertical line divides two scales, which are similarly graduated, but run in different directions. The circle represents the outer border of the cornea, the edges of which are in contact with the two heavy lines. The interval between the lines is 10°, counting down from the heavy line on the right side and up from the heavy line on the left side. When the head of the patient is held firmly in the proper position and the eye rotated strongly in any direction, the arc through which the border of the cornea passes may be accurately read upon the scale.

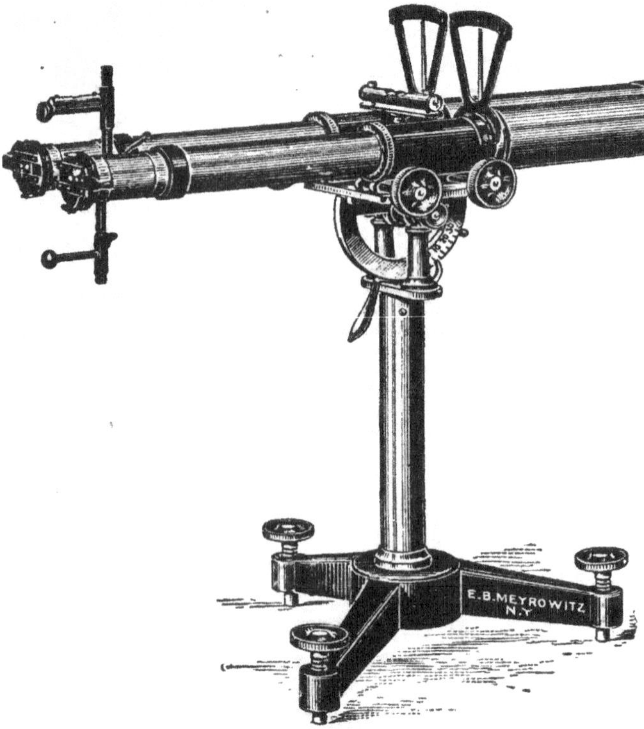

The Clinoscope

In the figure the curved dotted line represents such a rotation. The patient has been asked to look strongly *upward,* which causes a movement of the cornea *down* the scale, and reaches the point in this case of 50°, which would represent the measure of this rotation.

By means of a small lever the scale can be placed horizontally, vertically or obliquely, and by means of the two gradations, measurements can be made in opposite directions

In measuring the upward rotation the border of the cornea is made to coincide with the heavy line at the upper right-hand side, and for the downward rotation with the heavy line at the lower left-hand side. These adjustments are made by means of the milled head at the side of the standard. As the eye rotates in one direction the image appears to move in the other.

The customary rotations are as follows:

Upward	33°
Downward	50°
Inward	55°
Outward	50°

The above represent the four principal secondary positions, in addition to which there are rotations up and in, up and out, down and in, and down and out. The above figures will not be the same for every individual, on account of the variations in the normal power of the muscles of one person as compared with another, and also depending on the amount of effort and attention that is given to the exercise.

THE CLINOSCOPE

This instrument is also an invention of Dr. Stevens. It consists of two tubes of about twenty inches long, mounted

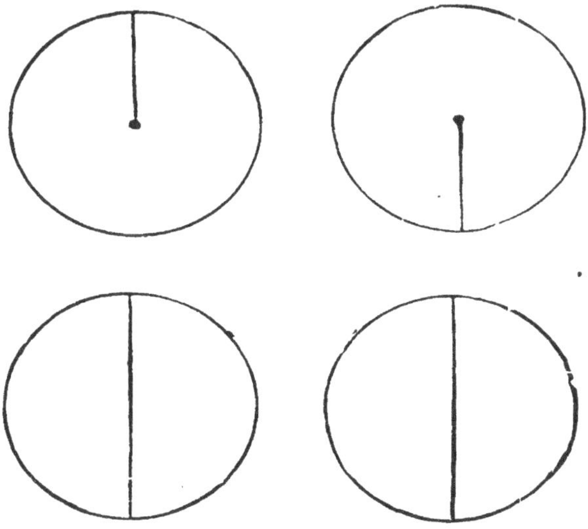

on a brass stand. The mounting of the tubes is such as to permit of a change in their adjustment from parallelism to convergence or to divergence, and at the same time they can be inclined to any desired angle.

The tubes are also susceptible of rotation about their longitudinal axes by thumbscrews, which motion can be measured by means of an index-pointer above each tube. At the extreme end of each tube provision is made for maintaining the diagrams in position.

These circles are blended in their normal position, and the amplitude of torsion is measured by rotating in opposite directions until the diameters begin to separate.

Dr. Stevens finds the amplitude of extorsion for each eye to be 11°, and of intorsion slightly less, when both eyes are simultaneously extorted or intorted.

THE PERIMETER

This instrument may also be used to measure the rotations of the eye, or what might be called the motor field. It consists essentially of an arc marked in degrees which rotates around a central pivot, which latter at the same time is the fixing point for the patient's eye, placed at 30 centimeters away or at the center of curvature of the perimetric arc. The test object should be small, 1 cm. to 2 cm. in diameter, and fastened upon a carrier, which is moved from without inward, and the point noted on each meridian where it first becomes visible. Usually the examination is begun with the arc in the horizontal position and then moved to the next meridian, and so on until the whole field has been investigated. Generally it is sufficient to examine eight meridians, two vertical, two horizontal and two oblique in each direction.

The result is noted upon a chart, prepared for the purpose by having ruled upon it radial lines to correspond to the various positions of the arc, and concentric circles to note the degrees.

The size of the field varies considerably within normal limits, being influenced by the character of the light, by the attention of the patient, and by his physical and mental condition, as well as by the size of the pupil and the condition of the refraction.

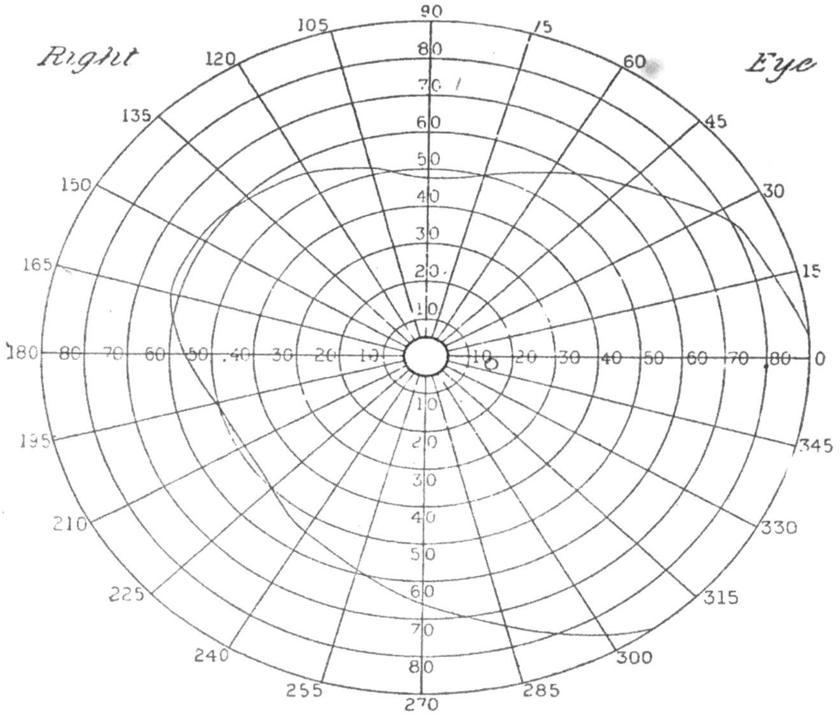

Perimetric Chart

The average physiological limits of the field are as follows:

Upward	50°
Upward and inward	55°
Upward and outward	70°
Downward	72°
Downward and inward	55°
Downward and outward	85°
Outward	90°
Inward	60°

From the foregoing figures it is evident that the field is not circular, showing the greatest mobility downward and outward, and the greatest restriction upward and inward. This restriction depends not so much upon a lessened mobility, as upon anatomical and physiological causes, viz., the edge of the orbit and the nose and the lessened sensibility of the outer portion of the retina, this latter condition being due to the fact that this part of the retina is less used than the inner and its functions are therefore less developed.

The determination of the visual field by means of the perimeter, is sometimes of value in obscure cases of muscular imbalance.

TESTS FOR CONVERGENCE

The power of convergence may be measured by determining the strongest prism placed *base out* before the eyes which can be overcome by the action of the internal recti

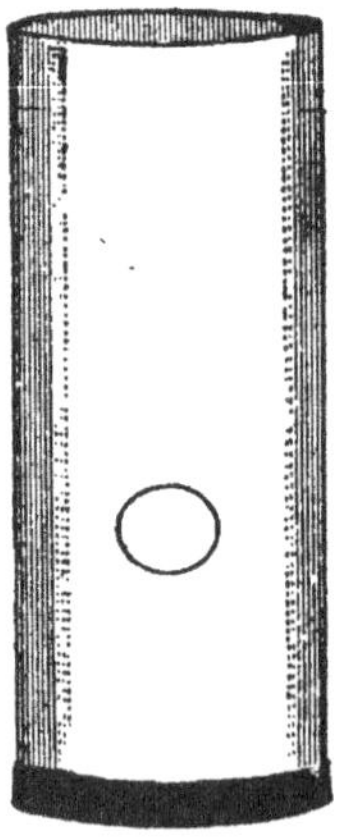

muscles, or in other words with which binocular vision can be maintained of an object at a distance.

It is customary to use a light of some kind placed at the usual distance of the test card, viz., twenty feet. A Welsbach mantle or an electric light with a frosted globe, in each case covered with a perforated chimney, makes a most satisfactory test object. The prisms are gradually interposed in increasing strength as long as the light remains single until the maximum strength is reached.

This action of the internal recti muscles is called the power of *adduction*, and shows variation not only from day to day, but even from hour to hour in some cases, and thus tends to confuse the study of muscle strength. It should be noted that there is a difference between the power of adduction as shown at the first trial, when the patient scarcely understands what is expected of him, and that which can be developed after repeated trials in a patient who has become familiar with the procedure.

If the patient can at the outset overcome a prism of 15° to 18° with ease, it is fair to assume that this convergence is not abnormal, and that he can readily learn to do twice as much after some exercise. The power of adduction may be said to range from 15° of primary effort to 100° of trained convergence.

If a prism of 10° or 12° is as great as can be overcome even after repeated trials, and that this represents an effort that is hard to make and still harder to maintain, then the power of convergence is shown to be intrinsically weak.

In contrast with the variation in the convergence, the other three rotations are fairly constant as follows:

Abduction	6° to 8°
Supraduction	2° to 3°
Infraduction	2° to 3°

TESTS FOR DIVERGENCE

The diverging power of the eye is measured by the strength of prism *base in*, which can be overcome while looking at the light twenty feet away. A divergence of less than 5° indicates insufficiency, and more than 9° an excess of abducting power.

TESTS FOR SURSUMVERGENCE

By sursumvergence is meant the power of the eye to turn up or down, and it is determined by the strength of the vertical prism that can be overcome while looking at the distant light.

Supraduction is measured by the strongest prism *base down*, with which single vision can be maintained. Infraduction by the strongest prism *base up*, with which single vision can be maintained.

A very marked difference between infraduction and supraduction, or an excess of either one over 3°, indicates the probable existence of hyperphoria.

The power of duction of the various muscles can be easily and quickly measured by the Risley rotary prism, which consists of two 15° prisms mounted in two cells and controlled by a milled head screw. The value of this instrument depends upon the principle first suggested by Sir John Herschel, that two prisms placed in apposition and rotated in opposite directions, produce the effect of a single increasing prism.

Risley Prism

When the base of one prism lies over the apex of the other, there is exact neutralization and the indicator of the instrument points to 0. As the screw is turned both prisms rotate in opposite directions, and any desired strength of prism can be obtained up to 30°, which is constantly shown by the indicator pointing to the numbers on the graduated scale marked on the blackened front of the containing cell.

This rotary prism is made of the size of an ordinary test lens, so that it can be readily used in the trial frame, and can be rotated so as to present the base of the increasing prism either up or down, in or out.

VALUE OF VARIOUS TESTS

The *screen* test can always be relied upon, and is besides universally applicable, being especially available in the case of children and also in those cases where binocular vision no longer exists.

The *parallax* test is scarcely less reliable and precise, showing clearly very slight deviations.

The *phorometer* is a useful instrument, especially valuable for the convenience with which the correcting prism can be rotated over the eye, but it possesses the disadvantage of displacing the image from the macula in each eye.

The *Maddox rod* is more to be depended upon, although there is a tendency, very strongly shown in some patients, to unite the line of light and the flame, even in the presence of an unmistakable heterophoria. This source of inaccuracy may, however, be guarded against by screening one eye for a moment and then suddenly removing the screen, and determining the relative positions of the line of light and the flame immediately, before the patient has had a chance to unite them. In hyperphoria the Maddox rod is usually very accurate.

HETEROPHORIA AT A NEAR POINT

It is exceedingly important that any existing heterophoria should be measured as well at a close point as at distance. A comparison of the results for distance and for near will show whether the deviation increases or decreases with the distance, quite an important factor in distinguishing anomalies in convergence and divergence.

The *dot and line test* was devised by von Graefe for determining insufficiency of the internal recti muscles. It has already been described in the chapter on Method of Examination.

Maddox has suggested a scale for close use, graduated in degrees to the right and left of a central zero, the right hand figures being black and the left hand red. From the central zero a vertical arrow projects. The numbers represent the ordinary degrees of a prism.

The scale is held about ten inches from the patient's eyes, and an 8° prism placed base down before right eye, with the result of producing two scales and two arrows, the upper one of which belongs to the right eye. If this deviates to the left it indicates divergence of the visual axis; if to the right convergence. The patient is asked to look at the lower arrow and to name the figure to which it points, and whether the figure is red or black.

In the illustration below the arrow points to the black figures, showing a crossed diplopia and indicating an exophoria of 4°.

A slight exophoria at the reading distance can scarcely be considered abnormal, varying in different individuals and in the same individual at different times. Such variations are

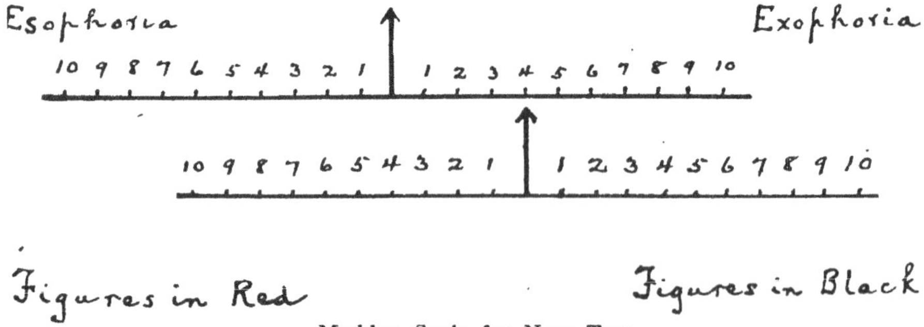

Maddox Scale for Near Test

not nearly so significant as in distant vision. It is impossible to fix a limit where exophoria passes beyond the physiological limit and becomes pathological. Every case must be considered on its own merits, and a conclusion arrived at, not from this test alone, but from a comparison of all the tests, and especially must weight be given to the relative strength of each of the vertical muscles.

An exophoria of 4° as shown by the phorometer or Maddox rod should not suffice as the basis for treatment by prisms or otherwise; but this diagnosis should be confirmed or disproved by a comparison of the power of adduction and abduction as developed by a prism base out and base in. If exophoria really existed it would be proven by a diminished prism convergence and an increased prism divergence.

It might be well to repeat that in these examinations, as in all tests to determine the muscular balance, vision should be as nearly normal as possible, and when an error of refraction exists the proper correction should be worn, because of the influence upon muscular relations of an uncorrected refractive error.

RELATIVE IMPORTANCE OF CORRECTION

A persistent hyperphoria calls more urgently for correction than any other form of heterophoria. Next in importance stands esophoria, and lastly exophoria. Maddox states "that in distant vision hyperphoria is at least four times more worthy of notice for each degree than horizontal deviations."

In near vision exophoria is comparatively unimportant, but esophoria cannot be ignored.

A heterophoria that causes no symptoms can usually be left alone as far as special prismatic correction is concerned, but a knowledge of its existence may be of value in the correction of refractive errors. When esophoria exists with hypermetropia, the latter should be fully corrected; if exophoria is present the hypermetropia should be undercorrected. Presbyopes with esophoria can bear stronger lenses than with exophoria.

In the prismatic correction of the various forms of heterophoria, the following suggestions have been made, subject of course to the judgment of the prescribing optometrist:

In persistent *hyperphoria*, from three-quarters to a full correction.

In *esophoria*, two thirds of the distant defect and all of the near.

In *exophoria*, one-half to one-third of the distant defect, and one-quarter of the near.

METHOD OF EXAMINATION OF EYE MUSCLES

Inspection for the purpose of detecting any obvious anomaly.

Noting the eye movements as they follow a pencil moved in different directions.

The *screen test*, followed by the *parallax test*, first with the test object at twenty feet and then at the ordinary reading distance.

The *prism test* or the *phorometer*, both for distance and for near.

The *Maddox rod*, testing first for horizontal and then for vertical deviations.

Tests for convergence, divergence and sursumvergence.

These comprise the tests that are necessary in average cases, and they can all be completed in probably ten minutes. In obscure or complicated cases, some of the other tests described may be employed.

NEW SUGGESTIONS IN THE TREATMENT OF HETEROPHORIA

Some new ideas have recently been advanced in the management of heterophoria, based upon the following predications:

1. That the movements of the eye are not simply an exhibition of muscular strength, but rather of nervous energy. This is proven by the fact that in a little while the internal recti muscles can be taught to overcome a much stronger prism than at the first effort. On commencing the test the muscles may not be able to show a prism strength of more than 10°, which in the course of an hour can be increased to 20° or 25°. This increased power can scarcely be attributed to an actual development of the muscles in such a short time, but is rather the result of a voluntary increase of the nervous supply to these muscles.

From the above facts we assume that the direction in which the nervous energy can be turned, is determined by the position of the apex of the prism. Therefore a prism of moderate strength may be used as a stimulant in accordance with the above principles.

2. In a great many instances organic changes commence as functional disturbances. If the nervous supply of a muscle is increased the blood supply will be similarly affected, and if continued long enough the muscle is better nourished and grows in size and strength. Whereas if the nervous supply be diverted, the blood supply diminishes, the muscle is less actively nourished and it becomes smaller and weaker. In both cases there has been a structural change, but in opposite directions.

Therefore it is argued that if a prism of not too high a degree is placed over a weak muscle, its nervous and blood supply is increased, and under favorable conditions a heterophoria may be cured.

For example, if the internal recti can easily overcome 25°

of prisms, while the external can scarcely overcome 4°, we have evidence of insufficiency of the latter, which is corroborated by the Maddox rod, showing an esophoria of 4°. According to the old methods, this would call for correcting prisms with their bases out. The apices being over the internal recti increases convergence to that extent and thus adds to the esophoria.

If, however, in this base the prisms be placed bases in, in a little while the esophoria will have lessened or entirely disappeared, and the external recti will be able to overcome a stronger prism.

If with the prism in the former position the patient has not been able to use his eyes with comfort, in the latter position relief may soon become apparent and the eyes restored to a condition of great utility.

If, on the other hand, it is found that the external recti have been disproportionately innervated and are able to overcome a prism of 9° or more, a pair of weak prisms bases out will tend to divert the nervous supply from the external to the internal recti, and restore the natural equilibrium.

In cases of hyperphoria a weak prism (.50 to 1°) before one or both eyes, with the apex placed towards the insufficient muscle, will probably restore the lost balance with a reasonable expectation of affording relief.

The reports as to the benefits that have been derived from prisms that have been reversed in accordance with the foregoing principles, are very encouraging, and the promise is held out that such prisms will greatly diminish the number of cases of tenotomy. The latter will still be applicable in those cases in which the muscle has become abnormally enlarged and strengthened with a structural change of its tissues, as they are then too far advanced to be influenced by this method of treatment.

These prisms should be worn constantly, in combination with any focal correction that may be necessary, or as plane prisms in simple heterophoria, and continued for weeks or months as may be necessary. When the normal balance has been restored, they may be discontinued tentatively, to be resorted to again if the conditions seem to demand it.

[THE END]

APPENDIX.

Optical Symbols and Abbreviations

Ac.	Accommodation
Aet.	Age
Am.	Ametropia
An.	Anisometropia
As.	Astigmatism
Asth.	Asthenopia
Ax.	Axis
Cc. or — (minus)	Concave
Ce.	Centigrade
Cm.	Centimeter
Cx. or + (plus)	Convex
Cyl.	Cylinder
D.	Diopter
D. Cc.	Double Concave
D. Cx.	Double Convex
D. T.	Distance Test
E. or Em.	Emmetropia
H. or Hy.	Hypermetropia
In.	Inches
L. or L. E.	Left Eye
M. or My.	Myopia
Mm.	Millimeter
N.	Nasal
N.v.	Naked Vision
O. D. (Oculus Dexter)	Right Eye
O. S. (Oculus Sinister)	Left Eye
O. U. (Oculi Unati)	Both Eyes
P. or Pb.	Presbyopia
P. Cc.	Periscopic Concave
P. Cx.	Periscopic Convex
P. D.	Inter-Pupillary Distance

Pl.	Plano
p. p. (Punctum Proximum)	Near Point
p. r. (Punctum Remotum)	Far Point
Pr.	Prism
R. or R. E.	Right Eye
R. T.	Reading Test
Rx.	Prescription
Sb.	Strabismus
S. or Sph.	Spherical
T.	Temporal
Ty.	Type
V.	Vision
Va.	Visual Acuteness
W. P.	Working Point
+	Plus—Convex
—	Minus—Concave
⌒	Combined with
L	At Right Angles
°	Degree
△	Prism-Diopter
′	Foot and Minute
″	Inch and Second
‴	Line, the twelfth part of an inch
=	Equal to
∞	Infinity, 20 feet or further

Glossary of Optical Terms.

Abduction........Movement of the eyeball outward.
Aberration........Wandering from normal.
Accommodation...Adjusting of the eye for near vision
Achromatic.......Without color.
Achromatopsia....Color blindness.
Adduction........Movement of the eyeball inward.
Albinism.........Abnormal deficiency of pigment in iris and choroid.
Amaurosis........Partial or total loss of sight.
Amblyopia ....Impairment or loss of vision without any apparent local cause or anomaly to account for it. Defective sensibility of the retina.

Amblyopia, Subdivisions of:

Congenital........Existing from birth.
Exanopsia........Loss of sight from continued disuse of the eye.
Hemeralopia .....Night blindness, due to blood degeneration.
Hysterical........Effect of nervous reflex. A sympathetic condition.
Nyctalopia ....Day blindness, due to same cause as hemerlopia.
Toxic............Due to poison absorbed into the system, as nicotine, alcohol, etc.
Traumatic........Produced by a blow.

Ametropia........The condition when parallel rays of light will not focus in the eye. Opposite of emmetropia or normal vision.

Amplitude (as applied to accommodation)......Power or extent.
Anæsthesia of the Retina.........Insensibility of the retina.
Aniridia..........Absence of the iris.
Anisometropia....The condition when each eye has different refracting power, necessitating two different lenses for correction.
Anophthalmia.....Absence of eyes.
Anopsia..........Disuse of the eyes.
Aphakia..........The condition when the crystalline lens is removed, as after operation for cataract.
Aplanatic.........Without aberration.
Arcus senilis......Ring of corneal opacity in aged.
Asthenopia.......Weak sight due to weakness of the muscles controlling the eye.
Astigmatism......The condition when, by malformation of the cornea or of the crystalline lens, or other cause, the rays of light from a point will not focus at a point after passing through the dioptric media.
Biconcave........Double concave.
Bifocal...........Double focus.
Binocular........Pertaining to both eyes.
Blepharitis........Inflammation of edges of eyelids.
Blind Spot........Entrance of optic nerve on retina.
Brachymetropia...Another term for myopia.
Canthus..........Angle of the eye.
Caruncle.........Small fleshy growth.
Cataract.........Opacity of crystalline lens.
Catoptrics........Laws of reflection of light.
Centrad..........Toward the center; unit of measurement for prisms.
Chalazion.........A cyst of the eyelid.
Chemosis.........Swelling of the conjunctiva.
Choroiditis.......Inflammation of the choroid.
Chromatism......Coloration.
Cilia.............The eyelashes.

Ciliary ....Pertaining to the cilia.
Concentric........Having a common center.
Concomitant ......Accompanying.
Conjugate ....Joined together.
Convergence......Turning to a point.
Co-ordination......Harmonious action.
Cortical ....Pertaining to outer layer.
Coquille..........A shell.
Cyclitis...........Inflammation of ciliary body
Cycloplegia ....Paralysis of ciliary muscle.
Dacryocystitis.....Inflammation of lachrymal sac and duct.
Day-Blindness ....Impairment of vision on bright days.
Decenter ....From the center.
Depilation ....Plucking out a hair.
Dilation...........Expansion or widening.
Diopter ....Unit of measurement.
Dioptric..........Pertaining to the diopter.
Dioptrics ....Science of refraction by transparent media.
Diplopia..........Double vision.
Disk.............A circular plate; the papilla
Divergence ....To turn from.
Ecchymosis.......Extravasation of blood into tissues.
Emmetropia ......Normal vision.
Entoptic ....Within the eye.
Entropion ....Inversion of margin of lids
Enucleation.......Removal of eyeball.
Epiphora.........An undue secretion of tears.
Esophoria ....Deviation of visual line inward.
Exophoria........Deviation of visual line outward.
Exophthalmos.....Protrusion of eyeballs.
Far Point ....Greatest reading distance.
Focus............Meeting Point of refracted rays.
Fovea............Yellow spot.
Fundus ....Bottom of the eye.
Glaucoma ....A disease of the eye characterized by hardening of the globe.
Granular Lids.....An aggravated form of conjunctivitis.
Hemeralopia......Inability to see at night.
Hemianopsia......The loss of vision in one-half the field.

Heterophoria......Abnormal tending of vision lines, due to want of balance or co-ordination of ocular muscles.

Heterophoria, Subdivisions of:

Esophoria......Tending of the visual lines inward.

Exophoria......Tending outward.

Hyperphoria....Tending of the visual line of either eye above the other.

Hyperesophoria.Tending up and inward.

Hyperexophoria.Tending up and outward.

Heterotropia........A deviation or squint.

Heterotropia, Subdivisions of:

Esotropia......Convergent squint. Turning in.

Exotropia......Divergent squint. Turning out.

Hypertropia....The condition when one eye deviates above the other.

Hypersotropia..Deviation up and in.

Hyperexotropia.Deviation up and out.

Homocentric.......Having a common center.

Hordeolum........A stye.

Horopter..........Boundary of vision.

Hydrophthalmia...Increase of fluids of eye.

Hyperæsthesia.....Oversensitiveness of the retina.

Hypermetropia....Far-sightedness.

Hypopyon.........Pus in anterior chamber.

Insufficiency.......Incapacity of normal action within the eye.

Intraocular........Within the eye.

Intraorbital.......Within the orbit.

Iridectomy........Cutting part of iris.

Iritis.............Inflammation of the iris.

Keratoscope.......An instrument to measure the cornea.

Keratitis..........Inflammation of cornea.

Keratocele........Hernia of cornea.

Keratoconus ...... Protrusion of cornea.
Lachrymation ..... Excessive secretion of tears.
Leucoma .... Opacity of cornea.
Macula Lutea ..... Yellow spot.
Megalopsia .... Seeing objects larger than normal.
Meibomian .... The glands of eyelids.
Meniscus .... Crescent-shaped
Metamorphopsia .. Seeing objects distorted.
Meter-Angle .... Angle of visual axis for one meter distance.
Micropsia .... Seeing objects smaller than normal.
Monocular .... Belonging to one eye.
Muscæ Volitantes .. Floating specks or imperfections in field of vision, due to shadow of vitreous cells.
Mydriasis .... Unnatural dilation of the pupil.
Mydriatic .... A drug that dilates the pupil.
Myopia .... Near-sightedness.
Myosis .... Unnatural contraction of the pupil.
Myotic .... A drug that contracts the pupil.
Nebula .... Opacity of cornea.
Neuritis .... Inflammation of optic nerve.
Nictitation .... Excessive winking.
Night-Blindness ... A form of retinitis.
Nyctalopia .... Day-blindness.
Nystagmus .... Oscillations of eyeball.
Ocular .... Pertaining to the eye.
Oculomotor .... The third cranial nerve.
Ophthalmia .... Inflammation of the eye.
Ophthalmic .... Belonging to the eye.
Ophthaldynameter . An instrument to measure accommodation.
Ophthalmology .... Science of the anatomy, physiology and diseases of the eye.
Ophthalmometer .. Instrument to measure corneal curvature.
Ophthalmoplegia .. Paralysis of ocular muscles.
Ophthalmoscope ... Instrument to examine interior of eye.
Optic Axis .... Imaginary line through center of cornea and lens.
Optic Disk .... Entrance of optic nerve.
Optics .... Science of light and vision.
Optometer .... Instrument to measure refraction of eye.

Orbit.............Bony cavity for eyeball.
Orthophoria.......Co-ordination of the visual lines of the eyes. Perfect muscular equilibrium in both eyes. Opposite of heterophoria.
Orthotropia.......Normal as relates to squint. Opposite of heterotropia.
Palpebral.........Pertaining to eyelids.
Pannus...........Vascularization and opacity of cornea.
Panophthalmitis...General inflammation of eyeball.
Papilla............The optic disk.
Papillitis..........Inflammation of optic disk.
Perimeter.........An instrument for measuring field of vision.
Periscopic.........To look around.
Phosphenes........Subjective light sensations caused by pressure on eyeballs.
Photometer........An instrument for measuring intensity of light.
Photophobia.......Dread or intolerance of light.
Pink-Eye..........Conjunctivitis.
Polyopia..........Multiple vision.
Presbyopia........Decreased power of accommodation, somewhat vaguely called old sight.
Prismoptometer....An instrument for estimating ametropia.
Pterygium.........Thickening of conjunctiva at inner canthus.
Ptosis.............Inability to lift the upper eyelid.
Pupilloscopy.......The shadow test.
Pupillometer.......Instrument for measuring the pupil.
Reflection.........Throwing back light.
Refraction.........Deviation of light.
Retinitis..........Inflammation of the retina.
Retinoscopy.......A method of measuring ametropia.
Scleritis...........Inflammation of the sclerotic.
Scotoma..........A dark spot in the visual field.
Skiascopy.........The shadow test.
Snow-blindness....Partial blindness from reflection of snow
Spectroscope.......An instrument for decomposing light.
Squint............Deviation of one eye.
Staphyloma.......Protrusion.
Stenopaic.........Having a narrow opening.

Strabismus . . . . Squinting of the eyes.
Stye . . . . A small boil in eyelid.
Subjective. . . . . Pertaining to one's self.
Supraorbital . . . . . . Above the orbit.
Symblepharon . . . . Adhesion of lid to eyeball.
Synechia . . . . Adhesion of iris to crystalline lens.
Tarsal. . . . . Belonging to the eyelid.
Tenotomy . . . . Division of ocular muscle.
Tension of Eye . . . . Term applied to hardness of eyeball.
Trachoma . . . . Granular lids.
Trichiasis. . . . . Inversion of eyelashes.
Uvea. . . . . Choroid, ciliary body and iris as a whole.
Yellow Spot. . . . . . . Point of retina possessing most acute vision.

INDEX

A

B

C

Lightning Source UK Ltd.
Milton Keynes UK
UKOW06f1805220715

255649UK00019B/531/P